Good Stock

Life on a Low Simmer

For Jim + Peggy,
Enjoy the stories + recipes
Good Cooking!
Sandy D'Amato

Good Stock

Life on a Low Simmer

Sanford D'Amato

A MEMOIR, WITH RECIPES

MIDWAY

AN AGATE IMPRINT

CHICAGO

Printed in China
Photography © Kevin J. Miyazaki
Design by Brandtner Design

Library of Congress Cataloging-in-Publication Data

D'Amato, Sanford.
  Good stock : life on a slow simmer / by Sanford D'Amato.
     pages cm
  Includes index.
  Summary: "A memoir/cookbook from the founder of Milwaukee's Sanford restaurant"-- Provided by publisher.
  ISBN 978-1-57284-150-5 (hardcover) -- ISBN 1-57284-150-8 (hardcover) -- ISBN 978-1-57284-728-6 (ebook) --
ISBN 1-57284-728-X (ebook)
  1. Cooking, Italian. 2. Cooking--Wisconsin--Milwaukee. 3. D'Amato, Sanford--Anecdotes. I. Title.
  TX723.D276 2013
  641.5945--dc23
                    2013019120

13 14 15 16   10 9 8 7 6 5 4 3 2 1

Midway is an imprint of Agate Publishing. Agate books are available in bulk at discount prices. For more information, go to agatepublishing.com.

FOR ANGIE

My Love, My Life,
My Friend

Still Makin' 'Um
After 30 Years

TABLE OF CONTENTS

◆

PROLOGUE **8**

INTRODUCTION **11**

CHAPTER ONE The Radiator **12**

CHAPTER TWO The Grocery Store **40**

CHAPTER THREE Flew the Coop **74**

CHAPTER FOUR The CIA **100**

CHAPTER FIVE Dutch Treat **126**

CHAPTER SIX Olfactory Emporiums **162**

CHAPTER SEVEN Mexico City **186**

CHAPTER EIGHT French Connection **210**

CHAPTER NINE Transition: Long Island **242**

CHAPTER TEN Back to Milwaukee: John Byron's **264**

CHAPTER ELEVEN Sanford: Who's the Boss **294**

CHAPTER TWELVE My Dinners with Julia **324**

CHAPTER THIRTEEN Continuing Education **352**

CHAPTER FOURTEEN Table 3 **388**

ACKNOWLEDGMENTS **426**

RECIPE INDEX **428**

ABOUT THE AUTHOR **431**

PROLOGUE

"ONE'S COOKING IS AUTOBIOGRAPHICAL," JULIA CHILD SAID FAMOUSLY. "IT REVEALS a lot about who you are." Navigate a plate of well-made food and you have a decent map of the soul of the person who made it. It's unmistakable: the training, craft, and taste level of the cook, as well as heritage, personality, and sexual preference (well, maybe not that)—the DNA of the cook is right there on the plate. Then again, to paraphrase Freud, sometimes a grilled cheese sandwich is just a grilled cheese sandwich.

Julia, as it turns out, knew what she was talking about, which is why she held Sandy D'Amato's cooking in such high esteem. She knew he was the real deal. No one has a better sense of who he is and where he comes from, and the proof, as they say, is in the pudding. If you are what you eat—or at least what you cook—then Sandy is a five-star banquet.

I first encountered him somewhere off the coast of Istanbul in September 1994, aboard a luxury liner bound for Sodom and Gomorrah. (I think it was for passengers with low-salt diets.) I was nursing a bout of seasickness that recalled *The Perfect Storm* and the last thing in the world I wanted to think about was food. Sandy appeared through the morning fog, rhapsodizing about sea bass and ratatouille and celeriac foam and what-have-you in a soliloquy that both horrified and fascinated, thus cementing a friendship for the ages. I was captivated by his passion and intelligence. The guy was a master of culinary refinement. He had great insight into the mysterious realms of cooking—the objectives, inspiration, and thought processes that combine to beguile our tummies. Moreover, he radiated charm and was full of humor and warmth, and except for a misguided fondness for the Milwaukee Brewers there was no way I was letting him out of my sight.

That night, Sandy cooked dinner on the ship, an intimate, cozy affair for maybe 250. Fine-dining at sea is an oxymoron; it veers somewhere between institutional provisioning and nuclear waste disposal. The kitchens are notoriously chaotic and short of essential ingredients, all of which conspired against him. But the meal Sandy prepared was a revelation. His cooking was full of imagination, fresh, delicately made yet intensely flavorful, elegant, unfussy, and oh-so-satisfying. It told me everything about him that I needed to know.

Or so I thought.

Combing through these pages one plunges into a lost world of indelible ancestry, tradition, rebellion, and self-discovery that go toward defining a singular vision. From his grandfather's corner grocery store, where the customs of southern Italy clashed with New World conveniences, Sandy got a first-hand look at the tyranny inherent in restaurant kitchens, let alone families with a strong patriarchal core. But the food he grew up on was life-affirming. It was home-schooling of a most essential kind. All those time-tested recipes laid a foundation to build on, and over the years Sandy has given them his own imaginative spin. But his enlightenment came elsewhere—as a member of one of the first graduating classes of the Culinary Institute of America, and later in the galleys of restaurants in New York and Mexico, In each of those sojourns, you begin to see the education of a master chef, and that is where this book finds its groove. Sandy developed his swing early—he was a threat at the plate. Expertise and innovation merged into a powerful talent marked by finesse and sophistication that ordained Sandy as one of America's greatest chefs.

I think it's poetic justice that he and his wife, Angie, wound up back at his grandfather's store in Milwaukee. That they transformed the bodega into a fine-dining Mecca would have tickled the old guy something fierce. But I'm getting ahead of the story. In between these covers is the personal odyssey of a man determined to take all that he had learned and to fashion it into more than a goal, more than a meaningful career—Sandy D'Amato developed his own unique expression, a sensibility about food and cooking that has delighted people for more than 30 years.

You are in for a treat. Sandy's story is inspirational, heartwarming, honest, and profound. And while you're at it, try taking a few of his recipes for a spin. I tried a few out on my wife, and let's just say that the payoff was, um, delicious. You never know where a Rémoulade can lead.

Dig in. Open the first chapter. Smell the food on every page. *—**Bob Spitz***

INTRODUCTION

WRITING WAS NEVER A PART OF MY LIFE.

Not the best line for an author to lead with, but, in my case, it's very true. From grade school through college, the mere notion of putting my thoughts on paper had me sweating like a death row inmate.

About 15 years ago, my wife, Angie, and I were having a lovely dinner with Russ and May Klisch, the owners of Lakefront Brewery, a short tumble down the hill from Sanford Restaurant (our business and home at the time). After a scrumptious Korean hot pot and a whole lot of Lakefront Stein, May suggested that I pitch the *Milwaukee Journal Sentinel* an idea to write a weekly food column with a recipe.

I'd had many recipes published over the years for major magazines and newspapers, and was confident that I had a knack for writing workable, delicious recipes. But the next day, with a clearer head, I realized that writing prose might be a stretch.

Apprehensively I put together a sample recipe for Rice Pilaf and a 120-word column with a technical and historical slant. I then met with Diane Bacha, the entertainment managing editor, and food editor Nancy Stohs.

Thankfully, they liked my idea. It was decided that I would write a regular Sunday food column for the newly developed Entrée section. In June of 2000, "Kitchen Technician" debuted. I still struggled with the title of writer, but my close friend (and real-deal writer) Bob Spitz helped me with that. He said to me, "You tell great, rich stories. Don't try too hard—just write as you speak, tell a story."

Over the 13 years I wrote the column, it morphed from a technical how-to to a weekly peek into my life as a cook. It regularly answered the most basic question that I have been asked about my career: Where does your food come from?

The more I wrote, the more I started to understand that there was not one specific answer. My food is an unfolding journey, and for me, a recipe is a roadmap on that journey. Try a menu of my dishes, and you will start to understand my odyssey, which will continue as long as I'm still breathing. I have also learned from the many cooks and chefs who have mentored me, both at home and professionally, that the real genius of cooking is in a person's soul.

I'm very proud of the fact that, for better or worse, I wrote every word of this book, and developed every recipe. It is a symbiotic relationship between the stories and the recipes, as I feel that without one, the other doesn't exist.

1

THE RADIATOR

IT'S ALL ABOUT THE HANDS. BOTH OF MINE WERE WRAPPED HEAVILY IN GAUZE-LIKE giant Q-Tips. I was wearing only a white, form-fitting pinned diaper as I roamed the tiny ring, shaking the railings like a caged animal. I'm sure I looked like a baby boxer waiting for his next opponent. Actually, I was just strolling in my playpen. But I was agitated and upset because, even at this early age, I was used to working with my hands.

My parents had set up the playpen in the most prominent and brightest spot in the apartment, the living room, right in front of the east-facing windows and the radiator. As the bright Wisconsin winter sun streamed through the half-frosted windows, the mammoth radiator enveloped the playpen in its maternal warmth; I always felt soothed and safe.

One morning I was spending my time figuring out how to get myself up the amazingly high pen rails to get a closer look at the front window. The radiator was so inviting that I placed both palms on the screaming hot cover. I think I went into shock as my hands swelled like taut, bright-red helium balloons.

I was just shy of two years old, and we were living directly above my father and grandfather's grocery store on the lower east side of Milwaukee (which, some 37 years later, became Sanford, the first restaurant my wife Angie and I opened). This was a time before Playskool puzzles. My dad made sure there were plenty of better items to play with in my playpen like a nonfunctioning transistor radio that he would watch me take apart and put back together. He was always a tinkerer, so I was quickly indoctrinated into ITI (Infant Tinkerers International). I would be perfectly content to while away the day, patiently trying to figure out any physical task thrown my way. I was possibly a bit obsessive, but giving up wasn't in my vocabulary—actually there was nothing in my vocabulary, as I did not utter my first word until about age three, a good year-plus later.

I think burning my hands was my first setback in life. And thinking back, the trauma should have kept me from ever getting within 100 feet of any heat source, let alone spending my entire adult life bent over an open flame as a professional chef. But from an early age I

Rocking on toy horse in my playpen in my childhood
apartment above D'Amato's Grocery, 1951

was always drawn to heat and fascinated by fire. With a different upbringing, I might have become a pyromaniac. But instead, I learned to tame and control the flame (as well as my harmful impulses), and my curiosity and inner drive only got stronger.

◆

GROWING UP I WAS FORTUNATE TO BE SURROUNDED BY A LOT OF REALLY GOOD—EVEN extraordinary—cooks, who shaped my culinary path without me ever consciously realizing it. My first meals, up to the age of three, were taken in my deluxe dining chair, which towered over our family's small '50s Formica table that took up a good three-quarters of the available floor space of the kitchen. As I sat upright nibbling on my Zwieback and perusing my fiefdom, my mom, dad, and sister would all smile my way, ready to jump at any mere utterance. All I needed to say was a quick "wah," and those wispy little pasta stars called pastina would appear. Mounded with a bit of Wisconsin butter and showered with grated Romano, it was the ideal "mac and cheese" Italian baby food. This was a wise choice, as the mostaccioli and meatballs that the serfs consumed might have been cause for a quick Heimlich maneuver on a tiny toddler.

When I was three, our family moved from the small apartment above the store to the Promised Land—our own house. It was a Dutch Colonial on the northwest side of Milwaukee, located on a quaint elm tree-canopied street, appropriately called Elmhurst Road. That is, until Dutch elm disease wiped out almost all of the trees in the late '50s and early '60s.

Before we lived above the grocery store, my parents had been living in Los Angeles, where my dad worked as a machinist. They were extremely happy and doing quite well there when a call came from home. My grandfather needed help back in Milwaukee at the family grocery store, D'Amato's Grocery, and for my dad, as the eldest son in a Sicilian family, well, there was no real choice. So my mom, Kathleen, and my dad, Sam, moved above the store, and my sister and I were born. And when the opportunity to put a bit of breathing room between the store and the home came about, my parents were primed. It was imperative to move in order to keep my mother happy—and if my mother was happy, the world was happy. Quite the opposite from my dad, a lot of my mom's happiness was predicated on appearances, which fit in perfectly with the general '50s psyche. The house was truly the foundation of it all.

The move brought about many exciting changes. My sister Stephanie and I each got our own rooms, and the hierarchy of our family shifted. When we lived above my dad's work, he would pop up regularly to help manage the brood—a real democratic co-parenting state. After the move, with him working seven days a week and leaving the house around 5 a.m. and returning near 7 p.m., we settled into an autocratic world with my mother as the ultimate despot. This was a role she was born for—and did she ever thrive in it! She immediately started to flourish in our new life. The ultimate reward for us, with the installation of the new Universal stove in the kitchen, was a repertoire of exciting new dishes flowing from my mom's hands.

◆

THE STARCH OF CHOICE AT THE NEW D'AMATO HOUSE WAS ALWAYS POTATO. I RARELY remember a meal that had rice, and despite how much pasta I had at my grandparents' house, it was only an occasional sighting at home.

Universal Range similar to the one in my childhood

My mother's potato of choice was the russet, and the preparation was almost always baked. Our baked potatoes were never the foil-wrapped pretenders that steamed in their shiny armor. They were washed and baked crispy wonders that, when a knife slashed a gorge through their tops, virtually exploded with atomic wisps of steam.

I was always a bit frightened by the railroad spikes that my mother inserted through the middle of the potatoes before baking. They were actually thick aluminum skewers about six inches long that helped the inside of the potato cook as fast as the outside. They produced a dry, white interior that sat up and screamed for the addition of salt, pepper, creamy Wisconsin butter, and a bit of pure set sour cream, if the butter wasn't enough. It was always a test

*From left to right: my paternal grandfather, my aunt, and my paternal
grandmother in front of D'Amato's Grocery, sometime in the 1940s*

of asbestos fingers as I tried to thoroughly mix in the seasonings while holding the red-hot boulder. We would eat the insides and then reseason the crispy skins and finish those off.

As much as I relished the perfect baker, my mother had one even better trick in her arsenal: her legendary stuffed baked potato. I say legendary because it took a few tries before I actually got the chance to sample one. They first started appearing at my parents' early 1950s Saturday night dinner parties. Early one Saturday morning (I mean *early*, about 5 a.m.), my sister and I were awoken by the exclamation, "Everyone *up*!"

My mother was on a mission. We helped clean as much as we could but mostly just stayed out of her way as she invaded room after room, set up the dining area, and then settled into her command post in the kitchen.

She started baking potatoes at about noon. After pulling out the big Mixmaster, she scooped out the potatoes; added globs of butter, sour cream, and a good dose of seasoning; and mixed it all together. Then she filled the empty potato shells with the ambrosia and, with a final dusting of paprika, put them into the fridge for later. I thought about trying to liberate one of those creamy boats; but my sister reminded me of the possible consequences, and we decided it would be worth the wait.

I couldn't believe it when my mother looked over at me and said, "You're in charge of canapés." She handed me a box of Ritz crackers, a jar of peanut butter, and a jar of Welch's grape jelly.

First of all, I didn't know what a canapé was. But peanut butter, jelly and crackers? This was going to be fun. She showed me the precise amount of peanut butter to put on each cracker.

"Don't forget the slight well in the middle to hold the jelly." I got ready to slap another cracker on top, but she said, "No, this one is done. Now make 11 more."

While I was toiling away, she was working on the centerpiece. She mixed pretzels and nuts with a combination of three types of Chex cereal, tossed it all with butter and a bit of secret seasoning, and put it in the oven to bake (this was back when you had to make your own Chex mix). Along with cream cheese-stuffed celery, pitted black olives, and the pièce de résistance, a chafing dish chock-full of Vienna franks smothered in barbeque sauce. By the time it was all ready, I was doing my best imitation of one of Pavlov's famous dogs, even though my sister and I had eaten dinner 30 minutes before. We then realized we wouldn't be indulging, as my parents spoke the dreaded words *grown-up party*.

I was more than a little miffed. As the party started, my sister and I were quickly introduced to the revelers. Then something was muttered about bedtime, and we were banished to the upstairs. I was reluctantly tucked in, and all I could hear was the hooting and hollering, only interrupted by what must have been the crunching of the Ritz. It was hard to sleep with all the laughing and commotion, but mostly because they were down there eating my stuffers and wieners.

Well, as all good kids do, I fell asleep. And when I woke up and walked downstairs, it was like a mini hobo Christmas. Between the overflowing ashtrays (this was the '50s after all) were big pieces of chips, slightly crusted dip, Chex mix—minus most of the nuts (though there were a few Brazils)—and the grand prize: 14 mini Viennas. I ate, I got sick, I didn't care! It was great!

It took a bit of whining, but at the next party we sold our souls so my mother would make a few extra "stuffers" that we could enjoy the next day. And I'll tell you, it was worth keeping my room clean for weeks just to get a bite of those legendary potatoes.

◆

AS WE GOT OLDER, MY SISTER BECAME THE SITTER, AND MY MOTHER WOULD LEAVE THE dinner up to her. Now, my sister's repertoire at that time consisted of two dishes. One was a magnificent glazed ham. Well, actually it was a whole Spam that was diamond-scored, studded with cloves, covered with brown sugar and a half bottle of 7UP, and baked to a crispy turn. The outside caramelized pieces were quite fine; but the middle, where you could actually taste the Spam's flavor, was a bit gaggy.

The alternate dish was tuna casserole. This was the hit of the two. We always had good-quality Italian canned tuna from the store, and I really liked the peas and noodles. The closer was the thick crust of crumbled potato chips on top. But a new favorite was just over the horizon, and my sister wouldn't even have to raise a spatula.

◆

THERE ARE PEOPLE WHO THINK THAT TV DINNERS ARE A HUGE STAIN ON THE FABRIC OF dining. They look with disdain at the compartmentalized meals as the downfall of the family supper. Well, they may be right. But I have to say, I loved TV dinners! I remember when the first one came into my dad's store—I think it was the Swanson turkey. We couldn't wait to bring the four shiny boxes home. My mother had the oven preheated when we arrived, and the Cal-Dak TV trays were in place in the sunroom (all offering a prime view of the television). As the foil was carefully peeled back, we each had our boxes in front of us to compare the picture to the steaming contents. Just brilliant how they do that! From the first tongue-burning taste of the potatoes—mixed with a great episode of *Father Knows Best*—we were hooked.

As each new TV dinner was introduced, it was like the unveiling of the latest Armani collection at the D'Amato household: fried chicken with corn, peas and carrots (especially good with the option of folding back the foil in the last 10 minutes of cooking so that you may enrobe the chicken with a BBQ sauce topcoat); roast pork with a tasty apple compote;

and meatloaf with chunky tomato sauce, green beans and (have I died and gone to heaven?) a chocolate brownie.

As we grew up, the frozen dinners also grew up with the introduction of the upscale Stouffer's dinners. These were reputed to be the replicated specialties of the famous Stouffer's Restaurants (one of which was located on the top floor of the old Marine Bank building on Water and Wisconsin Avenues in downtown Milwaukee). If you couldn't afford to eat at Stouffer's, you could still have a small taste of the experience in your own home.

The macaroni and cheese was the most popular, but my favorite was the turkey tetrazzini. This was a creamy concoction of bubbly turkey, noodles and mushrooms, with a crusty, buttery crust that almost cracked when you put a spoon to it. Talk about patience. The aluminum pan held its heat like a glowing cast iron stove, and I'd almost pass out as my head would get light from my continuously blowing on each forkful to cool it down enough to eat.

As much maligned as TV dinners have been over the years, in those times, they were as entertaining as the TV shows they were meant to accompany. After the foil containers were disposed of (no dishes!), it was on to the finale.

◆

MY SISTER AND I WERE BORN INTO A HOUSE OF SQUARE CAKES. MY MOTHER WAS NOT A baking aficionado, but that did not get in the way of her love and consumption of baked goods.

During the '50s most mothers were homemakers, which meant a regular *Leave It to Beaver*-style sit-down meal most nights. I always suspected this was a time for parents to pry out vital information from us kids as we were in a nirvana-like stupor from consuming every delicious morsel in sight.

Every night in our house, the flow of dinner always led up to the 8-by-8-by-6-inch white cardboard box sitting on the kitchen counter. What did it contain tonight? Cream cheese kolache, streuselkuchen, or a special cake? It was like *Let's Make a Deal*: You want the box? You clean your plate. The box always came from Lindmair's, our local bakery on 41st and Capitol. I would usually go up there with my bike in the morning before school to pick up the pre-ordered box. I was always excited when I saw scribbled on top of the box "Chocolate Jimmy Cake" (my mother's favorite).

One evening, after the much-anticipated opening of the box, my sister and I made a shocking discovery: there sat a square cake with no frosting or jimmies on the outside. It took us several cakes to figure out that the four outside slices of the round cake disappeared during the day and that they weren't actually made that way.

To this day we call the outside frosting-covered piece the "mother slice."

◆

THE INDIANAPOLIS 500 MEANT THE BEGINNING OF SUMMER. AS A CHILD, I WOULD WORK in the backyard picking up the trimmings and leftover leaves from last year, that my father would pull and rake. This was the one annual full day of yard work at the D'Amato homestead. In my immature lazy mind, the only thing worse than the boring yard work was the stupid drone of those racecars broadcast live on my dad's transistor radio. We're on lap 25,001, and they're still going around the oval and (surprise!) here they come again. The only thing worse than car racing on the radio might be golf.

The good part of Memorial Day weekend for me was that it kicked off a second race that I liked to call the Roosevelt 500. Once it got hot, and thereafter anytime the temperature was over 75 degrees, my mother would go into semi-hibernation in the sunroom in front of the fan. After dinner on some days, she would sweetly ask my dad if he would go pick up a cooling dessert. This would not have been a big deal, but she had very particular tastes. The only thing that would satisfy Mama Bear in the sunroom was the dreaded dipped cone. This was a soft-serve cone that was dipped upside down in chocolate to form a crispy outer shell. When my mom made these requests, my dad would turn slightly pale and then start to get red as the adrenaline began building. He might as well have just listened to a tape from *Mission: Impossible*; he knew if he got back and—heaven help us—the cone was melted, my mother would start clawing the nearest bystander to death.

I was often recruited to be the mope who would procure the cone. Boy Blue (formerly Carvel), at the intersection of Roosevelt and Fond du Lac right past Sherman, was the target. Gentlemen, start your engines.

Here's how the Roosevelt 500 worked. We would get in the Chevy Bel Air, race up Roosevelt past Sherman about seven blocks, then two more blocks to Fond du Lac. We would make good time! My dad would bark, "Sandy! Order the cone, pay for it, and tell them not to make it until you have the change in your pocket. Keep the car door open, grab the cone, and run back as fast as you can!" I would order, pay for the cone, and they would dip it; I'd grab it, run back, jump in the seat, and my dad would take off before the door was closed. He would time the lights perfectly as the Bel Air's tires burned. He'd pull up in front of the house, and I'd run to the front door that my sister would be holding open. If I noticed a drip on the side of the cone, I'd look at my dad as he would mouth in slow motion, "Just lick it but don't leave any marks on the chocolate shell!" I'd take a whisper of a swipe and round the corner of the sunroom. I'd be totally out of breath, trying to control the slight tremor developing in my hand, as I would offer the cone over (swipe side towards me) for inspection. During the debriefing we'd learn that the cone was a bit softer than expected—but thanks for getting it!

WE HAD AN INCREDIBLY EXPANSIVE BACKYARD THAT WOULD HAVE PUT THE PONDEROSA to shame, from my child's point of view. To the right were the Fredericks. He was a local landscaper whose well-manicured and always-blooming yard was surrounded by a white picket fence and guarded by bellowing twin beagles. To the left, behind drawbridge-high hedges, were the Bansemers.

Just about every morning, beginning in late spring, I would hear the incessant clip-clip-clip of Mr. Bansemer manually trimming his green barricade. He would never talk or make eye contact, and he would do this every morning throughout the summer. After two or three years, it really started to creep me out. I just knew there was something sinister happening on the other side of those hedges, but they were so thick and full that I couldn't see a thing.

A few years after moving in, my mother was preparing her signature cinnamon ribs for the Fourth of July. The fragrance of the floral cinnamon intertwined with crispy roasting pork was irresistible, so after the third time that I popped open the oven door to gaze at the ribs, my drooling face was banished into the yard to play until they were ready.

As I wandered around the yard figuring out what to do next, I kept staring over at the hedges. I was all hopped up after my third Nesbitt's orange soda, and I decided I had to see what was on the other side. I purposely threw my small wooden glider over the hedge and then took a running start and plowed right through. I fell through to the other side and found Mr. Bansemer sitting in a lawn chair with a beer and a transistor radio, listening to the Milwaukee Braves game. Not quite the demonic scene I expected. He did go a bit crazy, and within 10 seconds I was between my dad and Mr. Bansemer promising that I would never ruin the hedges again.

As the years went on, we actually started talking every summer. He explained to me that those hedges were his pride and joy and he always felt at peace when he was trimming. That early fear turned to respect and admiration, and the formerly annoying incessant clip-clip-clip cadence became as soothing as the crickets and fireflies at dusk.

Those cinnamon ribs are still a tradition every Fourth of July in our house, and each year, as I sit back in the chair with a stomach full of pork, I wonder if I could still get through that hedge.

AFTER DRIVING WITH MY FATHER FOR YEARS, I JUST KNEW I WAS BORN TO DRIVE. I WAS still in grade school, but I had a lot of experience being my dad's copilot, mentally helping him along as he column-shifted the Ford station wagon from first to second to third. I was

Here I am looking out of my parents' car window in front of D'Amato's Grocery, 1952

sure I didn't even need an automatic, as I felt I had absorbed all the mysterious nuances of a standard three-speed transmission.

If you're not yet convinced, I also had 12 years of drive-in experience. That's not walk-in—that's drive-in. The D'Amatos were well-known regulars at a multitude of drive-ins throughout the Milwaukee area, especially the Milky Way, which is no longer around, and Kitt's, which is still on 70th and Capitol today.

My driving obsession was based on two episodes. The first took place at Kitt's. As we pulled into the parking lot, off to the side was a small platform, which displayed the most perfect miniature racing car that any young guy could imagine. This was a dream machine, and my jockey-sized stature would fit very easily behind that wheel. My right leg started to quiver as I imagined my foot pushing right through the floorboard, quickly snapping my helmeted head deep into the driver's seat.

The second was the opening of one of the original go-kart tracks on Fond du Lac Avenue, next to Capitol Court. Every time we went to the drive-in and passed the Capitol Court track, I would plead my case. My mother, however, would look into the backseat and say, "Those are just too dangerous—forget about it."

After weeks of pleading, one night my dad and I went on a solo drive-in guy-night dinner. After we finished a four-pack of sloppy joes (washed down with a banana shake and a junior hot fudge pecan sundae), we pulled out of the drive-in, sped down the road, and sharply turned into the go-kart parking lot.

"Well, are you ready?" he asked. I thought he must have been on a custard high. But I didn't care—I was born ready.

It took a bit of persuading by my dad to convince the go-kart operator that his half-pint kid was old enough to drive. But he did, and with the din of the engines, the sweet smell of the hay bales mixed with the down and dirty scent of gas and oil, and the absolute exploding adrenaline of the starting line, we raced. I was certainly the youngest driver, and after a few practice runs, I was also sometimes the fastest.

This became a bi-weekly ritual—sloppy joes, shakes, sundaes, and go-karts—and the operator eventually gave me a racing handle: Shorty. I like to think even my mother would have been proud of my driving abilities, if she had known.

◆

IT WAS THE SATURDAY BEFORE CHRISTMAS WEEK. I WAS ABOUT EIGHT YEARS OLD AND was sound asleep, snuggly wedged into my soft, warm bed, dreaming of a huge twinkly Christmas tree. Suddenly, I heard an ominous rumbling to my left. I worried as the noise got louder and closer. Wait—snowplows? Yes, it was just snowplows. But it was getting really loud—like it was right outside the front door. Holy moly! It was coming through the door! My bedroom door snapped open, and I bolted upright in bed. It was my mother: "Go back to sleep—I'm getting ready for Christmas."

Go back to sleep? It was 4:30 a.m., and she'd just plowed through my door with a 424 horsepower Hoover. (Of course this is said in the safe confines of my brain.) I pulled the covers over my head to dim the overhead bedroom light and that slight respite lasts for about 30 minutes, until my mother asked me if I was going to sleep all day.

Leading up to Christmas, the normal obsessive cleaning quickly morphed into preparation boot camp at the D'Amato's. We all got into the act: First Lieutenant Stephanie (aka my sister), Buck Private (me), and Special Ambassador to the East Side (my dad, who was conveniently on working furlough) were all under the direction of General Kathleen Patton (Mom).

The only redeeming factor of this military experience was that we did have a say in the mess area. We took a verbal vote and the early returns showed a repeat for last year's winner: baked lasagna. This was a laborious venture that my mother would only attempt for Christmas. It was a stratified affair of creamy Falbo riccotta, ruffled noodles, Dentice sausage, and a true Sicilian, slightly sweet tomato sauce. This all rested under a crispy golden crust of fresh mozzarella and Pecorino Romano. But after all the precincts were heard from, our choice that year for Christmas dinner ended up being roast pork with oven-roasted vegetables. There was no disappointment, as it was, no doubt, the best dish my mother ever made. The pork was moist, juicy, and heavily crusted with dark crunchy fat, and the vegetables and potatoes were caramelized to a burnished turn. And after all the turmoil of Christmas preparation, the troops were more than satisfied. Mission accomplished.

◆

CHRISTMAS TRADITION AT OUR HOUSE HAD BEEN A VARIED AFFAIR OVER THE YEARS. Christmas Eve was for the adults, but as with most homes with young kids, we always celebrated Christmas on Christmas Day. My parents would wake my sister and me around 9 a.m. (my sister was actually asleep while I was in a vibrating coma of excitement). We were orchestrated down the stairs (we slept upstairs) as my father had the Bell & Howell movie camera going with 30,000 watts of handheld lights. After our third take of coming down the stairs, we actually got to tear into our presents. This was followed by the only formal breakfast we had all year.

I realized later in life that we never had breakfast besides cereal (Sugar Pops were my favorite) because my dad left the house around 5 a.m. to get to the vegetable market and my mother never ate breakfast herself. My dad was actually a breakfast hound who would occasionally stop at the old Broadway Bar and Grill at the Broadway Market, but usually settled for a trio of of donuts washed down with a shorty Coke when he got to the store around 6:30.

So the one day a year that we all sat down to early morning breakfast was the only day of the year that my dad wasn't working and the grocery store was closed: Christmas Day. Right after the grand opening of the presents, the unmistakable aroma of fatty smoked bacon would start to roll in from the kitchen. My mother extracted the Sunbeam electric skillet from the basement and, setting the dial to medium high, covered the entire bottom of the skillet with double thick slices of Patrick Cudahy sweet applewood bacon. As the rashers would start to get crispy, she broke the eggs right over the top and covered the skillet. The just-set eggs came out crackling crisp at the edges, heavily peppered and infused with the flavor of the bacon fat. As I took my first bite of this grown-up breakfast, an unexpected thought crossed my mind for the first time: Are Sugar Pops really tops?

◆

ONE OF MY FAVORITE FRUITS IS A VEGETABLE. THE FIRST TIME I REMEMBER HAVING IT was when my maternal grandmother was visiting us—as much as I saw my dad's mother, who lived next to the grocery store, I very rarely saw my mom's mother, except on holidays. I dreaded spending time with her because she didn't really relate well to children and I always felt like a huge burden. Hers were never "sit back, talk, and relax" types of visits. After she arrived, she immediately walked over to the kitchen window that overlooked the backyard. "Yes, it's ready. And if I wasn't here, it would rot."

I didn't have a clue as to what she was looking at. Through all the brush and bramble in our yard, my grandmother, with her falcon vision, had locked in on her prey: the rhubarb. As we walked outside, my grandmother carried a large kitchen knife in one hand, which she used to hack a small path through the overgrown weeds. Once she saw the bright red rhubarb stalks with large, wavy leaves, she quickly lopped them off from the bottom with one swift swipe and barked, "Gather it up!"

My grandmother immediately commandeered the kitchen. After years of living with my mother, we knew the drill. We gathered ingredients from the cupboard, refrigerator, local grocery store, or any other venue within a 10-mile radius that our bikes could reach. We returned out of breath, supplies in hand. But unlike my mother who demanded our help, we were relegated to the other room as my grandmother transformed the raw materials into a veritable dessert buffet. She went on to make various coffee cakes, kuchens, and pies, and it was almost worth it working with this taskmaster, whom my sister and I realized was the original kitchen general: Five-Star Nana. My favorite treat of all was the simply and quickly simmered chunks of tart rhubarb mixed with sugar; an instant preserve that puckered and then soothed in perfect balance. I would quietly sneak around the table to snatch warm chunks out of the bowl as they were cooling.

After the desserts were done and properly cooled, my sister and I were summoned to the kitchen by my grandmother, and she would say as warmly as she knew how, "Go on! It's not going to eat itself!" We didn't have to be asked twice.

◆

IT TOOK ME A FEW YEARS OF RATIONAL ADULT REASONING TO FIGURE OUT THAT THIS was where my mother's ordered precision came from. And, as regimented as my grandmother was when visiting, it was just a teaser for when you were in her personal confines. It was another "internment day" with my grandmother. I was never in military prison but that is the feeling I always got when my mother would drop me off at her mother's.

I would talk with friends and they would spin tales of their weekends with their grandparents. They would walk into the house and were immediately handed a giant Snickers bar as they were led to a roomful of the latest toys. Feeling bored? Well let's take a quick trip to the zoo, here's a large box of popcorn, hey, let's top it off with a double-dip custard cone. My experiences were a bit different. As I was "patted down and cleared" by my grandmother's roommate, my Aunt Martha, or "The Bull" as my sister and I referred to her, yelled ahead, "He's here!" My grandmother appeared in the entrance and said, "You know the rules." She sat me down, put a TV tray in front of me with a deck of cards and said, "Now have a good time."

Have a good time? Even though I was behind a TV tray there was no TV, no radio, no toys, no conversation, and I was thinking, just because YOU love to play solitaire—hey! I'm seven! I need more than cards! I'd sit there watching the clock on the mantle—9:00, 9:30, 10:00, 11:00, 11:59—and finally, thank God, it eventually became lunchtime.

"Grilled frankfurters with German potato salat," my grandmother would announce, as she'd plop the plate on my tray. The first time around, the franks looked good, but the potato salad wasn't what I was used to. No mayo? But then I tasted it—warm, tangy, and really good. Boy, that woman could cook. If not for that, I would have tried to escape.

◆

WHEN YOU'RE A KID, THINKING OF A PRESENT FOR MOTHER'S DAY CAN BE QUITE AN ordeal. I wanted to get a great present; but juvenile finances can be a nightmare, so I was limited in what I could come up with.

I tried breakfast in bed. The ingredients were already in-house, so the price was right. I guess I failed to take into consideration the fact that my mother hated breakfast, and even if she had been a connoisseur of the morning repast, I don't think Sugar Pops with big chunks of banana would have been her first choice. At least she was enthusiastic about the card—and I didn't realize how enthusiastic until the next year.

On the next Mother's Day, after my dad closed the grocery store at 1 p.m., he was instructed to pick up my mom's mother on his way home so she could spend the day with us. We pulled up in front of her house, and I ran up and rang the bell. My grandmother came marching out with a courteous, "Hello, Sanford" and proceeded to take the shotgun seat without even calling it. I climbed in back and after my dad traded a "Hello, Marie" for a "Hello, Sam," we continued to drive to our house, without her or my dad's heads ever moving from their locked-in, straight-ahead positions.

As we walked into the house, my mother was more agitated than usual (which was the case whenever her mother was around). She was particularly nervous, as she had made a schaum torte. My mother was a great cook, but rarely ventured into the scratch dessert arena. But she loved her mother's schaum torte and wanted to make a great impression.

When dinner was finished, she coaxed the torte out of the spring form pan and was visibly displeased with the results. My grandmother, looking somewhat comatose, said nothing positive or negative, which was her stoic M.O. I was happy, as anything draped with fresh crushed and macerated local strawberries and whipped semi-sweet heavy cream was fine with me.

After dessert my mother opened her Mother's Day gifts. Remembering last year, I had gone all out and purchased a bottle of Friendship Garden toilet water the day before at Carl's Pharmacy. She loved the gift but immediately asked, "Where is the card?" I had stupidly thought a big-time gift precluded a card, but as she proceeded to take my head off, I realized that the card was the whole deal.

With years of reflection and understanding more about the dynamics between parents and kids, I now realize the schaum torte might have had more than a little bit to do with how she reacted to the missing card.

CHAPTER ONE RECIPES

◆

Chicken Pastina

30

Fennel Sausage Lasagna

31

Fragrant Chili Pepper Cinnamon Ribs

34

*Turkey and Smoked Gouda
Tetrazzini with Kluski*

35

Sweet-Sour German Potato Salat

37

*Schaum Torte with Brown
Butter-Roasted Rhubarb*

38

CHICKEN PASTINA

The key to this soup is to make sure that it is rich and satisfying, which is accomplished by the use of a double stock. A double stock is made when you start with a chicken stock, then cook a chicken in it in order to enrich the stock. Also, make sure the vegetables are well cooked and not al dente so that they are completely infused with the flavor of the chicken.

SERVES 8

> 1½ pounds (681 g) on-the-bone chicken parts (leg, thigh, or breast)
>
> 2 quarts (1.90 L) unsalted chicken stock
>
> 1 bunch Italian parsley stems (reserve the leaves for garnish)
>
> 3 cloves garlic, peeled
>
> 3 bay leaves
>
> 2 sprigs fresh thyme
>
> 1 sprig fresh rosemary
>
> 1 cinnamon stick
>
> 3 tablespoons (45 mL) extra virgin olive oil
>
> 1 large onion (12 ounces [341 g]), diced small
>
> 2 carrots (10 ounces [284 g]), peeled and diced small
>
> 2 stalks celery (4 ounces [114 g]), diced small
>
> ½ of a trimmed fennel bulb (3 ounces [85 g]), core removed and diced small
>
> 4 cloves garlic, sliced
>
> Kosher salt and freshly ground pepper, to taste
>
> 5 ounces (142 g) pastina or acini de pepe, cooked 5 to 7 minutes in boiling salted water, drained, and rinsed
>
> Grated Pecorino Romano cheese, to taste

1. In a soup pot, place the chicken parts, chicken stock, parsley stems, the 3 whole garlic cloves, bay leaves, thyme, rosemary, and cinnamon stick. Bring up to a simmer and cook, covered, for 25 minutes.

2. Remove the chicken, and when cool enough to handle, take the meat off the bones; reserve the meat. Add the bones back to the stock and simmer for 20 more minutes. Strain the stock and clean the pot.

3. Place the cleaned pot over medium heat and add the olive oil. When hot, add the onions, carrots, celery, fennel, and the sliced garlic, then season lightly with salt and pepper. Sweat (cover and cook slowly) the mixture for 15 minutes, stirring every 5 minutes. Add the strained stock, bring up to a simmer, and cook for 10 minutes.

4. Shred the reserved chicken meat and add to the soup. Add the cooked pastina (or acini de pepe) and bring up to a simmer. Adjust the seasoning with salt and pepper to taste. Stir in the reserved parsley leaves and serve. Garnish with the cheese to taste.

FENNEL SAUSAGE LASAGNA

Angie and I have lasagna on Christmas Eve at our house. There are two reasons for this: First, I like to make a dish that is completely done ahead. And second, even though lasagna is a bit of work, it's really delicious. You can even make the lasagna ahead and freeze it, but make sure to place it in the refrigerator to defrost the day before.

SERVES 12

For the Tomato–Sausage Sauce: (Makes 12 cups [2.84 L] of sauce)

½ cup (119 mL) extra virgin olive oil

3 pounds (1.36 kg) Italian sausage links

2 large onions (1½ pounds [681 g]), diced small

Kosher salt and freshly ground black pepper, to taste

8 cloves garlic, finely chopped

4 bay leaves

4 sprigs fresh thyme

1 cup (262 g) tomato paste

1 bunch fresh Italian parsley stems, coarsely chopped

2 ounces (57 g) fresh basil leaves, coarsely chopped

2 cups (474 mL) unsalted pork or chicken stock

4 (28-ounce [784-g]) cans peeled plum tomatoes in juice, puréed in a food processor

1. Preheat the oven to 350°F (180°C). Place a heavy-bottomed pot over medium-high heat, add the olive oil, and brown the sausage for 4 minutes per side, or until golden. Remove the sausage to a plate.

2. Add the onions to the pot, season lightly with salt and pepper, and sauté, stirring, for 5 minutes, or until lightly brown. Add the garlic, bay leaves, and thyme and sauté for 1 minute. Add the tomato paste and sauté for about 3 minutes, or until the paste darkens. Add the parsley stems and basil and sauté for 1 minute.

3. Add the stock and puréed tomatoes, stir, and bring up to a boil. Add the sausage, cover, and bake for 45 minutes.

4. Remove and discard the bay leaves and thyme sprigs. Remove the sausage, and when they are cool, cut each link into ¼-inch (6-mm) discs; reserve in the refrigerator. Adjust the seasoning of the sauce with salt and pepper and cool.

(RECIPE CONTINUES ON PAGE 33)

(RECIPE CONTINUED FROM PAGE 31)

For the Lasagna:

> 3 ounces (85 g) fresh Italian parsley leaves (from about 2 large bunches)
>
> 2 ounces (57 g) fresh basil leaves
>
> 2 pounds (908 g) ricotta cheese
>
> 2½ teaspoons kosher salt, plus additional for the pasta water
>
> 1 teaspoon freshly ground black pepper
>
> ½ teaspoon grated nutmeg
>
> 3 large egg yolks
>
> 1 pound (454 g) mascarpone cheese
>
> 2 pounds (908 g) lasagna noodles
>
> Prepared Tomato–Sausage Sauce
>
> ½ pound (227 g) Asiago cheese, grated
>
> ½ pound (227 g) Parmesan cheese, grated
>
> 1½ pounds (681 g) whole milk mozzarella cheese, thinly sliced
>
> ¼ cup (59 mL) extra virgin olive oil

1. In a food processor, add the parsley and basil and process until fine. Add half of the ricotta, the 2½ teaspoons salt, the pepper, and the nutmeg, then process until fine, about 30 seconds. Add the remaining ricotta and the egg yolks and process until just mixed. Place the mixture in a bowl and mix in the mascarpone. Have the ricotta mixture, cheeses, and the Tomato–Sausage Sauce ready for assembling.

2. Fill a large (about a 3-gallon [11.4-L]) pot with water. Add about 2 to 3 tablespoons of kosher salt (until the water tastes like sea water) and bring up to a boil. Cook the lasagna noodles for about 4 minutes. Drain the noodles and re-cover them with cold water. When cool, drain the noodles. Place the noodles flat in 1 layer on a sheet pan that has been lined with plastic wrap. Cover the first layer with plastic wrap and repeat the process for all layers.

3. Preheat the oven to 350°F (180°C). Place 1½ cups (356 g) of the sauce on the bottom of a 12x16x4-inch (30.5x40.5x10-cm) baking pan. Place a layer (about 8) of the noodles over the sauce, just slightly overlapping each noodle. Spread 2 cups (474 mL) of the sauce over the noodles with a spatula. Sprinkle over ¼ of the sausage slices, ¼ of the ricotta mixture (I like to pipe it out with a pastry bag and lightly spread it to cover), ½ cup (50 g) Asiago, ½ cup (50 g) Parmesan, and ⅓ of the mozzarella slices. Place 8 more slightly overlapping noodles over the top and lightly press down. Repeat this sequence using the same measurements of the sauce, sausage, ricotta mixture, Asiago, Parmesan, and mozzarella 3 more times. Top the lasagna with a final layer of the noodles and mozzarella, then add more sauce to cover. Sprinkle the top with the remaining Asiago and Parmesan and the olive oil.

4. Place a piece of parchment paper (cut to fit the pan) over the lasagna, then cover the pan with aluminum foil. Bake for 1½ to 2 hours, or until an instant-read thermometer reads 150°F (66°C). Remove the parchment paper and aluminum foil, then place the lasagna back in the oven to brown slightly, for 10 minutes. Remove the lasagna from the oven and let it rest for at least 20 minutes before cutting. Serve with the remaining sauce on the side.

FRAGRANT CHILI PEPPER CINNAMON RIBS

I can't help but tinker with my mother's original dish, so over the years a bit of chili powder has worked its way into this recipe. If you're feeling a bit spicy, you can use the hot chili powder—but the medium chili powder combined with fragrant Saigon cinnamon will give you a wonderful taste combination.

SERVES 4

> 3 tablespoons (24 g) chili powder
>
> 2 tablespoons ground cinnamon
>
> 1½ teaspoons freshly ground black pepper
>
> 2 racks baby back pork ribs (4 pounds [1.82 kg] total)
>
> ¼ cup (59 mL) grapeseed (or corn) oil
>
> 2 tablespoons kosher salt

1. One day ahead, mix the chili powder, cinnamon and black pepper. Have your butcher remove the thin, inner membrane that covers the inside bones of the ribs (or you may pull it off by grabbing 1 end with a paper towel, then pulling across to remove). Place the ribs on a large piece of plastic wrap. Divide the spice mixture evenly over both sides of the ribs and lightly rub in. Place the racks on top of each other, bone side down, wrap in the plastic wrap, and leave in the refrigerator for at least 12 hours.

2. The next day, preheat the oven to 475°F (260°C). Unwrap and separate the ribs. Drizzle the oil evenly over the ribs and season both sides with the salt. Place the ribs meat side down on a rimmed baking sheet and bake for 15 minutes. Turn the ribs over and bake for another 10 to 12 minutes. Remove the ribs and let them rest for 10 to 15 minutes in a warm area before serving.

TURKEY AND SMOKED GOUDA TETRAZZINI WITH KLUSKI

Since a lot of my life is still spent in front of a TV, I'm more comfortable with a Cal-Dak tray than a table, and this Tetrazzini screams for a good one-hour show to give you time to let it cool down—if you can wait that long.

SERVES 4 TO 6

For the Turkey:

>   2 (1½-pounds-each [681-g]) turkey thighs, skin removed
>   3 cups (711 mL) unsalted chicken stock
>   1 tablespoon kosher salt

1. Add all of the ingredients to a small saucepan and bring up to a simmer. Cook slowly, covered, for 40 minutes.

2. Remove the turkey to a plate and reserve the poaching liquid. When the turkey is cool, pull the meat from the bones into medium bite-size pieces; reserve.

For the Tetrazzini:

>   5 tablespoons (71 g) unsalted butter (divided)
>   1 small onion (4 ounces [114 g]), diced small
>   ½ of a red bell pepper (2 ounces [57 g]), seeds removed and diced small
>   ½ of a green bell pepper (2 ounces [57 g]), seeds removed and diced small
>   8 ounces (227 g) baby portobello mushrooms, brushed clean and quartered
>   4 cloves garlic, finely chopped
>   2 bay leaves
>   2 sprigs fresh thyme
>   Kosher salt and freshly ground black pepper, to taste
>   3 tablespoons (23 g) all-purpose flour
>   ¼ cup (59 mL) dry white wine
>   1¾ cups (415 mL) reserved poaching liquid
>   ¼ teaspoon ground nutmeg
>   ½ cup (119 mL) heavy cream
>   Reserved poached turkey meat
>   8 ounces (227 g) kluski (egg noodles), cooked according to package directions, about 10 minutes, then drained, rinsed, and cooled

(RECIPE CONTINUES ON PAGE 36)

(RECIPE CONTINUED FROM PAGE 35)

> **8 ounces (227 g) smoked Gouda cheese, grated**
> **(reserve 2 ounces [57 g] for the Tetrazzini Crust)**
> **Tetrazzini Crust (recipe follows)**

1. Preheat the oven to 350°F (180°C). Place a large saucepan over medium heat. Add 3 table-spoons (43 g) of the butter, and when melted, add the onions, red and green peppers, and sauté slowly for 2 minutes. Add the mushrooms, garlic, bay leaves, and thyme, season lightly with salt and pepper, then sauté for 3 more minutes. Add the flour and stir for 1 minute. Add the white wine, bring up to a boil, and boil for 1 minute. Add the reserved poaching liquid and nutmeg, bring back to a simmer, then cook slowly for 3 minutes. Add the cream and bring back to a simmer. Adjust the seasoning with salt and pepper. Fold in the reserved turkey meat, then add to a bowl along with the kluski and the 6 ounces (170 g) of Gouda.

2. Use the remaining 2 tablespoons (28 g) of the butter to butter a 13x9-inch (32.5x22.5-cm) casserole dish. Transfer the mixture to the casserole dish and spread evenly. Sprinkle the Tetrazzini Crust evenly over the mixture. Bake for 25 to 30 minutes, or until golden and bubbly.

For the Tetrazzini Crust:

> **1 cup (108 g) plain bread crumbs**
> **½ cup (28 g) chopped fresh Italian parsley leaves**
> **2 ounces (57 g) reserved Gouda cheese**
> **2 tablespoons extra virgin olive oil**
> **¾ teaspoon kosher salt**
> **⅜ teaspoon freshly ground black pepper**

1. Mix all of the ingredients together.

SWEET-SOUR GERMAN POTATO SALAT

Every deli and grocery has their version of German Potato Salad and most taste like they were stamped out at the same industrial kitchen. This salat, unlike my maternal grandmother's, is smoky, tart, and satisfyingly creamy.

SERVES 4

> 1 pound (4 medium [454 g]) Yukon Gold potatoes
>
> 1 large egg
>
> 3 tablespoons (56 g) kosher salt, plus additional to taste
>
> ⅓ cup (79 mL) dry white wine
>
> 1 tablespoon grapeseed oil
>
> 4 slices thick-cut bacon (4 ounces [114 g]), cut in ¼-inch (6-mm) pieces
>
> ¼ cup (38 g) small-diced onion
>
> 1 tablespoon granulated sugar
>
> 1½ teaspoons all-purpose flour
>
> ¼ cup (59 mL) apple cider vinegar
>
> Freshly ground black pepper, to taste
>
> ¼ cup (59 mL) water
>
> 3 scallions, trimmed and cut in ¼-inch (6-mm) slices
> (6 tablespoons [38 g]; divided)

1. Place the potatoes and egg in a large saucepan, cover with water, and season with the 3 tablespoons (56 g) salt. Bring up to a boil, then turn down the heat to a light boil. Remove the egg after 8 minutes and cool in a bowl of cold water. Continue cooking the potatoes for about 25 to 30 minutes more, or until just cooked (when an inserted knife comes out easily).

2. Drain the potatoes, and when cool enough to handle, cut each potato in half, then cut each half in about ¼-inch (6-mm) slices, leaving the skin on. Place the potatoes into a baking dish, spread them out evenly, and pour over the white wine.

3. Place a sauté pan over medium heat. When the pan is hot, add the grapeseed oil, then the bacon, and cook the bacon until golden. Strain the fat from the bacon (reserve the bacon), then add the bacon fat back to the pan. Add the onion and sauté until tender, about 3 minutes. Add the sugar and flour and stir. Add the vinegar and bring up to a boil. Remove from the heat, add the ¼ cup (59 mL) of water, and stir. Add ¾ of the cooked bacon and adjust the seasoning with salt and pepper (this is the dressing).

4. Drain and discard any excess wine from the potatoes and season lightly with salt and pepper. Mix the potatoes with 4 tablespoons of the scallions and all of the dressing. Place the Potato Salat in a serving bowl. Peel and chop small the cooled egg, then mix it with the remaining 2 tablespoons of scallions and the remaining bacon to garnish the top.

SCHAUM TORTE WITH BROWN BUTTER-ROASTED RHUBARB

This is my variation on my mother's Schaum Torte, which she adapted from her bible, Milwaukee's own, The Settlement Cookbook. *A good Schaum Torte should have the combination of a crispy exterior with a creamy marshmallow-like interior. This recipe pairs it with a sweet-tart, brown sugar rhubarb compote, which should make any mother happy.*

MAKES 6 TORTES

4 large egg whites

½ teaspoon vanilla paste

¼ teaspoon cream of tartar

⅛ teaspoon kosher salt

1 cup (200 g) granulated sugar

1½ teaspoons cider vinegar

Brown Butter–Roasted Rhubarb (recipe follows)

1. Preheat the oven to 475°F (260°C). Place the egg whites in a mixer bowl of a stand mixer fitted with a whip attachment. Add the vanilla paste, cream of tartar, and salt and whisk on medium for about 1 minute, or until frothy. Add ⅓ of the sugar and continue whisking for 2 minutes. Add another ⅓ of the sugar and continue whisking for about 1 to 2 minutes. Add the remaining sugar and whisk until medium-soft peaks are formed. Add the vinegar and continue whisking to a slightly firm peak, where the tip just drops a bit.

2. Divide the mixture with an ice cream scoop into 6 removable-bottom straight-sided mini-cake molds (about 3 inches [7.5 cm] wide by 2 to 3 inches [5 to 7.5 cm] high). Even out the top and run your finger around the inside edge of the mold—about ¼-inch (6-mm) into the mixture—to clean the sides of the mold and form an inner circle. Place the molds directly on an oven rack and bake for 5 minutes. Turn off the oven, leaving the molds in the closed oven for at least 3 hours, or until the oven is completely cool.

3. Remove the molds from the oven and run a sharp knife around the sides of the mold, as close to the side as possible, to release the tortes. Push up through the bottom and run a knife under the bottom to release.

For the Brown Butter-Roasted Rhubarb:
(Makes about 2 cups [474 mL])

2 tablespoons salted butter

½ cup (3¼ ounces [92 g]) brown sugar

2 tablespoons sweet Muscat dessert wine

1 pound (454 g) rhubarb stalks, cut in 1-inch (2.5-cm) pieces

1. Preheat the oven to 375°F (190°C). Brown the butter in a large ovenproof sauté pan over medium heat. When the butter is deeply golden brown, add the brown sugar and Muscat. Bring up to a simmer, add the rhubarb pieces, and mix to coat.

2. Place the pan in the oven for 4 minutes. Mix carefully with a rubber spatula, trying not to break up the rhubarb. Cook 2 to 5 more minutes, depending on the thickness of the rhubarb (it should be just tender but not falling apart).

3. Pour and spread the rhubarb in a container large enough to just hold the rhubarb pieces and juices without stacking. Let cool and serve with the Schaum Torte, or refrigerate for up to 3 to 4 days.

2

THE GROCERY STORE

I **WAS SITTING BEHIND THE COUNTER OF MY DAD'S GROCERY STORE ON THE LONG** radiator, my legs dangling and squirming. I was looking at my scuffed-up revolvers, with their cracked, faux ivory handles, which were holstered at my hips. Bored and wallowing in a self-induced pity pot, I thought, *These are so last year*. On top of that hardship, our second-grade class had just seen *Ben-Hur*, and I was lamenting to my dad the fact that I wasn't born a Roman slave.

About 10 minutes later, my dad came along with the round wooden top from a bushel of bright green string beans that he had been stocking in the front vegetable case. He wrapped the outside of the wooden cover with a large sheet of butcher paper that he taped on the inside ridge. Then he cut up a wire hanger, fashioned and attached an internal grip, and handed it over to me. "You better start decorating your shield," he said. I unbuckled and dropped my holster on the radiator, grabbed a black grease pen, and started to draw a fine filigree outline of an ominous hawk on the shield; I just knew it would strike fear into any opponent's heart. By the time I had finished decorating, I realized that my dad had fashioned another shield as well as two large gladiator swords (from the sides of a heavy-duty corrugated cardboard iceberg lettuce box). He said, "Take these, get your cousin next door, and go play."

In front of the store was a good 20–25-foot stretch of prime sidewalk performance space. Usually we would race our small bikes around, coming within a whisker of the always-present audience firmly seated on their respective wooden fruit crates. We'd play, and they'd utter things like, "Those damma kids!" But being entertainers, we knew they really enjoyed the show. My grandfather and his brother, Uncle Turri, always took up two of the crates and interacted like a Sicilian Carson and McMahon. Baffu, who was married to their cousin Carmela, usually took the third seat.

I yelled through the screen and up the hall at my cousin, who lived next door in the flat above my grandparents'. I waited as my unsuspecting opponent appeared. I tossed him the other shield and sword.

Exterior corner of D'Amato's Grocery Store building, approximately 1920

"What's that on the front of your shield?" he asked.

"The Hawk," I replied.

"Looks more like a sparrow to me."

With those fighting words, the battle began. There was some awkward jousting, a brutal shot to my shield, a "stabbing" of my opponent's solar plexus, a clutched chest, and a winner. My cousin fell to his knees. I stepped back with my weapon and shield raised and turned to the gallery—two thumbs up from the audience. I was spared to fight again. Sparrow indeed!

The audience had a much deeper mission at the store, though. They were the regular greeting committee that chatted with every customer as they arrived and exited. This was back when everyone in the neighborhood knew one another and the store was the social center of this universe. Between their greeter duties, they passed the day by whittling, smoking Parodis (the small Italian cigars that look like dark brown arthritic pinkies), swearing in Italian at the kids, and solving the problems of the world.

◆

MY GRANDFATHER WAS STUBBORN AND FRUSTRATED WITH A PHYSICALLY MEAN, NASTY streak. He was not above chasing a family member down Jackson Street, wielding a thick banana stalk, which he found a much more effective and personally satisfying punishment than harsh words. He was against my father marrying my mother, as she was not Sicilian, or even Italian. As a result, he would not attend the wedding or even talk to or acknowledge her for quite a while afterward. About a year into the marriage, he decided to accept the situation and uttered a few words in my mother's direction. But being from a good German and English background, she did not reply to him for the next four years—she was inherently stubborn as well. So, right from the beginning, my relationship with my grandfather was completely influenced by my mother. As I think back, the only things I remember making him *really* smile were young beautiful women (especially Judy Marks, the Channel 4 TV weathercaster), cutting-edge cars (he used to race Indy-style cars), and cooking.

Growing up in this half-Sicilian family, tomato sauce was more familiar to me than Campbell's tomato soup. The three usual suspects to appear on the table were: a simple meatless sauce, a sauce with nicely browned Dentice Brothers sausage (from Tony and Pete, the butchers across the street), and a sauce sheltering perfectly light, bobbing meatballs.

I could usually tell which one was cooking as I entered my grandfather's house. If I didn't smell the lingering Filippo Berio olive oil, it was meatless. Otherwise, I would just have to distinguish between the tangy aroma of frying fennel-infused pork sausage and the sweet smell of the browning parsley, Romano, and breadcrumbs that meant meatballs.

About once every three months or so, a different bouquet would emerge and confuse me. Was that pork? No. Was it beef? Or sausage? As it turned out, it would become a favorite. It's what many Sicilian families call the Sunday meat sauce (sugu), or Sunday gravy, an over-the-top mixture of whatever combination of meats you wanted to add; it could be meatballs, spareribs, pork shoulder, beef chuck, or sausage. Whatever is chosen, it is all amalgamated with the sauce to truly make a Sunday dinner special. My favorite part was the succulent pork, browned and slowly braised to a marrow-like consistency. On a platform of exquisitely cooked al dente pasta, it became that perfect bite after bite that I still dream about.

I'M SURE MOST FAMILIES COOKED CARAMELIZED HAM WITH CLOVES, BROWN SUGAR, AND pineapple at Easter that would be ceremoniously carved in the center of the table for groups of hungry Easter-ites. In these same homes, about three hours after consuming their fill of this smoked porcine, folks would have a desert-like thirst that could only be quenched by massive amounts of water.

This is a cycle I'm quite at ease with because I love a great smoked ham. But I have to say, one of my most memorable Easter dinners had nary a leg in sight. It was back in 1957. I had on my suit and a dandy clip-on tie. I was walking stiffly because the suit fit like a cardboard cutout (they were cheaply made for kids because they would outgrow them in a year). My sister looked like she was going to her first communion—as that was the only other time I saw her with anything on her head—and we were all headed to my grandparents' for Easter dinner.

We ate at my grandparents' (over my mother's protest) on various family occasions, but this was a first for Easter. Even at that young age, the Easter ham culture was ingrained in us. When we arrived, I snuck in the kitchen to view the roasting ham, only to be shocked that there was nothing in the oven. However, a rolling rack next to the stove held the coveted Nesco, and it was hot.

So the situation wasn't as bad as I first thought, because at my grandfather's house, "Nesco" translated to "spiedini," those small Sicilian beef roll-ups skewered with onion and bay leaf that were, hands down, my favorite dish. My grandfather walked over and removed the lid. He had an out-of-character smile on his face. I looked in and saw what looked like the mother of all spiedini, slowly quivering in a sea of tomato bliss. I blurted out "Giant spiedini!" But my grandfather shook his head side to side and proudly said, "Braciola."

This meant nothing to me until he carefully lifted the mini roast out of the sauce and started to carve it for the table. He nestled the braciola into its silken tomato blanket as lov-

Interior of D'Amato's Grocery Store, sometime in the 1920s

ingly as a first-time mother cradles her newborn in a bassinet. It was a passion that he reserved solely for food. The braciola looked like spiedini, but it had an interior mosaic of salami, eggs, sausage, breadcrumbs, and herbs. And when you took that first bite, the meat had that melting rich texture that could only come from slow cooking in its tomato-rich bath.

◆

UNCLE TURRI, WHO LIVED BEHIND OUR ORIGINAL APARTMENT ABOVE THE STORE, SHARED a similar verbal temperament with my grandfather. But his was moderated by an inherent sweetness that blossomed when he nourished people. We always thought of his food as special treats that he would just bring downstairs with no notice.

Every year, as a chill came into the air, a large Department of Public Works truck came to our neighborhood. The truck was filled with large, dark-green wooden boxes, and the burly workers would deposit one on the northwest corner across from the grocery store. As soon as the box was in place and the truck pulled away, I, along with other people in the neighborhood, would make a pensive pilgrimage to the green idol. The older wise men of the neighborhood would pick up the cover to do the early inspection. A few comments would be thrown around like, "There was more sand last year," or "Looks like we got an older box," or "Hey, look! A new shovel!"

The box held sand meant for the cars that would invariably get stuck driving up the hill on Pleasant Street between Water and Jackson. But it became much more. For our family it meant my Uncle Turri would be roasting hazelnuts. With the ever-present Parodi dangling from his lips, he would leisurely walk over to the box, small bag in hand, and, almost in slow motion, scoop out about three or four nice handfuls of sand, all the while savoring every puff of his cigar. Once he had collected the sand, he'd walk back across the street, flick the Parodi into the accumulating snow bank on the lawn (no smoking in his house), and walk up to his kitchen.

He would then half-fill a metal pie plate with sand, embed a layer of hazelnuts (in the shell) in the sand, cover the hazelnuts with more sand, and invert another pie plate over the top. Then he'd place the hazelnuts in the oven for what seemed like an eternity (if you knew what was coming). I did repetitive reconnaissance from my outpost, the store counter, to the side door of the building, and as the overwhelming aroma of roasted nuts began to fill the entire upstairs and back hall, I'd know they were done. He would carefully pluck the nuts out of the sand with his asbestos fingers and bring them down to the store. My dad and I would sit behind the counter, cracking the hot shells and greedily popping the dark, crispy, almost-on-the-edge-of-burnt nuts into our mouths, one after another, until we were way past the point of being full.

As the snow bank started to melt and the layers of Parodi nubs were unearthed to eventually form what looked like the remains of a mini campfire on the parched grass, the green box was removed, and we knew that spring was coming. But one year it didn't return—probably because it had become obsolete; with better winter road maintenance and the advent of four-wheel drive, the number of cars getting stuck on Pleasant Street dropped dramatically. Now, anytime I make a recipe with hazelnuts, I always go back to that feeling of anticipation, followed by total satisfaction—but I miss the sandbox.

◆

MY DAD THOUGHT IT WAS A GOOD PLOY. "I'LL WAKE YOU UP EARLY, AND WE'LL GO FOR a real breakfast—just us guys—before we get to the store." How about, *"It's Sunday, and we will sleep in, then slowly roll out of bed and read the Sunday funnies?"*

Very early on, from when I was about five years old, my dad would take me down to the store at five in the morning. His Sunday always started at George Webb's, then located in the 20s on Capitol Drive, where he would have his regular eggs-and-bacon breakfast. I tried them a few times, but it never felt right.

One morning, right next to me at the counter, a fellow was digging into two burgers with fried onions. How could this be? Weren't burgers forbidden before noon? My heavy Catholic upbringing told me this had to be some kind of sin, or at least a crime. I wrestled with the fact that I wanted to be a part of this debauchery. I looked at my dad and pointed at the plate. "Can I have *that*?" I asked. I think he noticed that I was immediately bright-eyed and awake for the first time ever at this predawn hour and said, "Oh, OK."

The plate was put before me, and I felt like a lion invited to a gazelle pajama party. It was so wrong and perfectly tasty right at the same time. From that day on, I actually looked forward to getting up early.

◆

WITH MY WOOL MITTEN, I TRIED TO SCRAPE AWAY A SMALL PEEPHOLE THROUGH THE thick frost that had formed on the front windshield. It was so cold that even the blurry streaks coming from the passing street lights seemed to be frozen into grayish tentacles that grabbed the car and released as we slowly passed down the street. My father hunched over the wheel of his old Ford station wagon as he peered through the small personal porthole that the chugging defroster had formed.

We turned the corner and started down a narrow alley as Dad pulled the wagon side to side, trying to maneuver around the snow banks and frozen ruts.

"Ahh! There they are," he said as he slowed the wagon to a halt. "Go ahead and get 'em!"

I stumbled out the door and put both arms around a bag, which was a bit taller than I was. My hands didn't meet in the back. I slowly waddled back to the car.

I rested the bag on the floor in front of me, and the frost on the window quickly disappeared as the steam, like a magician's fog machine, rose from the brown crispy rolls. Right on top was a small piece of butcher's paper and wrapped inside was my reward: a bit of fresh, uncooked bread dough—an ideal gift for a strange kid.

We were at Rossow Bakery near 25th and Center. It was still Sunday morning, about 6 a.m., and we were on our way to the grocery store. The rolls, which we only got on Sundays, were for the baked ham that was already resting in the Nesco at the store, ready to be sliced for the hungry churchgoers from St. Rita's. This was my first behind-the-scenes bakery experience, and the raw dough became a weekly gift. The first time I met the old baker and asked

My sister (left) and two of my cousins with me in the buggy
in front of D'Amato's Grocery delivery truck

to try the raw dough, he was quite amused that I actually enjoyed eating it. The only thing better than the raw dough balls was what they yielded—the finished crusty, delicious rolls.

◆

EVERY WEEKDAY BEFORE THE GROCERY STORE OPENED, MY DAD WOULD MAKE HIS EARLY buying trip to the "Tooda Waada," what the older Italians called the Third Ward, where Commission Row, the old vegetable market, was located on Broadway. When I accompanied him, our first stop would always be Gagliano's to see his friend Nick "Gag."

"Hey, "WHAT'S GOING ON . . . WHAT'S GOING ON!" was always the first thing out of Nick's mouth—and then he would laugh. This was repeated by every person working there, right down to the older cashier behind the glass window who would check us out. I always thought it was a little weird, as I just didn't get the joke. As it turned out, my dad told me at some point, I was the joke. The first time I was with him at age four, we walked into Gagliano's, and there was a thunderous noise coming from upstairs. They were running the tomato boxing machines, and I was so frightened by the noise that I repeatedly screamed, "WHAT'S GOING ON!" From that point on, I had a new name.

This was always my favorite part of my day: cases upon cases of tomatoes, green beans, lettuces, grapes, cabbages, stacks of bananas on the vine; the unmistakable consoling smell of the mingling of these products in the various warehouses; the overriding sound of the out-of-sight packaging machines; and the huge metal-wheeled rolling wooden carts that moved the products from farmers' trucks into warehouses and then back out to the buyers' vehicles. It was an overwhelming symphony that truly encompassed all of my senses as I was handed a box of strawberries to munch on.

Every visit brought a new unidentifiable alien, in vegetable or fruit form, to learn about. One of the most memorable was the cucuzzi. These are long, gangly squash that range from six inches to over three feet, and are affectionately known as the "serpents of Sicily" for their coiled, snakelike appearance. When my dad brought them back to the store and put them in his refrigerated open display case, they looked alive as the ends dangled over the case in a defiant escape position.

The real excitement came later when my grandfather would pluck a particularly healthy specimen from the case and take it next door for dinner. He would slice it into thick coins and sauté them golden brown in olive oil, salt, and pepper. When they were done, he would bring a plate of the burnished green morsels back to the store for us to snack on. I always thought he was extolling his love of the squash when he would say under his breath, "Cucuzzi senza semenza." Only later did I find out the literal translation was "squash with no seeds," and the phrase was actually a Sicilian insult referring to people who were not very sharp. I'm happy that at least his cynicism never stopped him from being a great cook.

◆

ALL THE YEARS THAT I WORKED AT MY DAD'S GROCERY STORE, I REVELED IN MASTERING the tools of the trade. Starting with bagging, I learned to quickly eye up a customer's total haul and pick the perfect-sized brown paper sack for transport. The old register was set up like a typewriter, and with a combination of multiple fingers pushed simultaneously, the correct numbers popped up in the glassed-in top window. This triggered the ringing bell that signaled the customers to dig into their change purses. The Globe meat slicer (still in service at Sanford today) could be dialed up to shear a hefty slab of bologna ready to be crisply fried for a sandwich, and then dialed down to yield almost diaphanous slices of ham ready to be piled on a crisp Sciortino roll for a lunchtime treat. The scale is where I would challenge myself to guess the weight of the produce before the spinning slot machine dials came to a complete halt.

But my favorite tool was one of the simplest: the can stamper. You could set the revolving rubber wheels to come up with a correct price and then press down on the top when the dial would spin around from the concealed inkpad to stamp the price on top of the can with a signature "cha-ching" sound. The fun came in how fast I could do a case of cans, usually racing against my dad. I broke into a sweat as I blazed a cha-chinging trail across the can tops, only to look up and see my dad blowing on the end of his can stamper like a cowboy cooling down the end of his "peacemaker." Man, he was fast.

After stocking the shelves, we filled the wooden bread case with still-warm loaves of Sciortino bread that the driver had just dropped off, filled up the top of the milk case with the backup cartons lying below in the cooler, and then went on to my second-favorite task: arranging the display of fresh fruits and vegetables in the front window of the store.

The fruit and vegetable crates were the source of one of my favorite anecdotes in D'Amato Grocery lore. Once the wooden slats on the crate were removed (with the small, one-piece metal hammer/pry bar that was my dad's multipurpose tool for every task), often the fruits or vegetables were nestled in squares of beautifully printed wrapping paper. My father showed me how to unwrap each one, flatten out the sheets into a neat pile, and then place them into the corner of the window box.

During the Depression, everything had been utilized in the store, from the vegetable trimmings for soup to the papers used to wrap the fruit. A few of the thriftiest neighborhood women would ask my grandfather to save the fruit wrappings to be used to supplement their

*Joseph D'Amato (my paternal grandfather) calendar from
1951 for D'Amato's Grocery with original phone number*

toilet paper supply. For one particular customer, whom my grandfather did not particularly like, he saved a special bundle of papers from the prickly pears (cactus fruit that is very popular in Sicily). The outer skin of the prickly pear is covered in miniscule thorns that are hard to see. Needless to say, she never again asked him to save the papers.

◆

LOOKING BACK ON MY COOKING OVER THE YEARS, I NOTICE A FEW TYPES OF SEASONAL ingredients that always seem to work their way into my recipes—both sweet and savory. The big three are cranberries, rhubarb, and plums. They all have a common characteristic—with the rhubarb and cranberries, you certainly need a bit of sweetness to make them palatable; and with the plums, they are palatable by themselves, but the more tart varieties also need some sweetness to balance the flavor. This lack of sweetness allows for a greater range and flexibility of flavor, as you can always add sweetness to bring out the natural fruit flavor, but you can't unsweeten fruit without taking away from their inherent flavor.

I have always preferred the Italian variety of plums. These are the small, oblong purple fruit that are late bloomers and are most prominent in the market from August through October. And there is another, deeper reason for my love of plums: they are one of my three backyard fruits.

My first was the rhubarb that my grandma transformed into many delicious treats—but you couldn't just pick and eat that. My first experience with pick and eat (and run) involved my second backyard fruit: the raspberries from the raspberry bushes of our alley neighbors, the Lorres. I must have devoured half of their crop each year! And third, my grandfather had an Italian plum tree in his backyard. As children, my cousins and I would gorge ourselves on the plums in various states from green to overripe. I especially liked the firm tart ones with their bracing acidity. The tree is long gone, but to this day, when I'm at the farmer's market or in the local grocery, the sight of Italian plums brings me back to cool late-summer afternoons, just laying around the backyard and chomping away.

◆

MOST OF THE CUISINE OF THE IMMIGRANTS IN THIS COUNTRY IS BUILT ON FUSION. NOT having access to the products they were used to, families adapted to what was available in the United States. And as they felt more accepting of the dishes of their new home, they incorporated new techniques and products into older dishes that melded both cultures.

My first experience with this concept was at my grandfather's house. The dish that came with his exquisite olive oil fries was—what else?—a burger. Not your all-American ground-beef-and-American-cheese wonder, but a Sicilian man's homage to a newfound favorite. The pork and beef mixture, with bread crumbs, cheese, egg, onions, and garlic, kind of sounds like a meatball. And really, it was his variation of his meatballs, made into a patty, sautéed in olive oil, and then placed on a crusty hard roll with those crispy olive oil fries on the side.

The first time I dug into this beauty I was at first shocked at the difference, but that reaction quickly dissolved into amazement—this was the best burger I'd ever eaten. He never wrote down any recipes, as writing was not one of his strong points, so when I first started to recreate that burger, I just went through his movements from memory. Then I did a little fusion of my own by incorporating a natural tart accompaniment for my Sicilian-American palate.

Forget about pickles—the first tart flavor I remember was olives. My father would bring in cases of raw, bright-green olives. They looked so tempting and tasty, until I took a fatal bite of the bitter fruit. Of course they had to be cured or brined to be the palatable olive we all know and love. When I'm talking about cured or brined olives, I'm not referring to those bland, black canned ones that graced every supper club relish tray in the '50s and '60s; those olives, packed in water, have had almost every ounce of true olive flavor processed out of them—but they are usually everyone's first taste of olives. My first taste was from the crocks that sat on top of the deli case at our grocery. There were black brine-cured, green brine-cured, and black olive oil-cured—the most intense.

My favorite olive time of year was around the holidays when my grandfather would make his Sicilian green olive schiacciate to sell at the store. He would start with green brine-cured olives and crack each one with a light blow from an empty soda bottle to open the flesh and expose the pit. Then he would add diced onion, celery, dried oregano, salt, pepper, and olive oil to the olives and mix—simple, delicious, and the perfect foil for a juicy Sicilian burger.

◆

SOME PARENTS MAY HAVE BEEN STRICTER WITH THEIR KIDS WHEN IT CAME TO EATING sweets. But my dad was actually the biggest kid of all, with a diet to match. He started most days with three donuts: a long john, a cruller, and a maple Persian, all of which he washed down with the first of many eight-ounce Cokes. And as the day went along, it just got sweeter.

No day was complete until a trip was made to the deep, open freezer to the left of the grocery's front door. This held all the treasures of a properly outfitted ice cream truck, sans music. As kids entered the store, they ran right to the freezer, hopping high to peek over the top. My dad would hold the smallest ones up by their ankles as they perused the selection

Porth Pie pan

of popsicles, ice cream sandwiches, Push-Ups, Dreamsicles, Paddle Pops, and Drumsticks. I, of course, always had access to any sweets I wanted. I was the *real* kid in the candy store. But because of that I developed a take-it-or-leave-it attitude toward dessert—unless there was something particularly great.

My first dessert love (well, it verged on lust) was for pie. My earliest pie experience was with the individual Porth pies that came in little aluminum tins (for which the Porth Pie Company charged a deposit). In the beginning they were wonderfully flaky, full of fresh fruit, and tasted as though they'd been freshly baked that morning. As they became a bit more commercialized, they lost their edge, and I lost my interest.

Around 1960, a new diner-type restaurant opened near our house on 35th and Capitol. I went with my dad to the grand opening. They served simple, tasty food, all cooked to order on a flat grill and served at the counter. Behind the counter was a large, bright display case filled with incredible-looking pies that were made in the back by the owner. The one that caught my eye was a golden, sugar-glazed cherry number. I ordered a slice. As my fork broke through the crumbly lattice, an aroma of caramelized butter and sweet-tart cherries hit my nose. I took my first bite, and my hand started to shake. I moved the dish closer and thought, "Please, God, don't let my dad ask for a bite." I didn't realize until that moment that I had *never* tried pie before!

From that point on, every pie has been defined by that perfect slice. As I live and travel, I'm always in search of that dream pie.

◆

WE ARE SO AFFECTED BY WHAT WE WERE FED AS WE GREW UP THAT THE OLD ADAGE, "There's no accounting for some peoples' taste," should be, "There's usually a good reason for most peoples' taste."

I think about all the chefs and cooks I've worked with over the years, who have complete ego hissy fits if a customer wants to substitute something or, horror of horrors, dares to order a steak well-done. "We'll show you well-done. Leave that hunk of charcoal on the grill till it's cauterized." Heaven forbid they try to cook the steak to a perfect well-done (which takes the same skill as a perfect rare, medium-rare, medium, or medium-well) and give the customer what they want.

Taste is so affected by memory and I never forget how important it is as a chef to make the people eating my food as happy as I am about making it.

All the years that I ate at my grandparents' next to the grocery store, it was always my grandfather's food. He was an extraordinary cook, and I never had anything I didn't like.

Over the years, though, I'd heard stories—almost urban legends—about my grandmother's cooking. I'd never actually seen her near the stove, so you can imagine my surprise when one evening my dad said, "Dinner's ready next door. Your grandmother made pasta with peas—and I can't wait to eat."

As I walked through my grandparents' door, my grandfather was sitting on the couch, bolt upright and staring trancelike at the TV, a troubled look on his face. Without even looking over, he muttered under his breath, "Grandma cooked," and slowly shook his head.

I went into the kitchen, and she sat me down in front of a large bowl of the blandest, most watery pasta with gray peas imaginable. I immediately understood why she didn't cook. After soldiering through the bowl, we walked back, and I asked my dad why he was so excited about the dish. He said, "I know, I'm the only one who actually likes it. She made it because she knows that."

Invoice from D'Amato's Grocery

CHAPTER TWO RECIPES

◆

Braciola

57

Dark-Roasted Hazelnut Chocolate Tart

61

Italian Plum Tart with
Brown Sugar Almond Crust

63

Sicilian Burger with
Marinated Olive Schiacciate

65

Tart Cherry Lattice Pie

69

Pasta e Fagioli

71

BRACIOLA *(PRONOUNCED BRAH-JYOH-LAH)*

My grandfather didn't routinely make Braciola, but watching this disagreeable guy transform as he proudly served thick slices of the roll smothered in tomato ambrosia just made him a better person. I wish it had been a regular event.

SERVES 8

For the Tomato Sauce:

¼ cup (59 mL) extra virgin olive oil

8 ounces (227 g) Italian sausage links

1 large onion (12 ounces [341 g]), diced small

4 cloves garlic, finely chopped

2 bay leaves

2 sprigs fresh thyme

1 ounce (28 g) fresh basil leaves, chopped

½ bunch fresh Italian parsley stems, finely chopped (reserve the leaves for the Braciola)

2 tablespoons kosher salt

2 teaspoons freshly ground black pepper

½ cup (131 g) tomato paste

2 (28-ounce [784-g]) cans whole tomatoes in juice, puréed in a food processor until fine

1. Preheat the oven to 350°F (180°C). Place a heavy-bottomed pot over medium heat. When the pan is hot, add the oil, then the sausage and brown on all sides. Remove the sausage to a plate.

2. Add the onions to the pan and sauté until lightly brown. Add the garlic, bay leaves, thyme, basil, parsley stems, salt and pepper and sauté for 1 minute. Add the tomato paste and sauté, stirring, for 3 minutes, or until the paste darkens (do not let it stick to the bottom of the pan and burn).

3. Add the tomatoes, stir, then bring up to a boil. Add the cooked sausage, cover, and bake for 30 minutes.

4. Remove and discard the bay leaf and thyme. Remove and reserve the sausage. Adjust the seasoning with salt and pepper and cool.

(RECIPE CONTINUES ON PAGE 59)

(RECIPE CONTINUED FROM PAGE 57)

For the Braciola:

> 2 tablespoons extra virgin olive oil
>
> 2 ounces (57 g) pancetta, cut in small dice
>
> 1 onion (4 ounces [114 g]) diced small
>
> 3 cloves garlic, finely chopped
>
> Zest of ½ an orange
>
> ¾ cup (81 g) plain bread crumbs
>
> ½ cup (1 ounce [28 g]) fresh Italian parsley leaves, finely chopped
>
> ½ cup (50 g) grated Pecorino Romano cheese
>
> 6 ounces (180 mL) prepared Tomato Sauce
>
> 3 ounces (85 g) Italian salami, cut in small dice
>
> 3 ounces (85 g) cooked Italian sausage (reserved from Tomato Sauce), cut in small dice
>
> 2 egg yolks
>
> ½ teaspoon kosher salt, plus additional for seasoning
>
> ¼ teaspoon freshly ground black pepper, plus additional for seasoning
>
> 1 (1½-pound [681-g]) flank steak, butterflied into 2 pieces and pounded thin (about ¼ inch [6 mm] thick) between 2 sheets of plastic wrap

1. Place a sauté pan over medium heat. When the pan is hot, add the oil, then add the pancetta, and sauté for 2 minutes, or until lightly golden. Add the onions and sauté for 3 minutes. Add the garlic and sauté, stirring, for 1 minute. Add the orange zest and stir.

2. Strain, then press the mixture lightly with the back of a spoon to extract the oil from the mixture. Add the extracted oil back to the pan, add the bread crumbs, and sauté, stirring, until they are lightly golden. Stir in the parsley leaves and remove from the heat.

3. When the bread crumb mixture is cooled a bit, add the pancetta mixture and the cheese. Add 6 ounces of the Tomato Sauce, the salami, the sausage, the 2 egg yolks, the ½ teaspoon salt, and the ¼ teaspoon pepper and mix together.

4. Spread out the 2 flank steaks, season lightly with salt and pepper, and divide the stuffing evenly over each flank, slightly pressing down on the stuffing. Roll each flank jelly-roll-style, making sure that the grain is going from end to end on the finished roll. Tie each roll with string by making a knot every ½ inch (13 mm) (tie securely but not so tight that stuffing squishes out). Tie knots on the ends of the rolls so the stuffing will not leak out during cooking.

(RECIPE CONTINUES ON PAGE 60)

(RECIPE CONTINUED FROM PAGE 59)

To Finish the Braciola:

> **3 tablespoons (45 mL) extra virgin olive oil**
>
> **Prepared Braciola**
>
> **1 cup (237 mL) unsalted chicken stock**
>
> **Remaining prepared Tomato Sauce**
>
> **3 large eggs, placed into cold water and brought up to a boil, cooked for 8 minutes, drained, shocked with cold water, peeled, and sliced with an egg slicer**

1. Preheat the oven to 350°F (180°C). Place a pot, large enough to hold the 2 rolls of Braciola and the sauce, over medium heat. Add the olive oil, and when hot, sauté the Braciola on all sides until they are lightly brown, for about 6 minutes.

2. Add the chicken stock and remaining Tomato Sauce and bring up to a simmer. Bake for 45 minutes to 1 hour, or until the Braciola are fork-tender but not falling apart.

3. When they are tender, let the Braciola cool in the sauce, then refrigerate them until they are needed. Or, if serving immediately, remove the rolls from the sauce to a cutting board. Slice each roll in ½- to ¾-inch (13- to 19-mm) pieces, place on a serving platter, and, with scissors, cut the string and carefully remove it from the slices so they don't fall apart. Place 1 slice of the egg on each piece of Braciola and place the Tomato Sauce over all. If desired, Braciola may be served with pasta on the side.

DARK-ROASTED HAZELNUT CHOCOLATE TART

A few years back in Puglia, Angie and I stopped at a small gelato place where their specialty was dark chocolate studded with large chunks of toasted hazelnuts. The deepness of the hazelnut roast brought out a rich bitterness that reminded me of my Uncle Turri's hazelnuts—and they really rounded out the chocolate. When making the hazelnuts, you don't want to burn them, but don't be afraid to go to the edge.

SERVES 8 TO 10

For the Hazelnuts:

14 ounces (397 g) hazelnuts, roasted in a 350°F (180°C) oven for about 15–18 minutes, tossing every 5 minutes, until the hazelnuts are deeply colored, but not burnt, then rubbed with a towel while still warm to remove the skins (reserve 3 ounces [85 g] for the Tart Shell, 9 ounces [255 g] for the Filling, and 2 ounces [57 g] for the garnish)

For the Tart Shell:

(Note: Have all of the ingredients at room temperature.)

3 ounces (85 g) reserved roasted hazelnuts

2 cups (9 ounces [255 g]) all-purpose flour (divided)

2 tablespoons (½ ounce [14 g]) unsweetened cocoa

1½ sticks (6 ounces [170 g]) unsalted butter

7 tablespoons (3 ounces [85 g]) granulated sugar

1 small egg

1. Place the reserved hazelnuts and 2 ounces (57 g) of the flour in a food processor and process until fine. Add the remaining flour and the cocoa and pulse to mix together; reserve.

2. In the bowl of a stand mixer fitted with a paddle, cream the butter and sugar at medium speed for 1 minute. Scrape the bowl and beat for another minute. Add the egg and mix until emulsified, about 10 seconds. Stop and scrape the bowl. Add the flour mixture and mix for about 5 seconds.

3. Remove the paddle, turn the dough out onto a flat surface, and finish mixing with your hands until the dough just comes together. Press the dough into a 10-inch (25-cm) round removable-bottom pan that is 1½ inches high. Refrigerate the shell for 30 minutes to 1 hour.

4. Preheat the oven to 350°F (180°C). Bake for 10 minutes. (Do not prick holes in the dough—just press down with a towel after 5 minutes when the dough puffs.)

(RECIPE CONTINUES ON PAGE 62)

(RECIPE CONTINUED FROM PAGE 61)

For the Filling and to Bake the Tart:

(Note: Have all of the ingredients at room temperature.)

9 ounces (255 g) reserved roasted hazelnuts

Prepared blind-baked Tart Shell

2 large eggs

1 large egg yolk

½ cup (100 g) granulated sugar

½ cup (119 mL) light corn syrup

2 tablespoons unsalted butter

¼ teaspoon kosher salt

6 ounces (170 g) unsweetened chocolate, melted

1. Preheat the oven to 350°F (180°C). Place the reserved roasted hazelnuts in the blind-baked shell. In a mixing bowl, whisk together the 2 eggs and 1 egg yolk, then whisk in the sugar until smooth. Whisk in the corn syrup.

2. Melt the butter in a small saucepan until it turns medium brown, then add to the bowl and whisk together. Add the salt and melted chocolate and whisk until it is smooth. Pour the mixture evenly over the hazelnuts. Bake for about 25 minutes, or until the mixture is set on the outside and slightly trembling in the center.

For Serving the Tart:

2 cups (474 mL) heavy cream, whipped with 1 tablespoon confectioners' sugar to medium peak

2 ounces (57 g) reserved roasted hazelnuts, for garnish

Confectioners' sugar, for sprinkling

1. With a pastry bag fitted with a fine tip, pipe a thin line of the whipped cream around the inside border of the tart, then a small rosette in the middle.

2. Place the reserved hazelnuts decoratively on the whipped cream and dust with a bit of confectioners' sugar. Serve the tart with the remaining whipped cream on the side.

ITALIAN PLUM TART WITH BROWN SUGAR ALMOND CRUST

Plums are versatile—they are so good baked, dried, grilled, seared, puréed, juiced, and, of course, washed and eaten out of hand. The tartness comes in handy when you're making a dessert because you can control the sweetness level.

SERVES 8

½ cup slivered almonds (2¼ ounces [64 g]), baked in a 375°F (190°C) oven for 6 minutes, then cooled

¾ cup (4 ounces [114 g]) all-purpose flour

1 cup (5 ounces [142 g]) cake flour

½ teaspoon baking powder

⅛ teaspoon kosher salt

1 stick plus 2 tablespoons (5 ounces [142 g]) unsalted butter, at room temperature

½ cup (3 ounces [85 g]) dark brown sugar

1 large egg, at room temperature

¼ cup (1 ounce [28 g]) well-crumbled shortbread cookies

2–2¼ pounds (0.91–1.02 g) firm Italian plums, cut in half stem to tip, pits removed, then partially cut 4–5 times in each starting from tip and ending ¾ of the way down (don't cut all the way through)

2 tablespoons granulated sugar

½ teaspoon ground cinnamon

2 tablespoons plum jelly, melted (optional, for glaze)

2 cups (474 mL) heavy cream, whipped with 1 tablespoon confectioners' sugar to medium peak

1. Place the almonds and ½ cup (76 g) of the all-purpose flour in a food processor and process until fine. Remove from the processor and place in a bowl. Add to the bowl the remaining ¼ cup (38 g) of all-purpose flour, the cake flour, the baking powder, and the salt and mix together.

2. In the food processor, add the butter and brown sugar and process until well mixed. Add the egg and process until the egg is incorporated. Add the flour mixture and pulse until the dough just comes together (do not overmix). Remove from the processor and wrap in plastic wrap. Refrigerate for 20 minutes. Take out the dough and press it evenly into a 11x1½-inch (27.5x29-cm) removable-bottom tart pan. Allow the dough to rest in the refrigerator for 10 minutes, then remove.

(RECIPE CONTINUES ON PAGE 64)

(RECIPE CONTINUED FROM PAGE 63)

3. Preheat the oven to 350°F (180°C). Sprinkle the shortbread cookies over the bottom of the tart pan. Place the plums cut-side-up in a circular fashion starting with the outer rim until you end up in the center—it should look like a blooming flower. Mix the sugar and cinnamon together and sprinkle evenly over the plums. Bake for about 30 to 35 minutes, or until the crust is golden brown.

4. After baking, if desired, lightly glaze the tips of the plums with a pastry brush dipped in the melted plum jelly. Serve the tart warm or at room temperature with the sweetened whipped cream.

SICILIAN BURGER WITH MARINATED OLIVE SCHIACCIATE

My grandfather never wrote any recipes down so I've played with my memory of his original, in a "cheffed up" sort of way. The topper that works perfectly is the Schiacciate.

MAKES 4 BURGERS

For the Semolina Olive Buns: (Makes 4 Buns)

> ¾ cup (178 mL) warm water
>
> 4 teaspoons extra virgin olive oil (divided)
>
> ½ tablespoon barley malt
>
> ½ teaspoon granulated sugar
>
> 1 tablespoon active dry yeast
>
> 1½ cups (206 g) bread flour (divided)
>
> ¾ cup (125 g) semolina flour
>
> 1 teaspoon kosher salt
>
> ¼ cup (34 g) pitted and chopped oil-cured ripe black olives

1. In the bowl of a stand mixer, place the warm water, 1½ teaspoons of the olive oil, the barley malt, and the sugar and stir gently to dissolve the sugar. Add the yeast and stir to dissolve. Allow the mixture to stand and foam for 5 minutes.

2. Place the bowl with the yeast mixture on the stand mixer fitted with a dough hook. Add 1¼ cups of the bread flour, the semolina flour, and the salt and mix on low for 1 minute. Scrape down the sides of the bowl and continue mixing on medium-low until the dough is very smooth and elastic, about 5 to 6 minutes.

3. Place the dough on a lightly floured work surface, using the remaining bread flour as necessary. Flatten the dough. Place the olives on top, fold the dough from end to end, and knead the olives into the dough for about 2 to 3 minutes. Coat the inside of a 5-quart (4.7-L) stainless steel bowl with 1 teaspoon of the olive oil. Place the dough in the bowl and wipe the bowl with the dough. Cover the bowl with plastic wrap. Allow the dough to rise in a warm location until it has doubled in volume, about 1 hour.

4. Preheat the oven to 325°F (160°C). Place the dough on a lightly floured work surface. Use a sharp knife to cut the dough into 4 equal portions. Shape each portion into a ball. Place the balls on a baking sheet that has been lined with parchment paper. Loosely cover the dough with plastic wrap and allow it to rise in a warm location until doubled in size, about 30 minutes.

(RECIPE CONTINUES ON PAGE 67)

(RECIPE CONTINUED FROM PAGE 65)

5. Using a dough cutter or the back of a thin-bladed knife, press an X on the top of each bun (be sure not to cut the buns). Allow the buns to rise for an additional 10 minutes, then brush with the remaining olive oil.

6. Bake the buns for about 35 to 40 minutes, or until golden brown. Allow the buns to cool thoroughly before cutting in half. (The buns will keep fresh for 2 to 3 days if they are stored in a resealable plastic bag at room temperature, but are best used on the day of baking.)

For the Sicilian Burger:

¼ cup (59 mL) plus 2 tablespoons extra virgin olive oil (divided)

½ cup (75 g) finely minced onions

2 cloves garlic, finely chopped

¼ cup (59 mL) dry white wine

2 tablespoons sweet Marsala wine

1 bay leaf

1 teaspoon freshly ground black pepper, plus additional for seasoning

½ teaspoon kosher salt, plus additional for seasoning

1 pound (454 g) ground beef chuck

½ pound (227 g) ground pork

1 large egg, lightly beaten

¼ cup (59 mL) dry white bread crumbs

¼ cup (25 g) grated Pecorino Romano cheese

2 tablespoons chopped fresh Italian parsley

1 tablespoon chopped fresh basil

Prepared Semolina Olive Buns (right before the burgers are done, split the buns in half and brush the insides with extra virgin olive oil. Grill the buns oil-side-down in a sauté pan)

Marinated Olive Schiacciate (recipe follows)

1. Heat 2 tablespoons of the olive oil in a small nonstick sauté pan over medium-high heat. When hot, add the onions and cook until translucent, about 3 to 4 minutes. Add the garlic and sauté for 1 minute. Add the white wine, the Marsala wine, the bay leaf, the 1 teaspoon pepper, and the ½ teaspoon salt. Bring the mixture to a boil, then adjust the heat and allow it to simmer until most of the liquid has evaporated, about 4 to 5 minutes. Remove and discard the bay leaf. Transfer the onion mixture to a plate and place uncovered in the refrigerator to cool.

(RECIPE CONTINUES ON PAGE 68)

(RECIPE CONTINUED FROM PAGE 67)

2. In a 5-quart (4.7-L) stainless steel bowl, gently but thoroughly combine the ground beef, ground pork, chilled onion mixture, egg, bread crumbs, Romano, parsley, and basil. Gently form the seasoned ground meat mixture into 4 (7-ounce [199-g]) 1¼-inch-thick (3.2-cm) burgers. Cover the burgers with plastic wrap and refrigerate them until needed.

3. Just before cooking, lightly season the burgers with salt and freshly ground black pepper. In a large sauté pan that has been heated over medium heat, add ¼ cup (59 mL) of the olive oil. When hot, sauté the burgers for 6 to 7 minutes per side for medium-well. Place the burgers on the grilled buns and garnish with the Marinated Olive Schiacciate.

For the Marinated Olive Schiacciate:

1 cup (134 g) brine-cured Sicilian green olives, rinsed in warm water, drained, lightly crushed to crack open, pits removed, and quartered

¼ cup (38 g) whole pepperoncini, tops cut off, seeds removed, and thinly sliced

¼ cup (38 g) finely chopped red bell pepper

¼ cup (38 g) small-diced red onion

¼ cup (59 mL) extra virgin olive oil

1 tablespoon red wine vinegar

½ tablespoon juice from pepperoncini

1 clove garlic, finely chopped

Kosher salt and freshly ground black pepper, to taste

1. Mix all of the ingredients together and serve at room temperature.

TART CHERRY LATTICE PIE

I was having trouble finding my "dream pie." But as soon as I found myself in "cherry central" in Wisconsin's Door County and surrounded by orchards filled with sweet and tart ripe cherries, I thought, if I can't find my "dream pie," why not make it?

MAKES 1 (9½-INCH [24-CM]) PIE

For the Pie Crust:

> 2 cups plus 3 tablespoons (12 ounces [341 g]) all-purpose flour
>
> 1 tablespoon granulated sugar
>
> 1 stick plus 2 tablespoons (5 ounces [142 g]) cold unsalted butter, cut in ½-inch (13-mm) cubes
>
> 6 tablespoons (3 ounces [85 g]) cold leaf lard, cut in ½-inch (13-mm) cubes
>
> ½ cup (119 mL) cold water mixed with 1 tablespoon kosher salt
>
> 1 large egg yolk mixed with 2 tablespoons heavy cream
>
> 2–2½ tablespoons raw or turbinado sugar

1. In a bowl, mix the flour and sugar. Place the butter and lard on top and place the bowl in the refrigerator for 10 minutes.

2. Remove from the refrigerator and toss lightly with your hands to distribute the butter and lard cubes and flour. Place in a food processor and pulse about 20 times, until the butter and lard are pea-size. Add the salted water through the processor feed tube, while holding down the pulse button, and run for about 4 seconds (do not overmix).

3. Remove the dough from the processor (it will be very crumbly) and lightly gather it together into a square (do not overmix). Cover the dough with plastic wrap and refrigerate for 1 hour.

4. Remove the dough from the refrigerator and divide into 2 pieces, 1 slightly larger than the other (1 about 13 ounces [369 g] and the other 10 ounces [284 g]). Roll the larger piece into an approximate 13-inch (32.5-cm) circle with an even thickness of about ¼ inch (6 mm), dusting the top and bottom with enough flour so the dough doesn't stick to the surface or rolling pin. Carefully place the dough in a 9½-inch (24-cm) pie dish (the dough should overhang from 1 to 1½ inches [2.5 to 3.8 cm]). Crimp the edges to form a border around the top, cutting off any excess dough. Place in the refrigerator to chill.

(RECIPE CONTINUES ON PAGE 70)

(RECIPE CONTINUED FROM PAGE 69)

5. Roll out the other piece of dough, with enough flour so it doesn't stick, into an 8x12-inch (20x30-cm) rectangle that is about ¼ inch (6-mm) thick. Place the rectangle on a sheet tray that has been lined with plastic wrap. Brush the top with the egg/cream mixture (reserve the excess for glazing the crimped edges of the pie before baking). Evenly sprinkle the raw or turbinado sugar on top. With a pizza cutter, cut the rectangle into ½-inch (13-mm) strips lengthwise—you will need about 14 strips for the lattice. Refrigerate the lattice until you are ready to assemble the pie.

For the Pie:

> **6 cups fresh tart cherries (2½ pounds [1.13 kg]), pits removed with a pitter, or you may substitute IQF (Individually Quick-Frozen) tart cherries (do not use tart cherries in syrup as they will be too sweet)**
>
> **½ cup (100 g) granulated sugar**
>
> **¼ cup (38 g) Wondra flour (instant flour)**
>
> **Pinch salt**
>
> **Prepared Pie Crust**

1. Preheat the oven to 400°F (200°C). In a bowl, place the cherries, sugar, flour, and salt and mix together to evenly coat (if using frozen cherries, do not defrost them before mixing). Fill the prepared Pie Crust with the filling. Brush the reserved excess egg/cream mixture on the outside and inside of the crimped edges.

2. Top the pie with the lattice strips in a basketweave pattern: start with 2 perpendicular pieces in 1 corner of the pie and add 1 to each side toward the middle, weaving as you go along. Trim the excess lattice on the edges and crimp the lattice to the edges. Refrigerate the pie for 15 to 20 minutes.

3. Place the pie directly on an oven rack that has a pan underneath it to catch any drippings and bake for 15 minutes. Reduce the oven temperature to 350°F (180°C) and bake for an additional hour, or until it is deeply golden and bubbly.

4. Cool the pie on a wire rack for at least 5 hours, or until it is room temperature and completely set.

PASTA E FAGIOLI

Taste is so affected by memory and I never forget how important it is as a chef to make the people having my food as happy as I am about making it. You will thank me that this take on my paternal grandmother's pasta and peas is not her recipe, but I hope it's one that would make both her and my dad happy.

SERVES 8 TO 10

¼ cup (59 mL) extra virgin olive oil, plus additional for serving

8 ounces (227 g) smoked pork neck bones

1 large onion (12 ounces [341 g]), diced small

1 carrot (4 ounces [114 g]), peeled and diced small

2 stalks celery (4 ounces [114 g]), diced small

8 cloves garlic, sliced very thinly

For the sachet, mix together the following spices in cheesecloth and tie with butcher string:

> 10 juniper berries, crushed
>
> 1½ tablespoons anise seed
>
> 3 bay leaves
>
> 2 sprigs fresh rosemary (about 5–6 inches [12.5–15 cm] long)
>
> 2 sprigs fresh sage (about 14 leaves total)
>
> 1 cinnamon stick (about 2 inches [5 cm] long)
>
> 3 pieces orange zest (without white pith) (about 1x2 inches [2.5x5 cm] each)

2 quarts (1.90 L) unsalted chicken stock

2 cups (454 g) dried white beans (navy, pea, or cannellini), rinsed, soaked in 8 cups (1.90 L) of very hot water, placed in a covered container for 12 hours, then drained right before using

¾ teaspoon freshly ground black pepper, plus additional to taste

2 teaspoons kosher salt, plus additional to taste

½ pound (227 g) string beans, ends removed, cut in ½-inch (13-mm) pieces, blanched in boiling salted water until just cooked, shocked in ice water, and drained

½ pound (227 g) green peas (fresh or frozen), blanched in boiling salted water until tender, shocked in ice water, and drained

1 cup (105 g) ditalini pasta, cooked al dente according to package directions

1 (4–6-ounce [114–170-g]) piece aged Asiago cheese, to be grated for serving

(RECIPE CONTINUES ON PAGE 72)

(RECIPE CONTINUED FROM PAGE 71)

1. Place a soup pot over medium heat. When the pot is hot, add the ¼ cup (59 mL) oil, then the neck bones, and sauté for 3 to 4 minutes. Turn the heat to medium-low. Add the onions, carrots, celery, and garlic. Add the sachet to the vegetables. Stir, cover, and sweat the vegetables by stirring regularly without browning, for about 10 minutes.

2. Add the stock, the drained beans, and the ¾ teaspoon pepper and bring up to a very low simmer. Cover the pot and simmer slowly for about 40 minutes. Add the 2 teaspoons of salt and continue cooking until the beans are completely tender and creamy but not falling apart, another 15 to 20 minutes.

3. Remove the sachet and neck bones. Purée ¼ of the soup in a food processor, then add it back to the main soup. Adjust the seasoning with salt and pepper.

4. Mix together the cooked string beans, peas, and ditalini and season them lightly with salt and pepper. Divide the soup into bowls and garnish with the ditalini mixture. Grate the Asiago over the soup and sprinkle with the olive oil.

3

FLEW THE COOP

IT WAS 4 A.M. ONE BRUTALLY COLD WISCONSIN WINTER DAY AS MY DAD PULLED his '54 Ford station wagon up to the corner of 35th and Melvina, about six blocks from our house. He reached across me, opened the door, and waved me out, quickly wishing me good luck. Just as I was ready to apologize for whatever I did to make him drop me off, my sleepy head cleared and I remembered that this had been my idea. I walked toward a large, rusted metal hut and slowly lifted the latch on the door. The door was immediately ripped out of my hand as the wind blew it open. "Get in here and shut that door!" a voice shouted. This was my welcome to my first real job (outside of working for my dad in the grocery store). I was a paperboy for the *Milwaukee Sentinel*, the morning newspaper, and I had a route from Capitol Drive to Keefe, between 36th and 38th.

The ominous hut was the paper station, and Rollie and Ronnie, a stout pair of brothers, were the station captains. It was a large, uninsulated metal shed with a roaring potbelly stove on one end that kept it steamy warm. Music blasted out of a transistor radio in the other corner, and the middle was stacked to the ceiling with bundles of papers and tables to sort them.

The brothers immediately took me under their ample wings and showed me the tricks of the trade, from how to roll and rubber band my 40-some papers for delivery, to how to use the thick rubber thumb cover to "sub," putting together the sections of the weekend paper at blazing speed. These guys were Batman and Robin! They became instant mentors, and after I finished my route, I didn't want our time together to end. I asked if I could join them to eat. It was only 5:30 in the morning, but in the true tradition of the butchers of Les Halles in Paris, they were ready for a proper meal—no skimpy egg breakfast here. As the grasshopper in the equation, I was there to learn.

So that was how I started eating double pork steak and fried potatoes before the sun came up. And instead of washing it down with French wine, we threw back tall chocolate malts. As I sat back on my stool, surveying my ink-smudged clothes and inhaling the distinctive aroma of newsprint on my hands, I knew I had arrived.

Newspaper boy wire cutter

As the months went by, I found that the worst part of the job was getting up in the dark. I would do my best zombie imitation as I walked half-awake—actually, half-asleep—along my paper route. It usually took twice as long as it should have, as I'd miss complete blocks sleepwalking and only wake up as I stumbled off the curb at the end of the missed block.

But this sleep deprivation proved to be totally worth it when I went out to collect for the week's deliveries. I thought I was quite an enterprising entrepreneur as my metal changer, which was hooked to my belt loop, was so full I had to crouch over in a Quasimodo pose. So what does a young lad of 12 do with a pocketful of change? He goes to the legendary haven of goodness where they serve perfect hamburgers made with no less than a full block of butter on each patty: Butter Bun, on Wisconsin Avenue.

I talked my classmate Joseph into accompanying me on this epicurean adventure. We took the bus from 35th and Capitol and transferred on Wisconsin. As we got close to downtown, our faces were glued to the bus window as if we were going through the Grand Canyon. I spotted Butter Bun on the right side of the street and immediately yanked the buzzer. We leapt off the bus as it ground to a halt at the next corner. After a bit of shuffling at the Bun's front door, we entered and snagged the last two seats at the counter. We ordered, and two dripping beauties were placed in front of us. There was butter everywhere as we slowly ate around the buns. I had a plan, and it all ended with the most heavily butter-soaked portion of the bun: the money bite.

Most normal people would have been perfectly satisfied, but as hungry preteens (and both under five feet tall), we had a lot of growing to do. So it was only fitting to follow up with the best sensory palace in the city, the Buddy Squirrel. I had firsthand knowledge of this place. When Capitol Court opened in the '50s, I would catch a small whiff as I got off the bus and then literally float to the Squirrel's door as the heady aroma of roasted nuts melded with caramelized butter from the caramel corn, quickly turning me into a poster child for sensory conditioning.

I was always a sucker for roasted and grilled local corn, especially when it was prepared State Fair-style, the outside husks blackened; if you asked nicely, they would pick out a particularly charred one for you. And when delicious, fresh corn was dipped in Wisconsin's finest hot, melted dairy confection, it popped and became savory caramel corn. Yes, the only thing that could follow beef and butter had to be caramel corn and roasted nuts. Joseph and I split a bag of each, and I realized that the only thing better than eating them individually was eating them together.

◆

WHEN IT CAME TO FRIENDS, I WAS DRAWN TO PEOPLE WHO HAD THE SAME, ALMOST unnatural attraction to food above all else. My first real friend was TJ. I first met him at a horse race. He was so close I could feel his breath whoosh past my head as he lunged in front of me on a flowing graceful golden Palomino. I was a bit jealous of his handsome mount as I was bouncing along on Big Red, a boxy nag, but a gamer that had never let me down. Just as I was about to overtake him at the wire I heard a loud pop and was immediately thrown to the "carpet." I looked forward to see TJ cheering in victory and looked back to see Big Red listing to one side still attached to the frame by the three remaining springs. I was only four years old, but our friendship was cemented that day in his parent's living room.

Tony (Senior) owned Fazio's on Fifth with his brothers, and it was the ultra-special occasion place for our family. Fazio's was not only a restaurant, but also a cabaret and dinner theater that booked national signing and dancing acts and Broadway-type reviews. My dad grew up with Tony Sr., he was his best friend; and my mother's best friend from childhood was Eda Fazio, Tony's wife.

Both of our mothers had us involved in years of organized activities. Some I really enjoyed, especially swimming, diving, and tennis (which I still play today). I had mixed feelings about others.

We were marching in line, backs straight, eyes forward, when the music stopped and I was staring at what looked like a long raised horizontal ladder that was missing its rungs. I would have been happy if it were a ladder, as I never really had any fear of heights. But this was really bad. It was parallel bars.

My mother had enrolled TJ and me in gymnastics at the downtown Milwaukee Turner's. I know now they had our best interests in mind as a little physical activity was good, but after a bad karate experience, it seemed like an overload of military-school-type discipline was coming our way.

Surprisingly, we were not immediately smitten with the idea of dressing in gymnast's constricting stir-up pants and clingy tank tops that laid bare to the masses our scrawny appendages, then parading to the staccato beat of the bun-adorned ivory tinkler sitting properly erect at the upright piano. Every time she started to play, it meant we were on to a new pitiful display of gymnastic lack of skills. I had the natural flexibility of a concrete block and as bad as I was on the bars, the vault was worse. And the still rings, well those were just two wide mouths laughing at me. And no amount of bamboo pole coercing could get me up to the top on the freehand rope climb.

But I guess it wasn't all bad. I really liked the ritual chalking up of the hands and I felt almost masterful on the trampoline—until TJ told me I looked like a flailing dork.

Even bad gymnastics really works up an appetite, though. By the second week we figured out to tell our parents to pick us up 20 minutes past the time we were done so we could limp over to Heinemann's on Wisconsin Avenue at the bridge for hot fudge sundaes with deeply toasted pecans and extra fudge. It was just perfect for putting our defeated minds in a better place.

◆

MY SUMMERS IN HIGH SCHOOL WERE SPENT WITH MARK BAKULA, WHO HAD ATTENDED a grade school next to mine and had become a good friend as a result of proximity; he lived eight blocks from us. Mark's father, Andy, had owned a custard stand on Hampton Avenue and fancied himself an amateur chef—and Mark certainly shared his appreciation of well-made food.

During summers, we would hang out most days, filling the morning with baseball, biking, miniature golf, or basketball, and around noon, we'd begin a desperate search for food, as we were depleted and famished. One noon hour I told Mark about the great food and incredible pie I had eaten at the diner on 35th and Capitol. As we approached the diner, he looked across the street and saw that a new franchise roast beef sandwich place had just opened. Not completely trusting me about the food I'd had, he decided to go for the beef while I made my way to the diner.

At the diner, I had a burger and a slice of their incredible chocolate cream pie—a perfect smooth, deep, bittersweet chocolate filling with semisweet fresh cream on top. Mark walked over after his roast beef sandwich and told me how bad it was.

I replied "Oh, really? Well, try a bite of my chocolate cream pie." As soon as it hit his lips, he went crazy.

"I'll have a slice," he said to the waitress.

"Oh," she said, "that was the last slice, honey—try one of our fruit pies."

Mark looked as though Christmas has been called off.

"No, thanks," he replied. He then said, "Let's go up to Blankenstein's—I have to find a chocolate cream pie!"

When we got to the Blankenstein's (our local supermarket), the in-house bakery was void of cream pies. So Mark, quite obsessed by now, went to the frozen food section and picked out a Pet-Ritz frozen chocolate cream pie, and we went to my house to wait for it to defrost. After 20 minutes, Mark couldn't wait any longer. He took a fork and dug in, only to hit a concrete frozen center. In a twisted, teenage way, I was quite enjoying this. He chiseled away and dug out a good half-dollar-sized bunch of chards and crunched his thimble of pie down. Immediately disgusted, he threw the pie in the garbage and left.

◆

IN 1964, I WAS A FRESHMAN IN HIGH SCHOOL. I HAD JUST STARTED AT MARQUETTE HIGH on 35th and Wisconsin, and as every good high schooler can tell you, the most important question to learn quickly is, *Where do you hang out after school?*

At Marquette there were two places: Gilles on Bluemound, which was the main spot that was shared with our cross-Wisconsin Avenue rivals, Pius High, and Big Boy on Fifth and Wisconsin, which was shared with a friendlier rival, Holy Angels girls' school.

Two very defining moments in my life happened at Big Boy. Number one was my first cigarette. I was standing in line with a newfound friend who smoked Kools. He asked if I would like one. Well, of course, I would. I hid the fact that I didn't know whether to light the tobacco end or the white filter, and playing it "Kool," I took a deep puff. Surprisingly, I didn't cough much and got about halfway through the cigarette. Suddenly I got a bit dizzy and put the cigarette down in a nearby ashtray. Then I proceeded to drop right to the floor. Next thing I knew, I was looking up at a circle of faces. "Are you all right?" they asked. "Oh, sure. I skipped lunch, and I'm just over-hungry," I said, offering an acceptable excuse. My smoking days were numbered after that.

My second, and more professionally defining moment, was with Mark. We arrived at Big Boy and realized we had a dollar between us—and we were starving. I'd given up the notion of eating, but Mark said, "Just order two hot teas with the tea bags on the side." As the waitress set down the two stainless teapots, Mark channeled his inner vagabond and said, "Just pour a good amount of ketchup into the pot and stir it up." He finished it with a flourish of cream from the creamer, a touch of salt and pepper, and, of course, a hit of Lawry's seasoning salt (that was always on every table). "Voilà! Cream of tomato soup for 50 cents a person!" Washed down with unlimited free Big Boy ice water, a feast was in progress. Actually the faux soup was beyond bad—verging on disgusting—but as I choked it down, I had to admire the ingenuity and fearlessness that Mark exhibited in his freestyle/survivor approach to using what we had at hand. And this was a whole lot cooler than fainting in line.

◆

I DECIDED AT AGE 17 THAT I WANTED TO GET INTO THE COOKING FIELD. I WAS WORKING at the grocery store, and my dad asked his local Pabst salesman, Jerry, if he knew of any entry-level jobs in Milwaukee restaurants. About a week later, Jerry called and said that Kalt's, a German restaurant on Oakland near Locust, was looking for a kitchen helper.

I immediately got over there and spoke with Howard Kalt, the owner. I was nervous as I entered the darkened barroom in the front of the restaurant. The walls were covered with caricatures (drawn by Howard Kalt himself) of all the stars who had played at the J. Pellman Theatre, located next to the restaurant. This was Milwaukee's version of Sardi's (near the Broadway theater district in New York City).

We sat at the bar and talked, and just as I was ready to hear, "Thanks for coming by, but we need someone with a bit of experience," Howard said, "Can you start next Monday?" *Can I start next Monday? I can start right now! I'm going to be a cook!*

It was a Friday night, a month later, and I felt like I was floating in a pool of grease. I was trying to man Kalt's bank of fryers. I wasn't complaining, though, as that was what I had been working my way up to.

I started out as a daytime lunch helper, toasting bread, setting parsley on plates, and running the hand-pump mini steamer that reheated the corned beef and roast beef for sandwiches. Most of the latter part of my week was spent getting ready for that Catholic-inspired Milwaukee institution—Friday night fish fry. It started on Thursday as I spent the entire day working the electric slicer and transforming huge heads of cabbage into slaw ingredients; by day's end I had developed a Popeye-like forearm.

Friday morning was spent grating the dried bread for breadcrumbs and portioning the never-ending cases of Icelandic cod. For the first few months of working there, I would walk out at 3:30 after my shift and could only imagine the real-deal cooking that was going on there throughout the night. After pleading my case, I was promoted to the night breading station. Beyond a few orders of flaming breaded shrimp, my whole evening was taken up with the hand-breaded onion rings. Kalt's was known for them, and nary an order came in that didn't have a basket on the table. I felt I was fairly proficient at the process—flour, egg wash, bread crumbs— and thought, *This is a snap!* I had no fear of going into my first Friday night. But I should have. The night became a flurry of golden chunks of cod right from the 5 p.m. opening. The cook who originally trained me had to jump in as the clock hit 6:30, and I was behind by a good 30 orders. I backed away from the breading line, a little dazed, and looked at where my hands had once been. All I saw were what looked like two large, brown car wash mitts. My hands were so encrusted that they had become useless. I looked over at my replacement and could hardly focus on her hands; they moved so quickly and effortlessly that they became a blur.

Five minutes later, she was all caught up and looked over at me with a bit of a smirk while sipping her soda, "Not so simple is it, youngblood? I told you the first night—one hand for dry, one hand for wet." That's how I ended up in front of the fryers, as I was finished at the breading station for that night. I became a lot faster as the weeks progressed, and although I even began to look forward to the Friday night rush, I had learned to never underestimate the difficulty of any job.

After a few years at Kalt's, I decided to move on and took a job as a chef's helper at a new restaurant that was opening up, First Place East, on Oakland in Shorewood. I was excited to be part of the opening team. It was a daytime lunch job, and I was working directly with the chef so I could learn preparation and technique for all the dishes.

The menu was split between entrées and sandwiches with a couple of lunchtime specials thrown in. One of our early lunchtime specials was short ribs, which were new to me. The massive hunks of beef ribs, about six inches square, were tied off and braised. Braising is a process in which the meat and vegetables are well browned and then liquid is added to a level about two-thirds the height of the meat. The mixture is covered and slowly cooked in the oven until everything is tender and luscious.

After the daily special, the largest selling item at lunch was the Reuben sandwich. We usually cut up a good amount of corned beef to be ready for the rush, and as orders came in, I assembled the sandwiches. I laid out caraway rye bread and piled on Swiss cheese, sauerkraut, and the portioned corned beef. Then I lightly brushed the rye slices with oil and grilled the sandwiches until they were crispy on the outside and the cheese was molten on the inside. I felt very good about my new position, and my confidence grew as we experienced busier lunches and the food just flew out of the kitchen.

A few months after opening, the chef scheduled a day off so he could undergo outpatient surgery on a Monday. He felt that I would be able to handle the lunch alone, as Mondays were a bit slower. As Monday dawned, I was a bit nervous, but I just went about setting my-self up as best I knew how. I even preassembled a few of the Reubens, as they were the item that took the longest to put together. The chef helped me out by making a large pan of short ribs that I only had to reheat and serve.

The first orders started out fine, except the first two tables took all my premade Reubens. Next three tables: four more Reubens. Come on, folks! Doesn't anyone like short ribs? As I was assembling the new Reubens, another table came in. Five more Reubens. Now I had a huge problem. I was out of sliced corned beef so I ran downstairs to slice more. Meanwhile, the items on the grill were smoking, the French fries were turning into fossilized twigs in the fryer, and absolutely no food was leaving the kitchen.

Sadly, this was not a bad dream. It was a full-scale, real-life meltdown. By the time I had food ready to go out again, the tables had already left. I was devastated. The next day, when the chef returned, I was very cordially fired as a well-intentioned cook without enough experience. On the plus side, I have never since then been caught without my mise en place (preparation) being ready, and in spite of the memory, I've still never met a Reuben that I didn't like.

◆

WHEN IS THAT MOMENT WHEN YOU DECIDE YOUR FUTURE? IS IT A DEFINING MOMENT OF clarity when you stop and actually realize what's happening? Or, is it a continuing evolution through which you take unconscious steps in a direction that slowly becomes an avocation?

Even with my early interest in cooking as a trade, I still wanted my route to the food world to take me through college. The logical choice at the time was UW Stout, one of the few state schools that had a hotel and restaurant program. My plan was to spend a few years at UW Milwaukee for the preliminary courses that I would have to take at any college. This would be less expensive, as I was a resident; then I could transfer to Stout after saving money for a few years.

After my second year at UWM, I decided to just take a semester of courses that I enjoyed, so I signed up for drawing, design, and philosophy. It was a great year, as I found the fine arts courses very liberating, even though my natural drawing ability was surely in question. The drawing instructor mercifully told me that, although I had no natural skill, that wasn't necessarily a bad thing, as unlike the more talented students, I would have no choice but to be very teachable.

The philosophy courses were just as stimulating; thought-provoking debate was right up my contrary alley. One evening, about three-quarters of the way through the year, I was at my apartment on Locust and Weil. I had just finished a design project earlier that day and was studying philosophy when dinnertime came around. I was feeling peculiarly euphoric; throughout my years as a student, I had never really enjoyed studying—but that year, I had really enjoyed everything about my courses.

I put down my book, went into the kitchen, and grabbed a large cast iron Griswold (my only sauté pan). I heated it up and poured a bit of oil on the bottom. I took out some leftover boiled red potatoes, scallions, and garlic and started a crispy fried potato dish my roommate Tom made regularly. As the potatoes were turning golden brown, my euphoria shot into hyperspace. As happy as I was with the drawing, design, and philosophy, this moment of cooking was at another level. For me it was a moment of clarity, but it didn't come out of nowhere. Years and years of positive reinforcement and the influence of friends, family, and coworkers got me there.

I knew what I wanted to do; but I was pretty broke, and just coming up with enough cash to pay for half of the cramped quarters Tom and I called home, was a struggle. I needed some direction. After many inquiries I found out about a local cooking apprentice program run by the Jewish Vocational Service in Milwaukee. I called for information and found out it ran three nights a week, I could start immediately, and the best part—it was free!

I trekked downtown for my first night of class. The address led me to a large, slightly shabby, office building. I was a bit creeped out as I rode up the old elevator, hoping the door would reopen. It had pulled one of those bait-and-switch routines when I got on: open, then half close, then open again, and then grate slowly to a fully closed position. The building was completely deserted, as most downtown buildings were after 6 p.m. The elevator lurched to a halt, and I spontaneously broke into a prickly sweat, as the door wasn't moving. After five seconds it scraped open, and I scrambled out. I'm not usually neurotic; but that night was a big deal, and I was hoping that I had made the right decision.

The class was held in a small office/kitchen that was probably used as a building commissary. About six students surrounded the chef coat-clad instructor. I was easily the youngest by a good 15 to 20 years and the only student that didn't need a shave. I felt a tinge of intimidation, but the instructor, Chef Radcliffe, immediately welcomed me and had everyone introduce themselves. He laid down a few preliminary rules and jumped right into teaching. He was the head chef of Strucel's, an upscale westside restaurant known for its perfectly roasted prime rib. He had an easygoing style, but his knowledge flowed at the pace of water exiting a fire hose. By the time the first class is over, I knew I was in the right place.

The weeks went on and I noticed that I was the only regular volunteer for any extra duty and that my classmates changed regularly, with very few lasting more than a month. The ones who did attend regularly had a very lethargic rhythm, just doing the minimum required. There was also no class camaraderie and no hanging out after class or extracurricular "talking cooking," as I thought there would be. After the third month, Chef Radcliffe asked if he could talk with me after class. I didn't know if that was good or bad. After the rest of the students departed, we sat in the back office, and he said to me, "You're really interested in cooking, aren't you?"

Odd question, I thought. Then I replied, "Of course. This is the first step to becoming a chef—isn't everyone in the class interested in being here?"

"Oh my, you don't know!" he said. "You're the only one who doesn't have to be here—all the rest of these guys are on work release from prison!"

Well, that explained a lot! He asked what my goals were and recommended that I apply to a professional cooking school as his curriculum for the program only went so far. He told me about programs at Cornell, Michigan State, and Stout, all of which I knew a little about; they all offered a mix of cooking and management with a strong emphasis on the front of the house. He then told me about a small Eastern trade school that wasn't nationally known but had a major focus on training chefs, with a smattering of management. That would be his choice for me. The school, located on Yale's campus in New Haven, Connecticut, was called the Culinary Institute of America. Afterward, he wrote me a letter of recommendation, and I hoped the school would become my choice too.

CHAPTER THREE RECIPES

◆

Bitter Chocolate Cream Pie

85

Chilled Tomato Soup with
Maple Bacon Panzanella

87

Goujonettes of Perch with Potato Pancakes
and Chipotle Green Olive Sauce

90

Carbonnades of Beef with
Brown Butter Egg Noodles

93

Charred Corn, Zucchini, and Mussel Soup

95

Hot Fudge Toffee Nut Ball

98

BITTER CHOCOLATE CREAM PIE

For me, the balance in chocolate cream pie is when the chocolate filling is bitter enough to play off the sweet cream topping, so I think this pie should satisfy even the most over-indulgent chocoholic as it is loaded with balanced flavor. And if you're out there Mark, this pie's for you.

MAKES 1 (9½-INCH [24-CM]) PIE

For the Single-Layer Pie Crust:

> 1⅓ cups (6 ounces [170 g]) all-purpose flour
>
> 1½ teaspoons granulated sugar
>
> 6 tablespoons (3 ounces [85 g]) cold unsalted butter, cut in ½-inch (13-mm) cubes
>
> 2 tablespoons (1 ounce [28 g]) cold leaf lard, cut in ½-inch (13-mm) cubes
>
> ¼ cup (59 mL) cold water, mixed with 1 teaspoon kosher salt
>
> 1 large egg white, stirred with a fork with pinch of kosher salt

1. In a bowl, mix the flour and sugar. Place the butter and lard on top and refrigerate for 10 minutes.

2. Remove from the refrigerator and toss lightly with your hands to distribute the butter and lard cubes and flour. Place in a food processor and pulse about 20 short times until the butter and lard are pea-size. Add the salted water through the processor feed tube, while holding the pulse button down, and run for about 4 seconds (do not overmix).

3. Remove the dough from the processor (it will be very crumbly) and lightly gather it together into a square (do not overmix). Cover with plastic wrap and refrigerate for 1 hour.

4. Remove the dough from the refrigerator. Roll the dough into an approximately 13-inch (32.5-cm) circle with an even thickness of about ¼ inch (6 mm), dusting the top and bottom with enough flour so the dough doesn't stick to the surface or rolling pin. Carefully place the dough in a 9½-inch (24-cm) pie dish (the dough should overhang from 1 to 1½ inches [2.5 to 3.8 cm]). Crimp the edges to form a border around the top, cutting off any excess dough. Place in the refrigerator to chill at least ½ hour before baking.

5. Preheat the oven to 400°F (200°C). Place a piece of parchment paper (large enough to cover the inside of the shell) inside the shell. Fill with dried beans or rice to weigh it down (you will need about 3 cups [681 g]). Place the filled shell in the oven for 5 minutes. Turn the oven down to 375°F (190°C) and bake for another 10 to 12 minutes, or until the crust starts to look nicely golden.

6. Remove the parchment paper and beans or rice and continue baking for 8 to 10 minutes, or until the inside of the crust is lightly golden and fully baked (carefully press down the dough with a clean towel during baking if the crust starts to puff up). Before the last 2 minutes of baking, brush the inside of the crust with a thin coat of the salted egg white.

(RECIPE CONTINUES ON PAGE 86)

(RECIPE CONTINUED FROM PAGE 85)

For the Pie:

2½ cups (593 mL) whole milk

¼ cup (1.5 ounces [43 g]) plus 2 tablespoons granulated sugar (divided)

5 large egg yolks

3 tablespoons (¾ ounce [21 g]) cornstarch, sifted

¼ teaspoon kosher salt

8 ounces (227 g) good-quality (65% to 70%) bittersweet chocolate, chopped and melted slowly over a double boiler, plus additional to grate for garnish

2 tablespoons salted butter

1 prepared Pie Crust

1½ cups (356 mL) heavy cream

2 tablespoons confectioners' sugar

¼ teaspoon vanilla extract

1. Place the milk in a 2-quart (1.90-L) saucepan. Sprinkle half of the sugar over the milk and place over medium heat. Add the egg yolks to a mixing bowl and whisk them together. Add the remaining sugar and whisk in. Add the sifted cornstarch and whisk until smooth.

2. When the milk comes up to a full simmer, slowly add a couple of ladles of milk to the egg mixture, while whisking, to temper. Scrape all of the egg mixture back into the saucepan and whisk together.

3. Place over medium-high heat and whisk continuously, making sure to get the bottom and sides so they don't burn, until the mixture just comes up to a boil and gets very thick. Immediately pull the pot off the heat, add the salt, and continue whisking as you add the chocolate and butter. Mix until combined, pour the mixture into the baked pie crust, and even out the top with a spatula. Cover just the chocolate custard with a piece of buttered parchment paper or plastic wrap (do not cover the crust). Place in the refrigerator until the custard is cold.

4. Whip the cream with confectioners' sugar and vanilla extract to medium-firm peaks. Remove the covering from the chocolate custard and pipe or spread the whipped cream over the custard. Top the pie decoratively with the grated chocolate, and serve.

CHILLED TOMATO SOUP WITH MAPLE BACON PANZANELLA

In mid-summer you only have a few months to gorge yourself with as many ripe off-the-vine tomatoes as you can, so that is the time of the year to make this dish—the peak of local tomato season. Any other time it will just be a pale pretender.

SERVES 6

2 tablespoons extra virgin olive oil

2 stalks celery (4 ounces [114 g]), diced large

1 onion (6 ounces [170 g]), diced large

2 bay leaves

2 cloves garlic, finely diced

1½ pounds (681 g) ripe tomatoes, core removed and diced large

2 sprigs fresh oregano

1 tablespoon kosher salt

½ teaspoon freshly ground black pepper

½ teaspoon red pepper flakes

2½ cups (593 mL) unsalted chicken or vegetable stock

Panzanella (recipe follows)

Maple Bacon (recipe follows)

1. Place a saucepan over medium heat. Add the olive oil, and when hot, add the celery, onions, and bay leaves and sauté for 4 minutes. Add the garlic and sauté for 30 seconds. Add the tomatoes, oregano, salt, pepper, and red pepper flakes and sauté for 1 minute. Add the stock and bring up to a simmer, covered, for 10 minutes.

2. Carefully purée in a blender (not filling it more than ⅓ full as liquid is hot), then strain through a medium strainer. Chill in the refrigerator.

3. When the soup is cold, portion the Panzanella in the center of 6 bowls. Divide the soup around and garnish with the crumbled Maple Bacon.

(RECIPE CONTINUES ON PAGE 89)

(RECIPE CONTINUED FROM PAGE 87)

For the Panzanella:

> 1 cup (1½ ounces [42 g]) cubed good-quality stale dry bread, covered with water for 3 minutes, then excess water squeezed out (if bread is not dry, place in a 200°F [93°C] oven for about 15 minutes)
>
> 1 large ripe tomato (6 ounces [170 g]), stem removed and cut in small dice
>
> 1 scallion, trimmed and sliced, rinsed in hot water then cold water, and dried
>
> 1 clove garlic, sliced, rinsed in hot water then cold water, dried and finely chopped
>
> 1 tablespoon chopped fresh oregano leaves
>
> 3 tablespoons (45 mL) extra virgin olive oil
>
> 2 teaspoons red wine vinegar
>
> 1 teaspoon fresh lemon juice
>
> ½ teaspoon kosher salt
>
> ¼ teaspoon freshly ground black pepper

1. Mix all of the ingredients together in a bowl.

For the Maple Bacon:

> 6 slices bacon
>
> 2 tablespoons maple syrup

1. Preheat the oven to 350°F (180°C). Place the bacon slices on a parchment paper-lined sheet tray. Brush both sides with the maple syrup. Bake for about 10 minutes, turning once, or until golden brown, caramelized, and crisp.

GOUJONETTES OF PERCH WITH POTATO PANCAKES AND CHIPOTLE GREEN OLIVE SAUCE

While working at Le Chantilly in New York City, the chef proudly taught me how to make this French classic: breaded strips of sole deep-fried and served with a mustard hollandaise sauce. When he asked me what I thought of the dish all I could think was, "The French eat fish fry?"

SERVES 4

For the Chipotle Green Olive Sauce:

6 pitted green olives (about 1½ ounces [43 g]), rinsed and dried

1 small shallot, thinly sliced, rinsed under warm water, and dried

1 garlic clove, thinly sliced, rinsed under warm water, and dried

1 large egg yolk, at room temperature

1 tablespoon plus 1 teaspoon canned chipotle peppers in adobo sauce

2 tablespoons fresh lime juice (divided)

¾ teaspoon freshly ground black pepper

½ cup (119 mL) grapeseed oil

Kosher salt, to taste

1. Place the olives, shallots, garlic, egg yolk, chipotle in adobo sauce, 1 teaspoon of the lime juice, and the pepper in a food processor. Process until coarsely chopped, scraping down the sides, about 10 seconds.

2. With the machine running, start drizzling in the grapeseed oil. After half of the oil is in, add half of the remaining lime juice, then the remaining oil, then the remaining lime juice. Adjust the seasoning with salt. Add water by the teaspoon to adjust the consistency if the mixture is too thick (it should have the consistency of mayonnaise). Reserve in the refrigerator.

For the Potato Pancakes: (Makes 12 small pancakes)

½ pound (227 g) Idaho potatoes, peeled and diced large

½ Granny Smith apple (about 2 ounces [57 g]), peeled and diced large

½ small onion (about 2 ounces [57 g]), diced large

1 teaspoon kosher salt

¼ teaspoon freshly ground black pepper

⅛ teaspoon ground nutmeg

1 large egg

¼ cup (38 g) all-purpose flour

Peanut or canola oil, for frying

1. Place the potatoes, apples, onions, salt, pepper, and nutmeg in the bowl of a food processor and pulse 12 to 14 times, or until the mixture is coarsely and evenly chopped but not puréed (the pieces should be about the size of sunflower seeds). Remove the mixture and place in a mixing bowl. Mix in 1 egg to incorporate. Add the flour and stir.

2. Place a 12-inch (30-cm) sauté pan over medium heat. Add enough oil to come up the sides about ¼ inch (6 mm). When hot, carefully spoon the potato mixture into the oil using 1 heaping tablespoon per pancake (you should get about 12 2x1-inch [5x2.5-cm] oval pancakes). Pat down the tops lightly to even out the thickness. Let the pancakes sauté, undisturbed, for 2 to 3 minutes, or until the edges start to turn golden. Check under the pancakes with a spatula and continue cooking until they are deeply golden brown. Carefully turn them over so as not to splatter the oil and continue cooking the second side until it is golden, about 3 to 4 minutes per side total.

3. Place the pancakes on a wire rack (that has been placed on top of a sheet pan) and keep warm in a 200°F (93°C) oven until the fish is ready to serve. (Prepare the pancakes just before you fry the fish.)

(RECIPE CONTINUES ON PAGE 92)

(RECIPE CONTINUED FROM PAGE 91)

To Finish the Dish:

> 1 pound (454 g) boneless skinless perch fillets (4 4-ounce [114-g] fillets)
> (you may substitute walleye pike)
>
> ½ cup (75 g) all-purpose flour
>
> 2 large eggs, mixed together with a fork with 2 teaspoons milk
>
> 1½ cups (162 g) dry bread crumbs
>
> Kosher salt and freshly ground black pepper, to taste
>
> Peanut or canola oil, for frying
>
> Prepared Potato Pancakes
>
> Chipotle Green Olive Sauce

1. Cut the perch fillets diagonally (across the fillet from side to side following the contour of the top of the fillet) into ½-inch (13-mm) strips. Place the flour, egg mixture, and bread crumbs in 3 separate containers. Season the perch pieces with salt and pepper. Place about 4 at a time in the flour, cover well, and pat off the excess. Place in the egg mixture and coat evenly, lift out, and let the excess egg drip off. Place in the bread crumbs and coat evenly, pressing the bread crumbs into the fish pieces. Remove from the bread crumbs and place on a tray that has been covered with a piece of parchment paper (do not stack the fillets). At this point you may fry the fillets immediately, or place them in the refrigerator for up to 15 minutes before frying.

2. To fry, fill a large pot with the peanut or canola oil at least 4 inches (10 cm) deep, but not more than half the distance up the side of the pot. Place over medium-high heat, and with a deep-fry thermometer in the pot, bring the oil up to 380°F (193°C).

3. Fry the fish in batches but do not crowd the pan. Cook for 2 to 2½ minutes, or until golden. Drain the fish on paper towels and serve immediately with the Potato Pancakes and Chipotle Green Olive Sauce.

CARBONNADES OF BEEF WITH BROWN BUTTER EGG NOODLES

Carbonnades is a slow-cooked dish of beef chuck that is braised with dark beer. The true flavor and texture come from cooking it "low and slow"; that is, after searing the beef, you cook it at a slow simmer over a low heat. Be sure and use a distinctive, full-flavored dark beer with a slightly bitter flavor.

SERVES 4

6 ounces (170 g) bacon, cut into ¼-inch thick matchstick-sized pieces

3 pounds (1.36 kg) beef chuck, cut into 2x2-inch (5x5-cm) cubes

½ teaspoon kosher salt, plus additional to taste

½ teaspoon freshly ground black pepper, plus additional to taste

1 pound (454 g) onion, cut in half from top to bottom and sliced thinly

6 large cloves (112 ounces) garlic, finely chopped

¼ cup (66 g) tomato paste

¼ cup (38 g) all-purpose flour

¼ cup (59 mL) red wine vinegar

24 ounces (3 cups [720 mL]) dark beer (divided)

2 tablespoons brown sugar

2 cups (474 mL) unsalted beef or brown chicken stock

5 ounces (142 g) whole carrots

3 ounces (85 g) whole celery stalks

2 bay leaves

6 sprigs fresh Italian parsley

4 sprigs fresh thyme

Brown Butter Egg Noodles (recipe follows)

1. Place a Dutch oven over medium heat. When the Dutch oven is hot, add the bacon and render until lightly browned. Remove the bacon (reserve for garnish) and leave the fat in the pan.

2. Turn the heat to high. Season the beef with ½ teaspoon of the salt and ½ teaspoon of the pepper and brown in the pan on all sides. Remove the beef to a plate.

(RECIPE CONTINUES ON PAGE 94)

(RECIPE CONTINUED FROM PAGE 93)

3. Add the onions and sauté until golden brown, about 5 to 7 minutes. Turn the heat down to medium. Add the garlic and sauté for 1 minute. Add the tomato paste and sauté for 2 minutes, stirring. Add the meat back in along with the flour and cook for 2 minutes, stirring. Add the vinegar and cook for 1 minute. Add 20 ounces (600 mL) of the beer, the brown sugar, and the stock.

4. Tie together the carrots, celery, bay leaves, parsley, and thyme (bouquet garni) and add to the pot. Bring up to a boil, cover, and slowly simmer for 1 hour and 15 minutes, or until fork-tender.

5. Remove the bouquet garni and finish with the remaining beer and salt and pepper to taste. Garnish the Carbonnades with the reserved bacon and serve with the Brown Butter Egg Noodles.

For the Brown Butter Egg Noodles:

> **3 quarts (2.84 L) water, mixed with 2 tablespoons kosher salt**
>
> **8 ounces (227 g) kluski (egg noodles)**
>
> **4 tablespoons (2 ounces [57 g]) salted butter**
>
> **¾ teaspoon kosher salt, plus additional to taste**
>
> **⅜ teaspoon freshly ground black pepper, plus additional to taste**
>
> **¼ teaspoon ground nutmeg**
>
> **¼ cup (36 g) hulled sesame seeds, toasted in a 350°F (180°C) oven for 6–8 minutes, or until lightly golden**
>
> **3 tablespoons (11 g) chopped fresh Italian parsley leaves**

1. Bring the salted water up to a boil. Add the kluski and cook, uncovered, about 10 to 11 minutes, or until they are just cooked. Drain the kluski, rinse with cold water, then let drain in a colander.

2. Place a 10- to 12-inch (25- to 30-cm) nonstick sauté pan over medium-high heat. Slice the butter in ¼-inch (6-mm) pieces and place into the pan. Keep swirling the pan to let the butter turn a medium to deep dark brown color (do not let it turn black). When the butter is deeply brown, add the cooked kluski and quickly stir to coat.

3. Sprinkle over the ¾ teaspoon salt, the ⅜ teaspoon pepper, and the nutmeg and sauté for 1½ to 2 minutes. Add the sesame seeds, stir, and sauté for 1 minute. Add the parsley and stir. Adjust the seasoning, if necessary, with salt and pepper, and serve.

CHARRED CORN, ZUCCHINI, AND MUSSEL SOUP

There is only one time of year to make this soup: at the peak of sweet corn season when, after cutting the kernels off the cob, the cobs are still bursting with sweet corn milk that will eventually give the soup its backbone and sweet complexity. Don't blame me if you try it any other time of year.

SERVES 8

3 medium zucchini (1 pound, 4 ounces [567 g]), cut in quarters lengthwise and brushed lightly with extra virgin olive oil

Kosher salt and freshly ground black pepper, to taste

6 ears fresh corn (3 pounds [1.36 kg]), husked and brushed with extra virgin olive oil

2 tablespoons extra virgin olive oil, plus additional for brushing cobs

6 slices (4 ounces [114 g]) bacon, cut into ¼-inch thick matchstick-sized pieces

1 large onion (12 ounces [341g]), chopped in small dice

6 cloves garlic, coarsely chopped

3 bay leaves

3 sprigs fresh thyme

1 bunch fresh Italian parsley stems

1 tablespoon crushed peppercorns

1½ tablespoons dry mustard (medium-hot)

2 cups (474 mL) dry white wine

1 quart (948 mL) unsalted chicken or vegetable stock

2 pounds (908 g) small mussels, cleaned and beards removed (about 50–60)

1. Preheat the grill until you can hold your hand over the fire for no more than 3 seconds before pulling it off (the grates should be cleaned and oiled). Season the zucchini with salt and pepper and grill for 3 minutes on each of the 2 cut sides (do not grill the green side), or until just crisp-tender. Transfer to a plate and reserve.

2. Season the corn lightly with salt and pepper and grill about 3 to 4 minutes, turning regularly. Remove from the grill, and when cool enough to handle, cut the kernels off the cob and reserve the kernels. Brush the cobs with a bit of olive oil and grill the cobs to slightly char, about 3 minutes. Remove the cobs from the grill and reserve.

(RECIPE CONTINUES ON PAGE 96)

(RECIPE CONTINUED FROM PAGE 95)

3. Place a 1-gallon (3.80-L) saucepan over medium-high heat. When the pot is hot, add the 2 tablespoons olive oil. Add the bacon and cook until lightly brown and rendered, about 4 minutes. Remove with a slotted spoon and reserve for garnish.

4. Add the onions to the saucepan and sauté for about 3 minutes. Add the garlic, bay leaves, thyme, parsley stems, peppercorns, and reserved grilled cobs and sauté for 2 minutes. Add the dry mustard and mix in. Add the wine and reduce to 1 cup. Add the stock and bring up to a simmer. Cover and simmer slowly for 30 minutes (do not let it reduce too much).

5. Strain the stock. Add 2 cups of the stock to a clean pot along with the mussels (reserve the remaining stock). Cover and cook the mussels until they open, about 2 to 3 minutes. Strain the mussels. Add the strained liquid back to the reserved stock. Place the reserved zucchini and enough stock to cover the zucchini in a blender. Blend until very well puréed, then add back to the stock. Add the reserved corn kernels to the stock.

6. Shuck most of the mussels and reserve (you may leave a few in the shell for garnish, if desired). Heat the soup and season to taste with salt and pepper. Divide the shucked mussels between 8 bowls, divide the soup over, and garnish with the mussels in the shell and reserved bacon.

HOT FUDGE TOFFEE NUT BALL

One of my favorite desserts is one that I inherited when I started at John Byron's: the Hot Fudge Nut Ball. It was two scoops of Heinemann's Toffee Ice Cream rolled to resemble a softball, covered with fresh toffee and toasted almonds, served with their hot fudge. This recipe includes a rich bittersweet fudge sauce (if you like it sweeter, use a sweeter chocolate) to go with the toffee and nut-encrusted ice cream.

MAKES 8 NUT BALLS

For the Toffee:

> 1 cup (200 g) granulated sugar
> 1 cup (237 mL) water
> 3 tablespoons (43 g) salted butter, cut in pieces
> 2 tablespoons heavy cream
> Pinch salt

1. Place a piece of parchment on a baking sheet with sides. Mix the sugar and water in a saucepan. Stir to dissolve, bring up to a boil, and cook to a dark caramel stage, about 6 to 8 minutes. (Note: When working with caramel, use caution as it can give you an extremely dangerous burn.)

2. Remove from the heat and carefully stir in the butter, cream, and salt until the butter melts (be careful, this will create steam). Pour the mixture onto the baking sheet and freeze until it is firm.

3. Remove from the freezer and break the toffee into small pieces. In a food processor, coarsely chop them on pulse until they are peppercorn-size. Reserve the toffee in an airtight container in the freezer.

For the Hot Fudge: (Makes 1 quart [948 mL])

½ cup (43 g) unsweetened cocoa

½ cup (119 mL) hot water

6 ounces (170 g) (65% to 70%) bittersweet chocolate, finely chopped and melted slowly in a double boiler

½ cup (119 mL) heavy cream

½ cup plus 2 tablespoons (about 4 ounces [114 g]) brown sugar

1 stick (4 ounces [114 g]) unsalted butter

¼ cup (59 mL) plus 2 tablespoons maple syrup

1 teaspoon kosher salt

½ teaspoon vanilla extract

1. Mix the cocoa and hot water together in a small saucepan until smooth. Add the melted chocolate and stir until combined and smooth. Add the cream, sugar, butter, maple syrup, and salt and bring up to a simmer over low heat. Whisk with a small whisk for 6 to 8 minutes, or until the mixture thickens and can slightly stand up on a spoon. Add the vanilla extract and stir.

2. Pour the Hot Fudge into a heatproof container, cover, and cool in the refrigerator. Reheat the Hot Fudge to serve. (The Hot Fudge will keep for 1 to 2 weeks refrigerated.)

For the Nut Balls:

Prepared Toffee

1 cup (92 g) chopped toasted, salted almonds

2 quarts (1.05 kg) ice cream (I use butter pecan)

Prepared Hot Fudge

2 cups (474 mL) heavy cream, whipped with 1 tablespoon confectioners' sugar to firm peak (optional)

1. Mix 1 cup (150 g) of the toffee and the chopped almonds together. Put on plastic gloves and cut 8 pieces of plastic wrap, about 10x10 inches (25x25 cm) each, and lay them out flat on the counter. Scoop out 2 scoops of ice cream (for 1 portion) and quickly form into a ball so the ice cream does not melt. With approximately ¼ cup (45 g) of the toffee/almond mixture, coat the exterior all around, and then immediately wrap in the plastic wrap, maintaining a ball form, and place in the freezer. Repeat the process with the remaining 7 portions.

2. When you are ready to serve, microwave the Hot Fudge until it is just melted and serve with the individual nut balls and the optional whipped cream.

4

THE CIA

I WAS SIX MONTHS IN, AND THINGS WEREN'T GETTING ANY BETTER. I SPORTED black three-quarter-length knickers that almost covered my short legs, along with a billowy, white, three-quarter-sleeve shirt that was cut to the navel, and a bright red ascot. A three-inch-wide black belt and the pièce de résistance, a pair of shiny patent leather loafers festooned with large square brass buckles, completed the look. At the Hungry Lion, we "service blokes" looked like the love children of Henry the Eighth and a malcontent pirate—the absolute height of early 1970s fashion. Someone please put a saber through my belly!

Why put myself through this self-shaming? I'd had a perfectly normal apron-clad lunch cook's job at this faux English pub, and even though I had moved back in with my parents to save money, I would still need more if I were accepted at the Culinary Institute. Fortuitously, the Hungry Lion manager was kind enough to let me serve a few nights a week, even though I had no previous serving experience. I knew the inner workings of the menu, and once I had my blimey getup on, the customers couldn't help but feel bad for the sorry-looking sap standing before them—which was really good for tips. And whenever I was working with my friend Mike, a former high school football player, he became the Goliath to my David. Those knickers looked like tight Bermuda shorts on his offensive lineman thighs. Misery loves company.

Right before one of our nightly shifts, my dad walked into the restaurant. "I thought you might want to see this," he said, and handed me an envelope with The Culinary Institute of America (CIA) across the top. I carefully pried it open, thinking whatever was inside could make or break my life. I hoped to spend my first year at the school in New Haven, Connecticut, on Yale's campus, where the Culinary had resided since 1946 when it was called the New Haven Restaurant Institute, and then spend my second year at the CIA's newly purchased home of the Culinary in Hyde Park, New York. At first I was devastated by what I read, then I read on and found myself doing a very convincing, hopping Lucky Charms-leprechaun

My Chevy in front of the Culinary Institute of America prior to opening in Hyde Park, New York

tribute. The letter said that the classes were full for that fall, so I wouldn't be going to New Haven—however I had been accepted as part of the next year's first class at the new CIA in Hyde Park. I was going to New York!

◆

LATE FALL AFTER I RECEIVED THE LETTER, I DECIDED TO TAKE A QUICK TRIP TO CHECK out Hyde Park and look into housing options. I was talking to my friend Mike about the trip and he suggested we make a grand vacation out of it and explore the entire East Coast. That seemed like a great idea because by then I had saved a lot of money, which I wouldn't need for another year. My youthful logic said, *Spend now, and you can save again when you get back!* We packed up my Chevy Bel Air and took off.

We decided on two important criteria for a successful trip: mine was to try as much regional food as possible along the way, and his was to play a bit of basketball in every state we crossed.

Our trip took us from Wisconsin, east along the Great Lakes, through upper New York state and Vermont, to Hanover in New Hampshire, where we visited Dartmouth, Mike's alma mater. Then we drove up to the southern tip of Maine, down the Atlantic coast, across to New York City, and then north up the Hudson to Hyde Park. We got in a quick game of

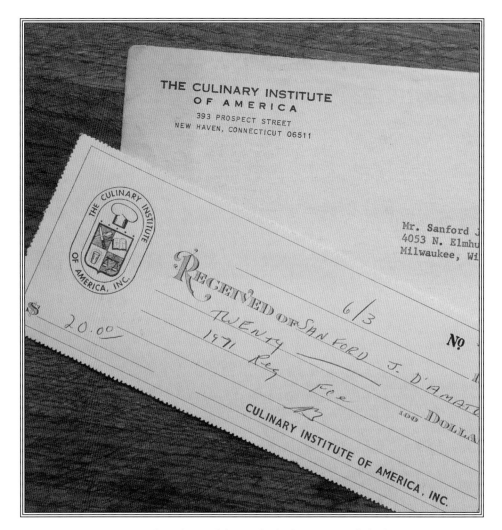

Original envelope and deposit slip for first semester of school
(with the old New Haven address as the school was moving)

basketball in each state (though we had to go back over the border in Maine when we forgot) and sampled great food along the way, from lobster rolls on the Maine coast to coal-fired pizza in New Haven near Yale's campus.

Besides visiting my future school, the highlight of the trip was experiencing a proper dinner in New York City. I had made a reservation at Mama Leone's, an old-school, red-sauce, tourist haven in the theater district. Being "worldly, sophisticated" 20-somethings, we entered the restaurant, bellied up to the bar, and confidently ordered two Black Russians. We were then seated along with a massive block of mozzarella whose sheer size made it feel like a third dining companion. The mozzarella was the most impressive part of the dinner as the rest of the food wasn't great. We didn't care—we were half in the bag in the middle of NYC.

On the way back to the car, which was parked in what I thought was an excellent space between Ninth and Tenth Avenues in the lower 40s, Mike mentioned that we had not played basketball in New York. He grabbed the ball out of the trunk, and we walked over to a nearby playground. We asked a group of guys if we could join in their game. All six of them stopped playing and walked over to the fence.

"You boys aren't from around here, are you?" said the oldest kid.

How did they know? Was it the white chinos and striped, short-sleeved shirts with big collars? The penny loafers? Or just the goofy grins on our faces?

"No, we're not," we answered. "We're from Milwaukee."

They started laughing and said, "You're in the wrong place, so I suggest you get your preppy asses out of here."

We didn't stop to banter and quickly moved ourselves and our intact asses out of the city.

The next day we arrived in Poughkeepsie, a few miles down Route 9 from Hyde Park, the future home of the Culinary Institute. This would be our home base for a few days so I could properly check out the campus and find housing for the fall opening. I was overwhelmed by a sense of anticipation as we drove up the tree-lined Route 9 highway toward the campus.

Would it be like the University of Wisconsin at Madison, an open-air student union on the waters of Lake Mendota? No, this is the East, and I had just seen the ivy-covered halls and quaint tree-lined passageways of New Haven's Yale, from where the Culinary was moving.

As we got closer, there was a worn sign that said "St. Andrews on the Hudson."

We turned onto the dry, dusty, dirt road that led to an abandoned Jesuit seminary, the future site of the Culinary Institute. The scene was a bit creepy; this one large building sat surrounded by golden tumbleweed-style dead vegetation. On the other side of a fence was a large graveyard in which lay the remains of past Jesuits. A path down to the river revealed a ramshackle gazebo, which did have a spectacular north-south view of the mighty Hudson.

On the drive back to Poughkeepsie, all I noticed were the dingy little motels and bars dotting the highway. By comparison, after having just seen Dartmouth and Yale, the sights of Hyde Park did not have an encouraging college aura.

◆

I WAS PLANTED IN MY CHAIR, WHICH WAS SO BIG IT TOOK UP A QUARTER OF THE available floor space in the room I was renting in Poughkeepsie. I was waiting to use the rooming house's shared bathroom and rooting for John, the 78-year-old guy across the hall, who was having his usual toilet challenges. I was pretty nervous. It was my first day at the Culinary Institute, and the jumble in my stomach reminded me of being five years old and clinging to the arms of my dad's overstuffed lounger with my mother beseeching me to follow her to the car so she could drop me off at my first day of kindergarten. All those years later, I had to beseech myself to move. After a half hour, I gave up on waiting for the bathroom and proceeded to wash and brush my teeth at the small sink in the corner of the room before taking off for school.

I entered the Great Hall and I was directed to the basement. In the old halls and stairs hung the entrenched institutional smell of preschool hot lunch blended with a physical prison-like feeling. I got in line, called out my name, and stretched out my arms to receive my folded uniform—white coat, checked pants, white apron, kerchief, and toque. Next was the rolled up "shiv" case, or knife set. Just when I was expecting a blast from a fire hose to shower us down, we were led into a large auditorium for a few words of welcome and a sample demo by Chef Czack.

It was 1972, and my only frame of reference for a decked-out chef was Chef Boyardee, who wore a big, floppy hat with his name emblazoned across the front in large capital letters. Chef Czack was no pretender. This was the poster boy for what a CIA chef should look like: a military dress-quality starched uniform, a towering toque, and a kerchief tied so flawlessly around his neck that the Duke of Windsor would have been jealous. The demo was a flurry of precise knife skills and technique that quickly yielded a photo-quality dish. *On second thought, I might just like it here.*

The location of the Great Hall, as it was named, was a former grand church with a spiraling ceiling and arched alcoves along the sides. This became the perfect setting for the grand opening of the newly located school. At most grand openings, the drinks are good and free-flowing, but the food can be suspect. At a culinary school grand opening, the food is everything, and the drinks are only there to wash it down. Each alcove was bursting with a specific country's food, which a corresponding chef from that country had prepared as the faculty included chefs from all over the world. And right in the prime center spot of the hall were the Scandinavian chefs. They were an imposing, impeccably groomed group of chefs surrounded by a cornucopia of pickled vegetables; all types of herring, sardines, and smoked shellfish; massive pork roasts studded with dried fruit; towering displays of Danish pastries; and in one small area, that other Danish delight, frikadeller. These are the traditional meat stretchers, a Danish comfort food. Like our meatloaf, the Danes frugally used all their butchered pork and veal scraps and transformed them, with the right hands, into a buttery, mousse-like crusted confection that melted in your mouth. As soon as I took a bite, I knew I was where I should be. I was ready to learn.

◆

I DIDN'T FEEL LIKE I FIT THE PROFILE OF THE AVERAGE STUDENT AT THE TIME. BEING A trade school, it attracted a lot of high school students who were looking to find their place in the working world or for whom college wasn't really an option. The school was founded in 1946 specifically to train returning WWII veterans in the culinary arts, so a large segment of students were older returning Vietnam War vets who chose to enroll because tuition was covered under the GI Bill. I never harbored any personal confusion or doubt about why I was there. My path had already found me in college when I decided to pursue a career in cooking. Knowing that helped me come to the conclusion that the fairly depressing, socially stunted location was a real plus when it came to focusing on the matters at hand.

Within my first few months at the Culinary Institute, I had learned that achieving success and standing out from the crowd required me to be fairly aggressive. That was quite contrary to my personality, which had been molded by years and years of being a polite Midwesterner. I like to think I had a "humble aggressiveness" that I used to jump ahead—without leaving a trail of bodies in my wake.

The Culinary Institute had regular class times, as in every school, during which the individual instructors pretty much stayed within the confines of the published curriculum. This made for a good, solid education but didn't always showcase their individual talents.

A lot of the faculty held outside positions that usually involved either weekend restaurant work or off-premises catering. Apparently, this is where they really showed their individual talents, unfettered by the in-school direction of the administration. Working outside of the school with the instructors became the plum jobs that everyone either did or should have aspired to. With some of the instructors, you could just mention that you were open to any kind of extracurricular work and they would bring you on board. But with the *chosen* chefs, the ones everyone wanted to work with, you had to be approached by them.

One of my classes was with a talented classic Italian chef named Marino, who had a reputation for scaring students senseless for the smallest mistakes. I apprehensively approached each class as focused as possible, having spent days going over the recipes that we would be covering. As the week went on, my fear was quickly dispersed. In this case, if you were serious, you were fine; if you were goofing off, you were crushed.

At the end of the week, the chef asked me if I was interested in working a catered party he was preparing near the school. Before he had even finished talking, I said, "Of course!" The party showcased elegant, traditional Italian dishes with techniques that were foreign to my unseasoned experience. One of my favorites was a dish of simple roll-ups of veal, cheese, and sage that were quickly seared, deglazed with a white wine-Marsala combination, and slowly reduced to a tender, sticky deliciousness. They were a sophisticated take on the "veal birds" my mother prepared; but with the addition of a glace de viande, a reduced veal glace, they were elevated to a level of depth and refinement I had not experienced.

The school had an austere, dog-eat-dog atmosphere. I think this had to do with the fact that the school had made a huge move from New Haven, and everyone—students and instructors alike—still had to get used to the new digs. That came with a learning curve; and their aim was to keep on budget along the way to make sure they could pay for those digs. One of the most notable areas of frugality came in the butchery class. We started with a couple of days of theory as the instructor, a master butcher from Poland, explained the intricacies of breaking down an entire pig, steer, or lamb into primal cuts, and then into portions that would be familiar to most folks as they'd see them in the supermarket. Most of this was done with large flip charts, but we were all waiting for the actual beasts to appear. I understood it probably was not feasible for every one of the 20-some students to have a personal side of beef to whale on, but we all expected a bit more than was delivered.

On our first cutting day, we had all sharpened our boning knives for the 16th time that morning. All those anxious students in their matching white uniforms wielding razor-sharp blades—it was like a scene out of *West Side Story*. We were the Sharks, and as the butcher turned over the box of Jets (actually, 20 whole chickens), the jabbing and slicing kicked into such high gear that even Maria wouldn't have been able to stop us.

That was a good start, but we implored Officer Krupke, played by the butcher, that we needed to see and learn on larger cuts. The next day he delivered, presenting a whole spring lamb. Everyone gathered around the table as he deftly cut through the lamb with a master's touch and knowledge, showing us just where to separate to produce the primal cuts: the legs, shoulder, loins, and so on. Then he gave each one of us the primal cuts to bone out. He would appear between us with the speed and grace of a ninja while keeping control of the whole group.

I had a shoulder, which the butcher explained was perfect for braising. When I had started cooking school, I didn't know the difference between a brisket and a bottom round. And if someone had asked me to make a braise or stew, I would have just used a large chunk of any kind of meat.

Part of understanding meat is knowing what cooking process to use for different cuts. As consumers, most folks will look for the leanest piece of meat with the least amount of connective tissue. So the bottom round, from the back of the animal, always looks better than the chuck or the brisket, from the front. But if you are braising a piece of meat, what you should look for is the marbling of fat and connective tissue that will break down through gentle cooking. This will keep the meat moist through natural internal basting, and as the tissues break down, they will form a slightly gelatinous texture that equates to richness and mouth-filling viscosity that will keep you going back for bites 2 through 16.

◆

I WAS GETTING REALLY TIRED OF THE ROOMING HOUSE, AND AFTER MY BIKE WAS STOLEN off the back porch, decided it was time to look for a new place. After asking around, I found out that one of my classmates, Roger, was looking for a roommate. After class I went to check out his place and we drove up to a mid-century modern glassed-in single-level freestanding house. He told me the owner built it for his mother-in-law who had recently passed away. It was located in a beautifully wooded part of Rhinebeck and actually closer to the school than my present cramped quarters. And it turned out that even though it was expensive, with us splitting the rent it was only a few dollars more than I was currently paying. Little did I know at the time that I was also inheriting a social director in the deal.

The second weekend after I moved in, Roger announced he was going to a party in Boston put on by some friends from his hometown in Connecticut. Did I want to go? Surprisingly I was free (as I had been for the previous five months). We barely got through the door when Roger, with his seemingly inherent brimming confidence (a trait I'm still trying to master), motioned to me to follow him. I couldn't mimic his signature swagger, but I did keep up as we approached two striking young ladies. "So, where are you from?" we asked. "Emerson College," they replied. "Are you in college here in Boston also?" "No, we just started at the CIA." Obviously a good answer as their eyes widened and they expelled a "WOW" in unison. "So you're training to be spies?" they asked. "Hell no, it's the Culinary Institute of America. We're training to be chefs!" we said. The wow quickly morphed into a furrowed, Hmmm. "So, you're going to learn to cook? Then what?" Before we could reply we got a, "Well, that sounds really interesting—oh look, there are our friends!" In less than a second, all that remained in their place was a blended scent of burning rubber soles and Arpege. You have to realize, this was a "bam-less" time, BTFN (before the Food Network), when being a restaurant chef had a bit less allure than it does today. In fact, it was considered one half-step up from being a circus carnie.

◆

ROGER INVITED ME FOR A WEEKEND AT HIS FAMILY'S HOME IN WESTPORT, CONNECTICUT. I knew he was from a fairly well-off family but as we pulled into the driveway past the Rolls Royce and were greeted at the door by a working non-family member, I realized they were fairly well-off in a "Kennedy" sense. If I was ever greeted by a non-member of the family at my house it would have meant I had stumbled into a robbery in progress.

I was shown to the guest quarters (which were the size of my apartment) and told to get ready, as we were going to his grandmother's for lunch. On the way over, he warned me that his Nana was a bit tough on new people, but he wouldn't elaborate.

We pulled up to a beautiful beachfront mansion and were ushered into the drawing room, which was filled with Roger's relatives, all of whom were sitting in ornate, almost palatial chairs in a semicircle around Nana. One particularly large chair directly across from her was the hot seat. My friend, her grandchild, was directed to this, and he sat explaining for about 15 minutes how his CIA school year was going, what he was learning, and so on.

Then she asked, "And who is he?" gesturing my way.

"Oh, that's my roommate Sandy. He's spending the week here."

She motioned for Roger to vacate the chair, and I was summoned to sit. As I climbed into the jumbo seat, I could feel the residual moistness exuding from the chair's mohair fabric—sweat left behind by the previous interrogatee. This immediately jump-started my own sweat glands, and I was almost drenched before The Nana's opening salvo of inquiries was unleashed: "Where are you from? What do your father and mother do to make a living? Where's your family originally from?" The "question machine" got more personal and ground me deeper into the seat. I thought, jeez, I was just here for lunch, not to marry into the family!

Just as I was ready to confess to just about anything to get out of the chair, Nana looked at her grandson and said, "Take him to the beach, and you two gather some clams for lunch."

As we walked to the beach I said to my friend, "A *bit* tough?" Since I was already soaking wet from sweating out my interrogation, the clamming process, which I had never done before, became a welcome relief as the cool water of Long Island Sound lapped over us. Since the only thing I had ever foraged out of our backyard was rhubarb, this was a defining moment.

Roger told me to look for the bubbles coming out of the holes as the water would recede and return to the sea after a wave. We dug at the holes, and before we knew it, the pail was brimming with hard-shell clams. A simple fish and clam mélange quickly became a delicious lunch, which I happily consumed, under-the-radar, in a question-free environment.

◆

GROWING UP IN MILWAUKEE, I NEVER HAD A CHANCE TO TRY INDIAN FOOD. THIS WAS because there were no Indian restaurants in Milwaukee. When I started at the Culinary Institute, I started reading in their vast library about Indian food. The combination of ingredients that I had never heard of—fenugreek, basmati rice, red lentils, and chick pea flour—being formed into mystifying dishes like biryanis, samosas, pilafs, dals, and chutneys was unfathomable to me. Within days I was having recurring curry dreams. I was going crazy—I had to try this food.

A week later I was talking to Roger about my Indian obsession, and he came up with a great idea. Miles Davis was playing in New York City at the old Fillmore East on the Lower East Side, within blocks of East Sixth Street, a hotbed of Indian restaurants. He suggested we get tickets to the concert and stop at one of the Indian restaurants for dinner beforehand.

We went to a place that Roger had been to a few times before. As we sat down, the waiter asked if we would like a drink or a lassi. *A Lassie?* I thought. Now I was suddenly scared. *No dog for me, please.* No, the waiter explained, a lassi was a mango yogurt drink. OK, bring it on. I ordered one—with relief.

From our first taste of onion fritters with tamarind sauce, I was hooked. We ordered three-quarters of the menu, and I couldn't (or wouldn't) stop eating. Every dish was a revelation of exotic spice tempered with tart-sweet chutneys and balanced by salty-bitter richness.

I didn't want the dinner to end, but we had a concert to go to. Given that I had consumed three times my body weight, it was a struggle to stay awake for the concert, though it was incredible. As I faded in and out and the improvisational rhythm of Miles Davis mixed with my Indian dreams, it finally all made sense.

◆

SINCE I'VE LIVED IN MILWAUKEE MOST OF MY LIFE, I'D SAY I'M NOT A COLD WEATHER neophyte. But the coldest day in my life was in Connecticut, not Wisconsin. Roger suggested we visit a high school friend of his one weekend. We began a beautiful, sunny ride, which ended on a long, winding, wooded road that snaked up a small, heavily forested mountain to a clearing surrounded by tree stumps.

A modest-sized, two-story log cabin stood in the center. Attached was a tiny barn with one cow, a couple of pigs, and a few strolling chickens. As we got out of the car, we saw a Jeep dragging a 12-foot log by a large chain emerge from around the corner of the cabin. Out jumped a husky, bearded gent in a heavy snowsuit who waved to us.

As I was introduced to him, his wife, and their two kids, I felt like I was in the middle of a *Grizzly Adams* episode set in a '60s hippy commune. The couple explained that they had dropped out of a well-to-do Wall Street lifestyle to start a simpler life on a highly sustainable miniature farm. No telephones. No TV. The kids were home-schooled, and we were surrounded by shelves of books. That afternoon we swapped stories and read around the central wood-burning stove that heated the entire cabin.

After dinner we were shown up to the attic bedroom and advised to grab a few extra comforters, as it could get a tad cold once the fire burned down in the stove. I was quite cozy as I got into bed, but at about two in the morning, I woke up shivering while a wind worthy of a polar ice cap whipped through the well-placed spaces in the log walls. I grudgingly got out of bed and put on every piece of clothing I had discarded before bed, including my parka and hood. I jumped back into bed and tucked every body part, my head included, under the comforters—any exposed flesh was at risk.

I fell in and out of sleep, determined not to lose what little heat I had managed to hold onto. But then the encompassing smell of frying meats permeated the comforter, followed by—*God, could it be?*—a slight flash of warmth. I carefully peeked my head out from the covers. Yes, it was warm. And better yet, there was bacon.

I ambled downstairs to what remains the best breakfast I have ever had: home-cured bacon, fresh milk, incredible whole-wheat pancakes with home-grown dried blueberries, fresh-churned butter, and natural maple syrup. The coldest night of my life turned into my warmest full stomach ever.

◆

THE WEEKEND IN THE CONNECTICUT COLD MADE ME HOMESICK FOR WISCONSIN, AND with Christmas approaching, I put my name up on the travel board to carpool back to the Midwest. I got together with a group of three guys who were from Detroit. For a nominal gas contribution, they would drop me off at the Detroit airport for an inexpensive puddle-jump flight to Milwaukee. I was looking forward to being back home again.

I took a corner in the back seat of their car and became the proverbial fly on the wall by either sleeping or feigning sleep through most of the trip. The had all gone to high school together, so the conversation consisted of very candid wrap-up of their first year of culinary education. It started with the chefs they admired, and then quickly digressed to a bitching session as the S-word was introduced. If you want to get a cook or chef really mad, you just need to utter one word: *shoemaker*. In the food world, the word *shoemaker* was an expletive of the highest order. It meant you were on the lowest tier of the cooking hierarchy, a cook who didn't have the technical or mental "game"—a slacker, a loser! I never quite understood the connection between a loser and a shoemaker as I've always had the highest regard for any craftsman. Spend some time in Florence or Milan where shoemakers are the royalty of Italy (think Prada, Gucci, Ferragamo, etc.). To add to this confusion, the name of one of my favorite chicken dishes, chicken scarpariello, loosely translates to "chicken shoemaker-style." I don't know if the dish has a culinary connection to the insult; I think it refers more to the style of the coarsely cutting of the chicken in small pieces before cooking. But it's an odd name nonetheless.

They went on to deduce that by working with about 10 different chef's each for two weeks since school started, they had ingested all that the chefs knew plus what they knew before they started school. They'd learned everything chefs knew by working with them for two weeks?! I was only three years older than most of those guys but jeez, when does maturity kick in? Never before had so many with so little talent sat as judge and jury for so few with a lifetime of skill. I'm sure any one of those neophyte car-mates soon found that they had "big shoes" to fill before they had half the skills they thought they possessed.

◆

FOR OVERLY ENERGETIC, FIRST-YEAR CULINARY STUDENTS, IDEAS FLOWED LIKE LAVA from Vesuvius—non-stop, partially formed, and fairly muddled. On my time off, I tested recipes and tried to incorporate my own ideas into them. Quite often they ended up in the trashcan; imagination without skill can have an ugly side.

I was really looking forward to Christmas, seeing my family, and trying my half-baked ideas out on them. Upon my return, my mother invited a few friends over for a dinner party to showcase my year's worth of skills. The dinner was a weird, overwrought culinary trip from savory Caribbean banana soufflé to Asian-marinated lamb chops; but I think both my parents were actually impressed with the meal. The tip-off came the next night, when my mother cooked. As we were eating dinner, she asked me, "How is everything?" I was stunned. When did it go from "Sit down and eat your dinner!" to "How is everything? Does it taste right?" I didn't think I had been gone that long, but things had obviously changed.

When I returned to school, I started the class I was least looking forward to in my time at the Culinary Institute: dining room service. Almost everyone at the school was dressed in their bright, crisp chef coat whites with checkered pants. A few awkwardly dressed people stood in ill-fitting white button-down shirts, clip-on ties, and black-cuffed pants or black skirts, wearing expressions that ranged from unconfident to downright embarrassed. They were the new dining room class.

The dining room students learned about service while serving to the other students the food that had been produced in the classrooms for lunch and dinner. The majority of dining room instructors were European and filled with almost mythic tales of the superhuman skills they had possessed in younger days—the ability to carry dozens of large wine glasses in each hand or stack a whole eight-top of full dinner plates on one arm.

When my time for dining room class came around, I was positive I would neither like the class nor be susceptible to the instructors' boasting. I was wrong on both points. Class was fascinating; it opened up a whole new way of looking at foodservice as *service*. Yes, there are people out there; it was very easy to overlook that fact when I was in my fairly egocentric and sheltered corner of the kitchen. When serving, I enjoyed receiving the immediate, one-on-one feedback from the customers and learning how to handle the problems and compliments with grace and humility.

The seemingly superhuman waiter tricks were really practical skills that were acquired by years and years of repetition and practice. (Hmmm, sounds a bit like in the kitchen.) My favorite part was the tableside service where I could use my cooking skills along with a flair for the dramatic and literally have people eating out of my hands (if I executed it well). As a result of these classes, I felt as at home in the front of the house as the back—just as long as I didn't have to wear those Hungry Lion knickers!

Spring came around quickly, and by my second year in school, and with Roger's guidance, I had come out of my self-imposed cocoon and transformed into a veritable social butterfly. I liked to think that, through my example, Roger had become a better student—a fair exchange. On a particularly beautiful spring day, the "fever" hit us hard on our way to school. I had maintained a perfect school attendance from day one, but when Roger suggested we blow off the day and meet up with some other like-minded students, I was in. So what crazy rebellious things do culinary students do on a skipped day from school?

Roger drove us up to a wooded area with a set of small rental cottages near our place. All together, there were about six of us, and we got right to it: a wild afternoon of food and conversation about food. I met an acquaintance of Roger's named Ruth, who was a year ahead of me and was well known at school. She was a fellow and sous chef at the Culinary Institute's Escoffier Room, working for Chef Peter von Erp. Chef von Erp was, in my mind, a legend, and he was reputed to be one of the most outrageous and talented chefs at the school.

Ruth had made perfectly proper and delicious watercress and egg salad sandwiches and other simple but elegant snacks. As we were eating, Ruth and I started talking about our backgrounds. As the conversation drifted into food and culinary philosophy, her questions started to expand beyond the realm of my limited expertise, but I did my best to hang in there. Little did I know that this flippantly skipped day would lead to my getting an interview with my first professional mentor.

CHAPTER FOUR RECIPES

*Frikadeller with Pickled Beets
and Marinated Cucumbers*
115

Navarin of Lamb
117

Dried Blueberry Oatmeal Pancakes
120

Chicken Scarpariello—My Way
121

*Wild Salmon on Potato-Sorrel Egg Salad,
Chive Vermouth Caviar Dressing*
122

FRIKADELLER WITH PICKLED BEETS AND MARINATED CUCUMBERS

(Danish Meat Patties)

Frikadeller is a traditional Danish comfort food. Like our meatloaf, the Danes frugally use their butchered scraps from pork and veal, and transform them into a mousse-like buttery-crusted confection that melts in your mouth. From my first bite I just knew, "There ain't nothin' like a Dane!"

MAKES 4 (7-OUNCE [199-G]) PATTIES

2½ tablespoons (37 mL) grapeseed oil (divided)

3 tablespoons (43 g) salted butter (divided)

1 Spanish onion (8 ounces [227 g]), diced small

1 bay leaf

1 sprig fresh thyme

1 clove garlic, finely chopped

1¼ tablespoons ground caraway

½ cup (54 g) dry bread crumbs

6 tablespoons (89 mL) heavy cream

¼ cup (59 mL) whole milk

½ pound (227 g) finely ground pork

½ pound (227 g) finely ground veal

⅓ cup (3 g) chopped fresh dill fronds (from 1 large bunch) (reserve the remaining dill fronds for the Marinated Cucumbers)

1 large egg

2½ teaspoons kosher salt, plus additional for seasoning

1 teaspoon freshly ground black pepper, plus additional for seasoning

Grated zest of ¼ to ½ lemon

Pickled Beets (recipe follows)

Marinated Cucumbers (recipe follows)

1. Place a sauté pan over medium-high heat. When the pan is hot, add ½ tablespoon of the grapeseed oil and 1 tablespoon of the butter. When the butter is melted, add the onions, bay leaf, and thyme and sauté for about 4 minutes. Add the garlic and sauté for 1 minute. Add the caraway and sauté for 30 seconds. Remove from the pan and cool.

(RECIPE CONTINUES ON PAGE 116)

(RECIPE CONTINUED FROM PAGE 115)

2. Mix together the bread crumbs, heavy cream, and milk in a large mixing bowl. Set aside for 2 minutes to moisten. Remove and discard the bay leaf and thyme from the onion mixture, then add it to the bread crumb mixture along with the pork, the veal, the dill fronds, the egg, the 2½ teaspoons salt, the 1 teaspoon pepper, and the lemon zest, and mix together very well until completely incorporated. Sauté off a flattened tablespoon-size portion so you may taste and check for seasoning Adjust the seasoning of the mixture with salt and pepper. Form into 4 oval patties, about 1 inch thick, and refrigerate for at least 1 hour.

3. For serving, preheat the oven to 350°F (180°C) . Place a sauté pan over medium-low heat. When the pan is warm, add the remaining 2 tablespoons of the oil and 2 tablespoons of the butter, and when the butter is melted and foaming, add the patties and sauté for about 7 minutes on 1 side. Turn the patties over, place in the oven, and bake for 8 to 10 minutes, or until the juices just run clear. Garnish the Frikadeller with the Pickled Beets and Marinated Cucumbers.

For the Pickled Beets:

2 beets (about 14 ounces [397 g]), roasted at 375°F (190°C) for 30 to 45 minutes until knife pierced in the center comes out easily, peeled, cooled, and cut into ¼-inch (6-mm) slices

1 teaspoon ground caraway

2 tablespoons fresh orange juice

2½ teaspoons red wine vinegar

1 teaspoon grapeseed oil

½ teaspoon orange zest

¼ teaspoon kosher salt

10 grinds freshly ground black pepper

1. Mix all of the ingredients together and let them marinate for at least 30 minutes.

For the Marinated Cucumbers:

½ seedless cucumber (about 6 ounces [170 g]), thinly sliced

1 scallion (about ½ ounce [14 g]), sliced very thin and rinsed

2 tablespoons chopped dill fronds

1 tablespoon plus 1 teaspoon cider vinegar

1 teaspoon granulated sugar

¾ teaspoon kosher salt

10 grinds freshly ground black pepper

1. Mix all of the ingredients together and let them marinate for at least 30 minutes.

NAVARIN OF LAMB

(Spring Lamb Stew)

In our "West Side Story" butchering class, I ended up with the shoulder of the lamb which, when boned, makes for a tasty tender roast. But it also happens to be the perfect cut for the French spring favorite Navarin d'Agneau, or Lamb Stew, with a mélange of spring vegetables. I made this dish regularly at Le Veau d'Or as it was always brought back around when the first spring lamb arrived right before Easter.

SERVES 6

For the Lamb Stock:

> **Reserved lamb bones and fat from lamb shoulder chops below**
>
> **1 onion (8 ounces [227 g]), cut in 8 pieces (peel left on)**
>
> **2–4 carrots (12 ounces total [341 g]) (use half, cut in 1-inch [2.5-cm] lengths, for stock, reserve the other half, peeled and cut in 1-inch [2.5-cm] triangular pieces, for garnish)**
>
> **2 turnips (12 ounces total [341 g]), peeled and cut in 1-inch [2.5-cm] wedges (use ¼ for stock and reserve ¾ for garnish)**
>
> **6 cloves garlic, peeled**
>
> **¼ cup (66 g) tomato paste**
>
> **6 cups (1.42 L) unsalted chicken stock**
>
> **2 bay leaves**
>
> **2 sprigs fresh thyme**
>
> **1 sprig fresh rosemary**

1. Preheat the oven to 400°F (200°C) . Place the lamb bones and fat in a roasting pan. Bake for 15 minutes, stirring once. Add the onion with peels, the half of the carrots for stock, and the ¼ of the turnips for stock. Continue baking for about 15 minutes, or until golden. Add the garlic and tomato paste, stir in, and continue baking for 15 minutes.

2. Remove from the oven and deglaze the pan with the chicken stock, then add the bay leaves, thyme, and rosemary. Bring up to a simmer and transfer to a stock pot, being sure to get everything out of the roasting pan. Simmer stock slowly for about 1 hour, then strain and reserve (you will need 4 cups [948 mL]).

(RECIPE CONTINUES ON PAGE 119)

(RECIPE CONTINUED FROM PAGE 117)

For the Navarin:

   3 tablespoons (45 mL) regular olive oil

   4 pounds (1.82 kg) lamb shoulder chops (1 inch [2.5 cm] thick), bones and excess fat removed and reserved, trimmed lamb cut into 1- to 1½-inch (2.5- to 3.8-cm) pieces

   Kosher salt and freshly ground black pepper, to taste

   1 tablespoon all-purpose flour

   1 cup (237 mL) dry white wine

   4 cups (948 mL) reserved prepared Lamb Stock

   6 radishes, trimmed and cut in quarters to about the same size as the turnips for garnish

   ½ cup (119 mL) water plus 2–3 tablespoons, if necessary

   1½ tablespoons granulated sugar

   1 tablespoon salted butter

   ⅜ teaspoon kosher salt

   ¼ teaspoon freshly ground black pepper

   6 asparagus spears, trimmed, blanched until tender in boiling salted water, shocked in ice water, drained, and cut in 1-inch (2.5-cm) pieces

   1 cup (63 g) sugar snap peas, blanched in boiling salted water 1 minute, shocked in ice water, drained, and cut in half lengthwise

   1 cup peas (140 g) (fresh or frozen), blanched in boiling salted water, shocked in ice water, and drained

1. Preheat the oven to 325°F (160°C). Place a large sauté pan over high heat. When the pan is hot, add the olive oil. Season the trimmed lamb pieces with salt and pepper and brown in 2 batches, about 6 to 7 minutes each.

2. When they all are brown, place them back in the same pan, sprinkle with the flour, stir and cook about 1 minute. Add the white wine, stir with a whisk, and bring up to a boil. Boil for 2 minutes. Add the reserved lamb stock and bring up to a simmer. Cover with a piece of oiled parchment paper and bake for about 50 to 60 minutes, or until the lamb is fork-tender but not falling apart.

3. While the lamb is cooking, place the radishes and reserved carrots and turnips for the garnish in a large sauté pan along with the ½ cup (119 mL) water, the sugar, the butter, the ⅜ teaspoon salt, and the ¼ teaspoon pepper. Bring up to a boil, covered, and let cook until all of the liquid is gone, about 5 minutes. Remove the cover and test the vegetables to make sure they are tender (if not, add 2 to 3 more tablespoons of water and cook until they are just tender).

4. Toss the vegetables so that they will glaze in the butter and sugar that remains in the pan and cook until well glazed. Remove from the heat and toss in the asparagus, snap peas, and peas. Adjust the seasoning with salt and pepper. When the lamb is done, adjust the seasoning with salt and pepper and add the vegetable garnish just before serving.

DRIED BLUEBERRY OATMEAL PANCAKES

I'm not a fan of breakfast as I've always felt it screws up lunch. So in my case, these pancakes could be a proper lunch or a weekend dinner, and for all you normal folks, they'll be quite satisfactory for breakfast or brunch.

MAKES 10 (2½–3-INCH [6.4–7.5-CM]) PANCAKES

¾ cup (68 g) uncooked rolled oats, lightly toasted in a small sauté pan in a 350°F (180°C) oven for 4 minutes, tossing once

½ cup (2½ ounces [70 g]) all-purpose flour

2 tablespoons (½ ounce [14 g]) brown sugar

1 teaspoon baking powder

1 large egg

1 large egg yolk

2 tablespoons salted butter, browned and cooled

¼ cup (28 g) dried blueberries

1 cup (237 mL) buttermilk

Grapeseed oil, for cooking

Butter and pure maple syrup, for serving

1. Sift the flour, brown sugar, and baking powder together in a bowl. In another bowl, add the oats to the egg, egg yolk, and butter. Add the sifted ingredients and dried blueberries and mix to distribute. Add the buttermilk (do not overmix). Let the mixture sit for 5 to 10 minutes.

2. Place a griddle over medium heat. When the griddle is hot, grease it lightly with the grapeseed oil. Add spoonfuls of the batter, about ¼ cup (59 mL) each (for small pancakes), to the griddle. Let the pancakes cook until bubbles form on the top, about 3 minutes. Turn them over and cook for 3 more minutes, or until cooked through. Divide the pancakes on plates and serve with the butter and pure maple syrup.

CHICKEN SCARPARIELLO—MY WAY

Shoemaker-style chicken is a standard in many Neapolitan restaurants and it has many interpretations. But I always liked it at its simplest, with just chicken, olive oil, garlic, parsley, and lemon. My version is like taking a great fried chicken and tossing it with a lot of garlic and parsley before serving.

SERVES 4

1 (4–4½-pound [1.82–2.04 kg]) fresh chicken, cut into 18 even pieces with a heavy knife: 2 thighs, 2 legs, 2 breasts with wings; wings detached at second joint, breasts cut into 4 equal chunks, thighs cut into 2 pieces through the bone, legs cut into 2 pieces through the bone (I like to use a wooden mallet to hit the top of a knife when it is set over the chicken bone to make for a clean cut [check for bone shards and remove].)

Kosher salt and freshly ground black pepper, to taste

¼ cup (38 g) all-purpose flour

½ cup (119 mL) regular olive oil (divided)

¼ cup (119 mL) extra virgin olive oil (divided)

1 cup (57 g) packed fresh Italian parsley leaves, chopped small

8 large cloves garlic, chopped small

Zest of 1 lemon, chopped small

1. Heat 2 (10- to 12-inch [25- to 30-cm]) sauté pans to hot. While the pans are heating, toss the chicken pieces with salt and pepper in a large bowl. Dust the flour over and toss to coat. Add ¼ cup of the regular olive oil and 2 tablespoons of the extra virgin olive oil to each pan. When hot, carefully add the chicken pieces. Cook over medium-high heat, turning as the pieces get very golden (turn on all sides to get an even brown), about 15 to 17 minutes.

2. While the chicken is cooking, mix together the parsley, garlic, and lemon zest in a small bowl. When the chicken is done cooking, scatter the parsley mixture over the chicken in the 2 pans, toss for 5 seconds, then place on a serving platter.

WILD SALMON ON POTATO–SORREL EGG SALAD, CHIVE VERMOUTH CAVIAR DRESSING

This dish is like a sophisticated stuffed egg with salmon and caviar. The dry and herbaceous vermouth balances nicely with the fattiness of the salmon and the tartness of the sorrel.

SERVES 4

For the Chive Vermouth Caviar Dressing:

> 1 large pasteurized egg yolk, at room temperature
>
> 1½ tablespoons fresh lemon juice
>
> 1 teaspoon dry mustard
>
> 1 cup (237 mL) regular olive oil
>
> 3 tablespoons (45 mL) dry vermouth
>
> ½ teaspoon kosher salt
>
> ¼ teaspoon freshly ground black pepper
>
> 2 tablespoons water
>
> 1 tablespoon red wine vinegar
>
> 2 tablespoons chopped chives (reserve for serving)
>
> ¼ cup (64 g) salmon caviar (reserve for serving)

1. Place the egg yolk, lemon juice, and mustard in a food processor. Turn on and in the following order add: ½ cup (119 mL) of the olive oil (in a steady stream to form an emulsion), the vermouth, the salt, the pepper, the remaining ½ cup (119 mL) of oil, the water, and the vinegar. (The dressing should be made the day before and refrigerated.)

For the Potato–Sorrel Egg Salad:

> 1 (12-ounce [340 g]) or 2 (6-ounce [170 g]) Idaho potatoes, peeled and cut in small dice, cooked in boiling salted water for 3–5 minutes, or until tender but not falling apart, drained and placed in a small bowl, covered with ½ cup (119 mL) dry white wine, cooled, and then drained before using
>
> 3 large eggs, covered with water and 1 tablespoon vinegar, brought up to a boil and lightly boiled for 8–9 minutes, drained, cooled under cold running water, peeled, and diced small
>
> 1 dill pickle (2 ounces [57 g]), diced (about ¼ cup)
>
> ¼ cup medium-pack sorrel leaves (about ¾ ounce [21 g]), thinly sliced
>
> 2 tablespoons drained capers
>
> Kosher salt and freshly ground black pepper, to taste

(RECIPE CONTINUES ON PAGE 124)

(RECIPE CONTINUED FROM PAGE 122)

1. In a bowl, mix the potatoes, eggs, pickles, sorrel, and capers with enough dressing to moisten. Season as needed with salt and pepper. Divide the salad among 4 plates.

For the Salmon Roulades and to Finish the Dish:

1½ pounds (681 g) center-cut salmon fillets

Kosher salt and freshly ground black pepper, to taste

2 tablespoons regular olive oil

Prepared Chive Vermouth Caviar Dressing with reserved chives and caviar

1. Slice the salmon fillets into 1-inch (2.5-cm) strips widthwise (you should have 8 strips total). For each roulade, lay 2 of the strips on their side, intertwining in a yin yang fashion and in a circle, and insert 4–5-inch (10–12.5-cm) wooden skewers though the center horizontally to secure.

2. Place a large sauté pan over medium-high heat. Season the salmon roulades with salt and pepper on each side. Place the oil in the pan, and when hot, cook the salmon fillets for about 2 to 3 minutes per side, or until cooked through.

3. Remove from the pan and top each salad with 1 salmon fillet. Stir the reserved chives into the Chive Vermouth Caviar Dressing and drizzle over and around the salmon. Garnish each plate with the reserved caviar.

5

DUTCH TREAT

"YOU COULDN'T BE A PIMPLE ON A CHEF'S ASS! COME ON! IS THAT ALL YOU HAVE?" It sounded like a child's taunt. It was such a stupid statement that it shouldn't have hurt, but it did. I did want to be a pimple, especially if it was on an accomplished chef's ass.

I was sitting on an overstuffed couch, my shirt damp from sweat. A shiny auburn wiener dog stared right through me. And next to the dog, in a recliner, sat Chef Peter von Erp. He too stared in my direction, looking over the slightly tinted glasses resting on his nose, waiting for my next response to his rapid-fire questions.

After Ruth's graduation, she and Peter had become a couple and taken over the management of food and service for the Dutchess Valley Rod and Gun Club in Pawling, New York, about 30 miles southeast of the school. Think New York socialites, old money, and tweed hunting jackets. The club had three overnight rooms above a post-and-beam great room with a professional-sized bar on one side and a massive granite walk-in fireplace anchoring the other end. This was a perfect place for the kin of the Roosevelts, Duchins, and Peales to soirée. On the weekends they held hunts for wild game—quail, pheasant, partridge, and mallard ducks—and trout fly fishing jaunts followed by lavish country lunches or dinners. The attached living quarters behind the kitchen for the live-in managers were quite sweet.

Peter was looking to bring on an apprentice to help with any and all duties that might come up, from shopping, prep work, cooking, and serving to dishwashing, mopping up, and changing the bed linens. After an hour of questions, Peter pushed his glasses down as far as they would go and said, "There is no pay, but you get room and board—are you interested?" I had never been offered a better deal in my life!

The club was the ultimate chef's playhouse, a private restaurant equipped with all the toys—heavy-duty Vulcan range with a built-in commercial hood, a 20-quart Hobart mixer with a meat grinder attachment, prep and butcher block tables, a walk-in cooler, and even a pass-through dishwasher with spray table and disposal.

Another perk of living there were the sporadic events during the week. The main room of the club became our living room, and the best feature was the fireplace. One night Peter set up a roaring fire and then disappeared into the kitchen. He returned hefting a half wheel of cheese, which he rested on a stone near the fire. Then he brought out a platter of baby vegetables—carrots, onions, turnips, and parsnips—that we had picked up at a farm stand a few days earlier. They had been quickly pickled and paired with tiny steaming boiled potatoes.

The half wheel was raclette, a pungent Swiss mountain cheese. Traditionally, in the mountain towns of the Alps, a half wheel of the cheese is rested near an open fire until the edge is soft and yielding. And before it literally melts off the wheel, the molten cheese is scraped over a plate of boiled potatoes, pickled onions, and cornichons. After adding a dusting of fresh pepper, you scarf it up while the cheese is still hot—kind of an inverted fondue.

The name *raclette* refers to both the dish and the cheese; it is a classic combination of rich and tart. Coming from a Velveeta background, I realized as we ate plate after plate draped over the miniature Hudson Valley vegetables, that this cheese actually tasted better than it looked. Forget about the room—I was there for the board!

◆

WE FINISHED THE RACLETTE AND WASHED IT DOWN WITH A FEW GLASSES OF CRISP WHITE wine, Peter grew more relaxed and started waxing dreamily about his time working in Manhattan, when he had first arrived in the United States. He asked if I wanted to visit the city that weekend, and I said yes. I had only been to Manhattan a few times before and had experienced overwhelming sensory overload, walking aimlessly in a wide-eyed stupor until it was time to leave.

This time around, with Peter as my guide, I was in more capable hands. I arrived in the city, he parked the car and said, "Let's take the subway downtown." GAUauAU-llee! I felt like Gomer Pyle as we descended into the tiled echo chamber surrounded by hoards of humanity. I heard a faint earthquake-like rumble in the distance. It got louder and bright lights appeared out of the dark tunnel at the end of the loading platform. As the door opened, I took one step, then felt myself floating as I was wedged then transported into the train car by the surrounding riders.

As we exited the station, Peter's gait changed from a casual walk to that of a man on an all-knowing mission. "Follow me," he said, taking off across the street into traffic. Cars miraculously stopped—he seemed to have control of all things in his proximity. We walked directly to Chinatown and into a small storefront restaurant that was his favorite. He shooed away the menu and just blurted out his order: winter melon soup, black bean clams, and Hunan lamb, among other dishes.

An intricately carved winter melon, about the size of a large watermelon, was brought to the table. Steaming hot soup was ladled from inside the melon, and the salty garnish of ham played off the richness of the fruit. The feast was underway; I had never tasted such full-flavored exotic dishes. The Hunan lamb, mixed with blazing hot peppers, was almost blackly caramelized. With the wok-charred eggplant with sweet-and-sour vegetables, the bitterness of the char on the eggplant played beautifully off the sweetness of the vegetables and the tartness of the vinegar. Everything was a revelation, but the one dish that I couldn't stop eating was the clams with deeply flavored, slightly salty, fermented black beans. I welled up a bit as the last clam was consumed.

My grief was short-lived, though, because next we went to a seafood restaurant for fresh blue crabs prepared with ginger and more fermented black beans—sweet crabmeat, spicy, salty, rich, and fulfilling—all masterpieces for the palate. This was just a small peek into the food that Peter loved and his way of showing me how great cuisine always has balance. His food was always a revelation. Never shy or demure, it progressed through each bite to reveal layer upon layer of flavor, from rich and creamy to hits of acidity, from a piquant middle to a hint of bitterness, mellowed with an almost imperceptible touch of sweetness that made the bitterness right. This is the way food is supposed to taste, but very rarely does.

My apprenticeship with Peter was always an exercise in self-evaluation, even if I was too dense to know it at the time. He had an encyclopedic knowledge of food. Not just from Holland, his homeland, as well as the rest of Europe, but from the entire world. He had spent his formative years working in foodservice for Royal Dutch Airlines (KLM) and the Holland America cruise line. His travels took him from the tip of Africa to the Far East, the Caribbean, and the Americas. His free time in these countries and ports was spent searching out the ultimate foods.

Working for him in the early '70s was a fast-forward through global food when the rest of the United States was completely enamored with great French and Italian cuisine. Knowledge of real ethnic food was limited, and a lot of the available examples were mere shadows of the originals, usually stripped down to appeal to the masses. What restaurants called "curry" at the time, was a French-styled cream sauce with a hint of timid, turmeric-heavy, manufactured "curry powder." By contrast, Peter would toast and grind fenugreek, hot pepper, coriander, cumin, and mustard seed together to add to gingerroot, onion, and garlic-infused lamb shoulder. Then he would sear the lamb in ghee and slowly braise it with lamb stock and coconut milk. He served the dish as it would have been eaten in a proper Indian home, with various homemade chutneys, pickled vegetables, Bombay duck, and toasted-almond basmati rice with saffron. His food captured the aroma, technique, taste, and soul of whatever cuisine he was working with.

Peter's teaching style involved a lot of hands-on learning by his students. For example, he and I once stopped at a local food market to pick up some fruits and vegetables for a weekend party. The cucumbers looked beautiful, so we picked up six. Peter said he would like to do an ethnically inspired cucumber yogurt soup and told me to do some quick research and come back to him that night with ideas. This was before the Internet, so I drove to the Culinary Institute's library and looked up different Asian and Middle Eastern recipes. After six hours, I came up with cajik from Turkey, maast-o-khiar from Persia, raita from India, jajeek from Iraq, and tzatziki from Greece—all cucumber-and-yogurt combinations, used as sauces, condiments, chutneys, salads, and soups. As usual with Peter, after I'd presented my ideas, he told me what we would be making (which he knew all along): tarator, a soup in Bulgaria and Albania and a sauce in Turkey. At the time I thought, "Why did I spend the afternoon poring through books if he already knew what we were making?" Silly me. It took quite a while to understand his method.

Not until Peter sent me to New York City to work did I start to realize the depth of knowledge that he had enabled me to acquire. But I did know I was on a journey to learn. Whether it was Chinese, Turkish, Indonesian, Hungarian, French, Indian, Thai, Italian, or Polish, every dish had that signature balance and palate explosion that formed the way I look at and prepare food to this day. When I finally figured that out, I never wanted to stop learning.

◆

BRILLIANT FOOD DOESN'T HAVE TO BE COMPLICATED. PEOPLE MIGHT THINK THAT CHEFS, because of their training, have an overly involved sense of comfort that carries over to their taste memories. But over the years, my experience has always been this: the simpler, the better. There are certain dishes that, when I take the first bite, make me feel as though I have settled into a familiar groove.

All through the three-plus years that I worked for Peter, he related many stories of how he started in cooking and his path from Holland to the United States. But he never mentioned his upbringing. One evening after putting out a small party, we were relaxing and well into our second bottle of wine. I asked Peter about his early home life. He reluctantly told me that his most vivid memories were of his mother whacking him with his own shoes and how he wished they could have been canvas sneakers instead of wooden shoes. When I asked him about the food of his youth, a dreamy restful smile snuck across his face. He talked about the big pots of potato leek soup and erwtensoep (pea soup) that would bubble on the stove, and how, as he sat down to the table all those years ago, his face shrouded in the mini steam bath of his bowl, he would know everything was all right.

Peter was a chef of unequalled brilliance who could cook the most elegant classic banquet and a moment later put out quintessential peasant fare that had the touch of a master chef wrapped around the soul of a grandmother—a humble elegance long practiced by the *grands-mères* of Europe.

The holidays were coming up, and with a touch of cajoling on my part, Peter agreed to make a large pot of erwtensoep (pea soup), the poster boy of Dutch cuisine. This was no watery, wimpy, uninspired version. The dish was bolstered with a bucket-load of smoked pork products—shanks, bacon, and cured sausage—filled with enough dried peas to steady your spoon between bites, and tempered with just enough root vegetables to add complexity without too much sweetness. It was so good that it would even cause an obedient Dutch child to pull their finger out of the dyke so they could hold the bowl with both hands. As he ladled out a few bites and we dug in, that elusive smile was returned, and a flood of good memories came rolling out late into the night, this time without any coercion on my part.

◆

IT FEELS GOOD TO BE TRUSTED, BUT NOT SO GOOD TO BE ALONE. AFTER I HAD WORKED parties at the club with Peter and Ruth for about eight months, a small group of six called in on a Friday for an early Sunday dinner. Peter and Ruth had already made plans, so Peter asked if I was ready to fly solo and do the party myself. "Of course! No problem!" came spewing out. Meanwhile my insides turned upside down—I didn't actually know if I could do it, but I wasn't about to let Peter down.

Peter was a perfectionist, so there was no room for error. He set me up for success by making sure two of the four courses were almost fully prepared: Hudson Valley melons with thinly sliced prosciutto for the appetizer and riz à l'impératrice, a molded rice pudding fortified with cream and a bit of gelatin, and studded with wine-poached apricots, for dessert.

Along with serving the food, I was responsible for sautéing the veal with chanterelles and tossing a simple local green salad with Belgian endive, which I had no experience with until working with Peter. I said good-bye to Peter and Ruth, and as the door shut behind them, I immediately had a *Home Alone* moment. What-ifs raced through my brain. But I pulled myself together and started to clean the lettuce, take out the plates, and set up the prosciutto and melon.

As the six guests arrived, I brought the appetizers right out and poured the wine a little more heavily than usual to foster congeniality. Everyone was happy so far. I cleared the plates and then tossed the salad (a bit too much dressing but pretty tasty nonetheless). After serving the salad, I ran back to start the veal. I had Peter's voice in my head as I went over the procedure: hot pan, season the veal, get a good sear on it, remove the veal, add chanterelles, sauté, add shallots, add white wine, reduce, add cream and just a bit of glace de viande, reduce, add veal and juices back in, season, plate, and serve.

The conversation stopped as the guests tucked into the veal—not a bad sign, as they were all eating. And now, the dessert. I placed the mold in warm, but not too hot, water to release it, but after two tries, it was not coming out. After breaking out in a massive sweat, I tried again. Voilà! The third time was the charm, and the complete dinner was done.

As I started to clean up the dishes, Peter and Ruth walked in—no "hello" or "How did it go?" He just walked over to the veal pan and swiped his finger across the remaining sauce. "Should be reduced more, but not horrible." Coming from Peter, that was like "You the man!"

As I was putting away the last dishes, Peter walked into the kitchen with two glasses of wine and handed me one. "Tough night," he said. "The first time I was left alone was on the cruise ship. There was a special captain's dinner for 12, and the main course was roast goose. The chef prepared the goose for the oven and placed it in. He then told me he had a meeting. I was in charge and should baste the goose regularly so it would acquire a deeply crisp, golden crust worthy of the captain's table. He said, 'Don't screw it up!' So after he left, I obsessively basted every five minutes, perched in a stooped position in front of the oven between bastings. I wished I were small enough that I could fit inside the oven so I could continually baste until that goose was ready!" With that, Peter drained his glass and said good night.

◆

DURING THE END OF MY LAST SEMESTER AT THE CULINARY INSTITUTE, IN ADDITION TO working for Peter at the club, I helped out at the Escoffier Room. Upon graduation, I would start a formal fellowship under Peter's direction at the Escoffier Room, which was, along with being the signature restaurant of the school, the last student class before graduation. The students completing fellowships were also teaching assistants, and those in the Escoffier Room were each in charge of a particular station, from garde-manger to saucier and everything in between. Our duties were to run the station for lunch and dinner services while instructing the students on how the station is run and how to produce the menu.

My last few months of school were the best for me because of the class I was really looking forward to: International Cuisine. In my and others' opinions, two chefs at the school were the best pure cooks with the deepest repertoire. One was Peter, and the other was Bruno Ellmer, who taught International Cuisine. They were slightly competitive, and over the years a budding rivalry had emerged between them. Both were considered to run the Escoffier Room. At first the administration wanted to split the lunch and dinner shifts between two chefs, but Peter said he would only take over if he had complete control over both of them.

Dinner menu from the Escoffier Room at the Culinary Institute of America

Chef Ellmer was the perfect European chef prototype, always impeccably starched and able to get tasty and consistent results from the students. He was also a favorite of the administration because he was extremely talented and played by the rules.

Peter, on the other hand, was a slightly troubled genius with his own playbook and agenda. Peter's detractors in the administration (the vice-president, etc.) really hated him, and if it wasn't for President Rosenthal, he might have been gone. He wasn't above going out after class to tip a few and then sleep in his car in the school parking lot. But he always woke up with enough time to get to class and teach. Peter was known for his "apron throw"; anytime he heard about a decision he thought was completely off base, his apron would come flying through the kitchen door, landing in the dining room in protest. The move was safer than a

Bobby Knight chair throw—but equally aggressive. If you screwed up in class, Peter would dress you down with the aplomb of a marine drill sergeant until you were left shivering like a live plucked chicken. He was given quite a bit of latitude because the school's president, Jacob Rosenthal, was totally enamored with his food and chose to overlook his temper, as it just came with the territory.

On my first day in International Cuisine, I was in charge of the plattar, Scandinavian silver dollar-sized pancakes griddled on a traditional seven-holed cast iron pan. As they started to come off the pan, Chef Ellmer ran over with a jar of preserved lingonberries and yelled with the childlike glee of a lemonade stand hawker, "PLATTAR! PLATTAR! STUDENTS COME GET YOUR PLATTAR! YOU MUST EAT THEM WHEN THEY ARE HOT!" He slathered the berries on top and dusted them with a snowy cap of confectioners' sugar that melted beautifully into the buttery, crunchy coins.

Since I had an uncompromising allegiance to Peter, enjoying the class made me feel like a culinary philanderer, but I really liked Chef Ellmer and was wowed by his cooking skills. But what really distinguished him were his teaching abilities. Along with chefs Sonnenschmidt, Czack, Kumin, Schreyer, and Metropolis, who were my personal favorites, his ability to teach was what I respected most. That component was missing in some of the chef-instructors; being a good chef didn't necessarily mean being a good teacher. A few of the chefs were very "old school" in that they would only dole out their knowledge to those whom they felt were worthy. Perhaps that is how they would have run their kitchens in the real world, but this was not in the best interest of any of the less-progressed students of the school who would just be left out in the cold.

Near the end of International Cuisine, we made moutabel, a Lebanese-style baba ghannoush, or eggplant dip. Chef Ellmer was happy with the results, and I thought it was really good; so I proudly took a portion down the hall to the Escoffier Room for Peter to try. He kind of scrunched up his face and said, "Not bad, but you broiled the eggplant. They need to be well-grilled to get that really smoky flavor." After class I stopped by to see Peter again, and he said, "Try this." It was a bowl of moutabel that he had made while I was finishing class. (Did I say he was slightly competitive?) "See the difference?" he asked. "*This* is *moutabel.*"

For me, this was exactly what set Peter apart from any other chef I had experienced. Peter would make a dish, revel in the moment, and then it was gone, ancient history, as if he was never satisfied with past accomplishments, always pushing to be better. His food had a modern, evolving fluidity that was always surprising. What was glaringly obvious watching him cook was his lack of wasted motion, every move seemed choreographed but also a picture of complete expressive freedom.

I gleaned from him an inner voice that I cannot turn off. It continually amplifies, like an oversized speaker thumping through my very being. *Now it's good—let's make it great.* There should be no doubt at that moment that it could be better. Taste, taste, taste, then taste again, until you're at a point that you can't wipe that smile off your face and anyone who tries it says, "Holy shit!" Only then do you know it's good.

◆

I WAS BURIED UNDER A LARGE QUILT IN MY BACK BEDROOM AT THE CLUB. IT WAS A freezing January day, and I would usually have done anything to eke out a few more minutes of womb-like sleep. But I uncharacteristically bounded out of bed, right onto the frosty wood plank floor. This was a special week.

It was 1974. I had worked my way through the Culinary Institute's two-year program and was ready for a first-degree graduation. There were a few other firsts going on too. My mother, who had implied in the past that she would rather be burned at the stake than set foot on an airplane, was taking her debut flight, along with my dad, from Milwaukee to New York's La Guardia airport. There they would pick up their first rental car to drive north up the Hudson.

The flight turned out to be the least stressful part of the trip. As you might remember, January 1974 was the sweet spot of the countrywide gas-rationing crisis. The rental car had a quarter tank of gas to start, and as my parents took off and passed station after station, they found—not even frustrating long lines of cars waiting to get gas—just signs saying "Out of gas." They took a chance, got off the main road, and literally rolled into a country station on fumes, where they pleaded to get a coveted fill-up. Peter had insisted on putting them up in a guest room at the club for their stay, and when they finally arrived, in a fairly frazzled state, they were instantly plied with calming cocktails and a welcoming fire crackling and glowing from the hearth.

Peter had also planned a special graduation dinner for us, and as it unfolded, the firsts kept coming. He quickly seared wild mallard duck, the breast cooked blood-rare on the bone, and then deftly removed the silky meat and lightly glossed it with a sumptuous, heady sauce melded from the remaining carcass, a bit of rustic red wine, and shallots, which were emulsified with ground fresh duck liver and a healthy dose of sharp pepper. My parents both looked at the ruddy red slices with a bit of trepidation but were soon mopping their plates with any remaining crusts of bread in the area. They loved the duck but had been absolutely blown away by the preceding dish—an appetizer of earthy wild mushrooms and slightly bitter artichokes balanced by small crouton-sized nubbins of sweet creamy goodness. After the dinner my dad asked what the nubbins were. Peter looked pleased and replied, "Sweetbreads." Graduation or not, if they had known that before, they would have politely filled their napkins rather than let one bit of offal cross their lips. But not knowing had turned them into believers.

For many people, *offal* is a perfect name for the variety meats that include, but are not limited to, liver, tongue, kidneys, tripe, brains, and most of the innards of a particular animal. The only real offal that has crossed over in a large way is liver. Sweetbreads were my first offal experience—and I have to say, it was awful.

We were at a "fine dining" place in Milwaukee in the late '60s. I had already developed a strong curiosity for anything different on a menu, and "sautéed sweetbreads in a sherry mushroom sauce" sounded perfectly different to me. When the plate was placed in front of me, I was confronted with a large, off-white globule (looking like a Michelin Man appendage) lounging in a watery, brown liquid with sliced mushrooms floating around it. Hoping that it tasted better than it looked, I started slicing and tearing, and a small chunk broke away from the mass. I popped it into my mouth, chewed a bit, and went for my napkin. It had the texture of a firm Nerf ball and the flavor of bitter, raw sherry.

I was a bit embarrassed, as I had thought I was the bon vivant for bravely ordering the adventure platter. As I looked wistfully at my parents' normal beef and chicken, which they were happily consuming, I did my best Houdini to cut and move the offending mass around the plate and under the decorative kale leaf, hoping to make it disappear.

Upon tasting Peter's sweetbreads that memory was annihilated. After the first bite I thought, "Oh, so *this* is what sweetbreads should taste like!" It's a shame that the first time we try foods, we don't always have the perfectly prepared versions; many folks go through their lives hating certain foods for no other reason than that they were prepared incorrectly.

◆

AFTER GRADUATION I STARTED MY FELLOWSHIP WORKING UNDER PETER IN THE Escoffier Room. The five of us new fellows changed stations every month. One of the harder stations was the entremetier—the vegetable, starch, soup, and garnish station. Every day for lunch and dinner, the entremetier was responsible for two different potatoes and two different vegetables. This really was not a lot, but Chef Von Erp did not like to see any repeats on the menu, so you had to garner a repertoire of 60 to 70 different classic potato and vegetable preparations.

We had two chef-approved literary sources for classic preparations: one was *Le Répertoire de la Cuisine* and the other was my bible, *Hering's Dictionary of Classical and Modern Cooking*. Every day the entremetier walked up to the kitchen board and wrote out the two potato and vegetable specials for the waiters. George was the fellow working the station that day. He was really behind in his work, so he put up cauliflower amandine (cauliflower with butter and toasted almonds) as one of the vegetables. This would not have been a problem except that he had run the same dish the week before.

When Peter walked in about five minutes before lunch started, he saw the cauliflower preparation listed on the board and frowned. He erased it and wrote, "cauliflower polonaise." George never looked up at the board, so when the first order came up, he put up a cauliflower amandine. Chef Von Erp looked at the cauliflower and yelled at George to put up the right garnish for the cauliflower. George protested and then turned toward the board. A look of horror came over his face. He said, "Chef, I don't have any polonaise garnish." Chef said, "Make it—and I want it in two minutes!" George just shut down, so the chef jumped behind the line and yelled, "Get me shallots, parsley, and hard-boiled eggs from garde-manger and bread crumbs from the saucier." He put some butter in a pan, let it brown, added bread crumbs, let them brown, added quickly chopped egg and parsley, and poured the mixture over the cauliflower in two minutes. Then he said to George, "Not so hard, is it?"

This was the way the fellowship went. We were supposed to be teaching the students, but in reality, we were still very much the students of Chef Von Erp.

When we started the fellowship, Chef Von Erp offered three of us—George, Danny, and me—free lodging at a house he owned that was connected to the Holiday Motel, also under his ownership. The motel, a place where Norman Bates would have felt at home, was about 32 steps below a Motel 6.

The free rent was great since the fellowship was continuing education with very little pay. But there was a small catch. We were also to be the management team and maintenance and cleaning crew for the motel. As you might imagine, single 19- and 20-year-old guys were not the best people to entrust with the cleaning of rooms. But in actuality, the price of the rooms reflected the slightly inferior cleaning team. Even though we hated cleaning, the upside was that the house was huge and had a great kitchen, which gave us a chance to try out all the recipes that were rattling around in our heads.

George was in possession of a one-ounce can of French Périgord truffles that had moved with him from rental to rental. Both Danny and I had been bugging him since we had first seen the can to open it up, as we had never tried real truffles before. So, with the Holiday Motel's great kitchen, we finally talked him into opening the can. It was like Christmas as we all huddled around; we were like archaeologists opening Tut's tomb to inspect the black diamond. We all agreed that we had to use it in a dish that would best show off the flavor, so we went classic and made truffle omelets. Was it worth the wait? In a word, no. The truffle was not the best quality, and it could have doubled for a slightly more tender hockey puck.

Hering's Dictionary and "The Settlement" Cookbook

After building it up in our minds for so long, nothing would have held up to the anticipation. But the omelets themselves were darn good.

George had mentioned that the Moody Blues were playing at the Spectrum in Philadelphia, and he knew a fellow student from Philadelphia who could get us all tickets. George wasn't scheduled to work on concert day, but Danny and I were. After a bit of finagling, we got off—and the road trip was on. This was my first trip to Philadelphia, so my personal mission was not to view the Liberty Bell, but to have the quintessential Philly cheese steak. Yes, young culinarians are a bit shallow.

George's friend was driving since he knew the city best. We left after he was done with morning class and got into the city as dusk was falling. He took us for a quick tour and then had to stop at his parent's house in the old Italian section of Philly to pick up the tickets. We waited for him in the car, but soon he came back out onto the small wrought iron porch and sheepishly waved us in. "My mom wants to meet you guys," he explained. Being in glazed-over concert mode, we weren't in proper shape to meet parents, but he said it would be quick.

As we walked in, his mother, a short woman with arms like a wrestler, was beaming.

"Come in, come in! You boys look hungry!"

"Ma, please! Were in a hurry!"

"No, no, sit, sit! I have a large pan of manicotti in the oven," she said, pronouncing the name of the dish "man-a-goat" with Italo-Philly ease.

She wedged us around the yellow Formica table that took up half of the kitchen; the other half of the room was occupied by the stove. I had the primo warm seat, so close to the stove that I could have served myself, but I was getting more than a little paranoid as the Sacred Heart of Jesus image hanging on the wall was pensively gazing down at me.

She served us all heaping plates and then sat down and quizzed us about our lives. She didn't eat, but she did listen as she watched us inhale everything on our plates. The pasta was fabulous—an herb-flecked luscious ricotta filling encased in thin, egg-rich wrappers, swathed in a golden-red amalgamation of sweet-tart tomato, creamy mozzarella, and sharp Pecorino. As we left, completely sated, she gave each of us a big smooch. In 20 minutes, we had become family.

We went on to the concert as full as we could be, and even though the Moody Blues were wailing away, we all slept through most of it. At the end of the concert, any chance of a Philly cheesesteak was off the board because our stomachs were still groaning. But at that point, I couldn't have cared less; I had had a Philly experience that I would never forget.

◆

FINE DINING HAS ALWAYS BEEN FIRST AND FOREMOST A PRODUCTION. YOU HAVE anywhere from 15 to 40 performers, and when they hit their marks and know their lines, there is no better show in town. The experience should feed the mind and soul as much as the stomach. Any proper fine-dining restaurant in the '70s would have had at least two to three items that were prepared or finished on the gueridon, that trolley of delight, which held a réchaud (or tableside burner), and had a bottom shelf of condiments ready to put the appropriate taste and flourish on one's selection. The perfect master of the gueridon is one-third waiter, one-third chef, and one-third ringmaster so he can prepare, plate, and serve a dish with the cool and aplomb of a Broadway performer. As dining room performance became more popular, there were fewer trained, qualified servers who could carry it out.

One of my first experiences with a complete dining room-cooked menu was at a restaurant called L'Auberge Bretonne, a few miles down the road from the club. I went there with a fellow student on the recommendation of one of our dining room instructors. We were seated at a bright-white, crisply coiffed, properly set table. We started with snails in puff pastry and salads, and finished with crêpes Suzette—all done tableside. The star of the show was the canard à la bigarade, a classic preparation of roast duck. The duck was delicious, but the show was masterful. A crisp duck was deftly broken down at warp speed and finished and glazed in a perfectly balanced sweet-tart orange sauce. Another pan mystically appeared and produced caramelized vegetables as an accompaniment. It was a treat to witness a real virtuoso of this old-school genre. I had limited school experience, but something clicked in this first real-world realization of the immense talent in the front of the house, a part of the restaurant that I had previously only thought of as a necessary delivery system for kitchens' masterpieces.

After that experience, the next time I entered the Escoffier's dining room, my eyes were immediately drawn to a squat, silver-plated contraption on four legs with a large crank wheel on top. It looked a lot like a medieval torture machine. Peter explained that it was a duck press, used for a classic French dish called caneton à la rouennaise, an over-the-top preparation in which a wild mallard duck is roasted quickly at high heat to very rare. The breasts and whole legs are removed in the dining room, and then the legs are sent back to the kitchen for further cooking. The carcass of the duck is placed into the body of the press, and the wheel is cranked to extract all of the internal blood and juices, which are mixed in a bowl with the pureed raw duck liver. Meanwhile, the breast is sliced quickly and seared with chopped shallots in a sauté pan over a réchaud. The sauce is made with cognac, wine, and duck stock, thickened with the liver-blood mixture—but it cannot be permitted to boil, as the sauce will coagulate and get grainy. After the breast is consumed, the leg and thigh are served as a second course. Done correctly, it's a magical tour de force of culinary wizardry. I was so enamored by the pomp and process that I went down to New York City and bought my own duck press. Not the deluxe silver model, but nonetheless, a handsome French nickel version.

As students we were shown the correct pressed duck presentation during a tableside class by Monsieur Bernard, the Escoffier Room maître d'. He had learned the process while working at Paris's La Tour d'Argent, where the dish is their specialty. I asked Chef Von Erp if we could put the dish on the menu at the Escoffier Room and he ran it past the maître d', who was shocked at the request. Without an incredibly huge staff, this type of preparation can be a real nightmare on a busy night.

He looked Peter in the eye and said, "Impossible! We only have one duck press, and the only way I would even consider it is if we had another press. But that won't happen." A sly smirk crept over Peter's face, and he shot back, "D'Amato has a duck press! So we have our second! It's settled—it's on the menu." Monsieur Bernard glared at me and said, "Well, then Mister D'Amato certainly should be in the dining room with us and his duck press."

As the first night started, I understood the glare. This was truly a nightmare with inexperienced students, such as me, preparing the dish. It would have been quicker for guests to fly to Paris, raise the duck, slaughter it, consume it with appetizers and dessert, and return to America, than to wait for my sad show to be finished. We did the dish for the longest two weeks of my life until it was finally retired from the menu along with my duck press. But I'm glad I had a chance to learn the right way.

That period got me thinking about my limited serving experience. I remember being given a large party of about 12 quite raucous people in the back room. Everyone ordered drinks I'd never heard of with special garnishes, and then a few of the people changed their orders on my way back to the bar. Then the manager told me my food was up on my earlier table and he had just seated me a new four-top. So, I ran to the bar to drop off the drink order and looked at my pad—but the order was gone. Suddenly I heard a screechy noise, which got louder and louder. I turned around and saw my alarm clock—time to get up for work.

Any cook or server who has been in the business for more than a few years has many stories of these kinds of nightmares. I've been jolted out of a deep sleep just as I burned my hand on the grill or was suffocated under an onslaught of order slips. You get the idea.

Working for Peter, I had an actual, conscious, waking nightmare. We had a new menu, and I was responsible for the shashlik, a Russian brochette of beef. I was using the recipe that Chef Von Erp had given us earlier in the year, which was a variation on the shish taouk, a Mediterranean kebab that was in the Culinary Institute handbook. I had prepared 15 of the brochettes for lunch service, and the dish was clearly a hot seller.

I had eight brochettes on the grill, and as I took the first one off, Chef looked at it and asked where the white truffles were.

I looked at him with my best Midwestern, wide-eyed, dumb-guy look and said, "Huh?"

"The white truffles!" he yelled. "Didn't you look at the original recipe in the handbook? This order is for Folsom!" (Folsom was the chef and administrator who wrote the handbook and recipes.) "Start over and get the truffles!"

I ran downstairs to the school commissary and begged the steward to give me a can of white truffles (no fresh ones in the 1970s). I had no requisition, so he just looked in my face and laughed. I ran back upstairs to ask the chef for a requisition. He just kept screaming, "D'Amato, you worthless IDIOT!" as he wrote it out. I ran downstairs and back up again with the truffles and started to put together new brochettes. Forty-five minutes later, they were ready, but everyone who had ordered one had already left the restaurant in brochette-less disgust. I was just hoping to hear that alarm and wake up, but no such luck. Thank heaven this was school, or I would've been out on the street.

Things took a bad turn from that day. Not long afterward, I was on fryer detail, which meant filtering and changing the 10 or so gallons of oil—a good job for the screw-up kid. After filtering and scrubbing out the fryer, I went to quickly pour the oil back in. I was about an hour behind on my nightly dinner prep for my station. I felt something strange at my feet, and simultaneously Peter started yelling, "D'AMATO! THE DRAIN!" As my feet and legs started to spread into a full split, I tried to reach the bottom drain but instead ended up on my back, flailing like a turtle in my own personal *Exxon Valdez* nightmare. Peter just walked out the kitchen door, shaking his head as he went.

The next week I was showing a group of students on my station how to prepare morel sauce for a lunch special. As I was pontificating, the morels behind me were taking on a more-than-darkened patina. I turned and quickly threw in a big splash of cream and then kept talking like nothing was wrong. Peter walked behind the line from the other side and stuck his finger in the sauce. He softly gestured and said, "Excuse me, students, gather around." All 18 students immediately surrounded me.

"Mr. D'Amato has made us a special morel sauce. Look at it and taste it so you all know what not to do in the future!" He took the sauce—pot and all—and flung it toward the dish-washing sink. He turned back my way. "Now make a proper sauce, *if you can*."

To compound the ordeal, I had to drive out to the club with Peter after class to work a party. He was dead silent for the first half of the 30-minute drive. My throat was dry, and my stomach was one big knot. I was a baseball fan and more than understood the concept of three strikes. "Am I done?" I asked.

Without even looking my way, he said, "You can start to worry when I don't yell anymore. That means I've given up on you."

◆

ABOUT A WEEK LATER, IT WAS THE FIRST NIGHT OF A NEW MENU AT THE ESCOFFIER ROOM. The first order for the evening was for President Rosenthal. He was always Mr. First Nighter at the new menu change so he could lend his critique. He started with a bowl of minestrone, which I had made, under Peter's direction, for the first time that morning. Peter took his inspiration from the Piedmont area, so we made a paste of pork fat, garlic, parsley, and cheese; we rolled this mixture up into small balls and popped them into the boiling soup at service to give that extra hit of garlic and pork richness. As I put up the soup for the server, somehow an extra ball of the pork-garlic mixture slipped into the bowl. After the soup went out, I mentioned the mishap to Chef Von Erp, who went slightly ballistic and kept murmuring, "Too much garlic, too much garlic . . ."

After dinner, Mr. Rosenthal stopped back in the kitchen and said "OK, who made the soup?"

Peter loudly responded in "throw him under the bus" mode, "D'AMATO."

"Well, Mr. D'Amato," Mr. Rosenthal proclaimed, "that minestrone was far and away the best soup I've ever had." He said the strong garlic flavor was perfect for him but could be too much for a non-garlic lover.

Chef Von Erp looked over at me and wryly said, "Well, D'Amato, sometimes it's better to be lucky than good." You can't build your career on luck, but I learned that once in a while it helps you break out of a slump.

◆

AT FIRST THERE WAS A FLUSH OF EXCITEMENT, BUT THAT RAPIDLY DETERIORATED INTO self-reflective doubt. Peter had just announced to all the fellows that the *New York Times* had been in for dinner and a review would be coming out at the end of the week. It was hard to concentrate through the lunch and dinner services after that. Working in the school under Peter, you never had an outside frame of reference for how good the food was (or wasn't). So this was a big deal—and not just because it was the restaurant's first review. This wasn't the *Rhinebeck Gazette*; it was the *New York Times*, the most influential paper in the world, and nobody wanted to be the one who prepared the dish or dishes that blew the review.

We were prepping for lunch one morning when Peter walked through the kitchen door with a stack of newspapers in his hands. We immediately huddled around his desk as he flipped to the review. "A Place Along the Hudson for Dining (If You're the Patient Kind, That Is)," the headline read—not a promising start. But the article went on to praise the "finest table appointments," "imaginative international dinner menu," "first-class hors d'oeuvres," "fine smoked partridge consommé," "glorious leek soup," "braised pheasant femiere, fairly tender and barely gamey," "delicate mousse of excellent shellfish with a superb fresh sorrel sauce, " "luscious array of elaborate desserts," and "a fabulous gateau." Nobody screwed up—a three-star review! And best of all, Peter was smiling.

◆

THOUGH I NEVER REALLY THOUGHT ABOUT IT, I HAD BEEN APPRENTICING FOR CHEF Peter von Erp for a little over two years, starting from a fledgling student, through graduation, and on to my fellowship. He clearly was not an easy man to please, but I always felt like

I was in a comfort zone. I was learning my cooking trade at an incredibly accelerated rate. Being an apprentice meant mistakes were expected, and the accompanying admonishment always came with the encouraging expectation of a lesson learned.

When Peter said I should move to New York City, I was crushed. *Was I screwing up too much? Wasn't I serious enough?*

"No," he said, "You're just ready to learn things you can't learn here. Most young cooks initially work at huge-volume food factories and can produce a lot of mediocre drivel, and to take the next step they have to develop a palate to go along with that speed. You learned a bit backwards. You have a great palate, but you're slow as shit and need to get out of your perpetual low gear—a high-volume French restaurant will do you good."

The next weekend he took me down to New York City to check out different areas to live. He suggested a location where he had first resided when he moved to the city from Holland in the '50s. As we walked around Yorkville, a Middle European enclave on the Upper East Side, almost every contiguous storefront held a new adventure to discover: the Berlin bars with their burnished fat knockwurst, frankfurters, and brats (I know those!), waiting to be paired with steins of real German DAB on tap; the Czechoslovakian restaurant on Second Avenue, with its kitchen window stacked high with the most impossibly crisp half ducks I have ever seen or subsequently consumed; and dinner at Café Geiger, where you could order a traditional German repast.

But the two places that sealed the deal and made me feel most at home were Paprika Weiss on Second Avenue and Lekvar by the Barrel on First Avenue, both Hungarian specialty stores. At Weiss, the pungent aroma of hanging fermenting salamis danced with the sweet, floral, deeply dusky smells of paprika, caraway, and marjoram. Lekvar was a cook's dream playhouse. You could look down and see large barrels of the namesake lekvar (prune and apricot purées) and large containers of crushed poppy seeds, all to be used to fill wonderful traditional pastries. Look up and you'd be dazzled by row after row of gleaming heavy-duty copper pots flanked by every imaginable type of utensil from hand potato presses and spaetzle makers to wooden cabbage cutters.

All of this, which should have been foreign to an Italian kid, was actually familiar and comforting. It brought me back to the scents of my grade school classmates' homes in our neighborhood near St. John de Nepomuc, a former Bohemian parish on the near west side of Milwaukee. That move made me realize that the comfort zone is not a particular place or even a spot on a chef's ass. It's your state of mind.

CHAPTER FIVE RECIPES

♦

Fermented Black Bean Clams
with Spicy Salami and Ginger
145

Juniper-Braised Short Ribs with Hutspot
147

Grilled Belgian Endive and Watercress
Salad with Tart Cherry Dressing
150

Rice Pudding with Late Harvest
Wine Gel and Apricot Sauce
151

Cumin-Dusted Sweetbreads, Lemon
Minted Peas, Glazed Carrots, and Morels
153

Maple-Glazed Duck with Burnt
Orange Vinaigrette
157

Minestrone
160

FERMENTED BLACK BEAN CLAMS WITH SPICY SALAMI AND GINGER

One of my favorite flavoring components for Asian food is salted black beans. They are made from soya beans and are dried and fermented. The best way of using them is to reconstitute them in a liquid. Some people like to rinse them to remove the excess salt but I think this also removes some of the flavor; it is easier to use them "as is" and adjust your final seasoning.

SERVES 2

¼ cup (1 ounce [28 g]) dried salted black beans

1 cup (237 mL) dry sake

3 tablespoons (45 mL) sesame oil

1 large shallot, thinly sliced

4 cloves garlic, thinly sliced

2 ounces (57 g) fresh ginger root, peeled and thinly sliced, each slice cut into thin strips (need ⅓ cup medium pack)

1½ ounces (43 g) spicy salami (I like to use hot Sopprasetta), thinly sliced and cut into thin strips (need ⅓ cup loose pack)

2 pounds (908 g) Manila clams, washed and scrubbed in cold water, then drained

½ teaspoon tamarind concentrate

⅛ teaspoon freshly ground black pepper, plus additional to taste

4 scallions, sliced in ¼-inch-thick (6-mm) pieces (need ½ cup [50 g])

1 cup (loose pack [16 g]) fresh cilantro leaves (divided)

Kosher salt, to taste

1. Place the beans and sake in a small saucepan over medium heat. Bring up to a simmer, then remove from the heat, cover, and steep for 15 minutes.

2. When the beans are steeped, place a large pot over medium heat. When the pot is hot, add the sesame oil. When hot, add the shallots and garlic and sauté for 1 minute. Add the ginger and sauté, stirring, for 1 minute. Add the salami and stir for 15 seconds. Add the clams, the bean mixture, the tamarind, and the ⅛ teaspoon black pepper and cover the pot. Raise the heat to high and cook until about half of the clams are open, about 1 to 2 minutes. Add the scallions, stir, and re-cover the pan until all of the clams are open (discard clams that do not open).

3. Mix in half of the cilantro with a slotted spoon. Divide the clams between 2 bowls. Adjust the broth seasoning, if necessary, with salt and pepper. Divide over the clams and sprinkle the remaining cilantro over all.

JUNIPER-BRAISED SHORT RIBS WITH HUTSPOT

Hutspot is a dish where potatoes, onions, and carrots are cooked together, then mashed into a totally satisfying mélange. A typical accompaniment might be long-stewed pears and kale, which I've quickly sautéed here to give the dish a touch of crispness. I'm sure that Peter would appreciate a bit of juniper and gin-infused ribs to even out the bites of Hutspot.

SERVES 4

For the Short Ribs:

4 pounds (1.82 kg) short ribs (need 12 pieces [2½x3 inches (6.4–7.5 cm) each])

Kosher salt and freshly ground black pepper, to taste

3½ tablespoons (52 mL) grapeseed oil (divided)

2 medium onions (1 pound [454 g]), diced large

3 stalks celery (6 ounces [170 g]), diced large

1 leek (4 ounces [114 g]), diced large

6 cloves garlic, peeled and left whole

2 tablespoons all-purpose flour

For the sachet, mix together the following spices in cheesecloth and tie with butcher string:

18 crushed juniper berries

2 sprigs fresh thyme

2 bay leaves

2 pears (12 ounces [341 g]), cut in half and cored (use 3 halves for stew and reserve 1 half for garnish)

1½ cups (356 mL) white wine

1 (14⅓-ounce [411 g]) can chopped tomatoes in juice

3 cups (711 mL) beef stock

½ cup (119 mL) gin

Hutspot (recipe follows)

Sautéed Kale (recipe follows)

1. Preheat the oven to 325°F (160°C). Place a large braising pot over high heat. Season the short ribs with salt and pepper. Place 3 tablespoons (45 mL) of the oil in the pot, and when hot, brown the short ribs on all sides until golden, about 7 to 8 minutes total.

(RECIPE CONTINUES ON PAGE 148)

(RECIPE CONTINUED FROM PAGE 147)

2. Remove the short ribs and pour out any oil in excess of 3 tablespoons (45 mL). Reduce the heat to medium-high. Add the onions, celery, leeks, and garlic and sauté for 3 to 4 minutes. Add the flour and sauté for 1 to 2 minutes.

3. Add the sachet, 3 pear halves for stew, and white wine and bring up to a boil for 2 minutes. Add the tomatoes, stock, and short ribs and bring up to a simmer. Bake, partially covered, for 45 minutes.

4. Remove the pot from the oven. Remove the short ribs to a plate and strain the sauce through a medium strainer, then a fine strainer, pressing on the vegetables to remove all liquid. Place the short ribs and sauce back into the same pot and bring back to a simmer. Cover and bake for about 1 hour to 1 hour and 15 minutes, or until the meat is fork-tender but not falling apart.

5. When tender, remove the short ribs from the pot and place, covered, on a plate. In a small saucepan, bring the gin up to a boil, carefully flame, cover to put out the flame, then add to the sauce. Reduce the sauce to your desired consistency, about 1½ to 2 cups (356 to 474 mL). Adjust the seasoning with salt and pepper.

6. Dice the reserved pear half for garnish. In a very hot sauté pan, sauté the pear quickly with the remaining ½ tablespoon of the grapeseed oil and lightly season with salt and pepper. Add to the sauce, then add the short ribs and any accumulated juices back to the sauce.

7. For serving, place a portion of the Hutspot on each plate, place the short ribs partially on the Hutspot, pour the sauce around, and garnish with the Sautéed Kale.

For the Hutspot:

> 1 pound (454 g) red potatoes (6 medium), cut in eighths
>
> 2 small carrots (8 ounces [227 g]), peeled and cut in 1-inch (2.5-cm) pieces
>
> 1 medium onion (6 ounces [170 g]), cut in 1-inch (2.5-cm) pieces
>
> 4 cloves garlic, thinly sliced
>
> 2 bay leaves
>
> 3 sprigs fresh thyme
>
> 1 tablespoon plus 2 teaspoons kosher salt (divided)
>
> ½ cup (119 mL) heavy cream
>
> ¾ teaspoon freshly ground black pepper
>
> ¼ teaspoon ground nutmeg

1. Place the potatoes, carrots, onions, garlic, bay leaves, and thyme in a pot. Cover with water and add 1 tablespoon of the salt. Bring up to a boil, then simmer for about 15 minutes, or until the carrots and potatoes are fork-tender. Drain and remove and discard the bay leaf and thyme. Place everything back in the pot and mash coarsely with a fork.

2. Add the cream, the 2 remaining teaspoons of the salt, the pepper, and the nutmeg and mix with a heatproof spatula over medium heat until creamy and thick, about 2 to 3 minutes. Serve immediately or reheat right before serving.

For the Sautéed Kale:

> 8 medium-sized kale leaves, stems removed and cut in ½-inch (13-mm) pieces
>
> 2 teaspoons grapeseed oil
>
> Kosher salt, freshly ground pepper, and ground nutmeg, to taste

1. In a large bowl, toss all of the ingredients together. Just before serving, place a heavy-bottomed sauté pan over very high heat. When the pan is very hot, add the kale and quickly sauté for about 45 seconds to 1 minute, or until just lightly scalded and crisp-tender.

GRILLED BELGIAN ENDIVE AND WATERCRESS SALAD WITH TART CHERRY DRESSING

Holland, Belgium, and France are the three largest consumers of endive with a good majority of it being used as a cooked vegetable rather than in salads. I've found it holds up well to grilling and it retains a distinctive crunch; it also blends beautifully with the Wisconsin tart cherries in this recipe.

SERVES 4

> **4 large Belgian endive, cut in half lengthwise**
>
> **2 tablespoons regular olive oil**
>
> **Kosher salt and freshly ground black pepper, to taste**
>
> **1 bunch watercress, large stems (about 1 inch [2.5 cm]) removed**
>
> **Tart Cherry Dressing (recipe follows)**

1. Preheat the grill to medium-hot. In a large bowl, toss the endive in olive oil and season with salt and pepper. Grill the endive for 4 to 5 minutes per side, or until crisp-tender, letting them brown very well but not burn.

2. Place 2 pieces of the endive on each of 4 plates. In a large bowl, toss the watercress with a bit of vinaigrette and season with salt and pepper. Divide the watercress among the plates. Drizzle the Tart Cherry Dressing over and around.

For the Tart Cherry Dressing:

> **8 ounces (227 g) fresh-pitted or IQF (Individually Quick-Frozen) tart cherries, defrosted and drained, juice reserved**
>
> **2 tablespoons balsamic vinegar**
>
> **¼ cup (59 mL) grapeseed oil**
>
> **½ teaspoon fresh lemon juice**
>
> **¼ teaspoon kosher salt**
>
> **⅛ teaspoon freshly ground black pepper**

1. In a small saucepan, reduce 3 tablespoons (45 mL) of the reserved cherry juice and the balsamic vinegar to 2 tablespoons of liquid.

2. Add to a bowl and whisk in the grapeseed oil, lemon juice, salt, and pepper. Add the tart cherries 15 minutes before serving.

RICE PUDDING WITH LATE HARVEST WINE GEL AND APRICOT SAUCE

This is a variation on a classic French rice pudding called Riz à l'Impératrice. It is an "old school" preparation of molded rice pudding fortified with cream, a slight bit of gelatin, and studded with wine-poached apricots. It can be made ahead and when serving, it should elicit a "retro" cheer, as it is unmolded.

SERVES 6 TO 8

For the Apricot Sauce:

> 12 ounces (341 g) dried apricots
>
> 3 cups (711 mL) plus 2 tablespoons late-harvest dessert wine such as Riesling, Semillon, Muscat, etc.
>
> 2 cups (474 mL) dry white wine
>
> 1 cup (237 mL) water
>
> ¼ cup (50 g) granulated sugar
>
> Juice of 1 lemon
>
> 2 teaspoons unflavored gelatin
>
> Rice Pudding (Recipe follows)

1. In a saucepan, place the apricots in 3 cups (711 mL) of the dessert wine. Bring up to a boil, reduce to a simmer, and let simmer for 8 minutes. Strain the liquid into a bowl (there should be about 1 cup [237 mL]) and reserve the liquid.

2. Add the white wine, water, sugar, and lemon juice to the saucepan and simmer for 5 minutes. With a slotted spoon, remove 8 apricots and set aside. Transfer the remaining contents of the saucepan to a food processor or blender and purée very fine. Strain the Apricot Sauce through a medium strainer and reserve in the refrigerator.

3. In a small heatproof cup, sprinkle the gelatin over the remaining 2 tablespoons of the dessert wine. Place the cup in a small saucepan or skillet that holds 1 inch of boiling hot water and stir the wine until the gelatin dissolves completely. Stir the dissolved gelatin into 1 cup (237 mL) of the reserved apricot cooking liquid. Pour half of the wine gel into the bottom of a 1-quart (948 mL) soufflé dish. Refrigerate until set. (Reserve the remaining wine gel at room temperature.)

4. Prepare the Rice Pudding and place it in a pastry bag that has been fitted with a large round tip. Remove the soufflé dish from the refrigerator and arrange the 8 reserved apricots decoratively on top of the gelatin in the bottom of the dish. Pipe the Rice Pudding into the center of the dish over the apricots, leaving about ¼-inch (6-mm) clearance around the edge (try to pipe it in an even thickness). Refrigerate for 30 minutes.

(RECIPE CONTINUES ON PAGE 152)

(RECIPE CONTINUED FROM PAGE 151)

5. Slowly ladle the remaining wine gel around the sides and over the top of the Rice Pudding (if the wine gel has solidified, slightly reheat it to room temperature). Cover the dish with plastic wrap and refrigerate overnight.

6. On the next day, unmold the dish by carefully cutting once around the side with a very sharp, thin-bladed knife. Place the bottom of the soufflé dish in about 1 inch (2.5 cm) of warm water to help release it (but not too long or the wine gel will melt). Place a large serving plate upside down over the soufflé dish and invert it to release the mold. Refrigerate the Rice Pudding. When you are ready to serve, pour the Apricot Sauce around.

For the Rice Pudding:

4 cups (948 mL) water

¾ cup (143 g) uncooked rice (I prefer jasmine rice)

1½ cups (356 mL) whole milk

⅓ cup (67 g) granulated sugar

1 ounce (28 g) fresh ginger root, peeled and cut into 4 pieces

Pinch grated nutmeg

Pinch ground cardamom

1 teaspoon unflavored gelatin

2 tablespoons Kirschwasser (clear cherry brandy)

2 large egg yolks

¾ cup (178 mL) heavy cream, whipped until soft peaks form and kept cold in the refrigerator

1. In a 2-quart (1.90 L) saucepan over high heat, bring the 4 cups (948 mL) of water to a boil. Add the rice, bring back to a simmer, and let simmer for 5 minutes. Strain and rinse the rice well. Return the rice to the saucepan and add the milk, sugar, ginger root, nutmeg, and cardamom. Cook over medium heat, stirring frequently, for about 20 to 25 minutes, or until all of the liquid is absorbed.

2. Meanwhile, in a small heatproof cup, sprinkle the gelatin over the cherry brandy. Place the cup in a small saucepan or skillet that holds 1 inch of boiling hot water and stir the brandy until the gelatin dissolves completely; set aside.

3. Transfer the rice to a stainless steel bowl and remove and discard the ginger root. Beat in the egg yolks and gelatin mixture. Set aside to cool.

4. When the rice is cool, fold in the cold whipped cream and immediately pipe into the soufflé dish.

CUMIN-DUSTED SWEETBREADS, LEMON-MINTED PEAS, GLAZED CARROTS, AND MORELS

Chef Von Erp made a quick appetizer of Sautéed Sweetbreads with Wild Mushrooms. He first soaked, then quickly blanched the sweetbreads, peeled off the outer skin and did a quick braise with vegetables and white wine to parcook them. They were cooled and pressed under a light weight, then he sliced, floured, and sautéed them to a perfect golden crispness. Alongside were sautéed wild chanterelles with a well-reduced pan sauce of white wine and lemon— offally good.

SERVES 2

For the Sweetbreads (prepare 1 day ahead):

> 10 to 12 ounces veal sweetbreads
> 2 tablespoons kosher salt
> 2 tablespoons white wine vinegar

1. Soak the sweetbreads in a bowl of ice water for about 1 hour.

2. Bring a large saucepan of water to a boil and add the salt and vinegar. Remove the sweetbreads to the boiling water and blanch for 3 minutes.

3. Place the sweetbreads in the ice water again, and when they are cool, remove some of the heavy outer membrane (do not remove all of it to keep the sweetbreads intact). Place the sweetbreads on a dish under a light weight (about 1 to 2 pounds [450–900 g]) and place in the refrigerator overnight.

For the Glazed Carrots:

> 1 carrot (3–4 ounces [85–114 g]), peeled and cut 2 inches (5 cm) long by ¼ inch (6 mm) wide
> ¾ cup (178 mL) water
> 1 teaspoon salted butter
> ½ teaspoon granulated sugar
> ⅛ teaspoon kosher salt
> ⅛ teaspoon ground cumin
> Pinch of freshly ground black pepper
> 1 teaspoon fresh lemon juice

(RECIPE CONTINUES ON PAGE 155)

(RECIPE CONTINUED FROM PAGE 153)

1. Place all of the ingredients, except the lemon juice, in a small sauté pan. Place the pan over medium-high heat and cover. Cook until all of the liquid is absorbed and the carrots are tender (if carrots are not tender, you may add a couple more tablespoons of water). Keep sautéing the carrots until they lightly color. Add the lemon juice, toss, and cook until dry. Reserve the carrots in the refrigerator until needed.

For the Lemon Oil:

> ½ cup (119 mL) fresh lemon juice
>
> Microplaned zest of ½ lemon
>
> ⅝ teaspoon ground cumin
>
> 6 tablespoons (89 mL) grapeseed oil
>
> 1 teaspoon granulated sugar
>
> ⅛ teaspoon kosher salt
>
> Pinch freshly ground black pepper

1. In a small saucepan, reduce the lemon juice, lemon zest, and cumin to 2 tablespoons of liquid.

2. In a small bowl, whisk together the grapeseed oil, sugar, salt, and pepper and whisk in the lemon juice mixture; reserve in the refrigerator. Bring the Lemon Oil to room temperature and whisk before using.

(RECIPE CONTINUES ON PAGE 156)

(RECIPE CONTINUED FROM PAGE 155)

To Finish the Sweetbreads:

10–12 ounces (284–341 g) prepared blanched Sweetbreads

½ cup (119 mL) milk

4 tablespoons (57 g) clarified butter (divided)

3 tablespoons (45 mL) grapeseed oil (divided)

1 cup (75 g) fresh morels or other wild mushrooms, cleaned, trimmed, and cut in half lengthwise

1 large shallot, thinly sliced

½ cup (119 mL) white wine

Prepared Glazed Carrots

½ cup (145 g) fresh or IQF (Individually Quick-Frozen) peas, blanched in boiling salted water for 30 seconds, shocked in ice water, and drained

Kosher salt and freshly ground black pepper, to taste

Prepared Lemon Oil

3 tablespoons (5 g) fresh mint leaves, thinly sliced

Ground cumin, to season sweetbreads

All-purpose flour, to coat sweetbreads

1. Cut the sweetbreads in ½-inch-thick (13-mm) slices and place in the milk.

2. Place 2 sauté pans (1 must be large enough to hold the sweetbreads in a single layer) over medium heat. Add 2 teaspoons of the clarified butter and 1 tablespoon of the oil to the non-sweetbread pan. When the pan is hot, add the morels and sauté for 1 minute. Add the shallots and sauté for 1 minute. Add the wine and reduce to dry. Add the carrots and peas, season with salt and pepper, and heat them through. Toss with 1 tablespoon of the Lemon Oil and the mint. (Keep the vegetable mixture warm while you sauté the sweetbreads in the second pan.)

3. Shake off the excess milk from the sweetbreads and season with salt, pepper, and cumin. Place them in flour to coat and pat off the excess. Place the remaining clarified butter and the remaining grapeseed oil in the sweetbread pan. When the butter and oil are hot, add the sweetbreads and sauté them until they are deeply golden on the first side, about 3 to 4 minutes. Turn them over and sauté until deeply golden on the second side.

4. Divide the vegetable mixture and sweetbreads onto 2 plates. Place a bit of the remaining Lemon Oil over and around the sweetbreads (but not too much so they stay crisp).

MAPLE-GLAZED DUCK WITH BURNT ORANGE VINAIGRETTE

This preparation is inspired by the theatrical tableside duck that I had at the former L'Auberge-Bretonne in Upstate New York. Although this recipe is a quick-to-fix low-keyed approach to the showmanship that I witnessed, you may, when presenting, roll out the plates on a cart, then (if you're experienced) flame the duck tableside.

SERVES 4

For the Maple-Glazed Duck:

> 2 shallots, thinly sliced
> ¼ cup (59 mL) pure maple syrup
> 3 tablespoons (45 mL) grapeseed oil (divided)
> 1½ tablespoons fresh lemon juice
> 1½ tablespoons fresh orange juice (reserve zest for Candied Orange Zest)
> 1 sprig fresh thyme
> 2 cloves garlic, thinly sliced
> 4 boneless duck breasts (7–8 ounces [199–227 g] each), trimmed and skin scored
> Oven-Roasted Broccoli (recipe follows)
> Kosher salt and freshly ground black pepper, to taste
> Burnt Orange Vinaigrette (recipe follows)
> Candied Orange Zest (recipe follows)

1. In a small bowl, mix together the shallots, the maple syrup, 2 tablespoons of the oil, the lemon juice, the orange juice, the thyme, and the garlic. Place in a resealable plastic bag along with the duck breasts and marinate in the refrigerator overnight.

2. On the next day, remove the duck breasts from the marinade and pat them dry. Prepare the Oven-Roasted Broccoli and when you put the broccoli in the oven, start the duck breasts.

3. Place a large sauté pan over medium-low heat. Season the duck breasts with salt and pepper. When the pan is hot, add the remaining 1 tablespoon of the oil. When hot, add the duck breasts, skin side down. Let the breasts sauté without moving them for 6 to 7 minutes, or until they are dark golden brown (check the skin once in a while—it should be dark but not burnt). Turn the breasts over onto the meat side and cook for 2 to 3 minutes, or until your desired doneness (I prefer medium-rare to medium). Remove the duck from the pan to rest for 2 minutes.

(RECIPE CONTINUES ON PAGE 158)

(RECIPE CONTINUED FROM PAGE 157)

4. Divide the prepared Oven-Roasted Broccoli onto 4 plates. Cut the duck breasts on the bias and place on the plates. Drizzle the Burnt Orange Vinaigrette over and around and sprinkle with the Candied Orange Zest.

For the Oven-Roasted Broccoli:

> **4 large stalks broccoli, stems peeled and cut lengthwise in ¼-inch (6-mm) thick slices to look like flat, bushy trees**
>
> **Extra virgin olive oil, to brush the broccoli slices**
>
> **Kosher salt and freshly ground black pepper, to taste**

1. Preheat the oven to 550°F (288°C). Place the broccoli slices in 1 layer on a sheet pan. Brush each side of the slices with olive oil and season lightly with salt and pepper. Bake for 5 to 8 minutes, or until crisp-tender.

For the Burnt Orange Vinaigrette:

> **1½ cups (356 mL) fresh orange juice, plus zest of 2 oranges**
>
> **½ cup (119 mL) fresh lemon juice, plus zest of 1 lemon**
>
> **¼ cup (50 g) granulated sugar**
>
> **¼ cup (59 mL) water**
>
> **¼ cup (59 mL) red wine vinegar**
>
> **¼ cup (59 mL) grapeseed oil**
>
> **Kosher salt and freshly ground black pepper, to taste**

1. In a small saucepan, reduce the orange juice and zest and lemon juice and zest to ½ cup (59 mL) and reserve.

2. Place the sugar and water in a small saucepan and bring up to a boil, whisking. Remove the whisk and let it boil until the sugar caramelizes. When the sugar is very darkly caramelized and just before it turns black, carefully add the vinegar. Reduce to ¼ cup (59 mL) and add the reserved orange-lemon reduction. Bring up to a boil, remove from the heat, and whisk in the grapeseed oil. Adjust the seasoning with salt and pepper. Reserve in the refrigerator. (Bring the Burnt Orange Vinaigrette to room temperature before serving.)

For the Candied Orange Zest:

Long zest of 1 large orange
½ teaspoon regular olive oil
1 teaspoon granulated sugar
Pinch salt

1. Cover the orange zest with water in a small sauté pan. Bring up to a boil for 5 seconds, drain, then refresh in cold water and drain well.

2. Place the pan over high heat. In a small bowl, toss the refreshed zest with the olive oil. When the pan is hot, add the zest, sugar, and salt and sauté for 30 to 40 seconds. Remove to a plate and reserve.

MINESTRONE

The first minestrone I made was with Chef Peter von Erp at the CIA, and it was inspired by the Piedmont region in Italy. We made a paste of pork fat, garlic, parsley, and cheese, rolled it up into small balls, and popped them into the boiling soup at service to give it that extra hit of garlic and pork richness.

SERVES 8

3 tablespoons (45 mL) extra virgin olive oil (divided)

5 ounces (142 g) pancetta, diced small

12 ounces (341 g) leg of lamb, diced small

Kosher salt and freshly ground black pepper, to taste

1 large (10 ounces [284 g]) onion, diced small

2 medium (5 ounces [142 g]) carrots, peeled and diced small

2 large stalks (5 ounces [142 g]) celery, diced small

6 large cloves garlic, thinly sliced

3 bay leaves

3 sprigs fresh thyme

¼ cup (14 g) chopped fresh Italian parsley stems

1 medium (4 ounces [114 g]) zucchini, diced small

1 medium (4 ounces [114 g]) yellow squash, diced small

10 plum tomatoes, core cut out, plunged into boiling water for 20 seconds, then placed in an ice water, peel removed, cut in half, seeds removed, and cut in small dice (or substitute with 2 [14½-ounce (411 g)] cans diced tomatoes)

2 quarts (1.90 L) unsalted chicken stock

2 cloves garlic, thinly sliced and rinsed under hot water

½ cup (½ ounce [14 g]) fresh basil leaves

1½ tablespoons (¼ ounce [7 g]) fresh rosemary leaves

¼ teaspoon kosher salt

¼ teaspoon freshly ground black pepper

Grated zest of 1 lemon

4 ounces (114 g) ditalini pasta, cooked according to package directions and drained

¼ cup (44 g) dry baby lima beans, rinsed, soaked overnight in hot water until 4 times their volume, drained and cooked in simmering salted water, partially covered, until tender (or substitute 1 [16-ounce (454 g)] can baby lima beans, drained)

6 leaves Swiss chard, cleaned, stems removed, and thinly sliced

Freshly grated Parmagiano Reggiano cheese, for garnish

1. Place a soup pot over medium heat and add 2 tablespoons of the oil. When hot, add the pancetta and cook for 2 minutes, stirring. Strain the pancetta and reserve.

2. Add the oil back to the pan, add the lamb, season lightly with salt and pepper, and cook 2 minutes. Add the onion, carrot, celery, garlic, bay leaves, thyme, and parsley stems, cover, and turn the heat to medium-low. Let sweat for 10 to 15 minutes, stirring every 5 minutes. Add the zucchini, yellow squash, tomatoes, and stock and bring up to a boil, then simmer for 25 to 30 minutes.

3. While simmering, place the reserved pancetta in a food processor along with the rinsed garlic, the basil leaves, the rosemary, the remaining 1 tablespoon of oil, the ¼ teaspoon salt, the ¼ teaspoon pepper, and the lemon zest and process until fine. Transfer the mixture to a bowl, form into ½-inch (13-mm) balls (you will need about 18 to 24), and reserve.

4. When the soup is done, mix in the ditalini, lima beans, and Swiss chard. Bring up to a boil. Adjust the seasoning with salt and pepper. Place 2 to 3 balls of the pancetta mixture into each bowl. Ladle the soup over and garnish with the grated cheese to taste.

6

OLFACTORY EMPORIUMS

I **MUST HAVE LOOKED LIKE MALCOLM MCDOWELL IN A *CLOCKWORK ORANGE*. I WAS** sitting completely rigid, leaning back with my eyes propped open, in a dark room. A film projector clicked away. My eyelids, unlike Malcolm's, were not being mechanically restrained—I just couldn't physically close them.

We were in the demonstration kitchen at the Culinary Institute about two months after I started. Chef Czack introduced a 15-minute documentary called *French Lunch*, which depicted a day in the kitchen of New York City's La Caravelle restaurant. It started innocently with cooks arriving in the kitchen. It then escalated into a choreographed modern dance; cooks moved around each other at controlled rapid speed, coordinating without any obvious communication as if they were wired together. As lunch started, the pace ramped to warp speed as spontaneous masterpieces were produced and repeated without any wasted motion. This was exquisite torture, a sort of culinary *Fear Factor*. Mesmerized, I so wanted to be that good, but I was also frightened out of my skull by what it must take to get to that level. It was like the first time I saw screaming people on a roller coaster at the state fair: *Who in their right mind would go on that?* And then *Who in their right mind could pass it up!* When I left that movie, not only did I know I had to eventually work at a French restaurant, I knew it had to be a *New York City* French restaurant.

When Peter suggested I move to New York, he thought a good place to get my feet wet and become acclimated to the city would be the Waldorf Astoria. That was where Peter had started when he first arrived from Holland in the '50s. At that time there were two main places that immigrating European chefs would start: the Waldorf and Luchow's on 14th Street. He said they were both like a United Nations clearinghouse of great European cooking talent. Each chef would stay long enough to feel assimilated in this new land and learn enough English to get by. The Waldorf had changed since Peter's time there and was not my first choice; but it would be an introduction to the city, and I really didn't have another good option.

After checking out an apartment on the Upper East Side, I made my way down to the Waldorf to interview. On my 35-block walk, I started to become consciously aware of the scents of the food emporiums. Not that I had previously been oblivious, but it just became so apparent as there were so many places situated side by side in a concentrated area. Walking down Second Avenue, you could see as many as 10 or 12 restaurants and food stores on each block. It was a warm day, so they all had their doors open, and the delicious scents all started to meld, the competing individual aromas casting a line around my head and hooking my nose as they tried to reel me in.

Thinking back on those times, I've been sad to see the gradual loss of distinctive food aromas as the country has gotten progressively food phobic. It is getting harder to find a food market that has any fresh product displayed without a protective plastic second skin. And in restaurants, where you could once actually inhale the menu as you crossed the threshold, the "sanitation" of the air, huge exhaust systems, and the proliferation of sous-vide preparations have prompted chefs to, at times, ingeniously *add* to dishes the aromas that used to be a natural occurring result of the preparation.

◆

I HAD GOTTEN A POSITION AT THE WALDORF AND JUST PENNED MY SIGNATURE ON A one-year lease, so I thought I would have a celebratory lunch. Realizing I was solo in a large, intimidating city took some of the "cele" out of the celebration, but I was starving. I decided on what looked like a small, quiet place that I had passed on the way to the rental office.

I walked through the door and was confronted with a full-tilt, high-noon New York lunch service. I was frozen like a statue, and the waitress behind the counter had my number in a second. "If you want a stool," she said, "you better grab one 'cause it's not going to grab you."

I sat down and realized my first priority was to find a bathroom. I shyly did a 180-degree turn, looking around when the waitress announced, "If you're looking for the can, it's down the hall to the left." I was both mortified and grateful at the same time as I loped back to the bathroom.

Finally I was ready to eat, and sat studying the menu. But the waitress didn't have time for my wide-eyed, gee-whiz, Midwestern hemming and hawing. "Try the clam chowder," she urged. "It's Manhattan—not like that creamy Boston crap." It turned out to be a delicious, briny tomato-and-pepper clam soup paired with a butter-grilled corn muffin—a perfect lunch.

I was feeling well fed and more at home in this town already. In my deepest most assertive voice, I called out, "Check, please!" Without even turning around she said, "Look next to your bowl and pay at the front counter. Thanks, babe!"

I started as a banquet cook at the Waldorf Astoria. On my third day there, I was assigned to a rather large party. I reported to the banquet chef, Willy, in the fourth-floor kitchen, along with 10 other cooks. Noticing I was new, he asked me what kind of experience I had. I told him with a slight bit of culinary swagger that I had graduated from the CIA and was most recently a fellowship saucier in the school's Escoffier Room.

"Hey everyone, we have ourselves a big time saucier here!" he proclaimed to the surrounding group. "So, *Mister Saucier*, how do you make a marchand de vin sauce?" As my swagger faded, I luckily rattled off a close-enough interpretation to satisfy Chef Willy for a quick second.

"So, Mister Saucier," Chef Willy continued, "do you know how to cook filets?" I replied that I had cooked a few in my time, so he led me over to a table in front of the bank of broilers that held 2,000 filets for the evening's banquet. This was a bit beyond my scope of four filets on the grill at one time, so I humbly asked for help. The chef paired me up with a veteran broiler man, and I learned how to get 2,000 filets ready for a seamless banquet. From that day on, I kept a very low profile. I had learned an important lesson: keep your mouth shut and learn what people have to teach.

I was hired for the princely sum of $100 a week, pennies above minimum wage. My monthly rent for my studio apartment on 89th and Second was $280 a month, leaving me a whopping $30 a week to feed and entertain myself.

Since I worked nights with Sundays off, I used to eat a regular two hot dogs for lunch from Grey's Papaya (under a dollar) and have all my dinners at work in the employee cafeteria. The hard part of that lifestyle for a young food person was the daily walk to work down Second Avenue. The area I passed through was known as Yorkville—a mix of inexpensive German, Czechoslovakian, Polish, Hungarian, Russian, and French restaurants and groceries. The aromas of the particular establishments were overwhelmingly heady as the daily walk commenced. All I could do was be frugal enough at the start of the month so that I could reward myself with a couple of Sunday meals at month's end.

My first Thanksgiving in New York City came a month after I moved into my luxurious budget apartment. Besides the view of Second Avenue, one of the most interesting attributes of the space was that, if you really stretched out, you could touch three of the four walls at once. I'm talking small. I've since had closets that were more welcoming, but it was home.

Since I was fresh out of cooking school and located in a culinary mecca for ingredients, I was really looking forward to doing some serious home cooking. The only problem was I had a stove the size of an Easy-Bake Oven with two, *almost* hot plate burners on top and a 12-by-12-inch area for food preparation. Thank goodness I was living alone.

Preparing Thanksgiving dinner in my New York City apartment

I only knew a couple of people in the city, and they were all former fellow students from the Culinary. One of them gave me a call a week before Thanksgiving and invited me over to her folks' apartment in the city, which was a crosstown bus ride away, on the Upper West Side near Columbia University. I was very excited to be with someone's family. Thanksgiving in a place like New York City, with its millions of people, can be a very lonely place.

I walked up to the old stately looking apartment building and was buzzed in. I was greeted warmly by half of the family and led into the expansive living room. Adjacent to that was the large Chippendale dining room table, set with bright, shiny silver as well as heirloom china, a lace tablecloth and a large silver candelabra at its center, surrounded by a cornucopia of fall's finest gourds and squashes. I thought, *Now* this *is a New York City apartment*. I couldn't wait to see a real kitchen. I was led through the swinging door and stopped short. *Man! Does everyone have Easy-Bake Ovens in New York?* I wondered. To be fair, the stove was a bit larger than mine, but one person had to leave the kitchen for me to get in to see it.

I learned two things that day: First, this was a typical New York City galley kitchen. And second, after consuming an amazing Thanksgiving dinner, I found that with forethought, ingenuity, and organization, you don't need all that extra space to create good food. From that day on, my mini kitchen became a hub of cooking experiments, and the next year I even had Thanksgiving with a few friends at my own little place.

◆

I WASN'T VERY HAPPY AT THE WALDORF. I WAS LEARNING HOW TO COOK FOR VOLUMES OF people, which could come in handy in the future, but my goal had not changed. I wanted to get into a great restaurant, preferably French—so things had to change.

I walked past the curtained front windows for the seventh time, looking casual and non-committal in case anyone inside was watching. It was cold outside, but I was sweating like crazy. Then, my hands shaking as though I were about to jump off a high dive, I yanked open the door.

"May I help you, Monsieur!"

"Yes, may I speak to Chef Fessaguet?"

"You may want to try the delivery door on the side, Monsieur."

Moments later, I was walking down to the basement kitchen at La Caravelle—yes, *that* La Caravelle, from *French Lunch*. As I walked past the front cooking line down to the chef's office, I could tell by the looks on the cooks' faces that they knew I didn't belong there.

"Oui? May I help you?"

It was Chef Fessaguet! "Yes, chef, a pleasure to meet you!" I said. "I'm Sanford D'Amato, a recent graduate of the Culinary Institute, and would love to work in any capacity for you—here's my resume."

"Have you worked in a French kitchen before?"

"I worked under Chef Peter von Erp at the Escoffier Room at the school—we received a three-star review from the *New York Times*."

"Hmmm, this Chef Von Erp doesn't sound French."

"No, he is Dutch but has an extensive knowledge of French cuisine."

"I'm sure he does, Monsieur D'Amato, but as you can see, I have many well-trained *French* cooks and do not need anyone right now—but stop back again in the future if you care to."

Once every two weeks I would stop back at La Caravelle to hear, "Oh, Monsieur D'Amato, I still have nothing, but stop back if you like." I kept going back, but I knew in my heart that it wasn't going anywhere. And it was the same at other French restaurants in the city. If you weren't French or didn't know someone there, forget about it.

At that point I decided to keep looking but knew I had to get another job for two reasons: I hardly had enough money to live on, and I had no social life—a bad combination. An ad in the *New York Post* would solve both problems. It read, "Chef wanted" and had been posted by Paxton's Public House on 73rd and Second Avenue, which was walking distance from my apartment. I decided to go there on my day off for Sunday Brunch to check out the menu and see if I wanted to apply. Paxton's was a classic singles' "fern bar" restaurant of the type popular

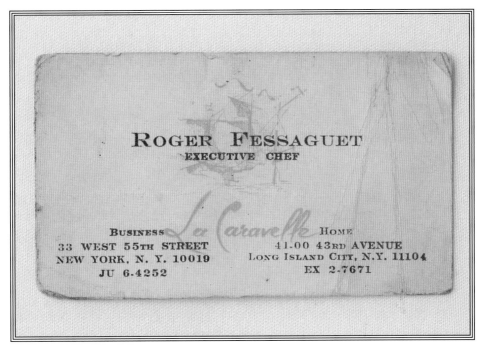

Business card of Chef Roger Fessaguet from La Caravelle

on the East Side of New York in the 1970s. This area was the birthplace of the original T.G.I. Friday's, P.J. Clarke's, and other restaurants that became national chains. The menus were similar, a small step up from diner food—spinach salads, chili, fish and chips, and oversized grilled burgers that teetered on crisp toasted English muffins, making them almost impossible to consume without a person looking like a contestant in a professional eating contest.

I interviewed for the job by making a straightforward Mediterranean red wine-marinated lamb shish kabob that the owners, Max and Richard, fell in love with. Richard then convinced me he was trying to make the leap to the next level so I would have free reign with the specials that were half the menu. This was not the type of food that I had moved to New York City to cook; but the pay was great, and it meant I could continue to live in the city and pursue my dreams. As a plus, the entire staff was my age, so the social aspect was a deal maker. I took the job and would start after I worked out my notice at the Waldorf.

Paxton's had an English public house theme. This was not really obvious from the décor or the menu, but one dish that Richard really wanted to keep on the menu was shepherd's pie. Paxton's shepherd's pie was essentially a beef sloppy joe slathered with watery instant mashed potatoes—not great.

I had never made shepherd's pie, so I did a bit of research (thank you, Peter) and found that it dated back to English and Scottish shepherds and was a casserole made with lamb and a potato topping. I changed the shepherd's pie at Paxton's to a dish of rich, red wine-braised lamb with a goat cheese-encrusted real potato topping. I tried to take each dish on the Paxton's menu and either upgrade the base ingredients or come up with a simple substitute dish that would appeal to the clientele. Such was the case with a dish that I had learned from Peter, braised beef rouladen. The dish consists of a flattened piece of beef spread with mustard, rolled around onion, pickle, and bacon, and tied up and braised in a wine-enriched broth until tender. It was perfect for the place because it was braised and thus reheatable. And it also was easy to explain, as it was beef, onions, and bacon with a pickle—only one or two steps from a burger.

We've all heard the cliché that all servers in New York or LA are actually out-of-work actors waiting for their big or small break. At Paxton's, the cliché was in full force. The restaurant was surrounded by a few small independent theaters, and a few of the soap operas were filmed nearby; so we had a staff of temperamental, overly dramatic thespians who would shift in and out of character between the soup and salad courses.

All of the orders were called in through the window/half-door to the kitchen, so if I didn't physically turn around to look, I would swear that the two blue cheeseburgers with the shepherd's pie had been ordered by a moaning Blanche DuBois from *A Streetcar Named Desire* instead of just Kim from Brooklyn. I actually found this slightly schizo character development to be quite entertaining during the usual repetitious night of order after order. My only in-character response was a weak Peter Lorre impression: "Excuse me, your order is ready. If you don't take it out now, I'm going to have to hurt you." Surprisingly, this never got a positive review.

The one server I really enjoyed working with was Stanley. He was a puffy, stout Tim Conway look-alike with a sharp wit and actual paid acting experience in a few soaps and commercials. He also fancied himself a culinary bon vivant, so we would regularly talk food.

One day he told me his favorite Italian dish was veal piccata, so the next night, a busy Friday, I put my version on the menu as a special, which usually meant we'd sell about four to six orders throughout the evening. The service started slowly. I was doing some last-minute prep, and John the dishwasher and salad maker, who hadn't yet decided what to make of this new chef in his world, was rhythmically swaying and singing along to the Hues Corporation's "Rock The Boat."

Stanley was so excited that his first 10 customers had no choice—they were all having the piccata. That would have been great, except that we had a two-person kitchen—just John and me. As I was getting buried under six flaming sauté pans filled with veal, I could hear Stanley at the window in his best Knute Rockne (played by Pat O'Brien) voice, compelling me to, "Dig deep. Plow through it. Win one for the Stanley!"

At the end of the evening, I didn't feel like I had won one; but everybody got fed, and I found out that John had some skills beyond salads and dishes as he jumped on the grill without any prompting and saved my ass. The omnipresent kitchen music was a huge difference for me. Actually the whole experience was different. Paxton's was like doing a touch of work during continual recess. I was internally motivated, but I could have been working at 50 percent and met expectations. The controls were very loose, and as long as the place was making money—and they were—everyone was happy.

In the mid-70s the only thing hotter than fern bars was disco. Even though this was pre-*Saturday Night Fever* and Studio 54—with their velvet ropes of decision only parting to let in the hippest and most well known of the NYC glitterati—disco clubs were still exclusive enough to ensure someone like me wouldn't be swooping through the door. Little did I know when taking the chef's job that Max, one of the owners of Paxton's, also owned Friends, an early disco club on First Avenue. Since I was Paxton's first pedigreed chef (by that I mean someone who had studied and graduated from an actual cooking school), I was somewhat of an odd celebrity in the company. So as a hiring perk, Max invited me over to the club for a night on the house. I walked up to the club's door wearing my flared jeans, platform shoes (a definite plus in my case), and my best '70s turtleneck pullover, feeling as Steve McQueen as possible. *Was I on the list?* Yes, Mr. D'Amato, enjoy yourself!

After the bouncer had confirmed I was on the list, I coolly sauntered over to the bar, channeling my old roommate Roger. After quickly downing a couple of cocktails, I was then pulled over to the dreaded dance floor by some new friends from the restaurant. My last dancing experience had been in high school, and I still had a historic grasp of the Mashed Potato, Hitchhike, and Tighten Up, but not a muscle in my body knew how to Hustle. As the thumping bass beat reverberated through my body and soul, I felt like a background dancer on the set of *Hee Haw* doing the prospector hop as the rest of the room was Hustling their way to smooth-dancing immortality.

Max walked up and wryly asked, "First time in a disco?"

"How'd you know?" I responded, laughing.

He said "Don't worry, I'm sure your first lamb kebab didn't taste like the one we had at the interview. Give yourself a few weeks on the dance floor, and I'm sure you'll be a disco machine."

Well, the machine part never happened, but I was starting to enjoy my new work life and the city.

◆

YOU JUST NEVER KNEW WHO WAS GOING TO WALK THROUGH THE DOOR AT PAXTON'S.
A lot of up-and-coming actors and some established actors like Kevin Conway and Mar-joe Gortner came through, and we had regular visits from Richie Havens, and even verified
Woody Allen and Diane Keaton walk-bys.

One of my most memorable walk-ins was on an unusually warm fall evening. A tall, quite
hairy, visibly sweating gent strolled into the bar. He was holding closed an oversized tweed
coat that draped past his ankles and slightly rested on his canvas sneakers. He smiled widely
and started to methodically extend the two sides of the coat! Just as I was getting ready for an
ugly exposure, everyone at the bar called out, "Doc!"

Turns out he was fully dressed, and the two inside flaps of his coat held multiple stitched-in pockets, each one holding a 750-milliliter bottle of wine. This was no Thunderbird and
Cold Duck vending machine—this was the Doctor of Wine. Each of his lushly padded pock-ets held a first-growth Bordeaux—Lafite, Margaux, Latour, Haut Brion, Mouton, Ausone,
Cheval Blanc, even a d'Yquem—'53s, '59s, and '61s. Money was flying, as the wines were
priced to move. I was dying to buy something, but even the bargain Bordeaux were too ex-pensive. Doc did have one half bottle of vintage champagne that I could afford, so I bought
it and put it in my refrigerator for a special occasion.

When New Year's approached, I realized I would be spending another holiday alone—
never a more suitable special occasion to crack open the champagne and make myself feel
better! I had enough money left over from a relative's Christmas check to buy a one-ounce
tin of beluga caviar and a package of plain French crackers.

After I got out of work around 10:30, I went home. I would have donned a tux if I'd had
one. Instead I put on a stack of B. B. King records (my wallowing music), turned on Dick
Clark, and made that champagne and caviar last well past the New Year's ball drop. I savored
every morsel. Anyone who has ever seen a professional cook eat knows that the word *savor*
is not in their vocabularies. Cooks usually eat at a frantic pace in large, voluminous bites, as
time is always at a premium. But I broke character and savored. Now, I've certainly had many
wonderful New Year's celebrations with friends and family over the years, but I'll always
remember how wonderful the combination of the champagne and caviar was—and how I
didn't want it to end. The only thing I did want to end was my "O Sole Mio" life.

The service window became my portal to the Paxton's life. I could casually lean on the
bottom half of the door and get an unencumbered view of the entire bar. This vista was only
interrupted when the soap opera stars from *All My Children* (led by Phil), with their Macy's

Thanksgiving Day Parade heads, would hang out at my end of the bar and virtually eclipse the room. During slow periods, the servers, bartenders, John, and I would trade gossip, stories, and observations of famous and quirky regulars. During one of these casual conversations I met Ellen. A native of Far Rockaway, Queens, who had lived in the city for years, she was an attractive, street-savvy, direct woman with an ironic quick wit—and I was interested.

◆

AFTER MY THIRD SCOTCH, I WAS FEELING VERY NEW YORK. ELLEN HAD SPENT YEARS serving at various hip East Side establishments. She seemed to know everyone and was quickly assimilating me into a brand-new lifestyle. Working at Paxton's quickly became a sidebar to my real life of barhopping and after-hour parties that would only end when the sun came out. From what I can recall, I was having the time of my life. Within months I proposed, and Ellen accepted. We were married at the transient church for NYC, St. John's Cathedral. It was a small ceremony—only 12 people, two of whom were her dad, whom I met that day, and Peter, my best man.

After the ceremony Peter asked me if I had a direction in mind for my career. I told him that since the French restaurant quest didn't look promising, I had spoken to a friend and restaurateur back in Milwaukee who had given me a couple of leads through the National Restaurant Association, in both San Francisco and Acapulco. I had sent resumes to both but had heard nothing. I had not thought about it for a while, but I wasn't going anywhere. The fun of Paxton's started to fade, and I was back to the want ads. I had four solid interviews for higher-paying jobs, but it all meant I would still be a chef at a mediocre food factory.

About two months after the wedding, the bartender at Paxton's called to me into the kitchen to tell me that I had a long-distance call. At the other end was someone with unexpected news.

CHAPTER SIX RECIPES

Manhattan Clam Chowder

173

*Olive Oil Confit of Turkey Thighs,
Cranberry Vinaigrette*

175

*Garam Masala-Spiced Kohlrabi Soup
with Tamarind-Glazed Almonds*

177

*Lamb Shepherd's Pie with Minted
Chevre Potato Crust*

180

*Chilled Lobster with Cauliflower
Scallion Cream and Caviar*

182

Skate Saltimbocca with Lemon Jam

185

MANHATTAN CLAM CHOWDER

Yankees or Red Sox. Giants or Patriots. Number three has to be Manhattan or New England (chowders that is)—let the trash talking commence. I'm a fan of both (chowders that is) but if you're making a pot of this in New England, and want a civilized dinner, just call it Clam Soup!

SERVES 8

For the Clam Broth:

4 ounces (114 g) bacon, cut into ¼-inch thick matchstick-sized pieces

3 shallots, thinly sliced

3 cloves garlic, thinly sliced

4 sprigs fresh thyme

3 bay leaves

1 bunch fresh Italian parsley stems (reserve 1 cup [57 g] of leaves for garnish)

20 crushed black peppercorns

1 cup (237 mL) dry white wine

10 pounds (4.54 kg) cherrystone clams, rinsed and scrubbed to remove sand (do not use soap)

2 cups (474 mL) unsalted chicken stock

1. Place a stock pot with a tight-fitting lid over medium heat. Add the bacon and render by half, or until it is just starting to brown. Remove the bacon and reserve for finishing the soup (leave the fat in the pot).

2. Add the shallots, garlic, thyme, bay leaves, parsley stems, and peppercorns and sauté for 3 minutes. Add the white wine, bring up to a boil, and cook for 2 minutes. Add the clams and stock and cover the pot tightly to steam the clams until they are all open.

3. Set a large strainer over a bowl and drain the clams. Strain the resulting clam broth slowly through 2 layers of cheesecloth (stopping at the end if you see sand) and reserve.

4. When the clams are cool, remove them from their shells, trim off the connective top and bottom if they are still attached, and cut into quarters. Cover and place in the refrigerator.

(RECIPE CONTINUES ON PAGE 174)

(RECIPE CONTINUED FROM PAGE 173)

To Finish the Soup:

> Prepared Clam Broth (reserve 1 cup [237 mL] for steaming Manila clams)
>
> 2 medium onions (1 pound [454 g]), cut in small dice
>
> 2 large (½ pound [227 g]) poblano peppers, stem and seeds removed, cut in small dice
>
> 2 stalks celery (4 ounces [114 g]), cut in small dice
>
> ¼ cup (66 g) tomato paste
>
> 1 pound (454 g) potatoes, peeled and cut in small dice, covered with water and 1 tablespoon salt in a large saucepan, cooked until tender, and drained (but reserve ¾ cup [178 mL] potato water for the soup)
>
> 1 (14½-ounce [411-g]) can small diced plum tomatoes in juice
>
> 1 tablespoon fresh thyme leaves
>
> Reserved trimmed cherrystone clams
>
> Kosher salt and freshly ground black pepper, to taste
>
> 24 Manila clams

1. Add the prepared clam broth to a large sauce pot. Add the onions, peppers, celery, tomato paste, and ¾ cup (178 mL) potato water, bring up to a simmer, and cook for 2 minutes. Add the tomatoes and thyme and simmer for 10 minutes.

2. Add the potatoes, reserved trimmed cherrystone clams, and reserved bacon and bring up to a boil. Turn off the heat, adjust the seasoning with salt and pepper, and cover.

3. Steam open the Manila clams in the reserved 1 cup (237 mL) clam broth in a large saucepan. Add the resulting Manila clam liquid to the soup. For serving, place 3 Manila clams in each bowl. Add the reserved parsley leaves to the soup and divide the soup among the bowls.

OLIVE OIL CONFIT OF TURKEY THIGHS, CRANBERRY VINAIGRETTE

Due to a turkey's anatomy, when cooking the breast to the right temperature, the leg and thigh need more cooking. One way to handle this is that when the breast is at the correct temperature, the leg and thigh should be removed so that they can finish cooking separately in the oven. So when I first began experimenting in my mini NYC kitchen, I came up with a dark meat alternative preparation. Inspired by duck confit, these meaty, moist turkey thighs fit the bill—and my small oven.

SERVES 8

> 1 cup (300 g) kosher salt
>
> ¼ cup (56 g) dark brown sugar
>
> 2 teaspoons freshly ground black pepper
>
> 4 bay leaves, ground
>
> 2 teaspoons ground fennel seed
>
> 1 teaspoon ground sage
>
> 6–7 pounds (2.72–3.18 kg) skin-on turkey thighs (4 large or 6 smaller ones)
>
> 2 heads garlic, each cut in half
>
> 2 cinnamon sticks
>
> 8 star anise
>
> 4 bay leaves
>
> 20 crushed juniper berries
>
> 6–7 cups (1.42–1.66 L) regular olive oil (you will need enough to cover the turkey thighs)

1. At least 1 day before, mix the salt, sugar, pepper, ground bay leaves, fennel, and sage and spread over the turkey thighs on each side. Place the thighs on a wire rack over a sheet pan and cover them with plastic wrap. Refrigerate for 24 hours.

2. Rinse off the salt mixture from the thighs and dry them with paper towels. Place the thighs in a pot large enough to hold them in 1 layer, then add the garlic, cinnamon sticks, star anise, bay leaves, juniper berries, and olive oil. Cover all with a piece of parchment paper and bring up to just before a simmer (about 165°F to 170°F [74°C to 77°C] on a deep-fry thermometer). Maintain that temperature for about 3 to 3½ hours, or until the thighs are fork-tender but not falling apart.

3. Remove the thighs from the oil and reserve the clear oil for sautéing. (Thighs may be prepared 2 to 3 days ahead up to this point.)

(RECIPE CONTINUES ON PAGE 176)

(RECIPE CONTINUED FROM PAGE 175)

To Finish the Dish:

Reserved clear oil for sautéing

Prepared turkey thighs

8 ounces (227 g) frisée or other tart greens

Cranberry Vinaigrette (recipe follows)

1. Preheat the oven to 375°F (190°C). Place about half of the reserved oil in a medium-hot sauté pan large enough to hold all of the thighs in 1 layer (or you can use 2 sauté pans). When hot, carefully add the turkey thighs, skin side down, and sauté them until the skin starts to get crisp and golden, about 2 to 3 minutes.

2. Place the sauté pan(s) in the oven and cook for about 8 to 10 minutes, or until the thighs are heated through and the skin is crisp (do not overcook as the turkey will dry out).

3. Serve the turkey with the frisée tossed with a bit of the Cranberry Vinaigrette and garnish with the reserved cranberries and pomegranate seeds. Serve the extra vinaigrette on the side for the Turkey Confit.

For the Cranberry Vinaigrette:

¼ cup (50 g) granulated sugar

¼ cup (59 mL) water

1 (12-ounce [341-g]) bag fresh cranberries

3 pomegranates, 2 of them juiced to yield ⅔ cup (158 mL) liquid, and seeds removed from remaining pomegranate and reserved for garnish

4 teaspoons red wine vinegar

¼ cup (59 mL) reserved oil from the turkey thighs or regular olive oil

½ teaspoon kosher salt

¼ teaspoon freshly ground black pepper

1. In a 1-quart (948-mL) saucepan over high heat, bring the sugar and water up to a boil. Add the cranberries, cover, cook for 30 seconds, toss, cover for 30 more seconds, and toss again—you want all of the cranberries to just crack but not be overcooked (it should take a total of 1 minute and 15 seconds time). Pour the cranberries into a bowl and let them cool.

2. When cooled, pour the liquid from the cranberries (about ½ cup [119 mL]) into a saucepan. Reserve the cranberries in the refrigerator. Add the ⅔ cup (158 mL) pomegranate juice to the cranberry liquid and reduce to ¾ cup (178 mL). Place in a bowl and add the vinegar, reserved ¼ cup (59 mL) oil, salt, and pepper. Reserve in the refrigerator.

GARAM MASALA-SPICED KOHLRABI SOUP WITH TAMARIND-GLAZED ALMONDS

Like curry powder, Garam Masala is a blend of spices from northern India. The word Garam *means warm or hot and* Masala *means spice mixture. Kohlrabi is at its best and sweetest from mid-spring to early fall and that is the time to make this soup, and the garnish of tamarind-glazed almonds adds a nice tart component to the slightly sweet and savory profile.*

SERVES 12

For the Garam Masala:

> 2 tablespoons ground coriander
>
> 4 teaspoons ground cumin
>
> 1 teaspoon ground cardamom
>
> 1 teaspoon ground cinnamon
>
> ¾ teaspoon freshly ground black pepper
>
> ⅜ teaspoon ground cloves

1. Mix all of the ingredients together and reserve.

For the Tamarind-Glazed Almonds and to Finish the Soup:

> 4 tablespoons (57 g) plus 1 teaspoon unsalted butter (divided)
>
> 2½ pounds (1.13 kg) kohlrabi, peeled and cut in small dice (reserve 1½ cups [203 g] for garnish)
>
> 3 stalks celery (6 ounces), cut in ¼-inch slices
>
> 1 carrot (3 ounces [85 g]), peeled and cut in half lengthwise, then cut in ¼-inch (6-mm) slices
>
> 1 large onion (12 ounces [341 g]), cut in small dice
>
> 1 Granny Smith apple (6 ounces [170 g]), peeled, cored, and cut in small dice
>
> 4 cloves garlic, finely chopped
>
> 4 bay leaves
>
> Prepared Garam Masala
>
> 1 tablespoon kosher salt
>
> 8 cups (1.90 L) unsalted chicken stock
>
> 2 teaspoons tamarind concentrate (divided)
>
> Kosher salt and freshly ground pepper, to taste
>
> 1 (2¼-ounce [64-g]) bag slivered almonds, for garnish

(RECIPE CONTINUES ON PAGE 179)

(RECIPE CONTINUED FROM PAGE 177)

1. Place a 1½-gallon (5.68-L) pot over medium heat. Add 3 tablespoons (43 g) of the butter, and when the butter is melted and hot, add the kohlrabi (less the reserved garnish), celery, carrot, onion, and apple and sweat, covered, stirring frequently, for 10 to 15 minutes (do not brown).

2. Add the garlic, the bay leaves, the prepared Garam Masala, and the 1 tablespoon salt and cook, stirring, for 2 minutes. Add the stock and 1 teaspoon of the tamarind concentrate, bring up to a simmer, and simmer, covered, until the vegetables are well cooked, for about 20 minutes.

3. Carefully process in a blender (only fill the blender ⅓ at a time and start on low, as the soup is hot), then strain through a medium strainer. Adjust the seasoning with salt and pepper.

4. Place a nonstick sauté pan over medium heat. Add 1 tablespoon of the butter, and when the butter is hot, add the reserved 1½ cups (203 g) kohlrabi and sauté until tender, about 3 to 4 minutes. Season the kohlrabi with salt and pepper and place in a bowl.

5. Wipe out the pan, and over medium-low heat, add the remaining 1 teaspoon of the butter. When the butter is melted, add the almonds. When the butter is just starting to brown after about 3 minutes, adjust the seasoning with salt and pepper, add the remaining 1 teaspoon of the tamarind concentrate, and cook 1 minute to glaze the almonds. Let cool at room temperature.

6. For serving, mix the almonds with the kohlrabi and divide among the bowls. Divide the soup among the bowls.

LAMB SHEPHERD'S PIE WITH MINTED CHEVRE POTATO CRUST

Over the years, I've made Shepherd's Pie both at home and at Sanford and the recipe has changed according to my taste at the time. This version is a combination of creamy goat cheese potatoes with tender succulent stewed lamb producing a homey, warming, highly spiced casserole that satisfies on many levels.

SERVES 4

2 tablespoons regular olive oil (divided)

1 pound (681 g) lamb leg meat, trimmed and diced small

Kosher salt and freshly ground black pepper, to taste

1 onion, diced small

4 cloves garlic, chopped

1 tablespoon ground coriander

1 tablespoon ground cinnamon

2 teaspoons ground fennel

1 cup (237 mL) red wine

1 can (14½ ounces [411 g]) diced tomatoes in sauce

½ cup (119 mL) unsalted chicken stock

Minted Chevre Potato Crust (recipe follows)

1. Place a large sauté pan over high heat. When the pan is hot, add 1½ tablespoons of the olive oil, season the lamb with salt and pepper, and add to the pan. Brown the lamb for about 6 to 8 minutes, then remove to a plate.

2. Add the remaining ½ tablespoon of the olive oil to the pan, add the onions, and sauté until they are translucent. Add the meat back in, then add the garlic, coriander, cinnamon, and fennel and sauté for 1 minute. Add the wine and bring up to a simmer, covered, and cook until reduced to dry, for about 10 minutes. Add the tomatoes and stock and simmer until the meat is tender, for about 15 minutes. Adjust the seasoning with salt and pepper.

3. Preheat the oven to 375°F (190°C). Place the lamb mixture evenly in an 8x10-inch (20x25-cm) casserole dish and cover with the Minted Chevre Potato Crust. Bake for about 25 to 30 minutes, or until golden and heated through.

For the Minted Chevre Potato Crust:

1½ pounds (681 g) Yukon gold potatoes

3 ounces (85 g) young chevre (goat cheese)

3 tablespoons (1½ ounces [43 g]) salted butter

1½ tablespoons heavy cream

1 tablespoon chopped garlic

3 tablespoons (45 mL) fresh chopped mint

½ teaspoon kosher salt

¼ teaspoon freshly ground black pepper

1. Preheat the oven to 400°F (200°C). Bake the potatoes for about 50 to 60 minutes, or until tender. Cut the potatoes in half while they are still hot and scoop out the flesh into a food mill or potato ricer, then rice into a bowl.

2. In a small saucepan, bring the chevre, butter, cream, and garlic up to a simmer, whipping. Add the mint, salt, and pepper, then add the mixture to the potatoes and blend with a spatula.

CHILLED LOBSTER WITH CAULIFLOWER–SCALLION CREAM AND CAVIAR

As Robin Leach would eloquently say, "Champagne wishes and caviar dreams." His tagline for Lifestyles of the Rich and Famous *embodies many peoples' perception of the ultimate in gourmet dining extravagance. Adding lobster into the mix is just the right thing to do. The opulent creaminess of the cauliflower-scallion cream is a match that I'm sure would make Robin proud.*

SERVES 4

For the Lobster:

   2 (1½- to 2-pound [681- to 908-g]) lobsters

1. Cut off the tips of the lobster claws with a heavy knife or cleaver (just ¼ inch [6 mm] of the tips). In a stock pot, steam the lobsters for 8 to 10 minutes, depending on their size; cool. Remove the meat from the shell, place in a bowl, and reserve in the refrigerator.

For the Cauliflower–Scallion Cream and to Finish the Dish:

   1 teaspoon grapeseed oil
   1 medium shallot, thinly sliced
   ½ small head cauliflower (5 ounces [142 g]), cut in small dice
   ½ cup (119 mL) dry white wine
   1 bay leaf
   ¾ teaspoon kosher salt, plus additional to taste
   ½ teaspoon freshly ground black pepper, plus additional to taste
   ⅛ teaspoon grated nutmeg
   ¾ cup (178 mL) heavy cream
   1 teaspoon crushed anise seeds
   6 scallions, sliced in ½-inch (13-mm) pieces (green part only)
   Reserved cold lobster pieces
   Lemon Vinaigrette: 3 tablespoons (45 mL) regular olive oil mixed with 1 tablespoon fresh lemon juice and kosher salt and freshly ground black pepper, to taste
   Unsalted chicken or vegetable stock, for thinning, if necessary
   2 ounces (57 g) good-quality caviar
   Fresh chervil sprigs, for garnish

(RECIPE CONTINUES ON PAGE 184)

(RECIPE CONTINUED FROM PAGE 182)

1. In a small saucepan over medium heat, add the grapeseed oil and shallots and cook 30 seconds. Add the cauliflower and cook 30 seconds. Add the wine, the bay leaf, the ¾ teaspoon salt, the ½ teaspoon pepper, and the nutmeg, cover, and cook until dry. Add the cream and anise seeds and bring up to a boil. Let sit, covered, for 3 minutes.

2. Remove and discard the bay leaf. Place the mixture in a blender along with the scallions and blend on high until very fine. Strain through a medium strainer and chill.

3. Ten minutes before serving, toss the lobster pieces with the Lemon Vinaigrette and adjust the seasoning with salt and pepper.

4. For serving, divide the Cauliflower-Scallion Cream among 4 plates (thin with a bit of chicken or vegetable stock if it is too thick—it should be the consistency of sour cream). Drain the excess Lemon Vinaigrette from the lobster and divide onto the plates. Divide the caviar over the lobster and garnish with the chervil sprigs.

SKATE SALTIMBOCCA WITH LEMON JAM

SERVES 4

    Regular olive oil, to fry sage leaves

    28 fresh sage leaves (20 for garnish and 8 for inside the Saltimboccas)

    Kosher salt and freshly ground black pepper, to taste

    4 very thin slices prosciutto

    4 skate fillets (about 6 ounces [170 g] each and ¼ inch [6 mm] thick), skinless and fully trimmed

    Wondra flour (instant flour), to dust fish

    ¼ cup (59 mL) extra virgin olive oil

    Lemon Jam (recipe follows)

1. Heat a wide sauté pan filled with ½ inch (13 mm) regular olive oil to 350°F (180°C). Carefully place 20 sage leaves in the oil for 5 to 10 seconds. Remove the leaves with a slotted spoon or skimmer, drain on paper towels, and immediately season with salt (sage leaves can be fried right before sautéing the skate).

2. Cut the prosciutto slices the size of half of a skate fillet and place them on half of each fillet. Place 2 sage leaves over the prosciutto and fold the other side of the fillet over the top to form a triangle. Score the butt end of the fold halfway horizontally through the fillet. Season both sides lightly with salt and pepper. Dust the skate with flour and shake off the excess.

3. Place a sauté pan, large enough to hold all 4 fillets without crowding, over medium-high heat. When the pan is hot, add the 4 tablespoons of the extra virgin olive oil. When hot, add the fillets and sauté them until golden brown and the skate is cooked through, about 2 to 3 minutes per side. Place the fillets on 4 plates and garnish with the fried sage leaves and Lemon Jam.

For the Lemon Jam:

    4 lemons, washed

    6 tablespoons (75 g) granulated sugar

    4 sprigs fresh mint

    1 star anise

    Kosher salt

1. Preheat the oven to 375°F (190°C). Wrap the lemons in aluminum foil in 1 layer and bake for 1 hour. Remove from the oven.

2. When cool enough to handle, cut the lemons in half and scoop out all of the flesh and juice (you should have 1½ cups [356 mL] total). Place the flesh and juice in a small nonreactive pan along with the sugar, mint, and star anise, and simmer until reduced to about 1 cup. Strain the mixture through a medium strainer and adjust the seasoning with salt.

7

MEXICO CITY

"BUENOS DÍAS Y BIENVENIDOS A MEXICO D.F." AS THE VOICE WOKE ME UP OUT OF a sound sleep, it took me a few seconds to recognize my surroundings.

I had received a phone call at Paxton's from Nick Noyes, the head of the Restaurant Association in Mexico. It was in response to one of the two resumes I had sent out, and he was looking for a chef for a new restaurant that he was opening in Mexico City. I told him I was very flattered but didn't really think I was qualified, as I was still fresh out of school. Plus, I was really looking and hoping for a position where I would be learning under a talented chef. After a long conversation, he told me that my experience was better than the majority of chefs in Mexico, and he eventually talked me into flying there for a few days to interview and see the city.

This was my first trip outside the Unites States. When I arrived that Sunday, Nick picked me up at the airport and did a quick-pace interview as we drove into the city. He then dropped me off at Chapultepec Park in the center of the city. The park was the social center of Mexico City (which at that time was reputed to be the second-largest city in the world). He gave me a short direction seminar, pointed out a few landmarks, and told me the address of the restaurant where we would meet. He said the best way to see a city was to dive right in; he assured me the people were friendly and willing to help.

"We'll see you in a few hours," he said. "Oh, as a last resort, here is my number."

Along the way I went from being frightened and apprehensive to becoming relatively calm and excited by the people, the architecture, the dress, and of course, the food. Nothing calms and satisfies me more than tasty food, and after an afternoon of "point and pay," I had tried many small dishes, one of which was grilled shrimp with green onions, potatoes, and chayote (a type of Mexican squash) bundled up in fresh warm tortillas and slathered with piquant salsa. Surprisingly enough, I did find the restaurant without calling. The people were incredibly friendly and helpful, and I was starting to realize that Nick Noyes was a smart fellow.

Relaxing in a hammock at the penthouse apartment in Mexico City, 1970s

We met in the offices above his main restaurant, Delmonico's, located in the heart of the Zona Rosa, the tourist center of the city. The restaurant was a fine-dining establishment with limited tableside service but was best known for the quality of its beef. American prime beef was a luxury in Mexico, and that separated Delmonico's from all others. Nick was a promoter and showed me a short commercial film of him in full John Wayne persona, complete with 10-gallon hat, chaps, and lariat, looking over his herd of hundreds of robust, ramblin' steers. He talked to me about his ideas for the new restaurant and how I would be a part of it from the ground up. In the meantime, I would get my feet wet by taking over as chef at Delmonico's.

The restaurant had been run for the last year by two sous chefs, both of whom had worked under the last departed executive chef. One handled the lunch shift, the other, dinner. They had a good handle on the day-to-day operations, so I would be free to just work on specials to upgrade the overall menu experience and get used to Mexico City's products, purveyors, and pace of life until the new place opened.

He walked me across the street to the strikingly classic Geneve Hotel and set me up for dinner at a traditional Mexican place, Fonda el Refugio.

"Just relax, have a great dinner, and think about the job," he advised. "Tomorrow you'll have a tour and dinner with the manager from Delmonico's—enjoy the city!" It was hard not to be swept up in his enthusiasm.

The next day I met up with the manager, and he took me on a whirlwind journey through the open and covered markets. The displays of unfamiliar fruits and vegetables—light green and darker chayote, nopalito, huitlacoche (corn fungus), guayaba, tamarind pods, tomatillo, and plantain that ranged from bright yellow to completely black—were all dwarfed by myriad examples of the soul of Mexican cuisine: peppers. My pepper experience at the time included green and red bells and an occasional pickled jalapeno; so these displays were making my head explode—in a good way. I had trouble just trying to comprehend the Cs—cascabel, chipotle, and chilaca—let alone the rest of the alphabet.

Next stop was my proposed living quarters, a penthouse apartment at 240 Londres, with unnecessary maid quarters and a very necessary and appreciated outdoor patio. Mexico City was starting to feel like home. By the time we arrived at Del Lago, an architectural wonder of a restaurant in the middle of Chapultepec Park, for the "wage talk" dinner, I was already in. That night I talked with Ellen. She too was on board, so two months into a new marriage, we were moving to Mexico.

◆

ELLEN AND I WERE IN FULL-SCALE CULTURE SHOCK AS THIS WAS ALSO HER FIRST TIME outside of the States. Immediately after moving into the penthouse, our first month in Mexico was spent in Cuernavaca, a warm, lush tropical town right outside of Mexico City. We were there to attend a full-immersion Spanish language school that had been set up by Delmonico's. The full-immersion aspect meant that you moved in with a Mexican family and only spoke Spanish during your entire stay.

The manager of the restaurant dropped us off at a modest, rustic home in the center of a sleepy residential neighborhood. I was introduced and handed over to Mariana, the head of the household, who lived there with her two children, sister, and grandparents. I was nervous (because of my lack of Spanish) but excited by the prospect of learning a new culture. Mariana, who spoke a bit of English, asked us to wait in the kitchen entrance. Soon I heard a major commotion in the background; then scowling grandparents walked past us on their way to the enclosed porch, with pillows and personal effects bundled under their arms. Mariana came back and directed us to the room they had just reluctantly vacated.

I looked at her and said, "I can't take this room! We'll stay on the porch." She just shook her head.

"Go in, this is your room. They were supposed to move yesterday."

Despite the tense start, it turned out that Mariana and her family could not have been more warm and lovely hosts. They were all more than helpful with the language, and most dinners were spent exchanging stories of our lives. That was the good news. The bad news was that Mariana was a pretty horrible cook. At immersion school, the other students would exchange stories of the incredible food they were having with their sponsor families: open fire-charred pork tacos, spicy fish stew, brightly verdant vegetable soups, and overabundant platters of ripe tropical fruit bursting with flavor. Back at Casa Mariana, however, the regular nightly repast was one quarter of a corncob bobbing in a liquid closer to water than soup. Alongside were crunchy refried black beans that had somehow missed their first cooking, with an added Mexican lagniappe that came from her not-so-secret method of leaving them out all night in the pan they were cooked in until they acquired a crust that looked like a dried-up black riverbed. The only highlight was the excellent warm corn tortillas that she picked up at the corner tortilla factory. After every meal we would politely excuse ourselves and go for a walk in the neighborhood. These nightly walks were actually a search for food, as man does not live solely on tortillas.

After our last morning of school, we got together with a few other students and treated ourselves to an afternoon and evening of luxury. Near the center of downtown was Las Mañanitas, an exclusive Relais and Chateaux property that included a small hotel and world-class restaurant. The crowning glory of the property was a tropical Garden of Eden where we plopped ourselves into overstuffed furniture in an outdoor gazebo, sipped champagne, and nibbled regularly replenished hot and cold hors d'oeuvres off silver trays as the peacocks and flamingos strutted by on their perfectly manicured runway. As dusk approached, a complete al fresco dining room appeared, and the hardest work of the day was moving our bodies 20 feet over to the impeccably set tables for a formal refection.

Cuernavaca was my first introduction into the disparity of the Mexican lifestyle. As we walked or drove through the town we saw the superrich, who lived in extensive haciendas hidden behind fortress-sized walls that cast shadows over shantytown neighborhoods comprised of hovels built from all manner of salvaged materials and fabrics, all centralized around a communal water spigot that barely quenched the collective thirst and water needs of the indigent inhabitants. What was missing from this scenario was a middle class—except for any tourists who might claim that label.

◆

WHEN DOES AN ITALIAN BOY FROM THE LANDLOCKED MIDWEST TASTE HIS FIRST ceviche? No, it wasn't at Sunday dinner at the grandparents'. It wasn't in Milwaukee in the

'60s or '70s (during that time you would be hard-pressed to find ceviche served anywhere regularly in the States). My first experience with ceviche was at Delmonico's. I was so green behind the ears that I should have had "Kermit" tattooed there. And I was "good gringo material" for the local staff at the restaurant—let's call it my initiation to Mexico.

When I walked in for my first day of work, the cooks were all together. A loud, "Buenos días!" rang out, and they led me to a small table behind the cooking line. It was set up with silverware, and they said I should eat first before starting work. A plate of scrambled eggs with green sauce was brought over, along with a cup of sliced scallops, shrimp, and diced fish that was glistening and uncooked. They were all eating and told me to dig in. I started with the seafood—tart, tangy, perfectly textured with a wisp of heat and a bit of sweetness and richness from some tomato and avocado—really great, even for breakfast. Then I plunged into the eggs. The green sauce was a charred tomatillo salsa, really delicious—*Wait, wait! Really hot, too hot!*

"Where's the water? I asked desperately. *Water makes it hotter?!* One of the cooks looked over and said, "Caliente?" or "Hot?" The whole staff fell out laughing.

When lunchtime came around, one of the cooks was working on the staff lunch. He took paper-thin slices of beef and charred them on a screaming-hot cast iron flat top. Then he smothered them in a striking vermillion sauce that had a brilliant, lacquered sheen and was made from seared dry ancho chilies, onions, and garlic blended with water and a good dose of citric acid. The sauce was blazing hot, but it was tempered by a charred sweet tomato salsa and creamy slices of avocado. This staff lunch made a mockery of all the stateside menus hawking "sizzling carne asadas." It felt like my heat tolerance had improved from breakfast to lunch.

Within weeks I was starting to crave the balance of heat, natural sweetness, bitterness, and acidity that reappeared in many dishes. If I had to hone in on one flavor that drew me in more than others, it would be the tart. I've always been an acid guy. Though I'm a child of the '60s, I'm not talking about the dropout, Dr. Leary, lovin' type of acid. I'm talking the unmistakable tartness from citrus and vinegar that brings so many foods into balance, and without which it would be a very, very bland world.

Choosing my favorite acid came down to a fight between red wine vinegar and lemon. These were the first two I tasted as a young child: Iceberg salad, with a long drizzle of olive oil, was awoken by a few shakes of tart red-wine vinegar. Deeply brown-crusted, rich Sicilian steak became perfect with a quick squeeze of bright lemon. Which was better? I'm still trying to decide.

I never really had a true understanding or respect for limes until I lived in Mexico City. One day, I was working on a new menu item and asked one of the cooks for a lemon. He brought me a lime. I said, "No, I need *fruta de color amarillo*"—yellow fruit. This got me a grapefruit. After many charade-like pantomime displays, I gave up and went over to the Mercado Central (Central Market) and walked the aisles. I saw all types of citrus except one—lemons. There were no lemons in Mexico City, so I learned how to substitute limes in anything that I cooked. This was a revelation to me in both savory dishes and pastry. While I didn't lose my love of lemons, I certainly had a new suitor to attend to.

Nick decided to do a publicity push and set up an interview with the local paper. I had never been interviewed before, so I was really nervous. Nick told me to relax and said we would go through a mock interview, with him acting as the reporter. He went through 12 questions that covered my background, what I thought of the city, what was in store for the menu, and so on. I felt slightly better as the real interview started, slowly getting more relaxed over the course of the first six questions, which were almost word for word what Nick had gone over with me. After that article appeared, I was invited to do my first cooking class at the upscale department store El Palacio de Hierro.

I started out the demo (with a translator) by letting my pan get too hot on the burner and subsequently browning the butter (unintentionally) for the pâte à choux. I quickly threw in the flour and started mixing vigorously, like nothing had happened. Most of the crowd didn't really notice. At the end of class one woman asked why I had browned the butter. I told her that I just wanted to add a little caramelized flavor to the pastry when it baked, which turned out, after tasting the finished pastry, to be true. I had never had to think on my feet in front of an audience before, and even though I had screwed up, it gave me a shot of confidence.

As some of the restaurant specials were getting some good feedback, I decided to try making a Yucatán specialty, cochinita pibil, a roasted baby pig. I had read about the dish, but had never seen it prepared or even tasted it. I put it on for a lunch special, not having a clue that it took a while to bake the pig. I arrived in the morning and was confronted with a 60-pound dressed hog staring at me from the walk-in. I half carried, half dragged it over to the worktable and tried to figure out where to start. The clock was ticking. Fortunately, I did have the ingredients for the marinade—Seville (or sour) oranges (another new citrus for me), annatto, spices, and garlic. I ground these into a paste that I slathered over the pig. I had the banana leaves I needed, but wasn't quite sure how to use them. I spent a good half hour walking in circles and fretting; I was in well over my head. All the while, the daytime sous chef Fernando had not taken his eyes off me.

Finally, I looked at him in desperation. "Do you know anything about cochinita pibil?"

"Sí, a little bit. I'm from the Yucatán."

"Why didn't you tell me that?"

"You never ask."

Within minutes he took over soaking the banana leaves and lining a large roasting pan with them. Then he swaddled the pig (after heavily tweaking the marinade) within the leaves and placed it into the oven. He made a batch of fresh tortillas, some quick-pickled, spice-infused crisp onions, and salsa xnipek (translated "dog's-nose sauce"), consisting of habaneros, onions, and sour orange juice. He explained that the pig should marinate overnight and be cooked in a dug-out stone pit, but assured me that my gringo facsimile would be edible. I engaged in quite a bit more collaborative consultation after that humbling day.

I was asked to work alternating day and night shifts to get an idea of the flow of the kitchen and to get to know the staff. I was really taken with how friendly and accommodating they were, especially the two sous chefs. The lunch sous had been there for 15 years, and Luis, the dinner sous, for eight. They both knew their stuff and had the respect of their peers, and I found myself getting an invaluable hands-on education in classic Mexican cuisine between working on the new dishes. After the first month, the day sous asked me a cryptic question, "Have you decided?"

"Decided what?" I replied.

"You know!"

"No, I don't know."

"Have you decided between Luis and me?"

It turned out that, unbeknownst to me, the management had told the two sous chefs that I would be deciding their fate—who would stay and who would go. Now it all made sense—that was why I had been welcomed like a returning World Cup soccer hero! I immediately talked with the manager to let him know I did not want or even feel qualified to let one of these guys go. It worked out in the end. One was promoted, but the other stayed on in his regular position—a good decision all around.

◆

THINGS WERE GOING PRETTY WELL AT THE RESTAURANT, BUT ELLEN WAS HAVING A LOT of trouble finding a position in the city. Waiting tables was pretty much out of the question, as one month of language school had not made her fluent. I talked with some of the people in the restaurant's office, and one had a friend at a local parochial school. They were looking for a fifth-grade science teacher. The main qualifications were a cursory knowledge of science and the ability to speak English, since the class was completely taught in English. Within a week, "Miss Ellen" had a class and a new career, and she actually seemed happy for the first time since we had arrived in Mexico.

I worked a lot of hours, so any free time was used to explore the city. Our apartment overlooked Londres Street, the main drag of the Zona Rosa, a tourist area filled with hotels, high-end shops, music clubs, and restaurants. One of the most surprising facts to me (since I knew nothing about Mexico City before I moved there) was the variety of ethnic restaurants, from traditional Swiss and regional Italian to Japanese and Middle Eastern.

There are two qualities that will immediately endear a restaurant to me: originality and a bit of wonderment. In a world of cookie-cutter franchise restaurants, you usually have a pretty good idea of what your experience will be before you even enter the door. I like to be surprised at some point in the experience. It could be in the beginning, with a well-written menu, or later, when the food arrives. When I read a menu I visualize the food and have certain expectations. At its best, my visualization is blown away, as I revel in a dish that exceeds anything I expected.

I walked into a small Italian restaurant called La Lanterna, located on Insurgentes, a main boulevard in the city. My expectations were not very high as I noticed the miniscule tables, bright lighting, sparse decorations, and simple menu matter-of-factly stating dishes like pasta with basil, artichoke salad, and veal with onion.

Dining Out *article from Mexico City when I was chef at Delmonico's*

I ordered the artichoke, and when it was placed in front of me, I met it with immediate surprise and wonderment. Impossibly thin raw artichoke slices shimmered under a gloss of young, green olive oil with shaved Pecorino, coarse sea salt, and a spritz of lemon. Pure perfection. Then a bowl of translucent, al dente linguini arrived; it was tossed with a verdant green amalgamation of the first (and to this day, the best) pesto I have ever had.

While I was dining, the older Italian chef was unobtrusively visiting tables. When he stopped to speak to me, I asked how he had ended up in Mexico City. He told me he had met his wife, a native of Mexico City, in his hometown in Italy, and at her urging, they had decided to move to her home country. So, there in Mexico City was an Italian restaurant that not only surprised me but also gave me a sense of wonderment that continued as I worked my way through the menu at subsequent visits.

When I first moved to Mexico City, I was warned by more than a few people to not drink the tap water and not eat the street food. The water I understood, as I spent many days there under the influence of Lomotil, an antidiarrheal medication. The street food was another matter. Since this was my first time out of the country, I didn't really know what indigenous street food was. People spoke of it as if desperados roamed the highways and byways and, upon finding road kill, set up impromptu burners, skinned and cooked the flattened carcasses, and served them up with a wink and a smile.

From my first day in Mexico City, when I took a taxi from the airport to the city center, I saw all along the way small tables with umbrellas shading the dreaded street-fooders from the bright sunlight as they plied their wares to the unsuspecting masses. After months of living in the city, I started to recognize the regulars. They weren't fly-by-night operations. On the contrary, they were outdoor restaurant operations, as primitive as could be, yet completely organized, with regular hours and an eager clientele.

I passed one particular setup near my apartment every night on my way home from work. I could see the glowing fire from about two blocks away, and as I got closer, the unmistakable scent of charred meat and onions would waft my way. By the time I got close enough to feel the heat of the grill and see the thin, flattened cuts of beef and pork and the long, charred spring onions, I'd be hungry. It took a while for me to realize that the surrounding area was not littered with retching sufferers and corpses, so I finally joined the crowd. That night, I realized what an idiot I'd been for missing some of the best food in the city. The fresh, warm corn tortilla was lightly piled with the grilled onions and glistening beef, and then you had a choice of five homemade salsas, each one better than the last.

After a few months I started to miss a lot of the foods I had previously taken for granted. I had enormous cravings for hot dogs with mustard and relish, juicy cheeseburgers, kosher dill pickles, and peanut butter. After I ruled out pregnancy, I realized I was homesick. Mexico City had hamburguesas from Burger Boy and chicken from El Pollo Kentucky to offer, but they were just strange, sad imitations of American fast food.

Since I worked so much, Ellen had become depressed and agitated in our new city. Occasionally, a movie was released in English, but there were no new English-language TV programs, just Spanish-language reruns of early *Brady Bunch* episodes. She did have her three fellow teachers to go out with, but that had its problems. The four ladies, who would think nothing of going out for drinks and dinner in NYC, ran into some very biased situations in the land of machismo—from male waiters ignoring them, to actually being asked to leave places because "their kind" wasn't wanted there. The common feeling was that single women or small groups of women having a drink at a bar were at worst prostitutes and, at best, amateur wenches. Ellen and her fellow teachers came up with snappy verbal comebacks to the incessant catcalls. My favorite was, "*Tu madre es una chuleta de cerdo!*" This always left their targets speechless, as it translates to, "You're mother is a pork chop!" Interestingly enough, in this very year, 1975, the first World Conference on Women—headed up by all the heavy hitters in the women's rights movement—was being held in Mexico City. The lack of attending female Mexican residents was glaring.

The end of our time in Mexico was a convergence of two forces. The country had experienced about 25 years of a stable economy and a strong peso. During the last year of President Luis Echeverría's term, however, the economy took a turn for the worse, and inflation was on the rise. When it became apparent that the next president would most likely be the current administration's finance minister, Jose Portillo—handpicked by Echeverría himself—the smart investment money dried up. Consequently, the new restaurant that I had originally been brought to Mexico to run was in heavy delay mode, if not dead in the *agua*.

The other, more personally frightening force was my wife. It was a regular routine for me to have to duck flying furniture before I could finish saying, "Hi, honey, I'm home!" Ellen was more than miserable, and the breaking point was a simple shopping trip. We were walking over to the indoor market with our de rigueur metal shopping cart. Crossing the street during rush hour in this frenetic metropolis was always an adventure, and on this particular day, as the light changed, we got caught in the crosswalk in a four-way gridlock of cars. Instead of letting us get through, one of the cars started edging forward toward us. Ellen just lost it. She started banging our puny metal cart repeatedly into the car's bumper and tires while screaming, swearing, and spitting. I pulled her and the mangled cart to the other side, but I couldn't calm her down. She only stopped crying when I said, "We're going home."

CHAPTER SEVEN RECIPES

◆

Sweet Potato Soup with Seared Tomatillos
197

Dungeness Crab Ceviche with Parma
Prosciutto, Candied Serrano,
Orange Garlic Dressing
199

Grilled Yucatan Pork Chop, Ancho
Potatoes, Orange Chili Emulsion
202

Pancetta-Stuffed Artichokes
206

Sauté of Boniato, Chayote, Shrimp,
and Wild Mushrooms, Cilantro Oil
208

SWEET POTATO SOUP WITH SEARED TOMATILLOS

The usual way to use sweet potatoes is to accentuate the sweetness with fruit juices, sugar, or honey, and subtle spices. What I've done with this soup is slightly de-emphasize the sweetness by adding acidity in the form of white wine, lime juice, tomatillos, poblanos, and jalapeños. This creates a soup that is smooth, silky, tart, smoky, piquant, and herbaceous that will have them coming back saying, "Mas, por favor."

SERVES 8

For the Soup:

2 tablespoons grapeseed oil

1 pound (454 g) smoked pork bones or ham

2 medium (1 pound [454 g]) onions, peeled and diced medium

1 (4-ounce [114-g]) poblano pepper, stem and seeds removed and cut in small dice

1 jalapeño pepper, stem and seeds removed and cut in small dice

2 bay leaves

1 (4-inch [10-cm]) cinnamon stick

3 cloves garlic, sliced (about 2 tablespoons)

1 tablespoon ground coriander seed

1 cup (237 mL) dry white wine

2 pounds (908 g) sweet potatoes, peeled and diced medium

7 cups (1.66 L) unsalted chicken stock

Kosher salt and freshly ground black pepper, to taste

40 grinds freshly ground black pepper

1. Add the grapeseed oil to a medium-hot pan, then add the smoked pork bones or ham and render for 3 minutes. Add the onions, poblanos, jalapeños, bay leaves, cinnamon stick, and garlic and sweat for 5 minutes. Add the coriander and sauté for 1 minute. Add the wine and reduce by ⅔.

2. Add the sweet potatoes, the stock, salt to taste, and the 40 grinds of pepper. Bring up to a boil, then simmer until the sweet potatoes are very tender, for about 25 to 30 minutes.

3. Remove the bay leaves, cinnamon stick, and pork bones or ham (reserve the pork bones or ham). Purée the soup in a blender. Adjust the seasoning with salt and pepper and keep warm.

(RECIPE CONTINUES ON PAGE 198)

(RECIPE CONTINUED FROM PAGE 197)

For the Seared Tomatillos and to Finish the Soup:

1½ pounds (681 g) small tomatillos, husks removed, washed, and cut in small wedges

2 tablespoons grapeseed oil

Kosher salt and freshly ground black pepper, to taste

2 jalapeño peppers, cut in half, stems and seeds removed, each half cut in very small dice (brunoise)

2 tablespoons fresh lime juice

2 tablespoons granulated sugar

1 cup (16 g) fresh cilantro leaves, coarsely chopped

Reserved pork bones or ham

1. Heat a sauté pan to very hot. In a bowl, toss the tomatillos with the oil and season them with salt and pepper. Add the tomatillos to the hot pan and sear for 1 minute (do not toss too much as you want to keep the pan hot). Add the jalapeños and cook for 30 seconds. Add the lime juice and sugar and reduce to dry. Remove to a plate for garnish.

2. Divide the tomatillos among 8 bowls. Sprinkle the cilantro leaves in the bowls. Ladle the hot soup over the leaves and around the tomatillos. Remove the meat from the pork bones and dice (if you're using ham, do the same) and use to garnish the soup.

DUNGENESS CRAB CEVICHE WITH PARMA PROSCIUTTO, CANDIED SERRANO, ORANGE GARLIC DRESSING

I learned to really love ceviche in Mexico City. In its simplest form, it is very fresh raw seafood marinated in an acid, usually lime, and seasoned aggressively with a bit of hot peppers or chili oil. The sweetness of the mango and the jicama play off the heat of the serranos and the saltiness of the prosciutto, and the tart orange dressing brings it all into balance.

SERVES 8

1 pound (454 g) fresh Dungeness crabmeat, picked of all shell and cartilage

1 small mango, peeled and diced small (you need ½–¾ cup [83–124 g])

1 small jicama, peeled and diced small (you need ½–¾ cup [60–90 g])

3 tablespoons (45 mL) regular olive oil

2 small serrano chili peppers (1 red, 1 green), stem ends cut off, seeds removed carefully without breaking the skin, and cut crosswise into very thin rings (wear rubber gloves when working with chili peppers or immediately wash your hands after cutting them and before touching your face)

2 tablespoons chopped chives

Juice of 2 limes

Cayenne pepper, to taste

Kosher salt and freshly ground black pepper, to taste

16 thin slices prosciutto

1 avocado, sliced for garnish right before serving

Candied Serrano (recipe follows)

Orange Garlic Dressing (recipe follows)

1. Mix together all of the ingredients, except the prosciutto, avocado, Candied Serrano, and Orange Garlic Dressing.

2. Place 2 slices of the prosciutto on each plate. Divide the ceviche among the plates. Cut the avocado in half and remove the pit. Cut each half into quarters from top to bottom and remove the skin. Cut each quarter in half to form 8 wedges. Cut each wedge in ⅛-inch slices, leaving the top intact, and lightly press to fan out. Season the avocado with salt and black pepper and place on top of the ceviche. Garnish with the Candied Serrano and Orange Garlic Dressing.

(RECIPE CONTINUES ON PAGE 201)

(RECIPE CONTINUED FROM PAGE 199)

For the Candied Serrano:

¼ cup (50 g) granulated sugar

¼ cup (59 mL) water

2 serrano chili peppers, stems removed and sliced into ⅛-inch (3-mm) rounds

1. In a small saucepan, bring the sugar and water up to a boil. Pour over the serranos in a bowl and cover with plastic wrap. (You may use them when they come to room temperature or store them in the refrigerator; remove them from the syrup before using.)

For the Orange Garlic Dressing:

1 cup (237 mL) extra virgin olive oil

1 cup (237 mL) fresh orange juice and fine zest of ½ orange, reduced to ¼ cup (59 mL)

1 tablespoon fresh lemon juice

½ tablespoon sherry vinegar

1 clove garlic, thinly sliced and rinsed under warm water

½ ounce (14 g) fresh Italian parsley leaves

1 teaspoon kosher salt

½ teaspoon freshly ground black pepper

1. Place all of the ingredients in a blender and blend until the parsley is finely puréed.

GRILLED YUCATAN PORK CHOP, ANCHO POTATOES, ORANGE CHILI EMULSION

After the first time I tried Cocinita Pibil, I was hooked. You might miss the traditional whole-roasting of the pig, but on the bright side, you don't have to dig a pit.

SERVES 6

For the Marinated Pork Chops:

> 1 (8-ounce [227-g]) orange, diced
>
> 1 (2½-ounce [71-g]) lime, diced
>
> 1 head garlic, peeled
>
> 2 tablespoons achiote (annatto seed) paste
>
> 1 teaspoon dried oregano
>
> ½ tablespoon ground cumin
>
> ¼ teaspoon cayenne pepper
>
> ½ teaspoon freshly ground black pepper
>
> 1 cup (237 mL) corn oil
>
> ½ cup (119 mL) dry white wine
>
> 6 (8-ounce [227-g]) trimmed pork chops or loins

1. Place all of the ingredients, except the pork, in a food processor and process. Place the pork chops in a large resealable plastic bag and pour over the mixture. Marinate in the refrigerator overnight, turning them once.

For the Orange Chili Emulsion and to Finish the Dish:

> (Note: All ingredients for the emulsion should be at room temperature.)
>
> 4 teaspoons achiote (annatto seed) paste
>
> 1 tablespoon chili powder
>
> 1 small seeded and roasted dried ancho chili
>
> 3 ounces (90 mL) fresh orange juice
>
> 1 clove garlic, sliced and rinsed
>
> 1 small shallot, sliced and rinsed
>
> 1 large egg yolk
>
> ½ cup (119 mL) regular olive oil
>
> ¼ cup (59 mL) corn oil

(RECIPE CONTINUES ON PAGE 204)

(RECIPE CONTINUED FROM PAGE 202)

>   2 tablespoons fresh lime juice
>
>   ½ tablespoon red wine vinegar
>
>   4 teaspoons fresh lemon juice
>
>   Kosher salt and freshly ground black pepper, to taste
>
>   Prepared Marinated Pork
>
>   Ancho Potatoes (recipe follows)
>
>   Pickled Chayote and Yellow Squash (recipe follows)
>
>   1 cup (16 g) fresh cilantro sprigs, for garnish

1. Add the achiote paste, chili powder, and ancho chili to the orange juice in a small saucepan and bring it up to a boil. Add to a food processor along with the garlic and shallots and purée. Add the egg yolk and process. Mix the olive oil and corn oil together and slowly add them, alternating between the lime juice, vinegar, and lemon juice to form an emulsion. Adjust the seasoning with salt and pepper.

2. Preheat the grill to medium-hot. Remove the pork chops from the marinade. Grill the pork chops (if you are grilling inside, on a heated grill pan) for about 3 to 5 minutes per side, depending on the thickness. Check the temperature with an instant-read thermometer so that the chops are at about 130°F (54°C).

3. Let the chops rest for 5 minutes, then serve with the Orange Chili Emulsion and Ancho Potatoes. Garnish with the drained Pickled Chayote and Yellow Squash that has been tossed with the cilantro sprigs.

For the Ancho Potatoes:

>   2½ pounds (1.13 g) russet potatoes
>
>   2 teaspoons regular olive oil
>
>   2 teaspoons finely chopped garlic
>
>   1 bay leaf
>
>   1¼ cups (296 mL) heavy cream
>
>   1 dried ancho chili (1 ounce [28 g]), stem and seeds removed, then toasted in a dry sauté pan over medium-high heat for 1 minute on each side
>
>   1 tablespoon kosher salt
>
>   ¾ teaspoon freshly ground black pepper
>
>   1 ounce (28 g) fresh cilantro leaves

1. Preheat the oven to 400°F (200°C). Bake the potatoes for 1 hour. While they are still warm, cut them in half, scoop out the flesh, and pass through a food mill into a bowl.

2. Place a small saucepan over medium heat. Add the olive oil, and when hot, add the garlic and bay leaf and cook for 30 seconds. Add the cream, ancho chili, salt, and pepper and bring up to a simmer. Cover and let steep for 10 minutes.

3. Remove and discard the bay leaf, then place the mixture in a blender along with the cilantro. Blend until fine, pour over the potatoes, and mix together with a spatula. Adjust the seasoning with salt and pepper, if necessary. (The Ancho Potatoes may be prepared ahead and reheated in a microwave just before serving.)

For the Pickled Chayote and Yellow Squash:

    2 cups (474 mL) water
    ½ cup (119 mL) plus 2 tablespoons apple cider vinegar
    2 tablespoons granulated sugar
    1 tablespoon kosher salt
    For the sachet, mix together the following spices in cheesecloth and tie with butcher string:
      2 bay leaves
      2 cloves garlic, thinly sliced
      1 cinnamon stick
      2 tablespoons cumin seeds
      1 tablespoon coriander seeds
      1 teaspoon whole allspice
      ½ teaspoon whole peppercorns
      ⅛ teaspoon cayenne pepper
    1 small chayote (4 ounces [114 g]), peeled, cut in half, core removed, and cut into ¼-inch thick matchstick-sized pieces
    1 small yellow squash (4 ounces [114 g]), ends cut off and sliced in ⅛-inch (3-mm) rounds

1. In a small saucepan, place the water, vinegar, sugar, salt, and sachet, bring up to a boil, and cover.

2. Place the chayote and squash in a container large enough to hold them and the hot pickling brine. Pour the brine along with the sachet over the vegetables, mix together, and cover. Leave at room temperature until it is cool, then refrigerate until needed (prepare 1 day ahead).

PANCETTA-STUFFED ARTICHOKES

This is my version of a dish of stuffed artichoke hearts that I had regularly at my favorite Italian restaurant when I lived in Mexico City. I like to use the whole artichoke and I look for the ones that have the thorns and pointy tips, as I'm not a fan of the texture and toughness of the thornless, rounder variety, which are more prevalent on the market.

MAKES 4 ARTICHOKES

> **4 large artichokes**
>
> **2 lemons, cut in half**
>
> **Kosher salt, to taste**
>
> **Pancetta Stuffing (recipe follows)**
>
> **Extra virgin olive oil, for sprinkling on the artichokes**

1. Cut off the top ½ inch (13 mm) of 1 artichoke. Cut off the bottom stem to level the artichoke so it can stand up. Cut off the tips (about ¼ inch [6 mm]) of all the leaves. Trim the remaining artichokes. Rub the cut surfaces of the artichokes with the lemons. Place the artichokes in a pot holding enough water to cover all 4 artichokes by at least 2 inches (5 cm).

2. Salt the water to taste (it should taste slightly salty) and squeeze the remaining juice out of the lemons into the water. Cover the artichokes with a towel then a heatproof plate to keep the artichokes submerged while cooking. Bring up to a boil and cook for 20 to 40 minutes, depending on the size of the artichokes. (Test the artichokes by pulling 1 out, placing it upside down, and when inserting a knife, the bottom should be knife-tender.)

3. When the artichokes are cooked, remove them from the water and immediately plunge them into a cold ice-water bath to stop cooking. When cooled, place them upside down in a colander to drain. When drained, grab 5 or 6 of the center leaves and pull them out, then carefully scrape out the fuzzy choke in the center with a small spoon.

4. Preheat the oven to 400°F (200°C). Stuff the artichokes by placing some of the Pancetta Stuffing inside each leaf and dividing the remaining stuffing between the centers of the artichokes. Sprinkle the artichokes with a bit of the olive oil. Bake for about 8 to 10 minutes, or until the bread crumbs are golden and the artichokes are warmed through.

For the Pancetta Stuffing:

4 ounces (114 g) pancetta, finely diced

5 ounces (142 g) onion, finely diced

1 ounce (28 g) garlic, finely diced

1 bay leaf

⅛ teaspoon cayenne pepper

1 teaspoon freshly ground black pepper

2 sprigs fresh thyme

Pinch nutmeg

½ cup (119 mL) white wine

¼ cup (59 mL) fresh lemon juice

⅓ cup (79 mL) extra virgin olive oil

1½ cups (162 g) dry bread crumbs

1 bunch fresh Italian parsley tops, finely chopped

4 ounces (114 g) grated aged Asiago cheese

Kosher salt and freshly ground black pepper, to taste

1. In a medium-hot sauté pan, render the pancetta until lightly crisp. Remove the pancetta with a slotted spoon and reserve.

2. In the same pan, sauté the onions until lightly browned. Add the garlic, the bay leaf, the cayenne pepper, the 1 teaspoon black pepper, the thyme, and the nutmeg and sauté for 1 minute. Add the wine and lemon juice and cook until they are reduced to a glaze but not dry; reserve.

3. In a separate hot sauté pan, add the olive oil. When hot, add the bread crumbs, mix well with a wooden spoon, and sauté until they are lightly browned and evenly toasted (do not get them too dark or burned). Immediately transfer the breadcrumbs to a large mixing bowl.

4. Remove and discard the bay leaf and thyme sprig from the reserved onion mixture. Mix the parsley, the reserved rendered pancetta, and the onion mixture into the bread crumbs. When the mixture cools, add the grated Asiago and adjust the seasoning with salt and pepper. (You may make the Pancetta Stuffing ahead and refrigerate until you are ready to use.)

SAUTÉ OF BONIATO, CHAYOTE, SHRIMP, AND WILD MUSHROOM, CILANTRO OIL

This dish is an ode to my "point and pay" carts in Mexico City that where brimming with the most mouthwatering items. The melded garlicky, herby, grilled masterpieces I would find in all combinations inspired this sauté, which is a seasonally changing standard on the Sanford menu.

SERVES 4

For the Cilantro Oil:

¼ cup (59 mL) extra virgin olive oil

¼ teaspoon kosher salt

10 grinds freshly ground black pepper

1 bunch fresh cilantro (about ½ cup [8 g] leaves) (reserve about ¼ bunch of sprigs for garnish)

1. Place all of the ingredients, except the cilantro garnish, in a blender and blend until smooth, about 15 to 20 seconds. Place in a plastic squeeze bottle and refrigerate until needed (bring to room temperature before using).

To Finish the Dish:

1 boniato (about 6 ounces [170 g]), peeled and cut in small dice (you will need 1 cup)

1 chayote (about 6 ounces [170 g]), peeled, cut in half top to bottom, core removed, halves cut in small dice (you will need about 1 cup)

1 tablespoon kosher salt

3 tablespoons (45 mL) regular olive oil

5 ounces (142 g) wild mushrooms (such as chanterelles, hedgehogs, black trumpets, etc., or mixed domestic mushrooms), cleaned and cut in medium dice (you will need about 2¼ cups)

6 ounces (170 g) peeled rock shrimp or other small to medium raw shrimp (if you are using larger shrimp, cut them in medium dice)

1 small jalapeño pepper, stem and seeds removed and cut in very small dice (brunoise)

2½ tablespoons (23 g) chopped shallots

2 teaspoons finely chopped garlic (about 2 cloves)

1½ teaspoons ground cumin

1½ teaspoons ground coriander
Kosher salt and freshly ground black pepper, to taste
Prepared Cilantro Oil
2 tablespoons pumpkin seed oil, for garnish

1. In a saucepan, just cover the boniatos and chayote with water. Add the 1 tablespoon salt, place the pan over high heat, and just bring up to a boil. Immediately drain and shock with cold water. Drain off the excess and make sure they are dry.

2. Place a large sauté pan over high heat. When the pan is hot, add the olive oil. When the oil is very hot, add the boniatos and chayote and sauté until they are lightly golden, for about 2 to 3 minutes. Add the mushrooms and sauté until they are lightly colored. Add the shrimp, jalapeño, shallots, garlic, cumin, coriander, and salt and pepper to taste and sauté for 30 to 45 seconds. Add about 3 to 4 tablespoons (45 to 59 mL) of the Cilantro Oil, remove from the heat, and stir together. Adjust the seasoning with salt and pepper.

3. Divide the mixture among 4 plates and garnish with more Cilantro Oil, the pumpkin seed oil, and the reserved cilantro sprigs.

8

FRENCH CONNECTION

I WAS SITTING WITH ELLEN IN MY NEW MOTHER-IN-LAW'S LIVING ROOM IN QUEENS, New York, watching Donny and Marie work their country/rock-and-roll magic. *How the hell did this happen? We're not visiting "Mamoo," we're living here!* This was, bar none, the lowest point in my working life.

First and foremost, I wasn't working. We had left Mexico (almost overnight) with the loser's trifecta: no work prospects, no place to live, and almost no money. In my depressed, selfish state, I couldn't get past the fact that this woman, whom I really don't care for, had saved our hides by generously offering us a place to stay in her one-bedroom apartment. Instead, I was obsessing about the ashtray next to her lounger that was filled with a tar-like substance I later found out was the mounded remains of hundreds of Good & Plenty licorice centers that had had their sweet, outer pink and white coatings sucked off.

I was making daily runs to Manhattan and had a few possible jobs lined up; but I didn't want to go backward, so I was not having much luck—that is, until I read in the paper that a fellow I had met upstate (while I was working with Peter at the club), Augustin Paige, had opened a small place on the East Side.

The Box Tree was a small, well-appointed restaurant in a beautiful brownstone, and Augustin remembered me from our visit to his original place, the Box Tree in Purdy, New York. It turned out that his head chef, Lee, my former classmate at the CIA, was taking a three-week vacation, and Augustin needed a temporary fill-in. At least I could make a few dollars until I found a permanent position.

I arrived at the Box Tree a little early on my first day, and a waiter ushered me into the kitchen to wait for Lee. He was going to give me the rundown on what my responsibilities would be while he was gone. The dining room was more than small—only 21 seats—and the kitchen was downright tiny: a six-burner range, an overhead broiler, and just enough room for one person to turn around.

I heard Lee's voice as he swept into the kitchen, looking much more like a Vegas magician, in his black satin top hat and cape, than a chef. Lee had made the crossover from flashy (in school) to confident flamboyance. I trained with him for three days, and the working culinary part was straightforward. He started with the menu: a five-course set menu with a few appetizers, followed by a set soup of the day; a delicious salad of endive, watercress, and grainy mustard dressing; choice of a few entrées; and a great group of desserts. It was basically a one-person kitchen with a back waiter to help with the plate-up and desserts.

The social part of the job was much more complicated, and this was where Lee's training was invaluable. Lee let me know that there was a lot of behind-the-scenes undermining and cattiness. The staff would do their best to take you down in a passive-aggressive manner if you weren't liked or didn't fit in, so he let me know that being the only straight guy working in the restaurant could be a problem for me. Most of the three days with Lee were spent in a capsulated course on the different personalities of the entire staff—and how to relate to each one for my survival. He then went out of his way to let everyone know I was a good guy, and asked them to play nicely until he returned.

Later that week, I called Peter to check in and tell him about the Box Tree and working for Augustin. He had some (possibly) good news on the job front. He had met two chefs, Clement Grangier (the former chef of Le Pavillon) and Jacques de Chanteloup (a master charcutier, also of Le Pavillon fame). I say fame because Le Pavillon in NYC was considered the first great French restaurant in the United States. It had been opened by restaurateur Henri Soulé, along with his chef Pierre Franey, in 1941 after a successful run at the 1939 New York World's Fair. Le Pavillon's former front- and back-of-the-house food superstars went on to create a legacy of French fine dining restaurants through the '80s. Chef Chanteloup had ended up at the Culinary Institute as a teacher and struck up a quick friendship with Peter, who years later let him know that Chef Grangier was thinking of going to the city's Park Lane Hotel. So Peter sent a letter of introduction for me to present to Chef Grangier.

As soon as it arrived in the mail, I ran, letter in hand, to the Park Lane. They knew nothing of Chef Grangier or where he might be. I thought if anyone might know it would be Chef Fessaguet. I hadn't even traveled all the way down the kitchen stairs at La Caravelle when Chef Fessaguet roared from in front of the hot line, "Monsieur D'Amato, we haven't seen you for a while!" (By this time I'd achieved a sort of mascot status: *There's that polite, spunky American that we will never hire—good to see him.*)

Then, without turning around, Chef Fessaguet said, "We don't have any openings."

I replied, "I figured that—I'm actually here because I have a letter for Chef Grangier, and I was hoping you might know how to reach him."

He did a quick 180 and said, "A letter for Clement? *You know Clement?*" Before I could reply, he said, "Well, Monsieur D'Amato, we still don't have a position here, but stop over at Lutèce and tell my friend Andre I sent you—I'm sure he will be able to help."

The conversation had spun so quickly I was having trouble differentiating between reality and a dream. *Did he say André? André Soltner?* "Thank you, chef!" I replied. "*Thank you!*"

I walked into the basement kitchen at Lutèce, and Chef Soltner couldn't have been more cordial. He had already received a call from Fessaguet and told me that he just filled a position, but he recommended that I go over to speak with his friend Jean Jacques Rachou at his recently opened restaurant, Le Lavandou.

Chef Rachou started the interview by having me stand next to the hot line during lunch to watch the service. It was a two-person line with a very encouraging sign, an *American* saucier (sauce and meat cook) along with a French poissonier (fish cook). I had arrived during the high-paced, one-hour power-lunch rush. After lunch Chef Rachou asked me what position I was looking for and how much money I wanted. He was very candid: "I need someone to replace my poissonier, who has been here for two years. He is sloppy and just doesn't care like he should."

I told him I had just graduated from culinary school and wanted to apprentice—the line position was probably a bit over my experience level.

He replied, "This is all I have. I'll give you a two-week trial."

This was a literal trial by fire. Even though I was a top student and had a one-year CIA fellowship under my belt, my introduction to a true, classic French kitchen with real Frenchmen was completely new and confusing. When I walked through the back kitchen door, I wasn't in New York anymore. I was in France. I reveled in the experience but hated the fact that I didn't have the skill level to hang with the French cooks.

There were a lot of basic skills exclusive to a deeply classical French kitchen that I had dabbled in at school but never became proficient in: turning potatoes, breaking down whole fish, French butchering, and so on. All of these skills, along with any kitchen skills, are mastered with a very simple process—repetition—the exact process that Peter had sent me to the city to accomplish. After two weeks, Chef Rachou took me aside and said, "You're a really hard worker and have a great attitude, but you don't have the experience to replace my poissonier. You need to learn more French basics, and I don't have that position—but my friend Roland, around the block at Le Veau d'Or, does."

So from there I started as the first American in Le Veau d'Or's kitchen, thankfully in a position that I could handle and grow from. Chef Roland Chenus was skeptical, as he had never had an American work for him, but he decided to give me a try. This was not an uncommon feeling, as the longer I worked for Roland, the more I found out about and started to understand the "French connection."

In the early '70s, the only New York City French restaurant that was hiring multiple Americans to work in the kitchen was Le Lavandou. At this time in New York, a French cook arriving from France could make more money on these shores, so most French restaurants had no need for young American upstarts who neither understood their kitchen language nor had a true background in French kitchen principles. But Chef Rachou realized that there was an untapped treasure trove of hungry Americans who would work any hours and didn't care about money; each one just wanted to get a foot in the door.

I was amazed at how, with a simple letter from Peter and my simply uttering the name "Chef Grangier"—abracadabra!—the portals opened. Even though Chef Fessaguet was responsible for me being at Le Veau d'Or, Roland would tell me that Fessaguet would call him up to verbally taunt him about having an American in the kitchen, as he would also do to Rachou, as that was something he personally (at that time) would never have allowed at La Caravelle.

♦

MY FIRST JOB AT LE VEAU D'OR WAS TO TAKE CARE OF THE PASTRIES AND AMUSE giveaways. The amuse were given to any patrons who ordered an aperitif, while they were looking at the menu. They were either given a slim slice of quiche Lorraine, a bit of chilled ratatouille, or a creamy celery root remoulade, which is celery root, or celeriac, that has been simply mixed with homemade mayonnaise and Dijon mustard to produce a crunchy, zesty salad. It was my first experience with celery root, which was very much at home in any self-respecting French bistro.

My first job as I arrived in the morning, before I started the amuse, was to fire up the ovens and make the pastries for the day. The two regular pastries that never changed were the fruit strips. Puff pastry was rolled out onto a rectangular sheet measuring about 14 by 18 inches and cut into two 6-by-18-inch strips. The remaining long strip was divided into four thin half-inch by one-inch strips that were attached to the edges of the two large strips using beaten egg. The sheets were docked (pricked) with a fork in the middle to control the rising and then baked in a hot oven until they rose, golden brown and crisp throughout. The thin strip formed a raised border on the edges, and the middle was filled with strawberries, raspberries, apricots, or other fruits, and then glazed.

The first time I was shown how to bake the tart shells, Michele, the sous chef, instructed me on the proper way to prop open the ancient oven door (which had an AWOL thermostat) to regulate the temperature. The next day, when I was flying solo, the makeshift oven propper, a stainless steel kitchen spoon, de-propped without my realizing it after I put the tarts in the oven. When I went to check on them I didn't even have to look inside the oven; the emitting smoke told the story.

I took the tray of blackened shells back to the pastry table. As Roland walked toward me, I said, "Sorry, Chef." (Mistake number one. Don't apologize.)

He fired back, "I don't care if you're sorry!"

"But, Chef! The oven's thermostat is broken, and the spoon fell out." (Mistake number two.)

"I don't want to hear excuses—make more shells!" he responded, and walked away. That propper *never* de-propped again.

I really tried to learn from that experience but this was all new territory for both Chef Chenus and me. I was trying to figure out my place in a French kitchen, which was quite different from an American one, and Chef Chenus was trying to figure out if I was an idiot or if I had some promise.

◆

I THOUGHT I COULD NEVER GO WRONG WITH A WELL-PLACED COMPLIMENT. AS FOOD has changed and evolved over the years, the art of the classic French saucier has changed and evolved along with it. With the emergence of simplistic, product-driven menus, it is becoming rare to see the long-simmered reduction sauces that at times actually "out-showed" the products that they were made to accompany, as guests would greedily scoop up every last drop with the de rigueur sauce spoon or the last crust of bread.

As easily as I can rattle off the starting lineup of the '57 Milwaukee Braves, I also have branded in my memory the great food I have tasted over the years. One revelation was Roland's vin blanc sauce (served with fish), with its off-white, almost luminous glow. It was the base for one of my new favorite sauces of his—Armenonville. With the addition of saffron, deeply browned mushrooms, reduced tomato concassé, and fresh, snipped chives, it was draped over a chunk of wild striped bass cooked to pearly translucence. It looked like an accessorized Gaultier belt, as it partially enrobed the golden filet with precisely spaced, visible grill marks, bringing the ensemble together.

The first time I tasted that fish sauce, it was as if I had never tasted a sauce before. I looked at Chef Chenus and said, "That's a really great sauce."

Instead of the expected "Thank you" or "So, you really like it?" he just looked at me strangely and said, "So, what do you know about sauces? Of course it's great—and maybe someday you'll know why."

Hence I quickly learned the pecking order in a French kitchen and that it was considered a bit insolent for an apprentice to judge the quality, good or bad, of his chef's dishes. From that time on, I was seen but not heard until I was asked for my opinion. Once this pecking order was established and Roland was convinced I understood my place and what I did and did not know, the education began.

On Fridays, our busiest lunch day, we took three pastry strips without the borders and layered them with fresh fruits and whipped cream or pastry cream (or both) to form a mille-feuille, or napoleon. *Mille-feuille* means "thousand leaves" or "thousand layers," and refers to feuilletage, or puff pastry, that is made by rolling and folding butter into a dough to encapsulate the butter between the layers, and then folding to create over a thousand layers. As the pastry bakes, the water in the butter—trying to escape as steam—pushes the dough layers apart, creating light, crispy layers kissed with butter flavor.

This towering sculpture was finished right at noon and carried out to the dining room on its silver tray. Promptly at 2 p.m., the empty tray, speckled with crunchy crumbs, was returned to the kitchen. I was telling Gerard, the Parisian lunch chef and saucier whom I worked with, how good I thought the napoleon was. Little did I know that he was a pastry addict. After work he took me on a pastry pilgrimage through Manhattan to find the best napoleon; we went to six or seven shops that day. Coming from the land of schneck, Danish, and kolache, the French pastry shop was virgin territory to me. Beyond the napoleon, many new favorites were found. We did find the ultimate napoleon at Patisserie Dumas, which, we discovered after traversing the island of Manhattan, was one block from Le Veau d'Or where we had started. Actually, Gerard already knew this, and had saved the best for last. The incredibly crisp layers were caramelized with the sheerest layer of caramel; the pastry cream and whipped creams were in perfect proportions, and there was no fruit between the layers—it didn't need it.

The other revelation, beyond the incredible mille-feuille at Dumas, was the tarte aux pommes (apple tart) at Bonté Patisserie. When I walked into the shop, it took my breath away. The display of fresh fruit tarts was laid out as precisely as finery in a jewelry store; the strawberry, raspberry, apple, pear, and apricot tarts shimmered in the perfectly stunning case. I've never put too much stock in the phrase "too beautiful to eat," but these tarts were as close as anything ever came to making a believer out of me.

But let's be real—this was food. And I could only revere for so long. I ordered two tarts: a raspberry and an apple. The raspberry was fabulous, but what struck my soul was the apple—crisp buttery crust and perfectly textured apples were in such perfect balance that you would have thought that the apples had been grown on the crust. After I devoured the tart in front of the store, covered with crumbs, all that remained was a wisp of caramelized butter and apple on my tongue and a big grin on my face. It was all such a delicious blur that I turned right around and purchased a couple more for the long walk back to the new apartment Ellen and I were living in.

Now that I was getting a regular paycheck and Ellen had secured a server position at a small restaurant on upper Madison Avenue, we had enough equity to get our own place in the city—a small one bedroom on 85th, between York and East End. At $425 a month it was a bargain, as rents were still in the realm of reality. We were a block from Carl Shurz Park and the East River—it wasn't quite Central Park, but it was a sweet niche for a touch of urban solitude.

◆

I HAD LEARNED THEORY ABOUT BRAISING IN MY TIME AT SCHOOL, ENOUGH TO MAKE me familiar with the concept, but I had little hands-on experience with day-to-day braising. That was quickly taken care of at Le Veau d'Or, where half the menu was braised—veal, beef, lamb, venison, pork from hoof to snout, including pigs' trotters, along with offal such as tripe, sweetbreads, and tongue, and all types of poultry. This is also where I learned that the greatest glories and most guarded recipes and techniques of classic cuisine were reserved for preserved and ground meats—pâtés, terrines, rillettes, rillons—perfect amalgamations of meat and fat brought about to transform and preserve the total animal.

At the top of my list in the world of preserving is confit, usually made with goose, duck, or pork. When properly prepared and aged, the transformed meat is silky, unctuous, and deeply flavored; it floats across the palette. We made duck confit for the cassoulet that appeared weekly. The confit was married with slow-braised beans, lamb, and pork shoulders, and then topped with coarse sausage and pork belly. A crisp, duck fat crumb crust lay across the top and was repeatedly broken into the interior during baking and replenished on top to add texture and richness. It was the true expression of rich, rustic hedonism.

The difference between braises at Le Veau d'Or and those at other restaurants I tried was the intensity of the flavor of the resulting cooking liquid or broth. I believe this was because Chef Chenus was a master saucier and wanted the same enhanced flavor from braises that he produced in his stand-alone sauces. These sauces were so good that you could push the main protein away and just drink the liquid that was left—but of course, if you did that, you would be missing the most delicious, succulent meat you could imagine.

My first braise at Le Veau d'Or was coq au vin, and this stalwart of French cooking is still a favorite of mine. Originally the dish was *coq* (or rooster) braised in red wine with lardons of bacon, pearl onions, and mushrooms. What made it so good was the technique of first marinating then braising the chicken in an already rich, previously prepared red wine-roasted chicken stock (which was itself started with a good primary chicken stock to yield a double stock). This is the only way to get that haunting, deep, rich essence that reverberates with layer upon layer of flavor.

All of the meats for the braises and charcuterie came from the world of Joseph, Le Veau d'Or's full-time butcher. This was the first time I had seen that position at a restaurant not connected to a hotel. There was always a line-up of various-sized heads, feet, shoulders, thighs, and organs in the walk-in, organized like an auto parts showroom and waiting for their ultimate destination: tête de veau vinaigrette, pied de porc panée, rognon de veau sauté moutarde, cervelle au beurre noir, and tripes á la mode de Caen. The employees of the nearby French consulate, who had grown up with these dishes, frequented us. They were knowledge-able customers and would order specific cuts of the tête du veau (poached veal head) such as extra cheek and brain—although there were not many calls for the brow.

I worked within eyeshot of Joseph, and we had an interesting relationship from the be-ginning. He was from the Pyrenees Mountains of southern France, in his mid-40s, husky, and slightly balding. His arms reflected years of hefting whole animal carcasses. He was generous with his knowledge and always ready to teach, but was also fiercely nationalistic, so many of our back-room conversations were USA-versus-France shouting matches. Everyone would join in, as it was open season on the lone American. In one heated exchange I played the WWII Normandy card: without the United States, they might all be German. Girard, who wasn't in the conversation but loved to fan the flames, said, "Jo-Jo"—his smart-ass name for Joseph—"tell him about Lafayette." Joseph immediately went into character (falsetto voice for the American and booming baritone for the French voice), presenting a one-man Ameri-can Revolutionary War play in one act.

"Mon-sieur La-fay-ette! We are soooooo cooooold—can you help us?"

"Certain-monte, George [Washington]. We have these theeck French woool blankets that will keep you and your men warm."

"Oh, thank you! Mon-sieur La-fay-ette, we are so hungry—can you help us?"

"Certain-monte, George. Take these delicious mountain snails with garlic butter and real French baguettes."

"Oh, thank you! Mon-sieur La- fay-ette, we need French guns and ammunition, as we are all out."

"Certain-monte, George, I have plenty! Take them . . . Now that you have defeated the British, enjoy your country—I was just happy to help!"

Girard just lost it behind the line—he couldn't stop laughing. Not quite the history I remembered, but it was that moment that broke the ice, and we could get back to the usual disagreements over American versus French butter, chicken, or beef.

I WAS JUST FINISHING UP MY SIXTH MONTH AT LE VEAU D'OR WHEN CHEF CHENUS decided it was not so bad having an American around. He decided to bring another "American foreigner" into this strictly French enclave.

I immediately felt bad for Richard, the new guy. He came with good credentials, having worked for a year at a small bistro in Paris. He wasn't fluent in French, but he did have a pretty good command of the language—well beyond my "Oui, chef" and "Non, chef," the pat exchanges that I considered conversations. Although I did understand *soigné*, a word Girard used to prompt me to finish a dish with a polished flourish, and *baveuse*—"slobbering on itself"—describing the proper custardy texture that I had to achieve with every omelet I prepared at lunch.

The reason I felt bad was the nonstop verbal hazing he was getting. That brought me back to my first weeks on the job, but the difference was that when I started, most of what I assumed were insults really didn't have much sting because I didn't understand them. With Richard, each tirade directed at him was visibly deflating. As the only two Americans in the kitchen, we became quick friends, and I tried to keep his spirits up after each verbal lashing.

On our days off, we would try to visit a new restaurant with a cuisine neither of us had ever tried. Richard lived off Second Avenue on the Lower East Side. He didn't have much money, and the rents were dirt cheap down there. His apartment was situated near a methadone clinic three doors away, and around the corner was the Hells Angels clubhouse. I always felt safer meeting him during daylight hours.

The upside of that neighborhood was the great amount of inexpensive ethnic food. There were Northern and Southern Indian, Czechoslovakian, Romanian, and Ukrainian restaurants. When we met at a small Russian place, Richard had an avalanche of pelmeni, exquisite-tasting tortellini-type stuffed dumplings in a pool of gorgeous, limpid broth. I had the shchi, a hearty cabbage soup with beef and root vegetables that was layered with rich, hauntingly deep flavors. Along with a good helping of homemade bread, all for less than two bucks, we were stuffed.

This became a farewell lunch as Richard said he was moving back home to Massachusetts to work; he just couldn't take living in a hellhole or receiving verbal abuse from the chefs anymore. As much as I tried to convince him that it would get better, he just countered with, "You're just lucky you don't understand a lot of French."

THE FAMILY MEAL SHOULD BE A JOYOUS OCCASION. YOU TAKE TIME TO SIT DOWN IN THE middle of a hectic workday to consume a hearty spread and reenergize for the coming busy evening. And for most staff in the beginning, it is usually just that; all the food is new and appreciated. But as the months and years go on, the staff can get restless and develop negative feelings about these gatherings. In New York City, some of the best restaurants were notorious (through the culinary grapevine) for serving poor family meals. This was especially common at hotels, where the leftover banquet food from a previous week might show up in a newly reconfigured form, way past its rational expiration date.

At Le Veau d'Or, our family meals usually consisted of stews and ground-meat preparations made from the trimmings of the many animals we used, paired with fresh vegetables and a salad—not bad. But there were those days when it was just a bit different. My first taste of veal tongue came with a zesty tomato sauce. I tried it with a bit of trepidation but was quickly in the positive camp. I actually started to look forward to tongue day. Gerard was much more picky, and he started to make an alternative dinner that he would share with me when he didn't like that day's fare. The only problem with this was that the bar manager (nicknamed Monsieur 10 Percent by Gerard since he owned 10 percent of the restaurant) would scrutinize the family dinner plates to make sure nothing was being eaten that shouldn't have been.

On split-roast-lamb-head day, Gerard decided we were having steak au poivre. One of my first experiences with steak au poivre was one of my first dinners in New York City after moving there. It was at a First Street restaurant near my apartment called simply Steak Frites. For $12.95, you got a nice green salad with mustard dressing and a seven-ounce New York strip coated with peppercorns in a creamy sauce with a mound of thin, crisp fries. It was an OK steak with a serviceable sauce, a touch chewy, but the large mound of fries made all the extra chewing worthwhile.

At Le Veau d'Or, Roland would make steak au poivre by request for special customers. He used a one-pound center cut of strip loin. He carefully crushed the peppercorns to the right size and then sifted out the fine pepper (as it would be too strong with it) and coated the steaks with the larger pieces of peppercorn. Then, in a heavy French steel pan over high heat, the steaks were well burnished and crusted. A large dose of brandy, some shallots, a good veal sauce, and a bit of cream were next. A small touch of mustard brought up the acidity, and a pat of butter finished the dish—it was steak perfection from a master. Even though he was as fiercely nationalistic as a Frenchman could be, in a weak moment he confided that he thought the United States did have better beef than France. So this dish was better than he could have made there.

Gerard was following Roland's script as he gently nudged two pepper-encrusted slabs into a large, black, smoking-hot steel pan. He told me to grab silverware, napkins, and drinks and follow him out the back door. We shimmied up a small ladder that led to the roof (which

Here I am in the Le Veau d'Or kitchen

I previously only saw used when Immigration would come in and I guessed that everyone who didn't want to meet with them would disappear up that ladder), settled our plates on the air conditioning unit, and dug in. The steak was everything my mind imagined it would be—sharp, creamy, rich, crusty. This was no Steak Frites special—it was the real deal.

◆

GERARD AND I WERE RIGHT IN THE MIDDLE OF THE DINNER RUSH, AND ROLAND WAS off for the evening. The line was full of tickets, slightly waving like mini-sheets drying in the backyard. That was if your backyard was 3 by 6 feet with an average temperature of 125 degrees. The orders were rolling in from the dining room. Bernard the waiter yelled, "This ticket is for Chef Jean Jacques Rachou." Immediately, I was nervous, as he was the one who had sent me over to Le Veau d'Or, and I wanted to impress him.

After dinner Chef Rachou stopped by the kitchen. Not only was he happy, it was like old home week! He had loved his dinner and in passing said to me, "Well, now you're ready—you can come back to Le Lavandou." So I figured that was how things worked and I was moving on to the next step.

The next day I saw Roland and said, "Chef Rachou was in last night, so I'll be going over to Le Lavandou."

He looked at me with an almost hurt expression and said, "You're not happy here? Is it money . . . you want more money?"

I replied, "You don't know anything about this?"

"How would I know?" he said.

I replied, "I just thought you all spoke together and decided it was my time to move."

It turns out the French connection had a few missing links. After a long talk, Roland not only almost doubled my wage (which was the furthest thing from my mind) but also told me about the new restaurant that he was working on. It was on the other end of the spectrum from Le Veau d'Or—a grand luxe, classic French restaurant in the style of Le Pavillon—and would be located right across the street from its former site on 57th between Park and Lexington. And his plan for me was to be on the opening team as his poissonier, the first position he had held at Le Pavillon when he had come to the United States. This was like going from summer stock to Broadway—in one fell swoop.

◆

I WALKED INTO THE KITCHEN AT THE DORCHESTER HOTEL RIGHT AROUND LUNCHTIME. The lighting was strangely dimmed by the years' worth of accumulated greasy patina that covered every surface. There was one cook behind the line, sipping a mug of coffee, and a diminutive fellow with a yellowed T-shirt and stained bib apron mixed a salad in the cold section. He ladled out a thick, gray-green mass and plopped it into the bowl with the wilted greens. "Green goddess!" he exclaimed, smiling.

Roland came walking over and said, "What do you think?"

I didn't know what to say. This was the future home of Le Chantilly, the grand luxe restaurant he had been building up for the last few months? It looked like a really dirty Veau d'Or with a much larger footprint, and it had that dead smell that was prevalent at restaurant auctions (in places where people had stopped caring for months or years before finally giving up and closing). I was starting to question my brilliant career decision when Roland started to explain how they would be gutting the entire kitchen and dining room— a six-month process. During that time I was to cook for any patrons of the Dorchester Hotel who desired room service. The hotel was a late-1970s condo, so most of the patrons lived there all year.

On average I would serve two or three single orders in an entire evening. It was like having my own restaurant (albeit not a very successful one). But I had complete control over the

Menu from Le Veau d'Or in New York

daily-changing menu, which included two soups, two salads, and two or three entrées, which I shopped for daily and prepared.

This was a two-man operation: I cooked, and Luis, the server/dishwasher, delivered all the orders and cleaned up. Every day, after prep was done, we would just sit waiting for the phone to ring. Luis and I didn't know each other very well in the beginning, but that changed quickly as we had a good four hours each night to pass the time. We played cards every night, and War was the game of choice, as it needed the least translation.

Luis was originally from Mexico and lived in the Bronx. He spoke at length about his neighborhood, which was very rough, and he told me the shining light of the neighborhood was the junkies. He loved the junkies. I was a bit confused; I had as much compassion as the next guy for addicts and addiction, but it had never crossed over to love. As I tried to explain my position, he looked at me strangely and then started laughing. "No, no, no! I mean the *junkies*! The New York *Junkies*! You know—base-a-ball." We shared many base-a-ball arguments after that.

Le Chantilly kitchen staff (I am in first row all the way to the right), 1970s

♦

"WHERE EEZ ZEE STAFF, ROLAND? WHERE EEZ ZEE STAFF?"

This was an almost surreal situation for a young cook. Le Chantilly had just opened, and I was standing behind the line as the opening poissonier. The gentleman standing in front of me firing the question was none other than Paul Bocuse, arguably the most famous chef of his time and the father of today's celebrity chefs.

He was in New York for a French chef's event and was visiting with Roland. In most two- and three-star restaurants in France, the number of staff members usually coincided with the number of guests served in a day. So when he saw our staff of nine cooks, he probably figured that an epidemic had spread through the kitchen, leaving us with a spindly skeleton staff. As he watched lunch service start up, he actually marveled at the amount of people that this "small" staff of ours could serve.

Le Chantilly kitchen crew making charcuterie (I'm on the left)

As the lunch hour came to an end, Chef Chenus told us to pull out a casserole that he had prepared before lunch. It was slowly braising in the oven, forming an impossibly crisp, golden crust. He escorted Chef Bocuse to the dining room and joined him for lunch.

What dish did Roland choose to serve this visiting dignitary? Well, it had to be classic. It had to be delicious. And it had to be from the heart of the chef. It was lamb Champvallon, a rustic mélange of seared lamb chops, buried and braised in glistening, crunchy potatoes and onions. The potato preparation by itself is classic boulangère, and when it is married with the lamb fat and meat juices, they are transported to another level of perfection. This is a real "chef's dish," from the hands and heart of an artisan craftsman. I thought, after partaking in this lunch, that Chef Bocuse must certainly see that it was not the size of the staff that mattered, but the size of their hearts.

◆

THERE WAS A TIME WHEN SERVING A MEAT-BASED SAUCE WITH FISH WAS A HUGE "non-non," as the French might say. That was pre-1970, back when French grande cuisine ruled the fine-food universe. The basis for most fish sauces was sauce vin blanc; a mixture of shallots and white wine is heavily reduced, after which fish stock is added before reducing the liquid again and finishing it with copious amounts of heavy cream. From this base sauce, myriad other sauces sprouted with the additions of herbs, purées, spices, vegetables, and other ingredients.

In the early '70s, a group of young French chefs decided to break with tradition, and nouvelle cuisine was born. The byword was "lighter." This style of preparation moved away from the heavy excesses of classic cuisine. Indeed some of the sauces looked light and ethereal, such as the ubiquitous beurre blanc. But as you stood over a pot mounting the sauce with a shovelful of pure butter, it was obvious things weren't as light as your tongue would have you think.

The efforts of a few of the nouvelle bunch—Bernard Loiseau with his "water sauces," Louis Outhier with his love of exotic spices, and Michel Guérard with cuisine minceur—were, by today's standards of modern cooking and molecular gastronomy, like lighting a sparkler at a Fourth of July fireworks finale. For that time, they really pushed the envelope.

When I started at Le Chantilly in 1977, Roland was rooted firmly in classic cuisine and teetered cautiously and reluctantly with the precepts of nouvelle cuisine. The sous chef at the time asked Roland if he could try a Michel Guérard-inspired dish of monkfish for a lunch special. Roland agreed, although later he attached himself to the sous chef's shoulder and critiqued every step of his preparation. Afterward, the sous chef told me he would never try a new dish again.

You almost had to shudder when the fish monger flipped open the delivery box and this head, with its wide-open mouth large enough to engulf your foot past your ankle, shoe and all, appeared. This revealed a fish with a head so big in proportion to its body that Disney should have considered it a perfect prototype for the big screen camera and a leading role in *The Little Mermaid*. But behind that huge, prehistoric-looking head and mouth and under the dark, dingy, warty skin lay a treasure trove of white pearly flesh.

Despite the angst involved in getting the monkfish ready, the dish was quite a success. Properly prepared, monkfish has the properties of meat; it can be pan-roasted, rested, and sliced like a mini roast. It caramelizes beautifully and retains a toothsome, moist character quite atypical of most fish.

In the end Roland admitted that he was surprised by the meaty veal stock-based sauce and how well it complemented the fish. The sous chef just looked my way and shook his head as if to say, "Too late—I'm already defeated."

◆

FRANC-COMTOIS IS A REGION OF FRANCE LOCATED ON THE EASTERN BORDER, WITH Burgundy to the west, Alsace up north, and the Rhône to the south. It is a very mountainous area with the Jura Mountains forming a natural border with Switzerland. The cuisine of this area is rustic and very similar to that of Switzerland, built on cheeses, hams, veal, cream, and mushrooms.

My familiarity with this area came from working with Roland, who was a native of the region. I was always excited to learn dishes that came from my fellow chefs' backgrounds rather than from their training. Since Roland was a classically trained French chef, much of what I learned from him was passed down from what he had learned in his formal training. But the food of his youth and region were the dishes that really touched his soul. When he passed those dishes on, he did so with a different tone and feeling for the history of the dish, his pride in the regional products, and the solace that the flavor of the finished dish brought him.

The signature dish of Le Chantilly when we opened was sauté de veau Franc-Comtois. This dish is a celebration of the region, with veal scallops enclosing Comté cheese (a type of French Gruyére) and French ham, served with a creamy morel sauce. Every time we put this dish up on the pickup line, Roland would carefully place it on the waiter's tray destined for the dining room, and a smile would cross his face. I'd swear it was the smile of a 10-year-old Roland sitting down to a dinner of his mom's veal Franc-Comtois.

❖

I REALIZED EARLY ON THAT THE KEY TO MY FOOD IS ACID. A TOUCH OF WELL-PLACED acid can take a mundane, flat, and insipid dish to the realm of the inspired. And interplayed with sweet, bitter, and salty, it can inspire a symphony on your palate.

These concepts are usually very clear to most when preparing savory food. But it seems that with desserts, most people are willing to settle for a very one-dimensional, sweet sensation. To me it's like the difference between a gummy bear and a Sweet Tart. I was always the guy who wanted Sweet Tarts, Lik-M-Aid, and Lemonheads, and I really lost interest when I ate nontart candies, which might explain why my dessert world is "bittersweet."

While I was working at Le Chantilly, I had the privilege and opportunity to work with the pastry chef Dieter Schorner in my off time. Besides being known as the chef who created the crème brûlée craze that swept across America, he was simply the best pastry chef I had ever seen—a combination of scientific technique and the hands and soul of an artist.

Since I was working six days a week, from 11 a.m. until close, my only off time when Dieter was also working was Saturday morning. We were closed for lunch, so from 6 a.m. until 2 p.m. (when I started my nightly fish preparation), it was just Dieter and me. He usually did all the pastries himself and didn't really need me, but he seemed to welcome the help and interest. He once apologized when he didn't have a lot to show me. *Apologize to me?* A few years back I was

Reuniting with Pastry Chef and CIA instructor Dieter Schorner after giving the commencement address at the Culinary Institute of America, around 2006

paying to be in a 20-person class to learn pastry, and now I had one-on-one attention from a pastry master—I should have been paying him!

The first few Saturdays he went over basics, but as I became more adept, it freed him up to try different desserts, dipped chocolates, and sugar work, all of which he patiently explained. The amazing thing about his pastries was the impeccable balance and complexity of flavor. I learned to make a lemon curd while working with him, and once I tasted the incredible purity and palate cut of the lemon brought out by the perfect ratio of sugar, I knew that, for me, it just couldn't get any better.

What became just as valuable was our developing friendship. Dieter had spent many years at the top of his field in the most competitive city in the world, and as I started to open up about my shaky home life and what my direction should be, our time together morphed into "Saturdays with Dieter." His wisdom and understanding of balance extended beyond the pastry realm, and those Saturdays became a master class in balancing life. He became a confidant, mentor, and guidance counselor—right when I needed personal life advice most.

CHAPTER EIGHT RECIPES

◆

Breast of Duck Smitane
229

Tarte Fine aux Pommes
231

Coq au Vin
234

Russian Shchi
237

Steak au Poivre
239

Lamb Champvallons
240

Lemon Curd Meringue
241

BREAST OF DUCK SMITANE

Smitane is an Escoffier-era sour cream sauce that was served with duck at La Caravelle in their heyday. Since I was obsessed with trying to work there, that dish became part of the obsession. I never did get a chance to try it but this dish that I made at Sanford was inspired by that time in my life—and it has all the angst and passion of never giving up.

SERVES 4

4 (8-ounce [227-g]) trimmed boneless skin-on duck breasts

Kosher salt and freshly ground black pepper, to taste

1 tablespoon regular olive oil

2 tablespoons chopped shallots (divided)

½ cup (119 mL) dry white wine

¼ cup (59 mL) brandy

1 cup (237 mL) veal stock (you may use consommé mixed with 1 tablespoon tomato paste as a substitute)

¼ cup (58 g) sour cream

1 teaspoon dry mustard

¼ cup (34 g) pitted brine-cured green olives, cut in half

1 cup (57 g) brussels sprout leaves (cut core from brussels sprouts and separate into leaves)

½ cup (68 g) small diced, roasted,* and peeled yellow beets (if in season, you may use roasted and peeled baby beets, cut in half after roasting)

1 tablespoon red wine vinegar

* For roasting: Season beets lightly with salt and pepper and roast at 375°F (190°C) for 12 minutes until tender.

1. Place a large sauté pan over medium heat. Season the duck breasts with salt and pepper. Add the oil to the pan, and when hot, add the duck breasts and sear, fat side down, until golden, about 5 to 6 minutes. Turn the breasts over and cook for 2 to 3 minutes, or until your desired doneness (I prefer medium-rare to medium). Remove the breasts from the pan and let them rest.

2. Remove and reserve all but 1 tablespoon of oil from the pan. Add 1 tablespoon of the shallots and sauté for 30 seconds. Add the wine and brandy and reduce by ⅔. Add the veal stock and reduce to ¾ cup (178 mL). Whisk together the sour cream and dry mustard and carefully whisk into the sauce, then add the olives. Adjust the seasoning with salt and pepper, cover the pan, and place in a warm area.

3. In a separate sauté pan placed over high heat, add 1½ tablespoons of the reserved oil. When the pan is very hot, add the remaining 1 tablespoon of the shallots and the brussels sprout leaves. Season lightly with salt and pepper and toss for 30 seconds. Add the beets and vinegar and cook until the vinegar is evaporated. Adjust the seasoning again and divide the vegetables on 4 plates. Place 1 duck breast on each plate and garnish with the olive/sour cream sauce.

TARTE FINE AUX POMMES (Apple Tart)

This tart, with its crunchy, caramelized crust and tart apple, will make you feel like a kid once you're covered with buttery shards from head to toe.

MAKES 1 (11X18-INCH [27.5X46-CM]) TARTE

For the Short Paste Dough:

> 8 ounces (227 g) all-purpose flour (2 cups loosely packed)
>
> 1 stick plus 2 tablespoons cold salted butter, cubed
>
> Pinch salt
>
> ½ of a beaten egg (reserve the other ½ for Frangipane)
>
> ¼ cup (59 mL) plus 2 tablespoons ice water

1. Add the flour, butter, and salt to a food processor and pulse until the butter is the size of peas. Whisk the ½ egg and ice water together and, with the machine running, add through the processor feed tube. Stop the machine when the liquid is all added.

2. Place the dough on a work surface and bring together with your hands (do not overmix). Cover with plastic wrap and refrigerate for at least 1 hour.

For the Tarte:

> Prepared Short Paste Dough
>
> ¾ cup (150 g) granulated sugar, to roll out the dough
>
> Frangipane (recipe follows)
>
> 1½ pounds (681 g) Granny Smith apples, peeled, halved from top to bottom, cored, and cut in ⅛-inch (3-mm) slices from top to bottom (do not cut the apples until you are ready to shingle them on the dough)
>
> Cinnamon sugar, to sprinkle over the tarte (1 tablespoon granulated sugar mixed with ¾ teaspoon ground cinnamon)
>
> ½ stick cold salted butter, cut in thin slices

1. Roll out the dough using the granulated sugar (so it does not stick to your work surface) into an 11x17x⅛-inch-thick (27.5x43x0.3-cm) rectangle (or the size of a nonstick baking sheet). Let the dough rest in the refrigerator for at least 20 minutes.

2. Preheat the oven to 375°F (190°C). Remove the dough from the refrigerator and spread with the Frangipane, leaving about ½-inch (13-mm) edge around the tart. Shingle the apple slices horizontally across the top, leaving about a ¾- to 1-inch (1.9- to 2.5-cm) reveal on the previous slice. On each progressive downward row, leave a ½-inch (13-mm) reveal on the upper row and stagger each row so the apple slices do not line up (like a roof). Sprinkle the apples with the cinnamon sugar and dot with the cold butter slices.

(RECIPE CONTINUES ON PAGE 232)

(RECIPE CONTINUED FROM PAGE 231)

3. Bake for about 20 to 25 minutes, or until golden brown. Serve the Tarte aux Pommes warm with your favorite accompaniment, like crème frâiche, ice cream, whipped cream, or yogurt.

For the Frangipane:

(Note: All of the ingredients should be at room temperature.)

2 tablespoons almond paste

2 tablespoons granulated sugar

2 tablespoons salted butter

1 egg yolk

1 tablespoon all-purpose flour

Reserved ½ of a beaten egg

1. Process the almond paste and sugar in a food processor. Add the butter and process until smooth, about 30 seconds. Add the reserved ½ of a beaten egg and the egg yolk to emulsify. Pulse in the flour until just combined (do not overmix). Refrigerate the Frangipane to firm it up, about 1 hour.

COQ AU VIN

Free-range organic chickens will yield a better texture and flavor than the supermarket variety. The breast pieces, which have little or no fat, can get over-cooked and quite dry. My solution is to remove the breasts when they are just cooked, then continue cooking the leg and thighs until fork-tender. Once they are done, you can add the breasts back in to infuse them with flavor. Don't be afraid to let the entire braise rest for a day or so—it will get better.

SERVES 4

For the Marinated Chicken:

1 (6-pound [2.72-kg]) chicken, either cut in quarters off the carcass (or you may have a butcher cut a chicken to yield 2 leg and thigh portions and 2 semi-boneless breasts with first wing joint attached) (Reserve the carcass cut into pieces, outer wing joints, and neck for the stock.)

3–4 large shallots, thinly sliced

8 cloves garlic, thinly sliced

½ bunch fresh Italian parsley stems

3 bay leaves

2 sprigs fresh thyme

20 crushed black peppercorns

8 crushed juniper berries

2 cups (474 mL) dry red wine

1. Mix all of the ingredients together in a bowl. Transfer them to a large resealable plastic bag and marinate for 2 days in the refrigerator, turning the bag every 12 hours.

For the Chicken Stock:

2 tablespoons regular olive oil

Reserved chicken carcass, outer wing joints, and neck

1 onion with the peel left on (10 ounces [284 g]), cut in half, then each half cut in 6 pieces

1 carrot (3 ounces [85 g]), cut in 1-inch (2.5-cm) pieces

1 stalk celery, cut in 1-inch (2.5-cm) pieces

6 cloves garlic

¼ cup (66 g) tomato paste

20 crushed peppercorns

2 sprigs fresh thyme

1 bay leaf

½ bunch fresh Italian parsley stems

2 cups (474 mL) red wine

3 cups (711 mL) unsalted chicken stock

1. Preheat the oven to 400°F (200°C). Place a sauté pan over high heat. Add the oil, and when hot, add the reserved chicken parts and sauté for 2 minutes. Place in the oven and roast for 25 minutes, stir, then roast for another 20 minutes. Add the onions and carrots and roast for 15 minutes, stir, then roast for another 10 minutes. Add the celery and garlic and stir. Add the tomato paste and roast for 5 minutes. Add the peppercorns, thyme, bay leaf, and parsley stems.

2. On top of the stove, deglaze the pan with the red wine and bring up to a boil. Transfer to a stock pot. Add the stock, bring up to a slow simmer and cook for 2 hours. Strain and reserve the stock in the refrigerator. (Remove the fat before using.)

For the Garnish:

6 ounces (170 g) pearl onions, peeled with ends kept intact

½ cup (119 mL) water

1 tablespoon unsalted butter

1 teaspoon granulated sugar

Kosher salt and freshly ground black pepper, to taste

6 ounces (170 g) slab bacon, cut in medium dice

8 ounces (227 g) button mushrooms, brushed clean and cut in quarters

1. Place the pearl onions in a sauté pan with the water, butter, and sugar and season with salt and pepper. Cover and bring up to a boil. Cook 1 minute, uncover, and cook until all of the liquid is reduced and the onions are glazed and tender; reserve.

2. Place the bacon in a separate sauté pan and cook over medium heat. When the bacon is rendered and just lightly golden, strain the bacon fat and reserve the bacon. Add 2 tablespoons of the fat back into the pan (reserve 3 tablespoons [36 g] of the fat to cook the chicken). Add the mushrooms and sauté over high heat until golden and tender. Adjust the seasoning with salt and pepper. Add the reserved onions and bacon to the pan and toss. Reserve the garnish in the refrigerator.

(RECIPE CONTINUES ON PAGE 236)

(RECIPE CONTINUED FROM PAGE 235)

To Finish the Dish:

> **Prepared Marinated Chicken**
> **Kosher salt and freshly ground black pepper, to taste**
> **Reserved 3 tablespoons (36 g) bacon fat**
> **1 cup (237 mL) red wine**
> **2½ tablespoons (23 g) all-purpose flour**
> **Prepared Chicken Stock**
> **Prepared Garnish**

1. Remove the chicken from the marinade and pat it dry with paper towels. Strain the marinade into a sauté pan, reserving the marinated vegetables. Bring the strained marinade up to a boil, then strain it again through 4 layers of cheesecloth (or a clean kitchen towel) to remove all of the scum and solids; reserve.

2. Place 2 (10-inch [25-cm]) sauté pans on the stove over medium-high heat. Season the chicken on both sides with salt and pepper. Divide the remaining 3 tablespoons of bacon fat between the sauté pans. When fat is hot, add the chicken pieces, skin side down, to the pans. Sauté the chicken for 5 minutes, turn over, then cook for 3 more minutes. Remove the chicken from the pans and place into a braising pot.

3. Deglaze 1 of the pans with the red wine and turn off the heat. To the other pan, add the reserved marinated vegetables and sauté for 2 minutes. Add the flour and stir to cook for 1 minute. Add the reserved strained/cooked marinade and wine/deglazing from the other pan. Bring up to a boil and cook for 1 minute.

4. Add the mixture to the braising pot holding the chicken along with the prepared chicken stock. Bring up to a simmer and simmer slowly, covered, for 20 to 25 minutes. Remove the breasts to a bowl when they are 165°F (74°C) on an instant-read thermometer, and cover. Continue to cook the leg/thighs until they are 165°F (74°C), about 45 to 55 minutes total. Remove the leg/thighs to the bowl.

5. Strain the sauce and reduce to 2 to 2½ cups (474 to 593 mL). Add the prepared garnish, bring up to a boil, and adjust the seasoning with salt and pepper. Pour the sauce over the chicken in the bowl and let it cool. Refrigerate the Coq au Vin, covered, and on the next day, reheat it and serve.

RUSSIAN SHCHI
(Cabbage Root Vegetable Soup)

Shchi is a Russian peasant soup that would fortify families when there was either plenty or nothing else to eat. There are as many recipes as there are families, but the constant is cabbage or sauerkraut. It's rich and filling but should always be balanced with an inherent tartness to play off the sweet root vegetables.

MAKES 12 SERVINGS

¼ cup (57 g) clarified butter

1 pound (454 g) rutabaga (1 large or 2 medium), peeled and cut in very small dice (brunoise)

1 pound (454 g) celeriac (celery root) (1 large), peeled and cut in very small dice (brunoise)

1½ pounds (681 g) yellow beets (4 medium), peeled and cut in very small dice (brunoise)

2 large onions (1½ pounds [681 g]), peeled and cut in very small dice (brunoise)

2 tablespoons kosher salt, plus additional to taste

2 teaspoons freshly ground black pepper, plus additional to taste

2 pounds (908 g) cabbage (1 head), cut in half, core removed, each half cut in 8 even pieces and those pieces cut in ¼-inch (6-mm) strips

2 tablespoons minced garlic (about 4–5 cloves)

⅓ cup (87 g) tomato paste

2 bay leaves

3 sprigs fresh savory, 2 sprigs fresh thyme, and 3 sprigs fresh marjoram, tied together with kitchen string

3 quarts (2.84 L) unsalted beef stock

¼ cup (59 mL) cider vinegar

2 tablespoons dry mustard

Sour cream, to garnish

Seared Brussels Sprouts (recipe follows)

Fresh dill fronds, to garnish

1. Place a soup pot over medium heat. Add the clarified butter. Add the rutabaga, the celeriac, the beets, the onions, the 2 tablespoons salt, and the 2 teaspoons pepper and cook, covered, sweating for 10 minutes, stirring every few minutes (do not let the vegetables brown). Add the cabbage and garlic and continue sweating for 5 more minutes. Add the tomato paste, bay leaves, and tied fresh herbs and cook for 3 minutes. Add the stock and simmer for 25 minutes.

(RECIPE CONTINUES ON PAGE 238)

(RECIPE CONTINUED FROM PAGE 237)

2. Mix together the vinegar and dry mustard and add to the soup. Adjust the seasoning with salt and pepper. For serving, garnish the soup with a dollop of sour cream, a bit of the Seared Brussels Sprouts, and a sprinkling of dill fronds over the top.

For the Seared Brussels Sprouts:

1 pound (454 g) brussels sprouts, core removed and sprouts separated into individual leaves

2 large shallots, finely diced

¼ cup (59 mL) regular olive oil

Kosher salt and freshly ground black pepper, to taste

Pinch nutmeg

3 tablespoons cider vinegar

1. Place a large sauté pan over very high heat. In a bowl, toss the brussels sprout leaves with the shallots and oil. When the pan is very hot, add the brussels sprout leaves, season with salt, pepper, and nutmeg, and toss the leaves quickly for about 5 seconds to just lightly sear. Immediately deglaze the pan with vinegar and remove the leaves from the pan and cool. Reserve to garnish the soup.

STEAK AU POIVRE

This has always been steak decadence for me and as I take that first bite, it once again becomes that guilty pleasure while "rooftop dining" at Le Veau d'Or.

SERVES 2

> 2 (10- to 12-ounce [284- to 341-g]) trimmed New York strip steaks
>
> ¼ cup (25 g) Tellicherry peppercorns, crushed with the back of a pot to about the size of ⅙–⅛ of a whole peppercorn, fine pepper sifted out (using a medium strainer) and coarse-ground pepper reserved (you will need about 1 tablespoon per steak and ½ teaspoon to finish the sauce)
>
> 1 tablespoon clarified butter
>
> Kosher salt and freshly ground black pepper, to taste
>
> 2 tablespoons brandy
>
> ¼ cup (59 mL) white wine
>
> 1 tablespoon chopped shallots
>
> 1 teaspoon red wine vinegar
>
> ¼ cup (59 mL) veal stock (you may use ¼ cup unsalted beef stock mixed with ¾ teaspoon tomato paste as a substitute)
>
> ¼ cup (59 mL) heavy cream
>
> 1½ teaspoons Dijon mustard
>
> 1 teaspoon whole butter

1. Invert a small plate over a larger plate and keep them in a warm place. Press a total of 2 tablespoons of the crushed peppercorns into both sides of both of the steaks. Lightly pound in the peppercorns with a meat pounder—the steaks should be about 1 inch thick.

2. Place a sauté pan over high heat. Add the 1 tablespoon clarified butter and reduce the heat to medium-high. Season the steaks on both sides with salt and sauté for about 3 to 4 minutes per side, to your desired doneness. Remove the pan from the heat, add the brandy, then place back on the heat to flame the steaks. Remove the steaks from the pan and place on top of the small, warmed inverted plate while you finish the sauce.

3. For the sauce, add the wine, shallots, and red wine vinegar to the pan and reduce to 2 tablespoons. Add the stock, heavy cream, and mustard and reduce by half, or until it is the consistency of heavy cream. Add any steak juices that have accumulated on the larger plate to the sauce. Add the 1 teaspoon whole butter and the ½ teaspoon of the crushed peppercorns and swirl the pan to incorporate the butter. Remove from the heat and adjust the seasoning with salt and black pepper, if necessary. Place the steaks on 2 plates and pour the sauce over and around.

LAMB CHAMPVALLONS

When I first saw Chef Chenus taking beautiful seared loin lamb chops and burying them in potatoes and braising them in the oven, I didn't get it. Why screw up those luscious chops! After lunch he let me try one and I had the answer—because they are incredibly delicious! Clearly, I had a lot to learn.

SERVES 2

> 2 (¾- to 1-inch-thick [1.9- to 2.5-cm]) lamb shoulder blade chops, about ¾ pound (341 g) each
>
> Kosher salt and freshly ground black pepper, to taste
>
> 4 tablespoons (57 g) clarified butter, warmed (divided)
>
> 1 large onion (10 ounces [284 g]), thinly sliced
>
> 6 sprigs fresh thyme
>
> 4 cloves garlic, finely chopped
>
> 3 bay leaves
>
> 2 cups (474 mL) unsalted chicken stock
>
> 1 pound (454 g) Idaho potatoes (2 large), peeled, covered with water, and just before mixing with the stock mixture, sliced in ⅛-inch-thick (3-mm) slices
>
> 1 teaspoon kosher salt
>
> ½ teaspoon freshly ground black pepper

1. Place a heavy-bottomed sauté pan over high heat. When the pan is hot, season the lamb chops with salt and pepper. Add 1 tablespoon of the butter to the pan and sauté the chops for 2 to 3 minutes per side to brown very well. Remove the chops to a plate.

2. Add 1 tablespoon of the butter to the pan, then add the onions. Season lightly with salt and pepper and sauté for about 2 to 3 minutes to lightly color. Add the thyme, garlic, and bay leaves and stir for 1 minute. Add the stock and bring up to a boil.

3. In a large bowl, toss the sliced potatoes with 1 tablespoon of the butter, the 1 teaspoon salt, and the ½ teaspoon pepper. Pour the hot stock mixture over the potatoes and mix together.

4. Preheat the oven to 350°F (180°C). In a 10- to 12-inch (25- to 30-cm) oval ovenproof casserole, large enough to hold both chops in 1 layer, layer the bottom with half of the potatoes and onions, then place the chops on top in 1 layer. Top with any remaining potatoes, onions, and stock. Press down the top to evenly layer the potatoes and drizzle the remaining 1 tablespoon of the butter over the top. Bake for about 45 minutes to 1 hour, or until the potatoes are golden and cooked.

LEMON CURD MERINGUE

Without Dieter's patient guidance, there would have been a great void in my pastry knowledge and personal life. And without his lemon curd, I would have missed out on my favorite citrus dessert—ever.

SERVES 6

For the Lemon Curd:

> 8 large egg yolks (reserve 3 whites for the meringue)
> 1 cup (200 g) granulated sugar
> 1 cup (237 mL) fresh lemon juice
> 1½ sticks unsalted butter, at room temperature, cut into pieces
> 1½ tablespoons grated lemon zest

1. Have 6 (8-ounce [240-mL]) ramekins ready for filling. Place a heavy, large non-aluminum saucepan over medium heat. Add all of the ingredients and bring up to a boil, whisking constantly, for about 5 seconds, or just until thickened. Continue whisking off the heat.

2. Divide the curd into the ramekins. Let the curd set in the refrigerator for at least 1 hour to cool. Cover the ramekins with plastic wrap and keep refrigerated until you finish the meringue.

For the Meringue:

> 3 reserved large egg whites
> Pinch kosher salt
> 1½ tablespoons granulated sugar
> 2 tablespoons plus 1 teaspoon confectioners' sugar
> Prepared Lemon Curd

1. In a clean stainless or copper bowl, whip the egg whites and salt until frothy. Add the granulated sugar and whip until a very soft peak. Add the confectioners' sugar and whip to a slightly firm peak.

2. When the tip of the peak just drops a bit, place the meringue in a pastry bag fitted with a large star tip. Divide the meringue over the top of the prepared lemon curds, covering all of the curd.

3. Preheat the broiler. Place the ramekins on a baking sheet and broil the Lemon Curd Meringues until they are just golden, for about 30 seconds to 1 minute, and serve.

9

TRANSITION:
LONG ISLAND

I HAD TONY MANERO'S SATURDAY NIGHT FEVER ANGST. IN ONE FELL SWOOP, I WENT from being a resident of Manhattan's Upper East Side to becoming a member of the Bridge and Tunnel Club (what Manhattanites called folks from Queens, Brooklyn, and New Jersey who "invaded" the city on weekends by crossing the Brooklyn or Queensboro [59th Street] Bridges or the Holland Tunnel). This was not a term of endearment but class warfare, a way for Manhattanites to express their self-proclaimed superiority and disdain for those so close but so unworthy. Even the waiters at the restaurant in which I worked (who were all French and, ironically, lived across the bridge in Long Island City, Queens) had an attitude as the weekend dining room filled up with all of those people. It was a caste system in which people from New York's boroughs were the best of the worst, the Jerseyites bordering on untouchable status, and those from Philly landing right at the bottom as unmentionables. Their M.O., in the waiters' minds, was to act as though they didn't even need a menu, as it seemed that the only items we sold on the weekends were onion soup and whatever steak was available. Nothing strange or unusual would leave the kitchen, and the checks, along with the tips, were way below what they were used to with the sophisticated weekday Manhattan diners.

I had experienced this silliness growing up in Milwaukee—or "Milburg," as some Chicago folks referred to it—so I understood border wars. And besides, Ellen was a steak-and-potatoes, bridge-y kind of gal. After many dinners with her, at which I would always order the most esoteric item on the menu, she sagely said one evening (as I was complaining about how my yak hoof wasn't properly braised), "You know, you always order something that only one or two people in the world know how to prepare, and you're actually surprised when it isn't right." Then she went back to her meltingly tender, crusted New York strip and sour cream baker with a smug look on her face.

We were looking for a slightly larger apartment, but rents in Manhattan had begun to skyrocket in the previous two years. Ellen's brother happened to be moving out of a two-bedroom in Jackson Heights, Queens, and it was still unrented. I had my doubts about Queens after our experience living with her mother, but the apartment was quite a bit larger and less expensive than where we were living. We figured that, with the extra money, we might be able to carve out a better social life.

Before we had gotten through our first week, I felt pangs of nostalgia for the good ol' days (last week) when my commute to work was a leisurely walk from 85th down Second Avenue, at a pace that gave me time to do a bit of window shopping and future planning, until I took the turn at 57th toward Le Chantilly.

Every nasty, claustrophobic subway cliché you can think of was my new reality on the morning rush hour F train from Jackson Heights into Manhattan. I was regularly cemented in place with my face plastered to some dude or dudette's armpit for the entire journey. It was only worse when I mistakenly got on the local E train and the nasal annihilation was extended by 10 or so stops. As I exited the 63rd and Lexington station, the Manhattan air never smelled so sweet. I would weave my way through the midtown crowd with my secret weapon, which had been passed on to me by a bartender at Paxton's.

I had been complaining to him how I always ended up ceding the sidewalk path to almost everyone as I was walking the streets. He told me to just never make eye contact or even look in the general direction of the oncoming people and act as if I were totally preoccupied. The first time I tried it, it was like I was Moses parting the Red Sea; the multitudes miraculously serpentined around my body. The only folks immune to this sorcery were Jackson Heights' roving gangs of older ladies. Armed with tank-like, armored, rolling shopping carts, with cackling glee, they were able to drive unarmed pedestrians like me off the sidewalk.

In truth, the worst part was that I had settled into a mid-shift job at Le Chantilly, and with Ellen leaving for work a few hours before I would get home, we would only see each other on Sundays and her day off (unless I hung out at the bar where she worked until she was done, which made me pretty worthless the following day at work). So even though we had extra money, the social parts of our lives were very separate.

During one of my "Saturdays with Dieter" sessions, I was unloading on him about my dilemma. My relationship with Ellen was quickly going south, and we were seeing a marriage counselor. But at the same time, I was very happy at work. The week before, I was closing the restaurant and sitting, sipping a beer as I waited for the evening's sauces to cool down in their ice baths before I put them in the refrigerator. I looked over the lineup—vin blanc, l'oseille, Armenonville, bordelaise, grand veneur, Americaine, poivrade, perigueux, morilles, diable—and it registered: I'm doing this. I'm making these sauces that a few years ago I could only dream of trying—I'm the guy in the French Lunch movie!

I really felt that I was poised to do well in the NYC restaurant scene, but something was missing. Dieter looked over at me and said, "Most chefs I know in this city, who are successful, have had to give up a lot in their family life. You have to figure out what is important to you and find that balance. I know from personal experience that you can't be totally happy with work alone."

◆

I WAS BEING KNOCKED AROUND LIKE A WEEBLE WITH NO BASE. MY CHEST AND CHIN were being jammed into the gravel, sand, and stones with such force that I started to ingest a mouthful. Then came an added flush of brackish water that completely ended any thought of breathing. My last conscious feeling was that of my feet heading toward my back.

"Sandy! Sandy!" I heard voices calling my name. I looked up, squinting, and saw that I was surrounded by a group of half-naked folks. Welcome to the Hamptons.

I had thought I was a better swimmer than that, but this was my first encounter with ocean undertow. Even though you can't see across Lake Michigan (my personal big-water experience), it's certainly not an ocean, so I had never acquired certain critical knowledge, like respect for huge waves.

The Hamptons, New York City's summer playground, was Ellen's happy place, and we had been invited out to Westhampton for the weekend to stay with a good friend of hers who had a seasonal rental. I was all for it, as happiness had not been an emotion pouring from either of us since we had made the move from Manhattan to Queens. The only positive for me was that our new area was a hub for ethnic food, especially Indian. This was the real deal. I walked into small places and was astonished by the quality and seriousness of the cuisine— the setting for my most memorable Indian food ever. Even a simple staple like mulligatawny had the soulful backbone that cooks dream about and a deep, brooding, floral broth that exploded with flavor and heat.

I didn't know it at the time, but Ellen had another plan for this Long Island weekend. It unfolded slowly as we unpacked our bags in a cute, rustic cottage and within a half hour found ourselves planted under a large beach umbrella with icy cold Rolling Rocks to quench our travel thirst. Even with my rude introduction to the ocean, it was hard to not be charmed by the peaceful beauty of the setting.

That night we went to visit Ellen's friend Peter. He was running a seafood restaurant near Hampton Bays, and we had a behind-the-scenes tour and a terrific al fresco dinner. The next few days were filled as Ellen took me to all of her favorite haunts; it was a "best of" tour that starred local crullers, sandwiches, fudge, ice cream, and lobster, which she hawked with the hard-sell zeal of a time-share broker. Then came the closer: she introduced me to her friend Bobby who was opening his first restaurant in Westhampton and just happened to be looking for a "young, talented cook" to take the leap to chef and run his kitchen.

By the end of the weekend, Ellen had closed the deal, and I found myself not just willingly, but excitedly, paging through the Southampton Press with her in search of a rental. It was hard to break the news to Roland because his reaction was not quite what I had expected.

He called his partner, Paul, into the room and said, "Sandy says he's going to be leaving us."

Paul, who never really said much to me over the years, said, "We thought you would be here forever!"

Roland added, "I was thinking of making you my first American saucier!" This made it even harder to leave, as I was overcome by the emotion coming from both of them. But after I explained why, they both let me go and wished me well.

We ended up with an affordable place in the tranquil village of Quogue. The village pretty much consisted of a few houses, a general store, a post office, and a road to the beach; it couldn't have been sleepier and, consequently, more perfect for me. Our small house included a rambling yard. It was the first time in my independent life that I'd had a backyard, and it got me thinking about the possibilities.

Immediately after unpacking in Quogue, the first thing I knew that I needed was a grill. I drove over to the local hardware store where they had a small lineup of Webers ready for the taking. But even at their discount pricing, they were out of my budget.

Then I spotted it. Lo and behold, for about half the price, the Happy Cooker. It looked like a Weber—shiny, black, wood-handled dome. The difference was the inferior weight and thickness of the metal. But the price was right.

Our stove in the house was run on propane and really didn't get very hot, so 80 percent of what I cooked at home was prepared on my Happy Cooker. In the beginning, every nightly dinner was a war. I was determined to be the master of the grill by controlling every nuance of that fire and the dishes that resulted. After months of grilling, I came to realize that you don't control the grill, you become one with the grill. Without sounding too Zen, you respect the grill for what it is; then you work with it. I became a very patient griller and slowly learned the code of the grill: Always wait until the fire is ready. Don't turn the meat before it is seared. Just let things cook.

I quickly learned that the biggest mistake was incessantly moving items around; I had worried that if they stayed in one place for more than six seconds, they would burn. The essence of grilling is the sear and crust you get on the items. If the fire is at the right heat level, you can let that crust form with confidence, and your food won't stick. I used that grill almost every day for the first few months, and as the seasons transitioned to winter, I found myself outside in my parka and gloves, charring away.

After the grill, we needed one more component to complete the suburban ideal, and since children were not immediately on the horizon, we decided a dog would help strengthen the relationship. We brought home Otto D'Amato, a terrier and springer spaniel mix. We thought we wanted a high-energy dog, but Otto continually blurred the line between active and psychotic, with a heavy dose of stubbornness—a perfect homage to his new parents.

An even bigger transition in my life was going from my high-volume, high-pressure job as poissonier at Le Chantilly to being a chef at a small local restaurant. After the first week, I discovered that there was really no transition at all, as these were the prime summer months when any and every self-respecting Manhattanite, also sick of the hustle and bustle, migrated to the Hamptons seeking relaxation. This was a good idea, in theory, but because of the absolute crush of people, it was like being shoved into an Upper East Side closet with 300,000 of your closest strangers, all of whom were annoyed and impatient because, even though they were on holiday, they still had to fight the crowds to get a dinner reservation, a cup of coffee, an ice cream cone, or just get to the other side of the street.

Bobby's restaurant was located right on Main Street in Westhampton. It was a turnkey operation, which meant we should have been able to walk in and just start operating. In this case it meant the key turned in the lock, the door opened . . . and good luck! The front of the house and the bar were in moderately good shape, but the kitchen needed some serious help. Bobby, being a bartender by trade, really had no idea of what the kitchen even minimally required to function, and after a few weeks of working with him, I was worried.

The kitchen was equipped with two small under-counter refrigerators (one with a sandwich top to hold individual ingredients for service), a four-burner range, and a char grill. I could and did work with the range and grill, but the lack of adequate refrigeration was a looming problem. There was a large walk-in about 30 feet from the back door, but that had its own problems—no shelving and no lights. But Bobby did spring for a really cool flashlight to keep right outside the walk-in's door.

Consequently, when business was slow I had just enough inside refrigerated storage for up to 15 customers, so I kept the menu small and picked up fish and vegetables daily at the local market. The dishes were French-influenced, and the menu products reflected the area: blushing pink, charred Block Island swordfish with sharp, billowy mustard mousseline; spicy saffron nage of tilefish and mussels; fresh pea potage St. Germaine; juicy bacon Gruyére burger; cruciferous chef's salad with house-pulled Long Island duck and tarragon-buttermilk dressing.

Bobby would invite people to the restaurant and tell them that, if our food wasn't the best they had on the island, they didn't have to pay. It was tasty enough that no one took him up on his offer, and within a few weeks, we started to generate good word of mouth. As the number of guests increased, it started to get crazy. Eight to 10 times a night I would have to run out to the walk-in to restock. One Saturday night, when I had my hands full, I was juggling the flashlight and digging in the boxes piled up on the floor of the shelf-less walk-in. The flashlight dropped and cracked; I tripped over a box and went flying into the eggs. With yolk and bits of eggshell dripping from my hair, I realized I had gone from fine dining to blind dining. The walk-in was a clown car with no exit. Bobby's answer was to get a new flashlight—the shelves and more indoor refrigeration would have to wait. I was deciding what to do about this dysfunctional situation when the next week my decision was made for me. I went to the bank to cash my check, and the teller told me there were no funds.

Ellen heard from another friend that a restaurant in nearby East Quogue was looking for a cook, so within three days I was behind the line at the New Moon Café on Main Street. At this small restaurant we were serving incredible numbers of people with a crew of fairly inexperienced kitchen and dining room kids. They were working just enough to pay for their food and housing so they could spend their off-hours spit-roasting themselves at the beach as they slept off the previous night's binge. The only professional was the chef/piano player who regularly had to (conveniently) leave the line right during the peak of the dinner rush to plunk out a few songs.

On the bright side, because I had a good pedigree in cooking by then, I could step into any available position on the line, and my time at the New Moon Café became an invaluable learning experience in scratch cooking. After a couple of weeks I was given free reign by the chef to try almost anything—but we were so busy that I barely even had time to get the regular menu items out of the kitchen.

I did get a chance to work on my shucking skills, as there were always a couple of clam dishes on the menu. While in school I had taken a job at a seafood restaurant called Mariner's Harbor, located on the banks of the Hudson River in New Paltz, right across the bridge from the school. It was a high-volume place with a typical week going from 200 people on a Monday to up to 400 or more on weekends. The food was fairly straightforward: simple cuts of grilled and baked fresh fish, the usual fried suspects, and a few simple shellfish casseroles.

The hardest part for me was the shellfish bar. We served fresh-shucked clams—littlenecks (the smallest), top necks (a bit larger), and cherrystones (larger yet)—and oysters, usually Blue Points from around Long Island, with other varieties making guest appearances.

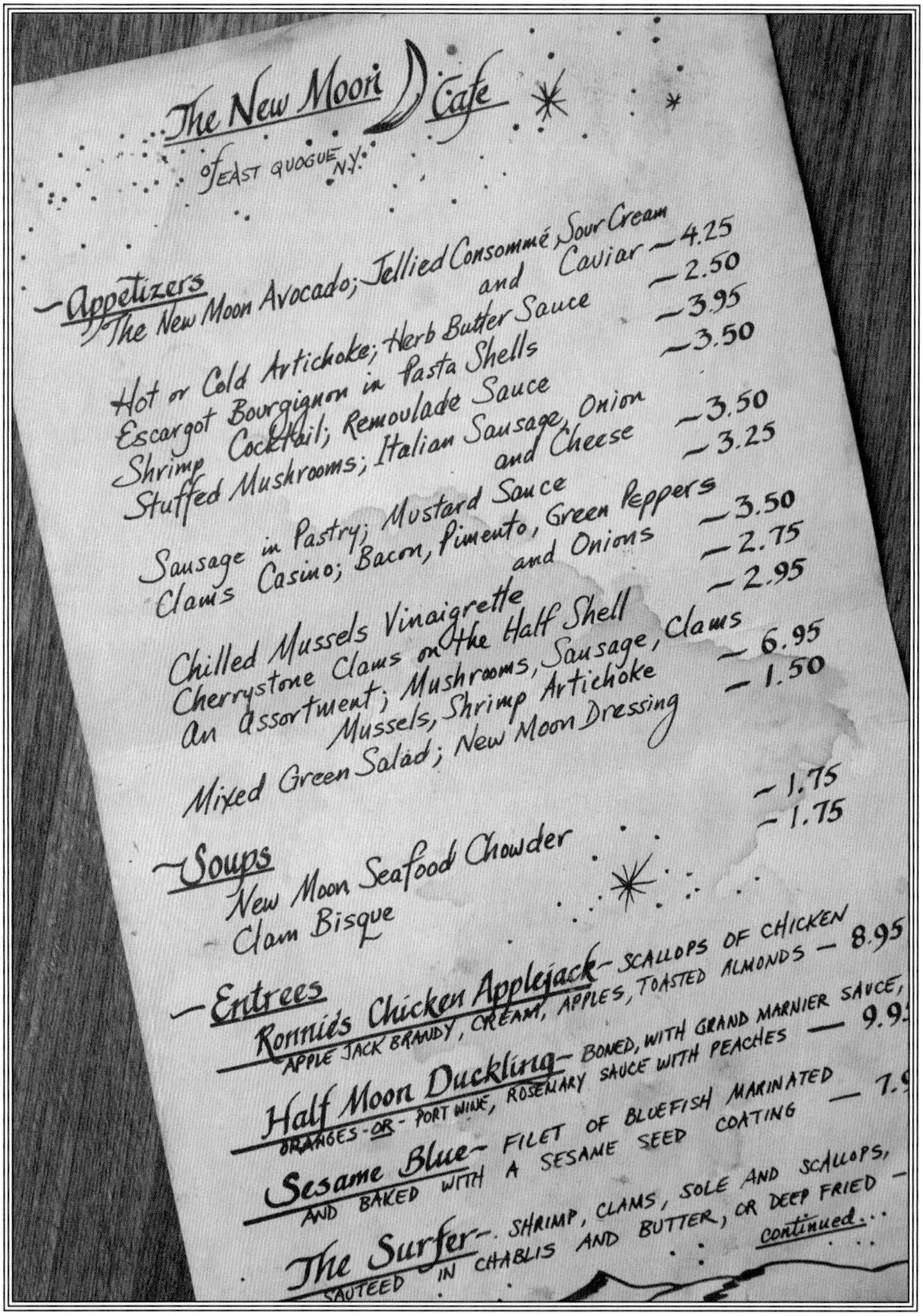

Menu from the New Moon Café in Long Island, New York

Being a Midwest guy, shucking clams and oysters was certainly not in my bag of tricks. I had opened two oysters at an early class at school (not quite the in-depth training I needed), so the Mariner's Harbor manager, Billy Reynolds, took me under his wing. He started by showing me the difference between a clam knife and an oyster knife and the sub-difference between a littleneck knife and a cherrystone knife.

Then came the important part: how to properly open the shellfish without impaling your hand with the blade. This is easier with a shucking glove, which is made of either metal mesh or heavy, cut-proof fabric that protects your hand. With clams, I found it easier to not use the glove as it gave me better control with the smaller ones. And since I was doing other cooking jobs along with shucking, it became a decision based on speed not to go back and forth putting on and taking off the glove.

After a few weeks, I had developed a good touch for shucking and was feeling fairly confident. This feeling proved short-lived as New Year's Eve arrived. As orders started flowing in, I was shucking and plating at a blurring pace. Then the rush hit, and the blurring pace just became a blur—this was the School of Hard Shell Knocks. Billy had to jump in and help dig me out, as I was, as we say in the business, "buried," "in the weeds," or "in the shit."

What I learned from my time there was that shellfish should be icy-cold to shuck and that you should have a professional oyster or clam knife (don't use a regular knife—very dangerous). And the final lesson was, after a New Year's Eve spent shucking shellfish and getting hundreds of tiny nicks in your hand, don't take a coworker's suggestion that straight lemon juice will remove the smell of shellfish from your hands. Yow!

When Labor Day and the end of the season came around, the New Moon started to slow down, and Ronnie, the owner, approached me to ask what my plans were. The chef was heading south to another seasonal job, and Ronnie wanted to know if I was interested in taking over. It turned out to be a pretty sweet deal, as we went from seven days to a low-season four-day (Thursday to Sunday) operation—just me and a dishwasher on Thursday and another kitchen helper added on Fridays, Saturdays, and Sundays. The regular menu was slashed, and I was given carte blanche to create any specials I wanted. It was as close to an ideal job as I had ever had.

By then I was also starting to fully comprehend the great natural resources of Long Island: ultra-fresh fish such as striped bass, swordfish, and bluefish; a plethora of shellfish such as scallops, clams, mussels, and oysters; and of course the lobsters, all a few steps from my front door. I became very familiar with the farms of the North Fork, the fish of the Peconic Bay, and the local Long Island duck farmers, from whom I could pick up fresh ducks daily. All of this was in addition to superb produce and a blossoming wine culture. I was in cook's heaven.

Working a full-time schedule in only four days was the deal-closer. Those three days off became my time to try out new recipes using whatever I picked up on my travels to the farmer's markets and various meat and fish vendors on the island, and to spend more relaxed downtime with Ellen.

◆

THE DAYS WERE GETTING CHILLIER, AND EACH WEEKEND YIELDED DWINDLING NUMBERS from the city. This was chili-time! My first taste of chili was out of a can at my dad's store. I think it was Hormel, and I couldn't have been more excited as lunchtime approached. I would scan the shelves, looking at the pictures on the labels, imagining what they would taste like. I remember the chili con carne having a really tasty-looking picture with big chunks of meat.

After a morning of incessantly bugging my father, he told me to grab a can of the chili and he would heat it up in back. The contents of the can didn't quite have the Hollywood look of the label, which was disappointing. But as we both sat on the hot radiator behind the front checkout, our backsides buffered by layers of the Milwaukee Sentinel, and our feet resting on the pulled-out wooden drawers of the front counter, there wasn't a cozier place to be found. I thought I was full, until my dad unveiled his best trick. He carefully extracted two large Hershey bars that he had placed between the sections of the Sentinel before we started on the chili. As I unwrapped the bar, the chocolate trembled, right at the point before it became molten, and the only sensible way to consume it was to lick it right off the paper. The chocolate blended with the taste of chili that lingered in my mouth—a duet that was sure to make an appearance in my future cooking.

Over the years I made many variations of chili, each one different from the last, as I couldn't come up with the totally satisfying, full taste I was looking for—until that winter in Long Island. I don't know if it came down to just having the time or if Ronnie's Texas drawl was rubbing off on me, but I came up with a chili that captured the round flavor I was looking for. It had a bit of heat but was tempered by the black beans and the richness. I used a small dice of beef chuck rather than ground beef; so it was like a mini stew, and the beef had a wonderful yielding texture that just soaked up the cocoa-laced spices.

By late October, we were strictly on local time, with all of our business coming from the older, year-round retired residents, local merchants, farmers, and fishermen. On many Thursday nights we would all sit at the bar—me, the dishwasher, the bartender, and the server—arguing about whether to watch *Laverne and Shirley* (with appropriate Milwaukee wisecracks directed at me) or *The Waltons*. We were only interrupted when a car would pull up in front of the restaurant, its headlights shining through our windows. We would all scatter to our respective posts, ready to serve; but half the time it was just someone asking for directions, and we would slowly slink back to our bar stools.

One morning a solid rap at the restaurant's back kitchen screen door caught my attention. I looked over and saw that the bright morning sun was completely eclipsed by the husky outline of a local fishmonger, self-named Chubby.

"I've got a surprise for you today!" he called out as he wedged himself through the doorway, each of his large paws grasping a three-foot fish. As he pointed one of the fish, as rigid as a board, toward my face, he proclaimed, "They're still in rigor mortis!"

Chubby was a local legend in the East Quogue area of Long Island. Customarily he would arrive daily with bags of the most pristine bay scallops I had ever experienced. I had always considered scallops a special treat. My first experience with them was similar to my first crab experience: a large box of Mrs. Paul's frozen, breaded scallops. Piping hot out of the oven and dipped in Kraft tartar sauce, they were a sublime experience for a nine-year-old. I tasted my first unbreaded scallops at Fazio's on Fifth during my 12th or 13th birthday party. Then I realized what the flavor of scallops was really like, as they had only been broiled in lemon butter.

Chubby's daily bag drop offered my first taste of fresh Peconic Bay scallops. These incredible morsels were harvested and shucked less than an hour before arriving at the back door. The best way to describe their natural sweetness is, as my friend Gayle would say, like a lush, briny candy; they didn't need any cooking, you could just pop them into your mouth. When they were quickly cooked, though, it only took me one bite to understand the fanatical devotion to fresh bay scallops in that area.

But today, Chubby had caught a beautiful 12-pound striped bass and a slightly smaller bluefish. They were, as usual, pristine, as if they were still swimming. "Well, do you want them both?" he asked. The striped bass was for sure, but as blue things go—I love blueberries, I'm a huge blues music fan, and I'm a true-blue friend. But I hated bluefish.

All my experiences with bluefish were from my time at the CIA. Students were responsible for receiving fish (steward class), prepping fish (butchery), preparing fish (kitchen class), and serving it (service class). Bluefish has high oil content and is very perishable, so the combination of slow and inexperienced student handling when the fish arrived, the slightly improper trimming and cooking of it, and the delayed serving usually meant that you were not tasting the fish at its optimal potential. It was the scourge of the lunch and dinner classes since we students also had to eat whatever we made. The mere mention of bluefish was enough to send student diners scurrying for the exits to escape the funkiness.

As I related my misgivings to Chubby, he said, "I'll give you this one for free because I know after you've had a really fresh bluefish, you'll be buying all I can get you in the future."

I filleted the glistening fish and removed the skin and its red outside bloodline to yield thick filets that looked like slightly darker-hued striped bass. I grilled up a piece with just a bit of salt and pepper. As usual, Chubby didn't disappoint. The oil content of the fish helped it grill up with a golden, crunchy exterior and a moist, flavorful interior. This bluefish had zero relationship to my previous frightening experiences, and from that day on, it became part of my repertoire.

◆

THE PAST FEW MONTHS HAD GOTTEN ME THINKING ABOUT WHAT DIETER HAD SAID, AND I was really feeling a balance and familiarity with the surroundings. It had never crossed my mind until then that the real inhabitants of the island—the farmers, merchants, and year-rounders—gave me a sense of community and place that I had never felt in New York. The last time I had had that feeling was during a stay in Milwaukee. Ellen and I had gone back for Christmas, and we'd really had a good time with the family and old friends. I had forgotten what the area had to offer.

One of the first nights back, my sister Steph and her husband, who had been regularly traveling a bit south of Milwaukee to Chicago's Greektown North neighborhood to get their "Opa!" on, dragged us along to dinner. They were raving about a place called Psistaria, on Lawrence near Western. In direct opposition to the turn-and-burn restaurants—where one's food is literally heaved at you (along with the bill), encouraging you to gulp it down, pay up, and vacate for the next sucker in line—at Psistaria you were encouraged to camp out for the evening, enjoy the impromptu floor show, order lots of food and even more wine, all of which was backed up by servings of a so-called digestif, Ouzo. This sounded to me like a perfectly sensible introduction to the Hellenic culinary arts.

It was a windy, frozen Great Lakes evening as we walked through their front door into a lively and bustling Mediterranean, street fare-type atmosphere. We were immediately seated; we ordered, and the food started to arrive. Even though it was a menu of the greatest hits of the country, being my first time, it was all Greek to me. Saganaki, taramosalata, moussaka, and pastitsio were all prepared with what seemed like a loving grandmother's touch. My favorite dish of the evening was the pan-fried squid, burnished and crisp, and rounded out with the simple, brilliant acid of fresh lemon.

The Greek wines were sturdy rustic reds served alongside the odd white retsina, with its characteristic resin-like taste. Along with the licorice-flavored Ouzo, it was a thoroughly aromatic beverage splurge.

After dinner, as we made our way back to the car, we passed a large, steamed-up window. I peeked in and spotted a line of bowling alleys in full swing. In our happy state we thought, "Why not?" and soon found ourselves, bowling balls in hand and fitted with the handsomest of shoes, whaling away at the pins. Within seconds our pores were oozing retsina, and our conversations were scented with what smelled like a mix of Pine-Sol and Nibs. I didn't remember the drive back to Milwaukee, as I was snoring in the backseat. But I'll never forget the combination of great food, family, and—who knew?—bowling. A heartland trifecta.

I had always thought when I left Milwaukee for cooking school that the direction I wanted to go in with my career would never lead back there. Part of my hesitance was that I had envisioned my eventual ideal restaurant to be a small fine-dining operation. That would be hard enough to sustain even in the largest of metropolitan areas with a lot of tourism like New York, Chicago, San Francisco, and Boston.

During our last few days in Milwaukee, Ellen and I were looking around at restaurants and made a last-minute reservation at Knut Apitz's restaurant, Grenadier's. This was a different experience from my last visits to the city—it turned out fine dining was actually doing quite well in Milwaukee.

I always thought it would have been easier to win the lottery than to personally own a restaurant in New York City. Sure, I could have been an "equity" partner with possibly 2 to 5 percent ownership of a place. But to be an outright owner, I would need to be in a city that was affordable and have local contacts as well. The idea of returning to Milwaukee at that stage of my career was not only starting to make sense, I was actually getting excited thinking about what could be possible there, such as local resources, family, friends, community, and balance. It seemed like a perfect future scenario that even Dieter would approve of.

I talked with Ellen about moving. Although our relationship wasn't Brady Bunch happy, we felt we were both in a better place since leaving New York City, so she agreed with me that it would be a good idea to try the Midwest.

Before we moved, we took a final walk down to Westhampton Beach. The winter surf was turbid and crashing. I thought about how I knew now to take the plunge and dive through the waves, instead of just standing frightened and letting them toss me like a toy. I thought, I guess I did learn something here.

CHAPTER NINE RECIPES

*Poached Oysters with Mint Cream
and Papaya Mignonette*
255

Mustard-Crusted Stuffies
257

*Black Bean Chili with
Cheddar Cheese Toast*
259

*Peppered Bluefish with Glazed Baby
Turnips, Lemon Turnip Green Broth*
262

*Sautéed Peconic Bay
Scallops with Applejack*
263

POACHED OYSTERS WITH MINT CREAM AND PAPAYA MIGNONETTE

Traditional mignonette is simply red wine vinegar, chopped shallot, and coarse pepper. This preparation is all dressed up for the New Year with a small dice of papaya and an herb cream, which helps keep the sauce and oyster flavor lingering on your palate after they disappear.

SERVES 4

> 24 large oysters in the shell (Blue Points, Malpeques, or Wellfleets) washed well in water
>
> 8 ounces (227 g) ripe papaya, peeled, seeded, and cut in small dice
>
> 1 jalapeño pepper, stem, seeds, and veins removed and cut in very small dice (brunoise) (optional)
>
> 1–2 shallots, diced very small (you will need ¼ cup [1 ounce]), rinsed in cold water and drained
>
> 1 tablespoon red wine vinegar
>
> 2 teaspoons fresh lime juice
>
> ¾ teaspoon coarsely ground black pepper, plus additional to taste
>
> ⅛ teaspoon kosher salt, plus additional to taste
>
> ½ cup (115 g) sour cream
>
> ¼ cup (½ ounce [14 g]) fresh mint leaves, very finely chopped

1. Carefully shuck the oysters. Reserve the oysters and liquid in a stainless sauté pan. (Rinse and reserve the bottom shells for presentation.) Place the sauté pan over high heat for about 30 seconds to just bring the liquid up to a simmer. When they just start to curl on the edges, remove the oysters, with a slotted spoon (do not overcook). Cool in the refrigerator.

2. Reduce the oyster liquid to ¼ cup (59 mL) and strain into a bowl. To the bowl, add the papaya, the (optional) jalapeño, the shallots, the vinegar, the lime juice, the ¾ teaspoon black pepper, and the ⅛ teaspoon salt and mix lightly. Refrigerate the Papaya Mignonette for 1 hour to blend the flavors. Mix the sour cream and mint, adjust the seasoning with salt and pepper, and reserve in the refrigerator.

3. Divide the reserved dry bottom shells onto 4 plates. Place a dollop of the reserved mint cream on each shell. Place 1 cold oyster on each of the dollops and top each oyster with 1 teaspoon of the Papaya Mignonette; serve immediately.

MUSTARD-CRUSTED STUFFIES
(Stuffed Clams)

Stuffies, or stuffed baked clams, are one of the great American contributions by New Englanders. I use cherrystone clams (with side muscles trimmed) that are one size smaller than the Quahogs and more tender when cooked. The clams are mixed with scalded spinach and mustard greens, then topped with a crisp, mustard breadcrumb crust. This is a light-handed preparation that lets the true flavor of the clams shine through.

A quick tip for sand-free clams is after steaming and removing the clams from the shell, give them a dunk in the reserved clam juice and lift them out to release any sand that might have been stuck in them after steaming.

MAKES 24 CLAM HALVES

>7 tablespoons (104 mL) regular olive oil (divided)
>
>1 large onion (10 ounces [284 g]), cut in small dice
>
>3 bay leaves
>
>2 sprigs fresh thyme
>
>4 cloves garlic, finely chopped (divided)
>
>¾ cup (178 mL) dry white wine
>
>24 cherrystone clams (about 5–6 pounds [2.27–2.72 kg])
>
>10 ounces (284 g) fresh spinach, stems removed
>
>½ teaspoon kosher salt (divided), plus additional to taste
>
>¼ teaspoon freshly ground black pepper (divided), plus additional to taste
>
>8 ounces (227 g) mustard greens, stems removed and cut in ½-inch (13-mm) strips
>
>1 tablespoon mustard seeds
>
>Grated zest of 1 lemon
>
>2 ounces (57 g) grated Parmesan cheese
>
>Mustard Crumbs (recipe follows)

1. Place a 2-gallon (7.57-L) pot over medium-high heat. Add 2 tablespoons of the oil and half of the onions and sauté for 2 minutes. Add the bay leaves, the thyme, and half of the garlic and stir for 30 seconds. Add the white wine and bring up to a boil.

2. Add the clams, cover, and cook for 4 minutes. Toss the clams and cook for 3 more minutes, then start removing the opened clams and place them in a strainer. Continue cooking and removing the clams until they are all removed from the pot (discard any clams that do not open). Slowly strain the clam liquid through 4 layers of cheesecloth, stopping at the end if you see sand, and reserve.

(RECIPE CONTINUES ON PAGE 258)

(RECIPE CONTINUED FROM PAGE 257)

3. Place a 12-inch (30-cm) heavy-bottomed sauté pan (I prefer a black steel pan) over very high heat. In a large bowl, toss the spinach leaves with 2 tablespoons of the oil, ¼ teaspoon of the salt, and ⅛ teaspoon of the pepper. When the pan is very hot, place half of the spinach in the pan and toss with a tongs until it is scalded (just wilted); remove to a tray. Scald the remaining spinach and remove it to the tray.

4. In the same bowl, toss the mustard greens with 2 tablespoons of the oil and the remaining ¼ teaspoon of the salt and ⅛ teaspoon of the pepper and repeat the scalding process. Place the tray of greens in the refrigerator to cool.

5. Wipe out the pan and reduce the heat to medium. Add the remaining 1 tablespoon of the oil and the mustard seeds and cook for 10 seconds. Add the remaining onions and cook for 1 minute. Add the remaining garlic and cook for 30 seconds. Add 1 cup (237 mL) of the reserved clam liquid and the lemon zest and reduce by ¾ (to ¼ cup [59 mL]).

6. Remove the cooked clams from the shells. Reserve 24 of the nicest shell halves, and rinse and dry them to prepare for filling. Trim off the side muscles and the top hard triangular part from the clams. Cut the trimmed clams in 2 to 3 pieces and mix with the scalded spinach and mustard greens, the reduction from the pan, and the cheese. Season to taste with salt and pepper.

7. Preheat the oven to 450°F (230°C). Divide the mixture among the 24 reserved shells and sprinkle with the Mustard Crumbs. Bake for about 5 to 7 minutes, or until the Stuffed Clams are brown and hot (do not overbake or the clams will get dry).

For the Mustard Crumbs:

½ cup (54 g) bread crumbs

2 tablespoons extra virgin olive oil

1 tablespoon Dijon mustard

1 tablespoon mustard seeds, toasted for 1 minute in a sauté pan, then crushed

¼ teaspoon kosher salt

20 grinds freshly ground black pepper

1. Mix all of the ingredients together.

BLACK BEAN CHILI WITH CHEDDAR CHEESE TOAST

One Saturday morning I woke up to my mother in the midst of a large production of making chili. The whole kitchen was in full swing with the electric skillet browning off the beef; the table covered with chopped onions, peppers, and tomatoes; and a huge soup pot in waiting on the stove ready to bubble away all afternoon until the chili was just right. My dad said my mother made the best chili—he was right, and I hope they would like my incarnation as well.

SERVES 4 TO 6

> 2 tablespoons grapeseed oil
>
> 4 ounces (114 g) bacon, cut into ¼-inch thick matchstick-sized pieces
>
> 2¼ pounds (1.02 kg) boneless chuck roast, trimmed of fat and cut in ¼- to ½-inch (6- to 13-mm) cubes
>
> Kosher salt and freshly ground black pepper, to taste
>
> 2 medium onions (1 pound [454 g]), cut in small dice
>
> 1 poblano pepper (4 ounces [114 g]), stem and seeds removed and cut in small dice
>
> 4 cloves garlic, finely chopped
>
> 3 tablespoons (24 g) medium chili powder
>
> 2 tablespoons ground cumin
>
> 1 tablespoon smoked paprika
>
> 1 tablespoon unsweetened cocoa
>
> 1 tablespoon achiote (annatto seed) paste
>
> 1 (12-ounce [360-mL]) beer
>
> 1 (12-ounce [341-g]) can diced tomatoes in sauce
>
> 1½ cups (356 mL) unsalted chicken stock
>
> 1 (15-ounce [426-g]) can black beans, beans and liquid separated
>
> Cheddar Cheese Toast (recipe follows)

1. Place a large stew pot over high heat. Place the grapeseed oil and bacon in the pot. Sauté the bacon until lightly golden, remove, and reserve.

2. Season the meat with salt and pepper and sauté in batches so it is not crowded in the pot. When the meat is browned, remove and reserve.

(RECIPE CONTINUES ON PAGE 260)

(RECIPE CONTINUED FROM PAGE 259)

3. Add the onions and poblano peppers to the pot and sauté for 3 minutes. Add the garlic and sauté for 30 seconds. Add the browned meat back to the pot. Add the chili powder, cumin, paprika, cocoa, and achiote paste and sauté for 30 seconds. Add the beer to deglaze the pot and simmer for 2 minutes. Add the tomatoes, stock, and bean liquid and simmer, covered but stirring regularly (do not let it scorch on bottom), until the meat is tender, about 45 minutes.

4. Add the beans and reserved bacon and bring back to a simmer. Adjust the seasoning with salt and pepper and serve with the Cheddar Cheese Toast.

For the Cheddar Cheese Toast:

> **4 ficelles or 2 baguettes**
>
> **¼ cup (59 mL) extra virgin olive oil**
>
> **Kosher salt and freshly ground black pepper, to taste**
>
> **4 ounces (114 g) sliced cheddar cheese**

1. Preheat the broiler. Cut the bread in half lengthwise. Brush the olive oil on the split sides and season with salt and pepper. Place the bread under the broiler and broil until it is golden brown.

2. Lay the cheese slices on the browned side, melt the cheese under the broiler, cut in serving pieces, and serve.

PEPPERED BLUEFISH WITH GLAZED BABY TURNIPS, LEMON TURNIP GREEN BROTH

This dish is best made at the peak of the farmer's markets when you can find a nice bunch of just-dug early turnips with really fresh green tops that will be used to enhance the broth (if you can't find turnips, radishes with tops will do). But the real key is just using the freshest fish you can find.

SERVES 4

4 small turnips with fresh green tops (about 4 ounces [114 g]), greens removed and reserved; turnips peeled and cut in 1-inch (2.5-cm) wedges

1 cup (237 mL) unsalted chicken stock

Pinch kosher salt

3 tablespoons (45 mL) extra virgin olive oil (divided)

Kosher salt and freshly ground black pepper to taste

1 teaspoon granulated sugar

Zest of ½ lemon and juice of 1 lemon (you will need 2 tablespoons plus ½ teaspoon juice, divided)

2 tablespoons Tellicherry peppercorns, crushed with the back of a pot to about the size of ⅙–⅛ of a whole peppercorn, fine pepper sifted out (using a medium strainer) and coarse-ground pepper reserved

4 (6- to 7-ounce [170- to 199-g]) skinless fillets bluefish (you may substitute striped bass)

2 shallots thinly sliced

2 cloves garlic, finely chopped

½ cup (119 mL) dry white wine

1. Cover the turnip wedges with the stock, add the pinch of salt and bring up to a simmer until the turnips are just tender, about 4 to 5 minutes. Strain and reserve the turnip stock.

2. Place a 12-inch (30-cm) sauté pan over high heat. When the pan is hot, add 1 tablespoon of the olive oil. When hot, add the cooked turnips, season lightly with salt and black pepper, and sauté until golden brown, about 4 minutes. Add the sugar and lemon zest and toss together. Add ½ teaspoon of the lemon juice, toss together to glaze, remove from the pan, and reserve warm.

3. Clean the pan and put it back over medium-high heat. Divide the crushed peppercorns evenly over the tops of the bluefish and press in. Season lightly with salt. Add the remaining 2 tablespoons of the oil to the pan and sauté the fish until it is golden brown on both sides, about 3 to 4 minutes per side.

4. Remove the fish, add the shallots and garlic to the pan, and sauté for 1 minute. Add the wine and the remaining 2 tablespoons of the lemon juice and reduce by half. Add the reserved turnip stock and reduce to ⅓ to ½ cup (79 to 119 mL). Place the stock and reserved greens in a blender and purée until fine. Adjust the seasoning with salt and pepper. Divide the fish and turnips among 4 plates and divide the turnip green broth around; serve.

SAUTÉED PECONIC BAY SCALLOPS WITH APPLEJACK

I've eaten a lot of wonderful fresh scallops in my lifetime but the best I've ever had, no question, are the Peconic Bay's. When I left Long Island and moved back to Milwaukee, I would still use the connections I had to get the Peconic's overnight air-freighted to use there. In 1984, that all stopped as a brown tide algae bloom covered the bay and they were about 90 percent wiped out. Thankfully they have come back (although in lesser numbers) and are worth searching out.

SERVES 2

> 3 teaspoons clarified butter (divided)
> 1 Granny Smith apple, peeled, cut in half, cored, then each half cut in 6 wedges
> Kosher salt and freshly ground black pepper, to taste
> 12 ounces (341 g) Peconic Bay scallops
> 2 tablespoons chopped shallots
> ¼ cup (59 mL) plus 2 teaspoons applejack brandy (divided)
> ½ cup (119 mL) heavy cream
> 1 tablespoon chopped chives

1. Place a nonstick sauté pan over high heat. Add 2 teaspoons of the clarified butter, and when the butter is hot, add the apple slices and season lightly with salt and pepper. Sauté the apples for 1½ minutes per side, or until golden brown, then remove from the pan and reserve.

2. Add the remaining 1 teaspoon of the clarified butter to the pan. When starting to smoke, season the scallops with salt and pepper, then slide them into the pan. Toss quickly and let them color for 30 seconds. Add the shallots and toss once. Add ¼ cup (59 mL) of the applejack, then remove the scallops with a slotted spoon (do not overcook the scallops).

3. Add the apples back to the pan, then add the cream and let it reduce by half. Pour any accumulated scallop juices back into the pan and reduce (you will need ⅓ cup [79 mL] of sauce). Add the remaining 2 teaspoons of the applejack and the scallops and turn off the heat. Adjust the seasoning with salt and pepper and add the chives. Remove the apples and divide onto 2 plates. Divide the scallops over the apples, pour the sauce over, and serve.

10

BACK TO MILWAUKEE: JOHN BYRON'S

"SANDY?"

"Trisha?"

Well, isn't this awkward.

When Ellen and I decided to make the move to Milwaukee, we needed to secure a place before we moved and decided to work with my mother to find a suitable apartment. She went through the rental ads with us over the phone, and we picked out places for her to check out. She found a reasonable one-bedroom in a nice residential east side village, Shorewood, which was right on the Milwaukee city line and tucked between the Milwaukee River and Lake Michigan. It was convenient, being only minutes from downtown Milwaukee. We were on the third floor of a brick 1930s apartment building with windows that overlooked the main drag, Oakland Avenue.

After we moved our furniture in, I took a few boxes down to the storage room and who is the very first person I run into after being gone from Milwaukee for 10 years? Trisha, my last girlfriend in Milwaukee, who had broken up with me a couple of months before I left for New York. She was now married, and she and her husband were the building's on-premises managers. After some really excellent small talk, I stumbled back upstairs trying to understand how that had just happened.

Now that Ellen and I had settled into our weirdly comfortable digs, the first order of business was finding gainful employment. Ellen found a waitressing position at a hot-spot restaurant, the Coffee Trader on Downer Avenue. I was looking for a cook's position and interviewed with the executive chef at the University Club. He had previously worked in New York City at the 21 Club, and after looking over my resume, he told me I was overqualified for a line cook position. He suggested that I should really be looking for a chef's position.

At the time there weren't any good chef positions to be found, so I took a line position at Harold's under Chef Axel Dietrich. I really liked working for him; besides being a talented chef, he was a real gentleman. About a month into my time there, I saw an ad for a chef posi-

Angie and me with entire staff at John Byron's, early '80s

tion at a place called John Byron's and went in for an interview with the manager, Stan, and John "Byron" Burns, the namesake owner of the restaurant. It was an interesting proposition but a tall order. The restaurant, located on the third floor of the 40-story First Wisconsin Center (the tallest building in the state), had been without a chef for the last six months, and John's aspiration for it was that it would become the main outpost for fine dining and wine in Milwaukee.

I wasn't sure how the interview went but found out quickly the next day when Peter called and said he had gotten a reference call from them. They had asked him if he thought I could handle the job, to which he replied, "Handle the position? You'll be lucky if he *accepts* the position!"

After Stan called me with an offer, I got really nervous about giving my notice to Axel, after only being there for a month. But he was genuinely happy for me and sent me off with nothing but good wishes—something I have never forgotten.

The next weekend we were at home watching hockey, a sport I usually have as much interest in as hacky sack, but this was the 1980 Winter Olympics. We were at the edge of our seats as Al Michaels made his iconic call, "Do you believe in miracles?" I thought, *Yes, yes I do!* I was so inspired: I taught myself how to install a new tile kitchen floor, worked really hard on Ellen's and my relationship, was starting a new chef position with the sky as my limit, and even noticed that Otto had a newfound serenity which he demonstrated with sporadic five-minute periods of actually lying prone and quiet.

◆

WITH THE HIGH OCCUPANCY OF THE FIRST WISCONSIN BUILDING AT ALMOST 7,000 people, John Byron's had a very good lunch business going. The dinner business was another story. At 5 p.m. the whistle blew, and they were all off to the burbs. Trying to get any of them to return to their place of work for dinner was a challenge. The lunch crew was pretty tight, as they were used to being busy. But the dinner crew was led by Tim, a fledgling student minister who was more interested in practicing Sunday sermons than in cooking and had the metabolism of a retired snail.

The main reason I was hired was to revamp the lunch and dinner menu and try to start building a dinner following. I knew I needed to bring in a stronger team, and that started with Kenny, a talented cook from St. Lucia, who became my first sous chef. After working with him for a few weeks, I put Kenny in charge of running the lunch line; then I started working on fine-tuning every dish on both menus.

The biggest seller at lunch was soup, and the house soup I inherited was a broccoli, bacon, and cheddar combination called Bode (*bow-dee*). It was named after the person who first made it for Heinemann's restaurants, which was an independent group of restaurant/bakery/ coffee shops that John's grandfather Byron Heinemann started in 1923. Bode turned out to be the catalyst for the first power struggle in my young position.

When I started at the restaurant, all of the soups where made at the Heinemann's commissary, which supplied all of the restaurants. I decided I wanted to make all of our soups in-house instead. After a couple of weeks, one of the owners walked into the kitchen and handed Kenny a recipe for Bode from the commissary. He came to me and asked if he should use it. I immediately went to Stan the manager and asked if I indeed was the chef at the restaurant (the ownership had gotten into the practice of micromanaging the cooks during the times when there was no chef). Stan relayed to me that the three owners had commented that the soup had changed, and I assured him that they were right. I was now using fresh broccoli instead of frozen and had refined the thick, stew-like broth (that had been filled with undissolved roux balls) into a silky, viscous broth.

After that day, our soup became broccoli-cheddar soup, and Bode was only seen sporadically on the Heinemann's restaurant menus. I told Stan I had no problem with criticism, but I had a large problem with anyone telling my cooks how to do their jobs and that if it didn't go through me first, I had no reason to be there. After that, all drive-by critiques came right to me and I was able to, for the first time, take total command of a kitchen.

In the beginning, dinner business on weekends was fine, but building the weekdays was a slow process. I looked at it as a chance to try out all the ideas I had used, or had hoped to use, while I was coming up. But there was only so much food I could prep for the five to eight customers who might show up. Most nights I would sit in the back room and play hangman with the waitresses between orders. Thankfully, that was short-lived; a few good reviews and stories about the place started a steady rise in dinner business.

◆

I'M ALWAYS ASKED WHERE MY INSPIRATION COMES FROM. WELL, IF YOU TAKE A WALK through any local farmer's market, part of that question will be answered. Whether it's a perfectly ripened cheese, a bronzed smoked slab of bacon, a deep vermillion side of tuna, or a bunch of tiny red radishes with vibrant green leaves, inspiration comes from a perfect product.

When I started at John Byron's in 1980, I began to source out any indigenous product the city and state had to offer. In the case of produce, that meant perfect *seasonal* product. A farmer's market is my candy store, and like a five-year-old, I'm hard to control. The most excruciating decision is what *not* to buy—I want it all. But I did, and still do, approach with a plan.

My first time to any new market, I get there early and walk up and down the aisles to see what's there. Then I go back and buy small samples of multiple fruits and vegetables from select vendors, trying to find the ones with the best flavor; this helps to expedite future visits because I find out which farmers have the soil and picking practices that yield, say, a perfect acid-sweet balance in a tomato, or a tender, snappy, sweet string bean with no trace of starch. This aspect of my palate was a direct result of those early mornings with my dad—I couldn't understand back then why, at 5 a.m., he was making me chomp down on a raw bean or a floret of broccoli when all I wanted was a short stack of pancakes and crispy sausage. But I learned that judging most products in their naked state gives you a true measure of their quality, as there is nowhere to hide any flaws. After my third or fourth visit to a market, I felt it was time to strike up a relationship with my favorite farmers and ask them what looked good in the fields and what was being picked in the coming week.

Upon my return to the restaurant, the cooks met my thrice-weekly jaunts to the West Allis market with a mixture of excitement and trepidation. I'd get back about 2 p.m. and had to get a few helpers to unload bag after bag of beautiful produce. This was the exciting part as each bag was an unexpected gift. Then came the trepidation as we scrambled to change the menu for that evening's service starting at 5 p.m. The payoff was the reaction we would get from customers, as they were as excited to be consuming produce that was hours away from the soil as we were preparing it.

Summer was moving into its prime. I had a few months as chef under my belt, and the job was going great. I loved the freedom I had to put together menus at a moment's notice based on the fresh local markets. I finally had the kitchen staff I wanted, and we were all on the same page. And I even had a really good relationship with the front of the house, as the entire restaurant was working together as a team with a common goal.

This wonderful work life stood in stark contrast to my marriage. All the positive feelings that were incubated around the winter Olympic time seemed to follow a parallel trajectory downward, with the country boycotting the Summer Olympics in Moscow. The only positive was that we had both really tried to make our marriage work. I had never quit at anything, but we both knew what we had been denying: we were great friends, but our relationship as husband and wife had been over for years. No one was to blame; we were just two very different people. After a mutual no-fault divorce, Ellen moved back to New York, and I once again found myself single.

By the time fall came around my family and friends were casually setting me up with various "chance encounters" and a few blind dates, and I quickly realized I hadn't lost it—I was still as awkwardly smooth as ever. I felt most at home with my fellow work crew, and they became the core of my social life.

A couple of my good new friends, Jeannie, a waitress at Byron's, and her husband, Tom, planned a large party at their house in the suburbs. I was looking forward to going and even had a date, of sorts. She was a close friend and had dated my friend Mark while they were in college. They had not been together for years, and she and I were so close for so many years that it was almost like dating a sibling for both of us; but we always had a good time.

Two days before the party, she came down with the flu, so I was soloing for the evening. The day before the party, I was passing time talking with a cocktail waitress at work whom I had been joking around with since she started. The cocktail waitresses at Byron's, because of the location of the bar and their erratic hours, were usually outside of the kitchen/dining room loop.

Because of that, she had not heard about the party, so I casually mentioned that it would be fun if she showed up. I gave her the address—all the while hoping she would be there.

About one hour after I arrived at the party, Angie appeared. We were just starting to pick teams to play charades, and in a low-key way, I made sure that we were on the same team. By the time we were well into the game, it was as if the room had gone quiet and we were the only people playing. I was enchanted: I was with this arresting, funny, sharp-as-hell woman, and she seemed interested in me. *Are you kidding me!* After a night of drinking and charades, we ended up being the last people at the party. Jeannie and Tom finally told us they were going to bed and to just let ourselves out. I eventually walked Angie to her car in the minus-10-degree weather, and we talked through the slightly lowered driver's-side window of her '70 Chevy Impala. After what seemed like an hour, we both reluctantly said our 35th goodbye.

As she backed out of the long, winding driveway, she went smack into a large snow bank. After 45 minutes of the Wisconsin heave-ho-back-and-forth ballet to try and release the car, I gave up and had to go back to the house to wake up Tom. He came to the door in his robe, glared at me, and then grunted where I could find the shovel. I dug the car out, and after our mini adventure, I wouldn't let her leave until she agreed to meet me the next weekend for drinks.

Cataldo's, located on Brady just east of Van Buren, was the site of our next rendezvous. We stopped in for a drink but stayed for the music. The owner, Carlo, had one of the best selections of '50s and '60s rhythm and blues music, both familiar and obscure, in the city. This was pre-karaoke, but after a few drinks, I didn't need a microphone to get me started. As retro hit after hit played, my voice started at a low hum. Then sporadic words started spilling out, and finally this evolved into my singing along with the chorus. And as "Under the Boardwalk" transitioned into "I Only Have Eyes for You," I had a big finish, with a face-to-face serenade, my voice at full tilt. It must have been love for Angie not to bolt for the door.

Our plan to have just a few drinks turned into our having dinner and staying until the bar closed. I found that singing really built a terrific appetite, so I ordered the breaded pork chops; and Angie chose the stuffed shells. The shells were homemade and delicious, and our assessment of the food was not influenced by our altered states. As Angie dabbed the corner of her mouth after decimating every shell in sight, I realized at that moment that I was with someone who had a similar affection for food. With the music in the background, I found that even with my mouth full, I could still hum along.

Our casual meetings were great, but I thought it was time for a proper date. I picked Angie up at her grandmother's home on the east side where she was living while she attended UW Milwaukee. I rang the bell on the back door, and she let me into the hallway. She quickly grabbed her coat off the hook and said, "Smell that? I have to eat that later." It was the unmistakable smell of cabbage. Her grandmother, Martha, with her Polish roots, was a cabbage maven. It was a biweekly experience, and I found that Angie had intended no disdain as she waxed lyrically about cabbage with melted butter in the same way I spoke about spiedini.

My first introduction to Three Brothers Restaurant had come through my sister Steph. I was still in my early teens at the time, but she was already a budding bon vivant around Milwaukee and had dined there on a date. She was so enamored with the place that she talked my folks into going for a weekend family dinner. I remember my dad driving around and around, trying to calmly follow her directions (she was a bit directionally challenged at that time), when he finally just turned sharply off her path and stumbled across the restaurant.

Upon entering, I was immediately taken by the warm glow of the shaded table lamps, each nestled on mismatched home-style dining tables; they softly calmed the packed dining room. I knew we were in good, confident hands as we were seated and made to feel like we were part of the family. As the food started to arrive, it was certainly clear this was a family I wanted to be a part of.

So Three Brothers became my logical choice for our date that night, as we were doubling with my sister and her date. It was Angie's first time, and the restaurant couldn't have been a better choice. She went straight for the goulash, and I went back and forth—the roasted lamb, the goose, the duck—before finally ending up with the crispy suckling pig. Along with the entrées we had an obligatory burek for the table. This was only obligatory because it was so perfect: myriad layers of crispy, buttery phyllo dough encasing wonderfully seasoned spinach and cheese. I think it was halfway through the burek when Angie decided I could be "The One."

Just to seal the deal, after we talked about a common love of circa-1980 Michael Jackson, it was off to Victor's for dancing—and a bit of Negroni slurping—that ended with a closing-time sing-a-long of "Camelot" (as performed by Robert Goulet) that never failed to get the stragglers (i.e., us) out. This date had been more than proper. Without that night of burek, goulash, Goulet, and Michael's "hee-hee-hee," the story of Angie and me might have had a different ending.

◆

BY 1982, ANGIE AND I HAD BEEN DATING FOR ABOUT TWO YEARS. WE HAD PLANNED A summer trip to visit my friend TJ in Florida for a week, followed up by a second week in New Orleans. My plan for this vacation was to propose to Angie, and I figured going to Florida first would give TJ (my future best man) a chance to meet Angie. Then I would pop the question on the last night in New Orleans at a restaurant where I had made a reservation two months earlier.

New Orleans had always had a very personal place in my memories. My paternal grand-mother's transplanted Sicilian family was from Gretna, a close suburb, so I had always felt a kinship with the city. After having visited many times, I became infatuated with its unique-ness and obvious charm.

The first week in Florida was perfect: great weather, great friends, and great food. Once we arrived in New Orleans, we checked in at a small guesthouse on Chartres Street in the French Quarter. We dropped off our luggage and walked a block down the street to see a small queue in front of a storefront. It was 4:30, and people were lining up to get into K-Paul's restaurant, which opened at 5 p.m. Chef Paul Prudhomme had opened his first restaurant a few years earlier; and it was a must-visit, so we jumped in line. At the time, many young American chefs were breaking away from the enclosed boundaries of French cuisine that had controlled the American fine-dining scene for decades. Although most were French trained, they were taking indigenous local products and mixing in regional techniques to be at the forefront of what came to be called New American cuisine and changed the way we looked at food—and K-Paul's was at the top of that list.

At 5 p.m. sharp, we were seated at a four-top; then surprisingly another couple was seated with us (our first experience with community seating). Conversation was strained at the be-ginning, but after the first martini with pickled jalapeños was drained, gosh darn if Marge and Harold from Montgomery, Alabama, hadn't become our best friends for life. Angie had the restaurant's signature blackened redfish (the dish that started the whole blackened rage around the country). I had soft-shell crabs, stuffed with lump crabmeat and served with bé-arnaise sauce.

Dinner was amazing and a perfect start to the week. The proposal—that didn't go nearly as well. At the hotel, before the last night's dinner, Angie started crying, and I asked what was wrong.

"I really thought you were going to propose on this trip," she cried.

"Well, I was . . . at dinner tonight—but how about now? You want to get married?"

Not as perfect as planned, but in retrospect that might have been for the best because the dinner that evening was a disaster. It was an evening of rude service—and the food! I had frog legs meunière that where served in a large bowl; there was so much butter that the legs were bobbing askew, as if they were screaming for a lifeguard to rescue them. The consolation prize was a clown-size loaf of pale, insipid bread-matter that would have made a perfect life raft for those drowning appendages. I couldn't believe this schlock house had made me mail ahead a $50 deposit to hold the reservation! After we finished, Angie asked if, considering the dinner, I would still have proposed. I told her no—I would have waited a few months for her birthday.

◆

INSPIRATION COMES IN MANY STRANGE FORMS. IN MY CASE IT USUALLY COMES WHEN I least expect it, or even want it. For instance, a rambling thought will emerge in the middle of the night. As I'm still three-quarters asleep, I'll fumble in the dark for the pen and paper that is always next to the bed, only to wake up the next morning to find indecipherable scribbling that almost requires an FBI code-breaker to decipher it.

Another time, it might just come when your wife drags you (under mild protest) to a small tearoom for what you just know won't be a proper or satisfying lunch. That happened to me at a small place called Bits of Britain, in Bay View, south of Milwaukee. I had visions of fluffy finger sandwiches piled on lace doilies as we sat surrounded by a bevy of wide-brimmed floral hats that would make it impossible to navigate a course from our table to the exit. I was pleasantly surprised to walk in and see a case filled with a trencherman's dream of deeply golden, glistening meat-filled pies, and rustic, crusty pastries. If they tasted as good as they looked, this would be a *more* than satisfying lunch.

We sat down and ordered, and along with the lamb and beef meat pies and requisite tea, Angie ordered a side of mushy peas—perfect pub fare. The pies were crisp and juicy, and the most surprising part was the mushy peas; coarsely mashed and savory, they really came to life with a bit of malt vinegar.

Back in the kitchen when I was putting together a spring dish of lemon-cured scallops, those peas were my inspiration. And a tart raisin vinaigrette was the link that brought the crusty seared sea scallops and the bacon-infused pea mush together. Bits of Britain helped me to get over my fear of tearooms.

◆

EVERYONE'S PERSONAL AND PROFESSIONAL LIVES CONTAIN DEFINING MOMENTS. AT times you make things happen. Other times, they just happen.

After going to culinary school and cooking in New York during my formative years, I had mixed feelings when I decided to move back to Milwaukee. I was a fairly competitive guy working at one of the best French restaurants in the country. It just seemed that New York City was the logical place to be. It was the epicenter of cooking and media attention, and if you wanted to jump-start your career, you were in the right place.

Milwaukee, on the other hand, was not the media center of the Midwest, let alone the country. But it was a place that could provide balance to a life that really had none. And I accepted the fact that I would spend my days working away in relative obscurity surrounded by family, friends, and a good quality of life. I had the freedom to cook as I wanted and the time to really enjoy my off hours.

Then one day the "relative obscurity" thing took a left turn. In 1984, during my fourth year at Byron's, I received a letter from *Food and Wine* magazine asking for my recipe for grilled veal with sundried tomatoes, olives, and fresh sage for the restaurant recipe column located on the beginning pages of the magazine. I happily sent in the recipe and included a few menus from John Byron's. I was flattered they had asked, but really didn't think much would come of it.

A few weeks later I received a call from one of the magazine's editors. She said, and I quote, "I don't mean to sound provincial, but what are you doing making this type of food in Milwaukee?" I nearly asked her to wait a moment while I put down the phone so I could turn down the fire under the big kettle of vittles and possum I had boilin' away on the stove. I assured her that folks in Milwaukee, and many other cities and towns between the culinary capitals of New York and Los Angeles/San Francisco, also enjoyed eating and supporting well-made food.

Less than a year later, from that small recipe placement, I received a letter letting me know that I had been included in *Food and Wine's* list of "Hot New Chefs of 1985," and surprisingly enough, the majority of the chefs were from national media-deficient areas around the country. Who said you could never go home again?

◆

IT'S ALL YOUR STATE OF MIND. AS LONG AS I'VE BEEN COOKING PROFESSIONALLY, EVERY one of those years has been packed with new thoughts and ideas. And along with gaining professional experience and working at mastering my craft, I've lived with the concept that there is always a better way. I'm not saying that I'm never satisfied with my work, but I'm always looking to improve it. This may explain the recurring feeling I have whenever I do any type of repetitive skill.

At times the prevailing attitude among young cooks seems to be that they've perfected a new skill after just two or three attempts. Often it's not long before you hear the confident statement, "I already know how to do that. How about something *new*?" As much as I understand the need for new knowledge, it rankles me that someone thinks they have mastered any skill after a second or third try.

After all these years, any time I'm chopping a bunch of parsley (one of my earliest repetitive jobs), I feel just like an apprentice as I wash the bunch, agitate, and lift the sprigs out of the water (to leave any dirt behind), spin them dry, pick off the tender leaves (saving the stems for stock), and start chopping with my chef's knife that has been previously sharpened (at home and off the clock, thank you). And while the parsley is being chopped in small, wispy, almost equal pieces, I couldn't be calmer and more focused as the aura of this simple task takes on a Zen quality. As I'm just waiting for the chef to come by and nab a pinch of parsley between his two fingers and flick it into the air, I realize that it's me doing the flicking; I'm judging my own work. Every day I become both judge and jury, and in my case, there's always a Sybil-like conversation going on between my past mentors—Peter von Erp and Roland Chenus—and me, all co-joined and swirling around in my head with every move.

When Roland would show me how to make simple and basic French dishes that he must have made hundreds of times during his 40-plus years of cooking, I could see in his eyes, words, and movements, the enthusiasm of the 15-year-old apprentice that was always inside of him, ready to make any dish the best it could be at that moment.

And what makes a good cooking apprentice? At the top of the list has to be attitude. After that, the recipe deepens: Sweat together two controlled hands (preferably of craftsman caliber), 50 pounds of endurance, 24/7 quarts of living and breathing food, and a large dice of common sense. Pour over enough inexhaustible enthusiasm to cover. Then add optional pinches of a varied strong palate, simmer, and finish with personal taste memories.

Only with these basics can an apprentice excel as a line cook. And a talented line cook has the moves and bravado of an NFL halfback blended with the grace and control of a ballet dancer. It's all about being able to control your body and mind in an unrestricted dance, because as soon as you have to consciously *think* behind the line, you start to fail. The road to cooking is all about repetition of movement, and you don't have time to think—you just have to react by muscle memory.

A great line cook is a culinary athlete. For example, consider properly sautéed soft-shell crabs: First a sauté pan, which will hold three nice-sized crabs with room to move but no excess space, is put over a screaming-hot burner. The crabs, resting in whole milk, are seasoned and quickly dusted in flour. Clarified butter is added to the pan, and before it implodes, the crabs are patted of excess flour and nestled in the pan. If the pan is the correct temperature, you can keep the crabs in a swirling motion without losing heat, which yields an amazing, deeply burnished, crackling exterior. Lightly shingle them on the plate before adding a pat of fresh butter to the pan and watching it immediately turn a bubbly hazelnut color; then add parsley and a squirt of fresh lemon to stop the browning. At that precise moment of destiny, drape that golden elixir lightly over the crabs and toss the pan to the side with the bravado of a Reggie Jackson bat flip as he's watching his Game 6 World Series rocket head for the center-field bleachers. Now repeat rapidly, 40 more times, before the crowd (the customers) heads for the parking lot.

To bat 400 in cooking is to be out of a job, and a 900 batting average is barely acceptable, as this is not a spectator sport. Customers do not know or care that you have had nine perfect plates go out before theirs; if you don't go 60 for 60 in an evening, it is considered a bust. Compound this by the fact that a restaurant is a team sport. Just having your finished dish is worthless if the other three or so dishes on the table are not at the same level or done at precisely the same time. Like a perfect double play, everyone has a part; and the food not only has to be hot and well executed, it also has to be brought to the table with the same speed, precision, and teamwork that produced the food. That is why there are so few consistently great restaurants. On the positive side, we are not surgeons saving lives, so a mistake here or there is possible to get over.

I've had many apprentices over the years. The overall majority I'm very proud of, although there have been a couple of failures, as not everyone is cut out for this business (or in chefs' speak, "They just don't get it"). I trained my first apprentice, Sarah, at John Byron's in the early '80s. She was an accomplished home cook, and what she lacked in professional kitchen experience was easily made up for by an incredible attitude, a genuine zest for learning, a razor-sharp palate, and a trunkload of taste memories from her Armenian background.

Putting together a dish for one of our early wine dinners at John Byron's one night, I was working with some jarred grape leaves. Sara came over and said her grandmother packed her own grape leaves when they were young and tender, and the next day she brought in a home-packed bottle. The difference between these leaves and the larger, more mature variety I'd been using was like night and day. I asked her if we could get enough for the nearly 100 people at the dinner. After Sara raided her grandmother's stash for the year, the guests that evening received quite a treat.

As Sara's apprenticeship went on, I learned a lot about her family's cooking, and to this day I use many of their techniques and recipes, including the one for her tasty tabbouleh.

Sara exemplified one other attribute of a great apprentice: the ability to bring something to the table. In the scheme of things, I will always be an apprentice, and in order to truly *get it*, a good chef never stops learning.

◆

BACK IN 1987 AND 1988, I HAD THE PRIVILEGE OF REPRESENTING WISCONSIN IN THE National Seafood Challenge. The competition was run by the American Culinary Federation (ACF), with 50 chefs (one from each state) cooking in a two-day contest. After the first day,

10 finalists were picked to cook the second day. Each contestant had four hours to prepare a menu of four to five courses with 12 portions each, and then had 15 minutes to plate up the courses for the judges.

The catch was that it was a mystery-box competition; at the start, you were handed a box with ingredients and given 15 minutes to pick what you would use and then write a menu. Today with the popularity of *Iron Chef* and its mystery ingredient, it is a format used in many cooking competitions, with the forerunner being the Culinary Olympics. But back then, it was new to me.

Competing was easily the hardest thing I have ever done in cooking, due to mostly self-inflicted pressure (I found that organization and good utilization skills were the key to doing well). Take some of the up-front pressure off, and this experience relates perfectly to the day-to-day operation of a restaurant, as a chef must be able to think on his feet to use new product as it comes in, and also fully utilize the products that are already there. In addition, it changes the way you look at food since 50 chefs will certainly produce 50 different dishes if given the same products.

Now, take this same concept into the home, and it can help to utilize leftovers, beyond the heated redux of the previous night's meal. For example, I made a touch too much of a prosciutto and grilled asparagus salad with Asiago, ricotta, and lavender honey for a party. The next night I wrapped the asparagus and the ricotta with the ham, sprinkled Asiago over the top, and then placed it in a very hot oven to yield a crisp, cheese crust and crispy-tipped asparagus. With a final drizzle of honey, I had the same ingredients, but realigned the leftovers into a new dish with a completely different and fresh feel and flavor profile.

The year 1988 was a big one for my career and for national recognition. Along with the Seafood Challenge, I was competing in the finals of the second Bocuse d'Or, and *Bon Appétit* magazine was doing a 10-page spread with 12 of my seafood recipes for their May issue. The magazine was so happy with the recipes that they were planning another 10-recipe holiday dessert spread for December.

With Angie and me working together at Byron's—where she had been the assistant manager helping to run the dining room for the past four years—we knew it was the right time to pursue our own place. We tried to work out a deal with Byron's to take over the restaurant, but there was a stumbling block. The bank, which owned the building, had fairly unreasonable expectations, and their 10-year lease had a rent escalator that would have had us out on the street by year three.

At the same time, my Dad was thinking of retiring and selling the grocery store, along with the family building in which it was housed. Gone would be my childhood home, filled with memories of my grandparents, family, and friends, and the store, where I had grown up and that was so instrumental in the many phases of my career. We approached my parents and asked, since they were going to sell, why not sell to us? At first they thought it was a terrible idea. When I was still in grade school my Dad had told me that whatever I decided to do in life, he would support me, except if I wanted to follow him in the store. He was so saddened about not having a choice in life, by having to come back from California to take over the store, that it was the only thing he would not allow me to do. We reasoned that it was not going to be a grocery store, but they still had their doubts, especially since it was outside of the downtown area and in a very residential neighborhood. We finally convinced them that the location was fine: first of all, we were only eight blocks from the city center, and second, it was the type of restaurant we wanted to open—small, 50 seats, fine dining—and could become a destination spot that people would travel to.

Now the only problem was money. We would have to gut the store and rear apartment to build the dining room, kitchen, and bathrooms. Our only option was applying for a Small Business Association (SBA) loan. In November I talked with John and his partner Ed, and told them of our plan to work toward getting a loan for a new restaurant. I gave them a year's notice, and Angie gave two months' notice so she could start working on the business plan. In that time period I agreed to train the new chef, who came on as my sous chef a few months later.

◆

I KNOW I WASN'T "BORN UNDER A BAD SIGN," BUT AS FAR AS MY LUCK WAS GOING, I WAS thinking more and more about Albert King's lyrics: "If it wasn't for bad luck, I wouldn't have no luck at all." After Angie and I had done our presentation to our 9th, 10th, 11th, and 12th banks, I had no illusions that presentation 13 would be any different. We had already taken the plunge and were all-in; we sold our house and moved in above the grocery store to get ready to convert it to our own restaurant. It was odd walking in the now-small hallway of my first home, which had seemed so vast when I was three years old. As soon as I got to the living room, flooded with the bright eastern sun, and saw the expansive front windows over the radiator, the odd feeling left, and the atmosphere became just as comforting and warm as it had been when I was a baby.

We had started to stock the basement with auction buys; we thought we were so *savvy* at the early auctions. At a Kenosha steak house auction, we were giddily euphoric as we felt we "stole" 50 feet of orange vinyl banquettes for the ridiculously low price of $35. At the end of the auction Mr. Savvy (me) pulled out my miniature Phillips-head screwdriver and started my agonizing trip to Carpal Tunnel Hell. No less than 100 three-inch screws held the booths in place.

The next step was for us to muscle the booths into the 16-foot rented open trailer (in the sleeting January evening) and quickly found out we couldn't do it alone. As we were grunting, a fellow came along and offered us help if we would just help him with his purchase. So after we piled all the booths on their ends and tied them together with 200 feet of clothesline that Angie had purchased while we were loading, I went back to help our "savior" and found out he had purchased the eight-foot stainless steel exhaust hood!

We finally got on the road about 10:30 p.m. for the 39-mile trip back to Milwaukee, worrying every second that the rusted chrome bumper on our '76 Cutlass would fall off from being wagged right and left by the off-balance loaded trailer. The two-hour bonus round started as we arrived home and had to insert the six- and eight-foot lengths of booth through the four-by-four-foot iron delivery door that led to the basement. We finally stumbled upstairs and collapsed onto the bed—before we could even change out of our work clothes.

That experience paled next to later auctions where I fried and fused a pair of pliers to the electrical disconnect of a walk-in (knocking out the entire building's power) and later, while disconnecting the pipes to a four-compartment sink, had the bright idea to cut off the lead-in water pipe on the wrong side of the shutoff valve, half flooding the space before we could find the main water shutoff.

This was just a microcosm of our naiveté throughout the entire process. The basement was filling up with auction lots consisting of plates, glasses, pots, and smallwares. We had larger auction equipment, like refrigeration, stored at various friends' warehouses throughout the city. This, along with preliminary architect plans, was all out of pocket, and we were getting down to the lint. Even though I had spent the last 10 years building up a fairly stellar food reputation in the city, banks were not interested. Even though we were debt-free and had a small, but dwindling chunk of cash available from our house sale, the closest we got to a yes was one bank asking for 125 percent collateral (if we'd had *that*, the bank would have been quite unnecessary).

This was happening for two main reasons: One, it seemed that the SBA rated types of restaurants according to risk level, and the small, fine-dining, nonethnic model supposedly had a large skull-and-crossbones, take-your-kids-and-run risk assessment attached—just about the most precarious restaurant loan out there. And two, although most of the loan officers were very complimentary about my cooking background and skills, their hang-up was, *What do you know about managing?* They completely discounted my lovely wife (excuse me, she's a *manager!*), who was sitting right next to me.

There was something amiss as we entered bank number 13, Brown Deer Bank. The loan officer, Mary Ann, was actually happy to meet us. We started to tell our story, and she pulled out the *Bon Appétit* article and said she was a big fan of my food at Byron's. Interestingly enough, she was the first female loan officer that we had spoken with and the only one who engaged Angie as we were talking.

A few days later we were in front of the building being interviewed by Carolyn Walkup of *Nation's Restaurant News*, who was doing a pre-opening story on the restaurant, when we received the call. After overcoming a touch-and-go zoning variance battle with the city and pleading our case to 12 banks, lucky 13 was the charm. We got the loan!

Everyone needs more than a bit of help in life and we were blessed with many angels. An especially large-winged one was our banker Mary Ann, who said that after looking over our plan, with me in the kitchen and Angie in the front, it was as solid a team and deal as she had come across. After I hung up the phone, I turned around and saw that my dad had disappeared from the room. As Angie and I went looking for him, I heard a thunderous crash coming from the back room of the grocery store. We ran toward the sound and found my dad in his best "Here's Johnny" pose from *The Shining*, wearing a weird, goofy smile on his face and holding a sledgehammer in his hands, the top half of which was embedded in the wall.

"I've been waiting a long time for this," he said. He had overheard the call and was as emotional as I had ever seen him. As strongly as he had felt about me being a grocer and stuck in this building, that had all turned around. The back wall came crashing down, as his years of personal frustration transformed into a new beginning for all of us.

CHAPTER TEN RECIPES

◆

*Grilled Prosciutto and Escarole Wrapped
Tuma Cheese with Anchovy Dressing*
281

Home-Style Pork Cabbage Rolls
283

*Sautéed Soft Shell Crabs with Morels,
Ramps, Fiddleheads, and Asparagus*
286

*Lemon-Cured Scallops on Bacon
Pea Mush, Raisin Vinaigrette*
288

*Lamb and Currant Stuffed Grape
Leaves with Spiced Yogurt Sauce*
291

GRILLED PROSCIUTTO AND ESCAROLE WRAPPED TUMA CHEESE WITH ANCHOVY DRESSING

This was a signature appetizer of mine at John Byron's and has never left my stable of go-to's, probably because, universally, I have never met a person who didn't like grilled cheese. It sure made me a few new friends in Umbria when Fabio's family could have turned at any moment. Wrapped in its coating of prosciutto and chard with a hit of anchovy, it's a small package of zesty pleasure.

SERVES 6

For the Tuma Packets:

> Freshly ground black pepper
>
> 18 ounces (510 g) tuma cheese, cut in 12 equal pieces (may substitute fresh mozzarella)
>
> 6 paper-thin slices prosciutto
>
> 12 large leaves Swiss chard, blanched in boiling salted water for 5 seconds, then shocked in ice water, drained, and dried
>
> Extra virgin olive oil, for covering the packets

1. Lightly pepper each piece of tuma. Wrap each tuma in half slice of the prosciutto, then wrap 1 leaf of Swiss chard around the prosciutto to make a neat package. Place the packets in a container, cover with the oil, and reserve covered.

For the Anchovy Sauce Reduction:

> 1 tablespoon extra virgin olive oil
>
> 2 teaspoons minced shallots
>
> ¾ cup (178 mL) dry white wine
>
> ¼ cup (59 mL) heavy cream

1. Heat the olive oil in a small saucepan. Add the shallots and stir for 20 seconds. Add the wine and reduce to a glaze. Add the cream and remove from the heat. Cover and reserve.

For the Anchovy Butter and to Finish the Dish:

> ½ teaspoon thinly sliced garlic, rinsed under hot water and drained
>
> ½ tablespoon thinly sliced shallots, rinsed under hot water and drained
>
> ¼ cup (14 g) packed fresh Italian parsley sprigs
>
> ¾ ounce (21 g) anchovy fillets
>
> ½ tablespoon fresh lemon juice

(RECIPE CONTINUES ON PAGE 282)

(RECIPE CONTINUED FROM PAGE 281)

⅛ teaspoon freshly ground black pepper

Pinch cayenne pepper

½ stick salted butter, at room temperature

Prepared Tuma Packets

Prepared Anchovy Sauce Reduction

1. Place the garlic and shallots in a food processor. Add the parsley sprigs, anchovy fillets, lemon juice, black pepper, and cayenne pepper and process to a paste. Add the butter and blend well.

2. Preheat the grill (or heat a grill pan). Drain the tuma packets on paper towels. Grill for about 1 minute per side, or until they are just soft and molten but not melting (if they get too hot, the cheese will melt out).

3. Meanwhile, heat the Anchovy Sauce Reduction, then whisk in the Anchovy Butter (do not boil). Place the grilled tuma packets on plates and spoon a small amount of sauce around each one.

HOME-STYLE PORK CABBAGE ROLLS

This recipe is inspired by an incredible stuffed cabbage dish that Angie and I had a few years back at Le Florimond in Paris. It is stuffed with seasoned pork forcemeat braised to a rustic turn, and served with a slightly tart broth that melds right into the cabbage. And if someone in the house should complain about the smell when you cook the rolls, send them out for dinner and you'll have more for yourself.

MAKES 8 LARGE CABBAGE ROLLS

For the Pork Stuffing Reduction:

> 3 tablespoons (45 mL) regular olive oil
>
> 2 medium onions (1 pound [454 g]), diced small
>
> 1 bay leaf
>
> 1 sprig fresh thyme
>
> 3 cloves garlic, finely chopped
>
> 1 cup (237 mL) dry white wine

1. Place a sauté pan over medium heat and add the olive oil. When hot, add the onions and sauté for 3 minutes. Add the bay leaf, thyme, and garlic and sauté for 1 minute. Add the wine and reduce to dry. Place on a plate to cool and chill in the refrigerator.

For the Pork Stuffing:

> Prepared Pork Stuffing Reduction
>
> 1 cup (108 g) dry plain bread crumbs, mixed with ¼ cup (59 mL) water
>
> ¾ cup (197 g) tomato paste
>
> 3 large eggs
>
> ½ cup (28 g) chopped fresh Italian parsley
>
> 2 tablespoons kosher salt
>
> 1½ teaspoons freshly ground black pepper
>
> 1½ teaspoons ground cinnamon
>
> 3 pounds (1.36 kg) ground pork

1. Mix all of the ingredients, except the ground pork, together until well mixed. Add the pork and mix with your hands until blended. Reserve the Pork Stuffing in the refrigerator.

For the Cabbage Rolls:

> 1 head Savoy cabbage (you will need 12–16 large leaves)
>
> Prepared Pork Stuffing

(RECIPE CONTINUES ON PAGE 285)

(RECIPE CONTINUED FROM PAGE 283)

1. Heat a large saucepan of salted water to a boil. Remove and discard the core from the cabbage and carefully peel away the whole leaves. Blanch the leaves in the water for about 2 minutes. Shock the leaves in ice water then drain in a colander until they are fairly dry. Cut halfway up each leaf to remove the heavy coarse part in the middle of the cabbage leaf.

2. Divide the Pork Stuffing in 8 portions. Lay out the leaves on a flat surface using 1½ to 2 leaves for each roll. Place the stuffing in the middle of the leaves and roll like you would an egg roll by folding the sides of the cabbage inward, then rolling to form a roll, about 5 inches (12.5 cm) long by 2 inches (5 cm) wide. Place the rolls in a non-reactive baking dish that is large enough to hold the 8 rolls. (If you are making the sauce immediately, you can leave the rolls out, but if you are making it later, refrigerate the rolls and remove them from the refrigerator when you start to make the sauce.)

For the Sauce and to Finish the Dish:

> ¼ pound (114 g) bacon, cut into ¼-inch thick matchstick-sized pieces
> 1 small onion (6 ounces [170 g]), diced medium
> 1 small carrot (1½ ounces [43 g]), diced medium
> 1 stalk celery (2 ounces [57 g]), diced medium
> 2 bay leaves
> 2 sprigs fresh thyme
> 1 cinnamon stick
> 1 whole star anise
> 1 teaspoon whole peppercorns, crushed
> 2 cloves garlic, thinly sliced
> ¾ cup (178 mL) red wine vinegar
> 1¼ cups (296 mL) dry white wine
> ¾ cup (197 g) tomato paste
> 3¾ cups (887 mL) unsalted chicken stock
> Kosher salt and freshly ground black pepper, to taste

1. Place a saucepan over medium heat. Add the bacon and cook, stirring, until it is lightly golden, about 2 to 3 minutes. Remove the bacon from the pan with a slotted spoon and reserve. Leave the fat in the pan.

2. Add the onions, carrots, and celery and sauté until lightly golden, about 4 to 5 minutes. Add the bay leaves, thyme, cinnamon stick, star anise, crushed peppercorns, and garlic and sauté 1 minute. Add the vinegar and reduce to dry. Add the white wine and reduce by half. Add the tomato paste and cook, stirring, for 1 minute. Add the chicken stock and bring up to a boil. Cover the pan, remove from the heat, and let it steep for 15 minutes.

3. Preheat the oven to 350°F (180°C). Strain the sauce through a medium strainer over the cabbage rolls. Cover the top of the baking dish with a piece of parchment paper, then cover the dish with aluminum foil. Bake for 1¼ to 1½ hours, or until cooked through.

4. Remove the stuffed cabbage rolls to plates. Add the reserved bacon to the sauce, adjust the seasoning with salt and pepper, and serve with the cabbage rolls.

SAUTÉED SOFT SHELL CRABS WITH MORELS, RAMPS, FIDDLEHEADS, AND ASPARAGUS

The main thing to remember with this dish is that sautéed soft shell crabs are like a soufflé—you wait for them, they don't wait for you, as when they get cold they lose their crispness. It's best to get fresh live soft shells so find out from your fish store when they will be available. A great American product with a tasty French preparation—this is what detente is all about.

SERVES 4

6 tablespoons (85 g) clarified butter (divided)

1 cup (4 ounces [114 g]) fresh morels, cut in half from top to bottom, plunged in a bowl of warm water, mixed around and removed quickly with hands, and drained on paper towels until dry

¾ cup (100 g) fiddlehead ferns, cleaned in room temperature water, ends trimmed, blanched in boiling salted water for 1 minute, shocked in ice water, and drained

4 medium spears asparagus, ends peeled, tough bottoms cut off, blanched in boiling salted water for 1 minute, shocked in ice water, drained, and cut in 1½- to 2-inch (3.8- to 5-cm) pieces

6 ramps, ends trimmed, cleaned in room temperature water, blanched in boiling salted water for 1 minute, shocked in ice water, drained, and cut in 1½- to 2-inch (3.8- to 5-cm) pieces

2 shallots, finely chopped (you will need about 1½ tablespoons)

1 clove garlic, finely chopped (you will need about 1 teaspoon)

Kosher salt and freshly ground black pepper, to taste

4 medium soft shell crabs, cleaned (bottom apron removed), and lungs under the side flaps removed (you may ask your fish market to clean the crabs)

½ cup (119 mL) whole milk

½ cup (75 g) all-purpose flour

¼ cup (14 g) fresh chervil sprigs

2 tablespoons salted butter

2 tablespoons drained and rinsed capers

1 lemon

1. Place a 10- to 12-inch (25- to 30-cm) heavy-bottomed sauté pan over high heat. When the pan is hot, place 2 tablespoons of the clarified butter in the pan. When the butter is hot, add the morels and sauté for 1 to 2 minutes. Add the fiddleheads and continue sautéing for 1 minute. Add the asparagus, cook for 30 seconds, add the ramps, and cook for 30 more seconds (if the pan is dry, add 1 more tablespoon of the clarified butter). Add the shallots and garlic and sauté for 15 seconds, stirring. Adjust the seasoning with salt and pepper to taste. Remove the vegetables from the pan and divide onto 4 plates.

2. Wipe out the pan and place it over medium-high heat. Place the crabs in the milk. Remove from the milk, one by one, seasoning each with salt and pepper. Place each crab in the flour, coat all sides, and pat off the excess flour.

3. Add the remaining clarified butter to the pan. When the butter is hot, carefully add the crabs, one by one, with the top shell down. Cook over medium-high heat until they are golden brown, about 2½ to 4 minutes per side, depending on their size.

4. Divide the crabs onto the vegetables. Divide the chervil over the crabs. Discard the butter in the pan, place back over the heat, add the whole butter, and swirl the pan. When the butter starts turning golden brown, add the capers and swirl. Cut the lemon in quarters and squeeze 1 quarter over the capers, then spoon over the crabs. Cut the remaining lemon quarters in half to be used for serving as desired.

LEMON-CURED SCALLOPS ON BACON PEA MUSH, RAISIN VINAIGRETTE

Years after Angie brought me to the tearoom, I was putting together a scallop dish and those mushy peas she ordered became my inspiration. The tart raisin vinaigrette is the catalyst that brings the crusty seared sea scallops and the bacon-infused pea mush together.

SERVES 8

For the Lemon-Cured Scallops:

8 (U-10) scallops or 16 (U-20) dry-pack scallops (you will need about 1½ to 2 ounces [43 to 57 g] per person)

Juice of ½ lemon

2 tablespoons regular olive oil

1. In a bowl, toss together the scallops, lemon juice, and olive oil and marinate for 1 hour before cooking.

For the Raisin Vinaigrette:

1 tablespoon granulated sugar

1 tablespoon water

¼ cup (28 g) dried currants

¼ cup (59 mL) plus 1 teaspoon cider vinegar (divided)

1 cup (237 mL) juiced fresh grapes, reduced to ¼ cup (59 mL)

¼ cup (6 g) fresh mint leaves (loose pack)

⅜ teaspoon kosher salt, plus additional to taste

¼ teaspoon freshly ground black pepper, plus additional to taste

2 tablespoons grapeseed oil

1. In a small sauté pan, add the sugar and water and cook over medium-high heat to caramelize. When the sugar turns deep dark brown, carefully but immediately add the currants and ¼ cup (59 mL) of the vinegar. Bring up to a boil, remove from the heat, cover, and let steep for 5 minutes.

2. After steeping, place the reduced grape juice, the mint, half of the currants and all of the vinegar from the currants, the ⅜ teaspoon salt, and the ¼ teaspoon pepper in a blender. Blend until fine. Remove the contents to a bowl. Add the remaining half of the currants, the grapeseed oil, and up to 1 teaspoon of the remaining cider vinegar to taste. Adjust the seasoning with salt and pepper to taste and reserve.

(RECIPE CONTINUES ON PAGE 290)

(RECIPE CONTINUED FROM PAGE 288)

For the Bacon Pea Mush and to Finish the Dish:

4 slices (2 ounces [57 g]) bacon, cut in ⅛-inch (3-mm) pieces

1 medium onion (4 ounces [114 g]), diced small

1 bay leaf

Kosher salt and freshly ground black pepper, to taste

2 cloves garlic, finely chopped

2 tablespoons dry sherry

½ cup (119 mL) dry white wine

1 tablespoon fresh lemon juice

8 ounces (227 g) fresh or IQF (Individually Quick-Frozen) peas, blanched in boiling salted water for 30 seconds, shocked in ice water, drained, and reserved

Prepared Lemon-Cured Scallops

Prepared Raisin Vinaigrette

1. Render the bacon in a nonstick sauté pan over medium heat. Remove the bacon when it is lightly golden and reserve. Remove all but 2 tablespoons of fat from the pan.

2. Add the onions and bay leaf to the pan, season with salt and pepper, and sauté for 2 minutes. Add the garlic and sauté for 30 seconds. Add the sherry, white wine, and lemon juice and reduce to almost dry (when about 1 tablespoon of liquid remains). Remove from the heat.

3. Add the peas and mix together until the peas are hot. Process the mixture in a food processor on pulse until chunky. Remove from the processor, add the rendered bacon, and adjust the seasoning with salt and pepper to taste.

4. After the scallops are marinated, place a heavy sauté pan over very high heat. Season the scallops with salt and pepper. When the pan is very hot, add the scallops to the dry pan and sear on one side for about 2 minutes, or until deeply golden. Turn the scallops over and sear the other side until the scallops are just warm on the inside, about 3 to 6 minutes total, depending on the size of the scallops. Divide the Bacon Pea Mush onto 8 plates, top with 1 or 2 scallops, and spoon the Raisin Vinaigrette over and around.

LAMB AND CURRANT STUFFED GRAPE LEAVES WITH SPICED YOGURT SAUCE

If you have access to fresh grape leaves, use the younger, more tender ones and blanch them quickly in boiling, well-salted water. When properly cooked, the stuffed leaves will have a snappy quality like a good hot dog casing, and the currants give a hint of sweetness that plays well with the tart yogurt sauce.

MAKES ABOUT 34 PIECES

For the Currants:

¼ cup (28 g) currants

1 tablespoon Anisette

1 tablespoon brandy

Zest of 2 lemons (2 teaspoons)

1. In a small saucepan, bring all of the ingredients up to a simmer and cover to allow the currants to absorb the liquid. Reserve.

For the Grape Leaves:

2 tablespoons extra virgin olive oil

½ cup (75 g) small-diced onions

1 bay leaf

1 teaspoon chopped garlic

½ cup (95 g) jasmine rice

½ cup (119 mL) dry white wine

Prepared Currants

1 pound (454 g) ground lamb

2 teaspoons ground coriander

2 teaspoons kosher salt, plus additional to taste

1 teaspoon ground fennel

½ teaspoon freshly ground black pepper, plus additional to taste

8 ounces (227 g) grape leaves (about 34), removed from the brine and rinsed in a bowl of warm water, drained, and stems removed just up to the leaf

4½–5 cups (1.06–1.19 L) unsalted chicken stock

Spiced Yogurt Sauce (recipe follows)

(RECIPE CONTINUES ON PAGE 292)

(RECIPE CONTINUED FROM PAGE 291)

1. Place a sauté pan over medium heat. When the pan is hot, add the oil. When hot, sauté the onions and bay leaf for 3 minutes. Add the garlic and sauté for 30 seconds. Add the rice, stirring for about 30 seconds to just coat the rice. Add the wine, cover, and let it reduce to dry. Add the prepared Currants, remove from the heat, and let cool in the refrigerator.

2. When cold, mix with the ground lamb, coriander, the 2 teaspoons salt, fennel, and the ½ teaspoon pepper. Sauté 1 tablespoon of the mixture to test for seasoning and adjust with salt and pepper, if necessary.

3. Place the grape leaves on a flat surface, shiny side down. Place about 1¾ tablespoons of filling on each grape leaf and roll up from the stem side, folding over and bringing in the sides like you would an egg roll. Place an inverted heatproof plate on the bottom of a pot large enough to hold the grape leaves in no more than 2 layers. Place the grape leaf rolls on top of the inverted plate, seam side down, right next to each other to form 1 layer. Place any extra rolls evenly on top. Cover the rolls with another inverted plate and pour the stock over. Bring up to a simmer and simmer until the rice is tender, about 45 minutes.

4. Let the Stuffed Grape Leaves cool in the liquid, then remove from the liquid and refrigerate, covered, until needed. Serve with the Spiced Yogurt Sauce.

For the Spiced Yogurt Sauce:

2 cups (490 g) plain yogurt

3 tablespoons (15 g) ground coriander

2 teaspoons grated lemon zest

1 teaspoon ground cardamom

½ teaspoon ground cayenne pepper

½ teaspoon kosher salt

¼ teaspoon freshly ground black pepper

1. Mix all of the ingredients together. Refrigerate the sauce for 30 minutes before serving.

11

SANFORD: WHO'S THE BOSS?

HARDEST YEAR OF MY LIFE? EASILY, THE YEAR ANGIE AND I OPENED Sanford. No matter how much you think you know about the restaurant business, there is almost nothing that can get you ready for owning your own.

About three months before we opened Sanford in 1989, I was assisting Jacques Pepin at a cooking class he was doing in Milwaukee. As we were prepping before the class, I told him how excited I was to be opening the restaurant and invited him to see the progress. The next morning I picked him up, and we went to look at the space. Demolition had been completed, so it was just a shell at the time, but we did have the kitchen, dining room walls, and equipment taped out on the floor so one could imagine the flow of cooking and service. He had some great suggestions on overall layout.

He asked about the menu, and I proudly told him I would be changing it completely every night. He replied, "That's very ambitious, but not really necessary. You don't have the same customers dining every night, and also your customers like to return and not only have the dishes they enjoyed before, but they want to be able to recommend those dishes to friends and guests that they bring with them." He was simply saying we should have a strong set of signature dishes that gave a sense of place and familiarity to our restaurant.

This advice proved invaluable. We did open with a regularly changing menu, but a few dishes became signatures from day one: provincial fish soup, grilled marinated tuna with cumin wafers (a dish for which I won a gold medal while representing Wisconsin at the 1988 American Seafood Challenge), and grilled pear and Roquefort tart (which I did as an hors d'oeuvre for Julia Child's 80th birthday in Boston). Those are the only dishes that started on day one and have never left.

After spending 10 years as chef at John Byron's, five of them with Angie as assistant dining room manager, we thought we had a grasp on what it would be like to own our own place, but we didn't—not to mention the issue of how we would procure the funds to start.

During pre-opening, we needed some serious guidance and didn't have a cache of cash to spend on consultants. Prior to Mary Ann, our original angel (and I do have a problem using that term as I grew up with him and know better) was TJ. After sharing much of my childhood with him, he was more of a brother to me than just a friend, and if there was any one person who primed us for our new reality, it was him.

He had spent years in the restaurant business, most recently as a troubleshooter for Steak and Ale during its heyday. He would travel to every troubled restaurant in the chain and in a matter of weeks get them on the right, profitable path, before immediately moving on to the next disaster. It was a thankless job where he never had a chance to step back and enjoy the fruits of his success. He was the perfect mediator, a reality check, and a devil's advocate between my optimistic pie-in-the-sky enthusiasm and Angie's one-foot-in-death's-door pessimism; he slid right in between our seesaw exchanges of "This will be great!" and "We're going to die!"

Apart from the finished business plan that he helped us with, the most attractive part to a lender had to be the fact that, with us living upstairs and feeding ourselves from the restaurant kitchen, we would have virtually no expenses and no time (even if we wanted to spend money). In our worst projected scenario of, say, a wintery February night when we might be serving four or five people total, with Angie in front and me in the back, we could handle that alone and stay open, as the two of us were drawing the major salaries of chef and manager. And even without drawing those salaries, we could survive.

Then there was the absolutely divine intervention of the Filo family. It started with Mike Filo who stepped in to take control of the entire construction project after we had to part ways with our architect, who was a really talented designer but just a bit over his head in the commercial restaurant area at that moment in his young career. Mike navigated the whole process, from helping me plot out the kitchen flow, to calmly working through every unknown disaster that could plague the makeover of a 100-year-old building. I coined the phrase "I want to be like Mike" a few years before the Jordan-era commercial. A mountain of a man with the even demeanor of Gandhi, he was a craftsman of the highest order; there was nothing that left his hands that wasn't impeccable. And when we needed a front desk and an eight-foot back service cabinet, he called his father, Louis Filo, who came out of retirement for a special appearance to fashion two masterpieces that were way beyond anything we could have purchased.

Our next angels appeared through family. My sister Steph was working as a carpeting rep at the Merchandise Mart in Chicago. Beyond helping us procure the carpeting, she also worked with colleagues to secure materials and fabrics. One of her friends, Jane, who was a designer for Skidmore, Owings and Merrill, was going to order the fabrics we had picked out. When she saw them together she mentioned to Steph that although they were individually nice on their own, they were in slightly different color families. After Steph showed her a picture of the chairs we were considering, she asked, "Would they be open to suggestions?" We were just overwhelmed at that point, having a lot of pieces to the puzzle, but no concrete solutions.

Steph and Jane floated up from Chicago the next Sunday, and after we explained to Jane that we didn't have much money left to hire a designer, she said not to worry, that we could work out any compensation in future trade. From that point on, she took over the design, helping us to find perfect, comfortable statement chairs (which are still in service today and inspired our logo), wall treatments, moldings, lighting, curtains, and the entire plan for the look of the exterior. We were so fortunate.

We started construction right after my dad closed down the store. Angie, my dad, and I did as much as we could do to save money. We asked Mike for direction, and he started us out on demolition, which it turned out we were very well equipped to do. The store was completely stripped down to the studs, and we filled dumpster after dumpster with old plaster, lath, and brittle linoleum tile. The bonus was that this was the first time my dad and I really had a chance to work together in adult life.

From demo we were promoted to staining the hundreds of trim pieces, drywalling and taping (in areas that were less conspicuous, like the basement), and a lot of painting. It was getting into November, and we had to paint the outside trim. I was still working at John Byron's, with my last day being the approaching Saturday, so we decided that because the weekend forecast was so great, Sunday would be the day. Somehow it slipped my mind as I finished up on Saturday and the kitchen staff wanted to take me out for "a drink." At nine on Sunday morning, Angie was shaking me awake; my dad was downstairs ready to help. I set up the 30-foot ladder on the Pleasant Street side of the building. My dad was the spotter, holding the ladder steady. (The street is actually a hill with the end of the building a full floor lower than the front.) As I shimmied up the ladder with the paint can in one hand and the brush in my mouth, I realized for the first time how high the trim was—and how hungover I was too. I tried not to look to my right, which overlooked the Milwaukee River and gave the feeling that I was twice as high as I actually was. I was just shaking as I stretched out to paint as much of the top trim and windows as I could before we'd have to move the ladder.

About an hour into the painting, I felt the ladder shaking, and yelled down, "What's going on?"

My dad asked, "Oh, can you feel that?"

"Are you serious?!" I shouted. Turns out my dad had picked that moment to scrape the specks of paint off the rungs of the ladder that had accumulated over the 20-some years of its life. No matter that his only son was dangling from the top edge hanging on for dear life!

He really had no choice but to scrape, though. Being a machinist at heart, his focus on detail and perfection was legendary in the family. He would see a speck of dysfunction and have to eradicate it. And while he was in focus mode, the rest of world stopped.

Working together was a different dynamic for both my dad and me. Even though we had spent many early years in the grocery together, as I got older, if I wasn't at the store, I really didn't see him except for Sunday afternoons and on Christmas Day. He worked all the other holidays, and even though we would sporadically vacation by renting a cabin up north, my dad only showed up one of the years (when I was about 10) by taking off two days on the weekend. In later years, we would vacation at the Holiday Inn about two miles

Working with my dad during construction of Sanford

from our house, and my dad would show up every night after work about 7 p.m. and leave at 4:30 every morning—which spurred rumors in the hotel that my mother was having a weeklong affair.

Because of this past, it was really a gift when the restaurant opened, because I got to spend almost every day with him. He was a man of few words and not really forthcoming with physical affection. So it came as a big surprise when during demolition I came across a large folder filled with every piece of press—mounted and down to minute clippings—that had been written about me since I returned to Milwaukee.

Since he knew every nook and cranny of the building, he became the handyman, caretaker, eyes, and ears of the business. When we would start new people, he knew within days if they would make it or not. From his years in the store he had heard every excuse and con and was consequently an impeccable judge of character. He became a mentor and father to all who passed through the Sanford family over the years, keeping many on the straight and narrow when they could have easily fallen by the wayside. Over the years we grew up together, and I had a chance to finally get to know what a wonderful, talented guy my dad was.

◆

WHEN WE LEFT JOHN BYRON'S, JOHN ASKED US NOT TO TAKE ANY OF THE CURRENT STAFF along with us. I assured him that we would not ask anyone to come with us as, besides the ethical question, we only wanted people who *really wanted* to take the leap, with their eyes wide open. Anyone who came along would be leaving a secure position for a restaurant with an unknown outcome. But if anyone approached us, they would be fair hires. In the end, six of our Byron's coworkers did approach us, and they became the nucleus of our opening team: Anthony and Dave in the kitchen, and Ralph, the two Nancys, and Perrie in the dining room. Anthony's friend Gumby joined the kitchen, and Kaarin, who slipped a note under the door during construction, became our fifth server. Except for Gumby and Kaarin, everyone had worked together for years and was intimately familiar with my food and Angie's service. This was our small family, and we all worked together to bring the restaurant to fruition.

For many years my goal was to have my own restaurant before I hit 40, and with four weeks to go in 1989, time was running out. We were already behind schedule and very anxious to open. For a little practice we organized a pre-opening hors d'oeuvre gathering for all the friends, family, and craftsmen who had helped us realize our dream of a restaurant. It went off without a hitch.

A few nights later, on Pearl Harbor Remembrance Day, December 7, a date that will live in infamy in my head, we opened for business. I thought I had put together a simple enough menu to produce well during the opening salvo from our invading guests (who were all good friends). Plus, we were only serving 30 in total; we hoped they would be understanding of any first-night jitters.

Well, if I had to pick the hardest night in our beginning months, it is definitely opening night. The dining room staff was in top form, and that covered a bit for the Hades-like situation in the kitchen. It was like one of my sister's first dinner parties, where the food never appeared. Everyone eventually did get fed, though they would have been better off sleeping over. But on the bright side, everyone said they loved the food (when it finally arrived)—probably because they were so hungry.

Angie and I were shocked and devastated and embarrassed by how badly the evening had gone. We were almost comatose as we mumbled good night to the staff and went upstairs to bed. The entire staff hung around in the dining room until almost morning, and broke down every part of the fiasco, why it had happened, and how it could be changed. The next day they sat down with us and rationally explained the simple systems they had figured out that we had been too brain-dead to even consider. By day two we went on to a more normal restaurant pace where people received food and service that were up to the standards and in the style that we had envisioned before opening. And we continued to live above the restaurant for the first four years; we went through a huge learning curve—which continues to this day and into the future. The six-day weeks became all consuming, especially since most days we never left the building.

◆

SANFORD WAS CLOSED ON SUNDAYS SO AS SOON AS MY HEAD HIT THE PILLOW SATURDAY nights, my mind would escape by dreaming of the carefree Sunday dinners of my youth. My mom's regular Sunday dinner was roast chicken. But on very special occasions, I would come in from playing outside and see the electric skillet set up, along with a container of flour, beaten eggs, and breadcrumbs on the table. Oh, boy—the breaded pork chops were coming. Just as I had cut a big, crispy chunk off the corner and brought it to my mouth, I would wake up to reality—it was Sunday, our only day off, about 11 a.m. The ritual had become: pull the TV in front of the bedroom door and do not leave the bed until hungry for dinner.

Sunday dinner out was our oasis for the week. But, because of our lack of motivation, we had strict criteria—we had to be able to walk to a restaurant within 3 to 5 minutes of our home so we could obtain instant gratification. Our two refuges that fit the criteria were John Ernst and Giovanni's. At Giovanni's, Angie would always try something different, but my regular Sunday treat was the Sicilian breaded pork chops. Sunday was a day of self-indulgence, and for this kid, nothing was more indulgent than those chops. They had the flavor,

First anniversary at Sanford with the original staff members

taste, and crispness that brought me back to my mother's and grandfather's cooking; the simple flavor of the crackling, crisp breadcrumb-and-cheese coating, the olive oil flavor, the slight pink hue of the chop, and a shot of lemon, was perfection.

◆

WHEN I TRAVEL, I DO EXTENSIVE, ALMOST SCHOLARLY, RESEARCH ON WHERE TO VISIT, stay, and especially, eat. If this research were a college course, I'm sure I'd have a PhD, or at least be a jolly good fellow by now. Over the years, all this probing has led to many incredible dining experiences. I've chronicled dinner after dinner with spectacular settings, ballet-like service, and otherworldly food.

As I think back, there is only one indulgence that overshadows all those evenings. That is the unexpected perfect lunch. Dinner is the expected time for a bacchanalian feast. Work

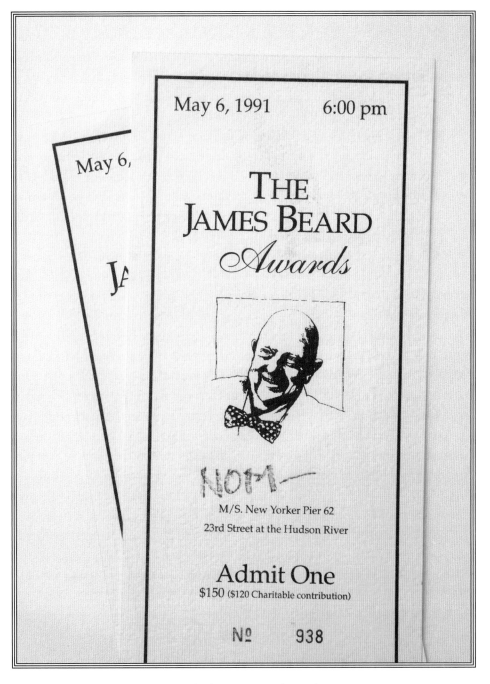

May 6, 1991   6:00 pm

THE
JAMES BEARD
Awards

NOM—

M/S. New Yorker Pier 62

23rd Street at the Hudson River

Admit One
$150 ($120 Charitable contribution)

№   938

May 6,

JA

Tickets from the first James Beard Awards in NYC

is over for the day, and time is not a factor, so the meal becomes the entertainment for the evening. On the other hand, lunch is usually a break in the day—a time to quickly restore before getting back to work—so having a no-holds-barred lunch is a guilty pleasure that feels so wrong it makes you giggle. Angie and I have had many amazing lunches in the Americas, Europe, and Asia throughout the years, but the ultimate was about 15 years back at Bouley in New York City, during the first James Beard Awards.

When I was nominated for the inaugural James Beard Awards in 1990, I thought it was a prank or a promotion. It was the first year for the awards, and I didn't even know they existed. I was notified of my nomination with a Western Union telegram. It was the first telegram I had ever received—and it looked suspiciously like a Publisher's Clearinghouse envelope as I opened it up and read: "You, Sanford D'Amato, are nominated for Best Chef—Midwest!" I called the number on the telegram and asked what I had to buy. The woman assured me that it was real and that, along with Rick Bayless and Charlie Trotter in Chicago, I was one of three nominees.

Craig Shelton, then the Chef de Cuisine at Bouley located in Tribeca, introduced himself to us during the awards and invited us to the restaurant the next day for lunch. We walked through the large wooden French provincial door and were immediately bombarded with the aroma of bushel after bushel of fall apples. We settled into a cozy, tapestry-covered booth, as golden streams of light came streaking through the opaque windows. The absolutely extraordinary plates of food were nestled before us on a thick, lightly starched European tablecloth. Course after course built to a crescendo with braised artichoke barigoule with red mullet. It would be impossible to recreate the setting—the light, the food, the wine, the service, and especially our euphoric mood as all these components aligned. Angie even said, after freshening up, that she wanted to live in the bathroom. We were in the middle of the thriving metropolis of New York City, and the only fitting end for this pure slice of serenity was a long nap in our hotel room.

As it went, Rick won the award the first year. In year two, I was again nominated with Charlie, but that year the nominees had expanded from three to five, with Jimmy Schmidt, Michael Foley, and Rex Hale rounding out our Midwest category. I think both Charlie and I thought we had a good chance to win as we had been previously nominated. And alas, Charlie won.

After the award ceremony, there was a party at Alice Tully Hall, but Angie and I had already decided to go to a bistro that served late. I saw Charlie and asked if he and his wife would like to join us, and he said, "Sure, but just wait one minute." He returned and said David Bouley had invited us, along with some other chefs, to his restaurant for a late-night dinner. We were thrilled to go back, and we all hopped into cabs. Along with Charlie and his wife were Frank Brigtsen and Emeril Lagasse from New Orleans, Frank Stitt from Birmingham, Lora Brody (a cookbook author from New York), a few spouses, and guests.

We arrived at Bouley after midnight, and although the kitchen was closed, a few of the staff stayed around to cook for this group of 12. It was an amazing meal that certainly helped soothe any disappointment that some of us may have felt.

◆

WHEN HOLIDAYS COME AROUND AND YOU ARE IN THE RESTAURANT BUSINESS, INSTEAD of enjoying the holidays yourself, you are usually working to make sure others enjoy theirs. That's why it's called the *hospitality* business.

Probably the three biggest holidays for the restaurant business are Thanksgiving, Mother's Day, and Easter. I was always fortunate enough to work at restaurants that were closed on holidays. But for a few years, before we opened Sanford, Angie was working at the Milwaukee Athletic Club, and she had to work on both Easter and Thanksgiving—two of their busiest days. So when we opened Sanford, it was a prerequisite that holidays were a "no-work zone" for us. Maybe that was not the best financial decision, but it was certainly worth its weight in quality of life.

There was one semi-holiday, though, that we had no choice about: the number-one biggest restaurant day, New Year's Eve. Since I started working in restaurants in 1967, I had never been off on New Year's Eve. In many of the early years, I'd get off work about 12:30 or 1 a.m. and then go out and try to play catch-up with friends. It always ended in a lost New Year's Day where I finally felt normal at around eight that night. As the years progressed, I finally learned to enjoy the after-work party yet still relax with a real robe day on New Year's.

One of my most memorable was in the early '90s when Wisconsin won its first Rose Bowl, under Barry Alvarez. Angie pulled out the sofa bed in the living room and got the TV situated while I made a quick run to the Burger King on Capitol to pick up the special breaded pork cutlet Whoppers that they ran for a short time. Not very chef-like, I know, so fast-forward to the past few years when we've decided to just have a champagne toast at the restaurant and then celebrate with a really nice but simple dinner at home. One of my favorite dishes to prepare is cacio e pepe, not just because it is easy and delicious, but also because it goes really well with, say, a special bottle of wine from our personal cellar, one that I put away when we originally opened Sanford. I guess we were maturing right along with the wine.

◆

ANGIE HAS ALWAYS BEEN MY BIGGEST SUPPORTER AND HARSHEST CRITIC; CONSEQUENTLY she has been a catalyst for many new dishes. When it comes to food, we have 80 percent symbiotic palates, so most of the criticism, even though I don't always react in a positive way, is usually shared by me.

A few years back, with Valentine's Day approaching, I naturally had desserts on my mind. German chocolate cake might evoke a vision: lederhosen-clad waiters dancing and hoisting large platters while exiting the Black Forest, followed by dirndl-corseted waitresses laden with multiple frothy steins of Teutonic bliss (to wash down the cake, of course). Although this would be quite idyllic in a slightly twisted, chocoholic, Milwaukeean, thirst-quenching type of way, there was a problem with the vision. The main ingredients of the cake's frosting—pecans and coconut—aren't quite Germanic staples.

Actually, German chocolate cake has nothing to do with Germany. It is said to have been first conceived in Dallas, Texas, in the '50s, which makes sense to me as it seems to be a Southern collaboration—as if a New Orleans praline rendezvoused with a traditional Southern coconut cake frosting. The wild card is the chocolate cake layers, which are achieved with the help of the optimal ingredient after which the cake is named: Baker's German's Sweet Chocolate, named after its creator Samuel German.

Angie has many desserts she favors, but number one for her is German chocolate cake. Her cake of choice is from our friends at Beans and Barley, but a while back I developed my take on an individual, warm German chocolate cake that we now serve at Sanford. It received Angie's Good Dessert seal of approval.

◆

WHEN DINING OUT, YOU LIKE TO THINK THAT THE RESTAURANT IS TREATING YOU AS WELL as they are capable of. After years in this business, I know that is not always true. When I was working in New York City, I learned there was a definite hierarchy of customers. The chef would announce the name of a special customer with a loud, "Attention!" (which sounded like "ah-tone-see-own"). That would be the signal that everything had better be perfect.

At times this really didn't affect the quality of the other diners' food; but there were crunch times where your full attention had to go somewhere, and you could be sure it would go where the chef wanted it. I personally vowed that, when I had my own restaurant, it would be an equal-opportunity server of quality. And if and when we screwed up, it would be for random reasons, not because we were giving special treatment to a few at the expense of others.

One of the most blatant examples of not being among the chosen happened when Angie and I dined at an Italian restaurant in Chicago. We were there on a Sunday, participating in the annual Meals on Wheels Celebrity Chefs' Brunch fundraiser with 30 other chefs from around the country, serving about 1,000 guests. Right next to our station was Angelo Auriana, the chef from Valentino in Los Angeles, along with his sous chef. Their flight arrived late to Chicago, and they only had about two hours to prepare all of their food for the brunch. I asked if they needed any help, as they looked really frazzled, and they said, "If you could—we're really in trouble!" So we all helped them crank out the 50-some frittatas they were serving.

The event went off well, and afterward Angelo invited us to lunch at an Italian restaurant in Chicago where he knew the chef. We made the reservation under our name and arrived a bit early. The hostess was in a deep conversation with the bartender, and when she finally noticed us at the desk, she walked our way (visibly perturbed that we were *interrupting* her), grabbed two menus, and curtly seated us, without even a hello.

Angelo was running late, so after a half hour, we ordered a few appetizers. The food that was literally thrown in front of us was insipid and tasteless. Just then Angelo arrived and was immediately recognized by the staff. It was like the footlights of Broadway clicked on! We were engulfed by doting waitstaff, and the food changed from mediocre to brilliant. This was a very sad commentary; mediocre food and service can mean a restaurant is having a bad day, but rudeness and indifference mean you have a restaurant at its worst. I learn as much if not more from the bad experiences, like that Jekyll-and-Hyde lunch, as I do from a perfect afternoon at Bouley.

◆

THE MONTHS WENT BY, AND ALTHOUGH WE WERE REALLY BUSY, IT STARTED TO FEEL LIKE a case of "be careful what you wish for." We had a bare-bones kitchen and dining room staff, so anytime we were busier than expected or someone was sick, there was no one to call in. Everyone in the restaurant worked five days except Angie and me, who worked all six days that we were open each week. We were both completely overwhelmed by the insistent, non-stop treadmill of not just running the restaurant, but also living in the same building, which made it a near 24/7 commitment. The only *real* down time was that 2 a.m. Sunday to 6 a.m. Monday window when the restaurant was closed.

Angie and I had a running dialogue in which, at any given time, either one of us would be at the end of his or her rope and say, "I quit." This was followed by the calmer one of us talking the other off the ledge by coming up with an idea or solution to the particular problem. We had to use each other, as there was no one else to listen. This was our stilted way of coping and bringing about change, and every outburst usually resulted in a new employee being brought on to lift the strain.

As we were closing in on the end of the summer, we figured out we needed a vacation. Since we couldn't leave the restaurant, we decided to close for the week after Labor Day so everyone could take their vacation at the same time. As vacation time approached, I was doing my usual obsessive trip-planning itinerary—5:30 p.m. arrival, 7:30 dinner, get up early, move quickly to the next lunch, then snack—when Angie decided to stage a solo intervention.

"I just want to go somewhere with no phone, no TV, no people, and be devoid of thought for the whole trip, even if it means no great food."

I was stunned. No great food? I couldn't get my face to reverse its massive pout position, but after a few days of rational thought, I planned a surprise trip to Virgin Gorda in the British Virgin Islands. There was no phone, no TV (gasp), and—heaven forbid—possibly mediocre food waiting at the resort in which we were staying.

Before I knew it, my eyes were the size of SUV hubcaps as we were seated in the front row of a 10-seat miniature prop, for lack of a better word, plane. We were looking over the pilot's right shoulder as he approached the island's landing strip, which was the size of an elementary school playground. This flying bus lunged down and stopped with the reverberating force of a roller coaster finishing an out-of-control ride—frightening, but very impressive. As the hatch door opened, an otherworldly blast of steam room humidity rolled into the plane.

It took me less than one day to get into a rhythm that previously had been unthinkable: Get up when a light tap is heard on the door, bring in the breakfast tray, smell the aroma of the hibiscus, pick at perfectly ripe tropical fruit, sip fresh-squeezed juices, walk out the front door, sink into the beach lounges under the large, propped-up, palm-frond umbrella. Read, have a libation, or just pop into the crystal-clear sea, five feet away. Go back to the chair— almost time for lunch! Eat and repeat 'til dinner. Three meals a day, all outside, with balmy trade winds continually lulling me into a trance. To my surprise, I was completely enchanted with this island paradise. Come to think of it, I'd been wrong. I was not just *getting* really good at the whole relaxation thing—I think I was actually born to do it.

After a few days of eating at the resort, though, I couldn't help myself as I started to ask the folks working at the resort (and any other islanders) where they would go for great, local, home-cooked fare. A place that came up a couple of times was the Crab Hole for really good chicken and rice. No one had exact directions, but they said any one of the few cab drivers on the island would know where it was.

The next evening we had the resort call us a cab, and as the driver took off, we told him we were going to the Crab Hole. He looked at us strangely and said, "Never hear of dis place, mon!" We went on to describe the food and approximately where it was. The driver was still puzzled—"Crab Hoe . . . Crab Hoe? Oh, oh, oh, you mean, Cggrhhaab, Hooooooooooaale!! No problem!"

In five minutes we were at a little Formica table in a tiny shack. The menu was limited; we went right for the chicken and rice. When it arrived at the table, Angie was less than enchanted. To me it looked like the basic NYC restaurant family meal, as backs, neck, feet, skin, and an errant beak made their appearances in the rice, with nary a piece of leg, thigh, or breast to be found. As bad as it looked, its appearance was well trumped by its inherently disturbing flavor and texture, as if they had vulcanized the bits of grizzle in the rice. Not the best beak we'd ever had!

As we took our cab back to the resort, I had no idea that the next day would change my career and life.

Angie and me on the beach on the island Virgin Gorda

CHAPTER ELEVEN RECIPES

◆

Veal Ragout Arancini with Smoked
Tomato and Mint Emulsion
309

Individual Warm German Chocolate Cakes
312

Waterzooï á la Gantoise
314

Pasta Cacio e Pepe
316

Rhubarb-Glazed Squab on Candied
Radish and Scallions, Rhubarb Essence
317

Seared Striped Bass on Green
Papaya Salad, Green Curry Broth
320

VEAL RAGOUT ARANCINI WITH SMOKED TOMATO AND MINT EMULSION

Every good Sicilian boy has a big soft spot for arancini as they can be the size of softballs. I put these on the menu in 1989 when we opened Sanford and along with the cannoli, they were a link to the past. With a twist of the red wine veal ragout with mint and formed into a poppable golf ball-size, you don't have to stop at one.

SERVES 8

For the Veal Ragout:

> ½ pound (227 g) trimmed veal stew meat, cut in small dice
>
> Kosher salt and freshly ground black pepper, to taste
>
> 2 tablespoons extra virgin olive oil
>
> 1 medium (½ pound [227 g]) onion, cut in small dice
>
> 2 cloves garlic, finely chopped
>
> 1 sprig fresh thyme
>
> 1 bay leaf
>
> ½ tablespoon grated orange zest
>
> ¼ cup (59 mL) red wine vinegar
>
> 3 cups (711 mL) dry red wine
>
> ¼ cup (59 mL) unsalted veal stock (you may use ¼ cup unsalted beef stock mixed with ¾ teaspoon tomato paste as a substitute)
>
> 2 tablespoons pitted cured black olives, diced small

1. Place a sauté pan over high heat. Season the veal with salt and pepper. Add the oil to the pan, and when hot, add the veal and brown well. Remove the veal, add the onions, and cook until they are lightly caramelized. Add the garlic, thyme, bay leaves, and orange zest and sauté for 1 minute.

2. Preheat the oven to 375°F (190°C). Deglaze the pan with the vinegar and reduce to almost dry. Add the veal and red wine and bring up to a simmer. Cover and bake 30 to 45 minutes until almost dry. Add the veal stock and cook until the mixture is thick and coats a spoon, but is not dry. Add the olives and adjust the seasoning with salt and pepper.

(RECIPE CONTINUES ON PAGE 310)

(RECIPE CONTINUED FROM PAGE 309)

For the Rice:

¼ cup (59 mL) regular olive oil

½ small onion, diced small

1 cup (190 g) jasmine rice

1 bay leaf

1¾ cups (414 mL) unsalted chicken stock, heated

Kosher salt and freshly ground black pepper, to taste

5 ounces (142 g) Parmesan cheese, grated

2½ tablespoons (4 g) fresh mint leaves, chopped

1 large egg yolk

1. Preheat the oven to 375°F (190°C). Heat a saucepan over medium heat. Add the oil, and when hot, add the onions and sauté until translucent. Add the rice and bay leaf and sauté until the grains of rice are glistening.

2. Add the chicken stock that has been highly seasoned with salt and pepper (it should be a little over-seasoned). Bring up to a boil and cover with an oiled sheet of parchment paper. Bake for about 16 to 18 minutes, or until all of the liquid is absorbed.

3. Fluff the rice with a 2-prong roasting fork and transfer to a shallow baking dish. When the rice is cool, mix in the cheese, mint, and egg yolk and season to taste with salt and pepper. Cover and reserve until you are ready to make the Arancini.

For the Tomato Vinaigrette:

2½ ounces (71 g) smoked dried tomatoes or sun-dried tomatoes

½ cup (119 mL) unsalted chicken stock

3 tablespoons (45 mL) fresh lemon juice

1¼ tablespoons balsamic vinegar

1 cup (237 mL) regular olive oil

1 cup (237 mL) extra virgin olive oil

Kosher salt and freshly ground black pepper, to taste

1. In a saucepan, bring the tomatoes up to a boil in the stock. Cool. Add the tomatoes to a blender along with the lemon juice and balsamic vinegar and purée. Add both of the olive oils and blend. Season the vinaigrette with salt and pepper.

To Finish the Arancini:

> 1½ cups (158 g) dry fine bread crumbs
> 1 cup (150 g) all-purpose flour
> 2 large eggs, mixed with 2 tablespoons regular olive oil
> Prepared Rice
> Prepared Veal Ragout
> Regular olive oil, to fry
> Prepared Tomato Vinaigrette
> Sliced fresh mint, for garnish

1. Place the bread crumbs, flour, and egg mixture in 3 separate containers. With an ice cream scoop, scoop out golf ball-size rice balls. Place a ball in your hand and flatten slightly. Place 1 teaspoon of the Veal Ragout in the center of the slightly flattened ball, then re-form back into a round shape. Continue the procedure with the remaining rice balls. Refrigerate the rice balls until they are firm.

2. Dredge the rice balls in the flour (lightly pat to remove the excess), dip in the egg wash (remove with a fork to drain the excess), and place in the bread crumbs and roll around to cover. Set the breaded rice balls on parchment paper. (You may refrigerate the rice balls at this point covered in the refrigerator until you are ready to fry them.)

3. Heat the oil in a large sauté pan to 350°F (180°C) to 375°F (190°C). Deep-fry the rice balls in batches in a 2-quart sauce pot (that is not filled beyond half-way high with oil) until golden brown and hot in the center, about 2 to 3 minutes (fry 1 for a test first to gauge the frying time).

4. Serve the Arancini with the Tomato Vinaigrette by placing 1 rice ball on a dollop of the vinaigrette. Place a drop of vinaigrette on top of each Arancini and top with the mint.

INDIVIDUAL WARM GERMAN CHOCOLATE CAKES

This recipe is all about Angie. I became tired of hearing how great this and that German Chocolate Cake was and finally came up with this cake for all of the Valentine's Days that we had missed over the years from being in the restaurant business.

MAKES 4 CAKES

> 6 tablespoons (3 ounces [85 g]) salted butter, plus some soft butter for buttering ramekins
>
> All-purpose flour, to dust ramekins
>
> 3 ounces (85 g) unsweetened chocolate, coarsely chopped
>
> 3 large eggs, separated
>
> ⅓ cup (67 g) granulated sugar (divided)
>
> German Chocolate Cake Frosting (recipe follows)
>
> Half and half, for thinning frosting, if necessary

1. Preheat the oven to 375°F (190°C). Spread the softened butter in 4 (6-ounce [180-mL]) ovenproof ramekins, coating the inside surfaces very lightly. Cut 4 pieces of parchment paper to fit the inside bottom of the ramekins. Butter the top of the parchment paper lightly and press the bottom into the ramekin to stick. Dust the ramekins with flour over the butter and tap out the excess.

2. Place the chocolate and the 6 tablespoons (85 g) butter in a bowl and place over a double boiler, making sure that the bottom of the bowl doesn't touch the water. Heat over medium heat until the chocolate and butter are melted. In another bowl, whisk the egg yolks with half of the sugar until smooth. In the bowl of a stand mixer, whip the egg whites and the remaining sugar to very soft peaks. Whisk the warm chocolate mixture into the egg yolk mixture. Whisk ⅓ of the egg whites into the chocolate mixture, then fold in the remaining egg whites until they are just mixed.

3. Fill the ramekins and bake for 3 minutes. Place 1 of the reserved pre-formed balls of frosting in the center of each cake and continue baking for 3 more minutes. Immediately remove the cakes from the oven and place in the refrigerator to cool.

4. For serving, preheat the oven to 375°F (190°C). Place the cakes in the oven and bake for about 10 to 12 minutes, or until just set on the outside. Remove from the oven, and holding the ramekin with a towel, run a knife around the inside perimeter, being careful not to cut the cake. Invert the cake into your hand from the ramekin and place right side up onto individual plates.

5. Serve immediately by pouring the German Chocolate Cake Frosting (that has been reheated lightly in a microwave or double boiler) over the top of each cake (you may adjust the consistency of the frosting with a little half and half if it is too thick).

For the German Chocolate Cake Frosting:

¼ cup (50 g) granulated sugar

2 tablespoons water

¼ cup (59 mL) heavy cream

1 small egg yolk

1 tablespoon salted butter, at room temperature

¼ cup (20 g) plus 2 tablespoons shredded coconut, toasted at 375°F (190°C) for 5 to 6 minutes until lightly golden

¼ cup (27 g) plus 2 tablespoons small-diced pecans, tossed with ½ teaspoon of grapeseed oil and lightly salted, then toasted at 375°F (190°C) for 7 to 8 minutes until golden brown

Pinch salt, if necessary

1. Mix the sugar and water in a small saucepan and bring up to a boil. Cook to a very dark vermillion stage of caramel but not burning. When the caramel is dark, carefully and quickly whisk in the heavy cream. (Caution: the sugar is dangerously hot.) Let the caramel cool slightly to about 180°F (82°C).

2. Place the egg yolk in a separate bowl and while whisking, temper the caramel sauce into the egg yolk. Add the soft butter and whisk in. Fold in the coconut and pecans. Let the frosting cool down.

3. When cool, form 4 balls (about 1 tablespoon each) of frosting and reserve to be placed into the cakes during baking. Reserve the remaining frosting in the refrigerator.

WATERZOOÏ Á LA GANTOISE

Waterzooï is a classic Belgian stew that by mere mention starts a country salivating. Belgians are serious about their food and there is about 200 years of tradition behind Waterzooï, or "water-zootje," literally meaning boiled (zootje) water (water). The name isn't overly appetizing but when you add the fixin's, you have a great dish.

SERVES 8

> 3 tablespoons (43 g) salted butter (divided)
>
> 3 tablespoons (45 mL) grapeseed oil
>
> 4 large leeks, 3 leeks sliced in rounds (reserve 1 whole leek for garnish)
>
> 1 large onion (12 ounces [341 g]), diced large
>
> 3 stalks celery (8 ounces [227 g]), diced large
>
> 2 medium (6 ounces [170 g]) carrots, peeled and diced large
>
> ½ bunch fresh Italian parsley (1½ ounces [43 g]), chopped coarsely
>
> 4 cloves garlic, thinly sliced
>
> 3 bay leaves
>
> 2 sprigs fresh marjoram
>
> 1 tablespoon crushed fennel seeds
>
> 1 tablespoon kosher salt, plus additional to taste
>
> Zest of 1 large orange (you will need 3 tablespoons [32 g], divided)
>
> ½ teaspoon freshly ground black pepper, plus additional to taste
>
> 1½ cups (356 mL) dry white wine
>
> 6 cups (1.42 L) unsalted chicken stock
>
> 2 pounds (908 g) bone-in chicken breasts, skin removed

1. In a large saucepot over medium heat, add 1 tablespoon of the butter and the grapeseed oil. When just hot, add the 3 sliced leeks, the onions, the celery, the carrots, the parsley, the garlic, the bay leaves, the marjoram, the fennel seeds, the 1 tablespoon salt, half of the orange zest, and the ½ teaspoon pepper and sweat, covered, over medium-low heat for 15 minutes, stirring every 3 minutes.

2. Uncover, add the wine, raise the heat to high, and simmer for 3 minutes. Add the chicken stock and bring up to a boil. Add the chicken breasts and turn to low. Cover and let the chicken poach for 20 minutes.

3. Remove the chicken and remove the meat from the bones; reserve the meat warm. Add the bones back to the pot and let them cook over low heat for 20 more minutes. Remove the bones and bay leaves, then carefully purée in a blender. Pass the puréed mixture through a medium strainer and reserve it hot.

4. Slice the remaining leek into rounds. Place a nonstick sauté pan over medium heat. Add the remaining butter, and when the butter is hot, add the leek rounds, season with salt and pepper, and cook for 1 to 2 minutes, or until crisp-tender. Add the remaining orange zest and toss together. Slice the reserved chicken breasts in ¼-inch (6-mm) slices and mix with the leeks and orange zest. Adjust the seasoning with salt and pepper. Divide the garnish among 8 bowls, ladle the hot broth around, and serve.

PASTA CACIO E PEPE

This dish was inspired by a simple pasta I had at Bottigleria da Gino in Rome that reminded me of the "high chair" pastas I had when I was little. The key is the texture of the pasta with sharp black pepper, combined with good-quality Pecorino cheese. I add a bit of potato starch to the pasta water to mimic the starch-rich water of restaurant kitchens where large batches of pasta are cooked.

SERVES 2

>   3 ounces (85 g) grated Pecorino Romano cheese
>
>   2 ounces (57 g) grated Pecorino Toscano cheese
>
>   Kosher salt, for the pasta water
>
>   8 ounces (227 g) dried spaghetti
>
>   ¼ teaspoon potato starch, dissolved in 1 teaspoon cold water
>
>   1 tablespoon freshly ground black pepper, fine, but not ultra-fine
>
>   2 tablespoons extra virgin olive oil

1. Mix the cheeses together in a bowl. Place a large pot of water on the stove for cooking the pasta. Add enough salt to the water so it tastes like sea water. Bring the water up to a boil, then add the pasta and stir (keep the pasta at a low boil). Cook according to the manufacturer's suggested time (10 to 11 minutes total for De Cecco), so that the past is al dente.

2. While the pasta is cooking, remove ½ cup (119 mL) of the pasta water and place it into a large sauté pan. Bring up to a simmer and whisk in the dissolved potato starch and the pepper. Bring up to a simmer and turn off the heat.

3. When the pasta is cooked, remove it from the water with tongs and place it directly into the sauté pan holding the starch water. Turn the heat under the sauté pan to low. Immediately sprinkle over the cheeses and olive oil and toss together with tongs until the pasta is coated and the cheese turns creamy (if necessary, add a couple more tablespoons of pasta water). Divide the pasta between 2 warm bowls and serve immediately.

RHUBARB-GLAZED SQUAB ON CANDIED RADISH AND SCALLIONS, RHUBARB ESSENCE

One of the greatest compliments I ever received was at a dinner in Detroit when one of the other participating chefs, Rocco DiSpirito, walked up to me after we put out the course and said, "Fuck You! I'm supposed to be the king of rhubarb—but that squab is great!"

SERVES 4

For the Marinated Squab:

> 2 New York-dressed squab (feet on), leg and thigh portions removed, boneless breast removed from carcass (keep the carcass for future stock or discard)
>
> 1 large shallot, sliced
>
> 1 large clove garlic, thinly sliced
>
> Juice and zest of 1 large lemon
>
> ¼ cup (84 g) molasses
>
> ¼ cup (59 mL) regular olive oil
>
> 2 sprigs fresh thyme
>
> 2 bay leaves
>
> 10 black peppercorns, crushed

1. Place all of the ingredients in a large resealable plastic bag and marinate overnight, turning once.

For the Rhubarb Essence:

> 2 cups (474 mL) fresh rhubarb juice (from juiced fresh rhubarb), reduced to ¼ cup (59 mL)
>
> ⅓ cup (79 mL) grapeseed oil
>
> 2 teaspoons granulated sugar, or to taste
>
> Kosher salt and fresh ground black pepper, to taste

1. Mix all of the ingredients together.

For the Candied Radish and Scallions:

> 8 radishes (4 ounces [114 g]), greens removed and cut in quarters
>
> 5 tablespoons (74 mL) water (divided)
>
> 2½ teaspoons extra virgin olive oil (divided)
>
> 2½ teaspoons granulated sugar (divided)

(RECIPE CONTINUES ON PAGE 319)

(RECIPE CONTINUED FROM PAGE 317)

> ⅜ teaspoon kosher salt (divided)
>
> ¼ teaspoon freshly ground black pepper (divided)
>
> ⅛ teaspoon ground cardamom
>
> 1 teaspoon fresh lemon juice
>
> 4 scallions, ends cut off and cut in 1-inch (2.5-cm) pieces

1. In a small sauté pan, place the radishes, 4 tablespoons of the water, 1½ teaspoons of the olive oil, 1½ teaspoons of the sugar, ¼ teaspoon of the salt, ⅛ teaspoon of the pepper, and the cardamom. Cover and bring up to a boil over medium-high heat, boil for 1 minute, remove the cover, and cook until the radishes are knife-tender and the water is gone (if the radishes need a bit more time, add a few more drops of water). Continue sautéing and let the radishes glaze for about 30 seconds. Add the lemon juice and toss until the pan is dry and the radishes are glazed and cooked; remove to a plate.

2. Rinse out the pan, add the remaining water, the remaining oil, the remaining sugar, the remaining salt, the remaining pepper, and the scallions and place over high heat. When the water is evaporated, toss the scallions to glaze for 30 seconds, then add to the cooked radishes.

To Finish the Dish:

> Prepared Marinated Squab
>
> Kosher salt and freshly ground black pepper, to taste
>
> Prepared Candied Radish and Scallions
>
> 1½ cups (75 g) fresh baby frisée
>
> Prepared Rhubarb Essence
>
> Candied Rhubarb (recipe follows)

1. Remove the squab from the marinade and season lightly with salt and pepper. Grill or sauté the squab breast and legs to medium-rare, or to your desired doneness. Place the squab on the Candied Radish and Scallions.

2. In a large bowl, season the frisée lightly with salt and pepper and toss with just enough Rhubarb Essence to moisten. Place next to the squab and garnish with the remaining Rhubarb Essence and the Candied Rhubarb over and around.

For the Candied Rhubarb:

> 1 stalk rhubarb (about 3 ounces [85 g]), cut in ¼-inch-thick (6-mm) slices
>
> Granulated sugar, to coat the rhubarb

1. Preheat the oven to 225°F (110°C). In a bowl, toss the rhubarb with enough sugar to coat it. Place the pieces on a parchment paper-lined sheet tray and bake for about 45 minutes to 1 hour, or until half dry. Reserve the Candied Rhubarb covered at room temperature.

SEARED STRIPED BASS ON GREEN PAPAYA SALAD, GREEN CURRY BROTH

In this dish, the curry can be made as hot as you like and the papaya salad gives a crisp, acidic balance to the richness of the curry sauce. You want to control the heat so you can still taste the fish. For my taste, two tablespoons of the curry paste is a good heat level, but you can start with one tablespoon and add more later.

SERVES 4

For the Marinated Bass:

> ¾ cup (178 mL) corn oil
>
> ¼ cup (59 mL) fresh lime juice
>
> 2 tablespoons brown sugar
>
> 1 tablespoon chopped garlic
>
> 4 (7-ounce [199-g]) skinless fillets striped bass (1 to 1½ inches [2.5 to 3.8 cm] thick)

1. Mix all of the ingredients, except the bass, together in a bowl. Place the bass in the bowl and marinate in the refrigerator for 4 to 6 hours.

For the Green Papaya Salad:

> 4 scallions, trimmed, sliced crosswise very thin, and rinsed (you will need about ½ cup [50 g] loosely packed)
>
> ¼ cup (59 mL) grapeseed oil
>
> 1 tablespoon plus 2 teaspoons buckwheat honey
>
> 1 tablespoon plus 2 teaspoons fresh lime juice
>
> 1½ teaspoons chili paste with garlic
>
> 1 teaspoon tamarind concentrate
>
> 1 teaspoon fish sauce (fish sauce is also known as Nam Pla in Asian markets)
>
> 1 teaspoon ground ginger
>
> ¼ teaspoon kosher salt
>
> ⅛ teaspoon freshly ground black pepper
>
> 1 green papaya, peeled, seeded, and cut in ⅛-inch thick long slices, then each slice cut into long ⅛-inch thick pieces resembling noodles (you will need about 2 cups [300 g])
>
> 2 nests vermicelli, covered with hot water for 15 minutes, drained, and reserved (vermicelli are also known as bean thread noodles and they come 8 nests to a package)

1. Mix all of the ingredients, except the papaya and vermicelli, together in a bowl. Add the papaya and mix in. Add the vermicelli and mix in. Let the salad set for 15 minutes before serving.

(RECIPE CONTINUES ON PAGE 322)

(RECIPE CONTINUED FROM PAGE 318)

For the Green Curry Sauce:

> 2 teaspoons sesame oil
>
> ¼ cup (24 g) chopped ginger root
>
> 2 cloves garlic, thinly sliced
>
> ¼ cup (59 mL) dry white wine
>
> 1 tablespoon fresh lime juice, plus additional to taste
>
> 1 (13½-ounce [405-mL]) can coconut milk
>
> 2 teaspoons green curry paste
>
> ½ teaspoon fish sauce (Nam Pla)
>
> ½ cup (8 g) fresh cilantro leaves
>
> Kosher salt and freshly ground black pepper, to taste

1. In a small saucepan, heat the sesame oil. Add the ginger and garlic and sauté for 30 seconds. Add the white wine and the 1 tablespoon lime juice and reduce to almost dry. Add the coconut milk, curry paste, and fish sauce and reduce to 1 cup (237 mL) of liquid. Cool down the liquid in an ice bath.

2. When the liquid is cool, place in a blender along with the cilantro leaves and blend until well blended, about 20 to 30 seconds. Strain the sauce through a medium strainer and reserve. When you are ready to serve, slowly warm the sauce, stirring, and adjust the seasoning with salt, pepper, and a touch of lime juice, if necessary.

To Finish the Dish:

> Prepared Marinated Bass
>
> Kosher salt and freshly ground black pepper, to taste
>
> Prepared Green Papaya Salad
>
> Prepared Green Curry Sauce

1. Remove the bass fillets from the marinade. Place a sauté pan over high heat. Season the bass with salt and pepper and sear about 3 to 4 minutes per side, depending on the thickness—they should have a golden caramelized color (do not overcook).

2. Divide the Green Papaya Salad among 4 plates. Place the bass on top of the salad and garnish with the Green Curry Sauce over and around; serve.

12

MY DINNERS WITH JULIA

"EXCUSE MOI!" "PARDON!" "CON PERMISO!" "PLEASE MOVE OVER A BIT!"

There were four of us fighting for position in front of an eight-by-eight-inch window located in the kitchen door leading into the dining room. We were at Le Veau d'Or in New York City in 1975: Joseph the Basque butcher, Gerard the Parisian saucier, Carlos the garde-manger from Santa Domingo, and me. We were all jockeying for position to catch a glimpse of a very special diner. With this international interest, one might think a US president? Or possibly the pope? At least a movie star or musician. No, just little ol' Julia Child.

I certainly understood why *I* was at the window, and the two Frenchmen were also well aware of her celebrity, as early on she had been very instrumental in bringing innumerable American novices under her Franco food spell (hence more notoriety and business in French restaurants). But Carlos from Santa Domingo, it turned out, had no idea who "Hoo-leo Sheeld" was but saw it as a good excuse to get away from prep work for a few minutes.

We all waited for her order, and it couldn't have been more classic: saucisson chaud en croûte (garlic sausage in puff pastry), poussin en cocotte "bonne femme" (small roasted chicken with white wine and mushrooms), and mousse au chocolat. After she masterfully consumed every morsel, even scraping the mousse cup, she appeared through the portal we had been using for viewing and gave us a big, "Bonjour!" She individually shook everyone's hand as her gracious compliments flew.

Little did I know at the time what an enormous effect Julia would have on my career. I'll never forget my first impression of her, which was truly larger than life; it brought me back to a sunny summer afternoon one Saturday in the early 1960s. Any self-respecting teenager would have been found lolling the day away at the park, playing a bit of ball, or just biking along to nowhere. But this teen was glued to his TV, waiting for the next installment of *The French Chef*. My friends were at the beach, but I was in the south of France, lounging in a hammock, watching a crispy, burnished, rosemary-encrusted leg of lamb rotate on a spit over the open fire of an ancient stone grill. My right hand was confused—should it be the rustic

Bandol or the blushing rosé? I went for the rosé, realizing that my left hand already contained a golden, crunchy, salty gougére to take the edge off until that gorgeous gam was *à point* (a flawless medium) and ready to accompany the waiting Bandol.

It was a perfect little world in the D'Amato's sunroom as I waited for Julia to take me on my next culinary voyage. The only difference between this and my usual fantasies of being a train engineer, bomber pilot, or sharp-shooting sheriff was that this fantasy would become a reality.

From those early shows and my early friendship with Mark, who was a like-minded cook in training, came my first real forays into scratch-food preparation. Crêpes were the first formal recipe I ever cooked. I had put food together before, like beans and wieners, and macaroni and cheese, and had even tried baked pork chops with apples. But I hadn't ever looked at a cookbook or actually tried to make a dish from one until I was about 12 years old. Since I didn't have a copy of Julia's book, the book of choice was my mother's copy of the *Old Settlement Cookbook*, where we searched for a recipe for those thin pancakes that are vehicles for any mixture of fillings and toppings, both sweet and savory.

The intent was quite natural. Mark and I were looking for a use for some fresh strawberries and a can of Reddi-wip that we had found in the refrigerator. I had seen my mother use the *Old Settlement Cookbook* regularly to come up with tasty wonders, so we eventually found a recipe for crêpes suzette—a classic French recipe for crêpes cooked and finished with orange, sugar, and various liqueurs. Not having the key to the liquor cabinet, we decided to just make the pancake part.

We took a large, square nonstick skillet and started cooking. The results were truly amazing for a first-time effort, and we came up with several 12-by-12-inch thin, crispy-at-the-rim crêpes that we packed with strawberries and whipped cream. From that point on, a whole new world was opened up; all those delicious dishes cooped up in that small book started my head spinning. This success was the embryo of a career that, unbeknownst to me, would lead well beyond the "good cook" stage and into a lifelong profession.

Not surprisingly, it was quite a few years before I saw Julia Child again (in person) after Le Veau d'Or—about 15 to be more precise. It was six months into our first year at Sanford, and I was a cofounder of the original American Institute of Wine and Food (AIWF) chapter in Milwaukee. We had planned a series of events, and the main part of the festivities, scheduled for September 4 to 7 of 1990, was to accompany Julia around the state to showcase the bounty of Wisconsin. Her first visit to the state was to conclude with the chapter's inaugural dinner at Sanford on her last night.

For her first evening we had a small dinner at Three Brothers. Over the years since my first date with Angie, the owners, Branko and Pat Radicevic, had become good friends. (I think

With Julia Child in Sanford's kitchen, 1990

it started one night, after dinner, when we emptied a bottle of Branko's aged slivovitz and shared common life and restaurant stories at their bar.) For Julia's visit, they pulled out all the stops, and Julia was eating with gusto as we dug into a family-style Serbian salad and stuffed grape leaves. Angie and I were asking Julia if there was anything, besides the lamb that she had ordered, that she wanted to try; if so, we would order it. She emphatically replied that we should order what we wanted, as she did not share or expect anyone else to. This got us talking about the ultimate pass-around—the very much in vogue "dessert wave"—in which everyone at the table received a different dessert, and then each took one bite and passed the plate to the next person, resulting in everyone eventually getting an undistinguished bite of an unrecognizable mish-mash.

On the second day of the visit we were set up to see a veal farm that supplied calves to Provimi Veal. Provimi's private jet whisked us away from the Waukesha airport to visit the farm. In previous visits around the country, Julia had been badgered (by protesters who charged animal cruelty in the production of veal), so this part of her itinerary was kept under wraps.

We landed and transferred to a bus that pulled up in front of the most immaculate, bucolic farm I had ever seen. Upon entering the calf barn, we were greeted by a half dozen puffball kittens intertwined and frolicking together. After a collective on cue "awwww," it was on to the calves, with their Kewpie doll eyes, all lounging in a designer barn that could have doubled for a Southern California spa—not much to protest here.

We also made stops at two cheese makers. At the first we tasted 5- and 10-year-old cheddars. This was a first for everyone involved, as at that time the only Wisconsin cheddars that achieved that kind of age were in the personal stashes of cheese makers, unavailable for public purchase. Then we moved on to an Italian cheese-making family that not only took us for a tour, but also welcomed us into their family for an afternoon of food and stories.

We were humming along on the return flight when Julia's aide, Gabrielle, called me to the jet's window.

"Sandy—what is that?" she asked.

I peeked out. "Oh my God! It's the Wienermobile! This is great! They sent the Wienermobile to pick us up!" I was enraptured, until Gabrielle replied, "I don't think so."

A flush of fear crossed my mind. Would this be the second time I missed the Wienermobile? When I was about five years old working (hanging out) at my dad's grocery, the Wienermobile used to make unannounced stops at local stores to promote their products. As it pulled up in front of our store, I jumped up on the front radiator to look out the window and saw the door rise. Out strode Little Oscar, all four and a half feet, dressed in his signature floppy-hatted chef outfit. He was headed for our front door when I panicked and ran screaming to the back room of the store. The rest of the neighborhood kids got a tour of the Wienermobile along with complimentary official wiener whistles. I always regretted missing my chance.

It seemed like the sun rose, as Julia leaned toward the window and said, "I think I'd like a ride in that wiener bus." *Julia, where have you been all my life?* And so transpired as surreal an experience as I've ever had: riding down I-94 in the Wienermobile with Julia Child, as the Oscar Mayer theme song blasted through the interior and exterior speakers. We blew along with our de rigueur wiener whistles, as drivers in passing cars honked and waved.

As we pulled up to our destination, the Pfister Hotel, a large, wiener-curious crowd had already gathered, and as the DeLorean-style flip-up door rose, Julia majestically strode out—

Standing with Julia Child and others in front of the Oscar Mayer Wienermobile

it was a vision of worlds colliding. The crowds, with their gaping mouths, surely thought this was the largest chef that had ever walked out of the Wienermobile. I think the aura of the Wienermobile even won Gabrielle over.

The most inspirational part of being with Julia for that trip was watching her passively educate everyone around her with the intuitive questions she asked. She had the enthusiasm of a food reporter and recorder, and as soon as she asked a question, I would think, *Of course! Why didn't I ask that?* It is the same commonsense brilliance that any great chef has when they produce a dish that is so simple and delicious that everyone chides themselves for not coming up with it. She had an inexhaustible need for knowledge and was always learning—a consummate professional.

The last event, held at Sanford, was the most important dinner I had produced up to that day, from the wild mushroom ravioli with smoked chicken essence, to the halibut, served with the last of the season's sweet corn and the first of the season's peppers blended in a zesty relish with Wisconsin roots. It was a menu I was proud of.

At the end of the evening, Angie's mother, Felicia, was waiting in front of the restaurant and introduced herself to Julia. Julia said to her, "So, you have the restaurant on the west side of Milwaukee—how is that going?" After four days of probably 20 separate events, and meeting and speaking with thousands of people, she recalled that snippet from a two-hour, first-night conversation with Angie and me at Three Brothers. Not only an extraordinary listener with an amazing memory, she genuinely cared about people.

◆

"TAKE THIS SHOPPING BAG AND JUST WALK BEHIND ME. AS I PASS BACK AN ITEM, JUST drop it in." Julia was back in Wisconsin, and we were on our way from Milwaukee to Madison for a tour of the Saturday farmer's market (one of America's best) followed by an event honoring Julia. The event was a dining walkabout, and I was Julia's bagman, so to speak. She told me that at these large events there was no way she could physically consume all the food that people offered her; but she didn't want to offend anyone, so she would take a small nibble, thank the person, move to the next booth, and then, conjuring up her inner spy, deftly pass the remaining food back to me for the bag.

Interestingly enough, as we were driving back to Milwaukee after the event, Julia was hungry since she actually had consumed almost nothing at the event. We pulled off the highway at the Johnson Creek exit and went into town looking for a restaurant. Nothing was open in town, but on the way back to the highway, Julia pointed to the left and asked, "What about that place?" A prickly chill ran down my spine as it came into view. She was pointing at the Gobbler.

I had first visited the Gobbler with my parents and sister in the late '60s right after it opened. Even at that time, it was the most oddly decorated new supper club in Wisconsin; it looked like the aftermath of a design death match between Frank Lloyd Wright and Austin Powers, an explosion of pink and purple shag and Naugahyde, topped off with a revolving, raised bar. Even the walls and stairway handrails were covered in purple shag. It immediately became a roadside attraction of the highest order and was the self-proclaimed "grooviest motel" and restaurant in Wisconsin. Their hook was turkey, as the owners, the Hartwig family, were among the largest turkey producers in the state and were probably looking to take roast turkey out of once-a-year Thanksgiving mode into an everyday restaurant dinner setting. By this time in 1991, the restaurant had played and worn out the turkey card a decade before, becoming merely a garish museum of past bad taste—what better place to stop with Julia Child.

It was about 1:30 p.m., and as we walked in, a young hostess behind the semicircular purple-carpeted desk was engulfed in a serious telephone conversation with a friend about what she was going to wear on a date that evening. All through the conversation, without ever looking at us, she kept her finger raised in the international sign of "This call is soooo important, and I'll be right with you." As we got into the second minute, she decided on the maroon cashmere sweater and inadvertently made eye contact with Julia. Her eyes widened, and she said to her friend, "I gotta *go*!" She slammed down the phone and stuttered, "C-Can I help you?"

We were led to our pleather swivel seats, and as I took in the whole empty scene, the only change I noticed was that the shag now lay under a permanent patina of years of cigarette smoke. The waitress came over for our orders. What does a food legend order at the Gobbler? "Dearie, I'll have a Gobbler Burger and a tall tapper." Of course!

◆

A FEW DAYS INTO OUR MUCH-NEEDED VIRGIN GORDA VACATION, I SAT ON A PADDED lounge chair, my feet buried in silvery white sand, while I used my nose to carefully nudge away a miniature umbrella so that I could refresh my parched palate with a sip of frothy piña colada. Angie and I kept conversation to a minimum but jointly decided that the Crab Hole, where we had eaten the night before, wasn't Virgin Gorda's best. It had emotionally scarred Angie, putting her off bird consumption for the foreseeable future. Amazingly after the third colada was drained, the breeze slowly carried away our angst. Angie was feeling so good that I bet she would have downed a bucket of necks without any protest. This was the perfect incommunicado week in paradise, time away that I hadn't even realized I wanted or needed.

Since we had told family and friends that they should only try to reach us for an extreme emergency, we were already contemplating a death in the family when the office contacted us on the beach to tell us that we had received a call. I immediately called my friend back, and she said, "I know you told us not to contact you, but you received a call from a representative of Julia Child's asking if 'that Andy boy from Milwaukee' would cook for her 80th birthday." Andy? Sandy? That was close enough for me—I was thrilled!

There were many dinners held in honor of Julia's 80th birthday, which was August 15, 1992, but there was only one for which Julia specifically picked out the chefs. That dinner was held on November 2, 1992, at the Copley Plaza hotel in Boston. There were 12 chefs in total, and we all collaborated on courses. The entire event was filmed for WGBH, Boston's public television station, and was called "A Birthday Tribute to Julia Child—Compliments to the Chef!" We were cooking for Julia and 650 of her closest friends. Of course, being on public television, you needed music, and the Boston Pops would have to suffice. As we were prepping for the event, members of the orchestra were rummaging through the kitchens, whirling, thumping, and tapping pots and other utensils to use later as instruments during the show. When a few of us walked over to listen to them practice on 40-gallon stockpots, pan-cover cymbals, and wire whisks, it crossed my mind that the end result might be just a bit cheesy.

The 12 chefs asked by Julia to prepare her dinner were Jody Adams, Daniel Bruce, Jimmy Burke, Marcel Desaulniers, Patrick Healy, Johanne Killeen, Cindy Pawlcyn, Caprial Pence, Dawn Sieber, Lydia Shire, Allen Susser, and me. We all were assigned specific courses, and I was responsible for dessert, along with Marcel and Johanne. I had brought along Nate from Sanford, and after borrowing a hooded parka and stepping into a six-degree walk-in freezer, we traded off prescooping 650 miniature balls of lemon ice cream that would be served with the dried cherry and mascarpone gingersnap cannoli—my signature contribution to the plate. This was actually the final step after two days of us baking off and forming the individual cannoli shells and whisking together hotel-sized bowls of filling.

It was great having Nate along. He was our first pastry chef at Sanford, and as detailed and precise as I was when I traveled with food, Nate was always one step ahead. Pastry is all about detail, yet all kitchen food personnel are not created equal. I like to separate them out—baking, line cooking, and pastry—as they each handle their craft differently.

Bakers are the nicest and most convivial of the bunch, as they are used to working together on joint projects such as mixing various doughs and rolling out proofed dough for breads and rolls. It's like a daily Amish barn raising—highly tedious and repetitive work that just begs for friendly conversation to pass the time, as the physical motions become second nature. There are formulas, but in the end, bread baking is about touch and feel because temperature and humidity change the game on a daily basis. Their unusual upper body strength belies their even temperament—not as goofy as the Pillsbury Doughboy, though (and usually possessing really soft hands).

Line cooks also have to work together, but they have their individual stations to worry about. And when they are working together, they have to count on the others to make sure all their food reaches the pass at the same time, so it comes out hot and at the right temperature. When the line is busy, there is no time for or inclination toward idle conversation, as a cook can easily lose his or her concentration. This can cause angst and ridicule, especially when a cook has to redo their food because someone else on the line screwed up. Because they are

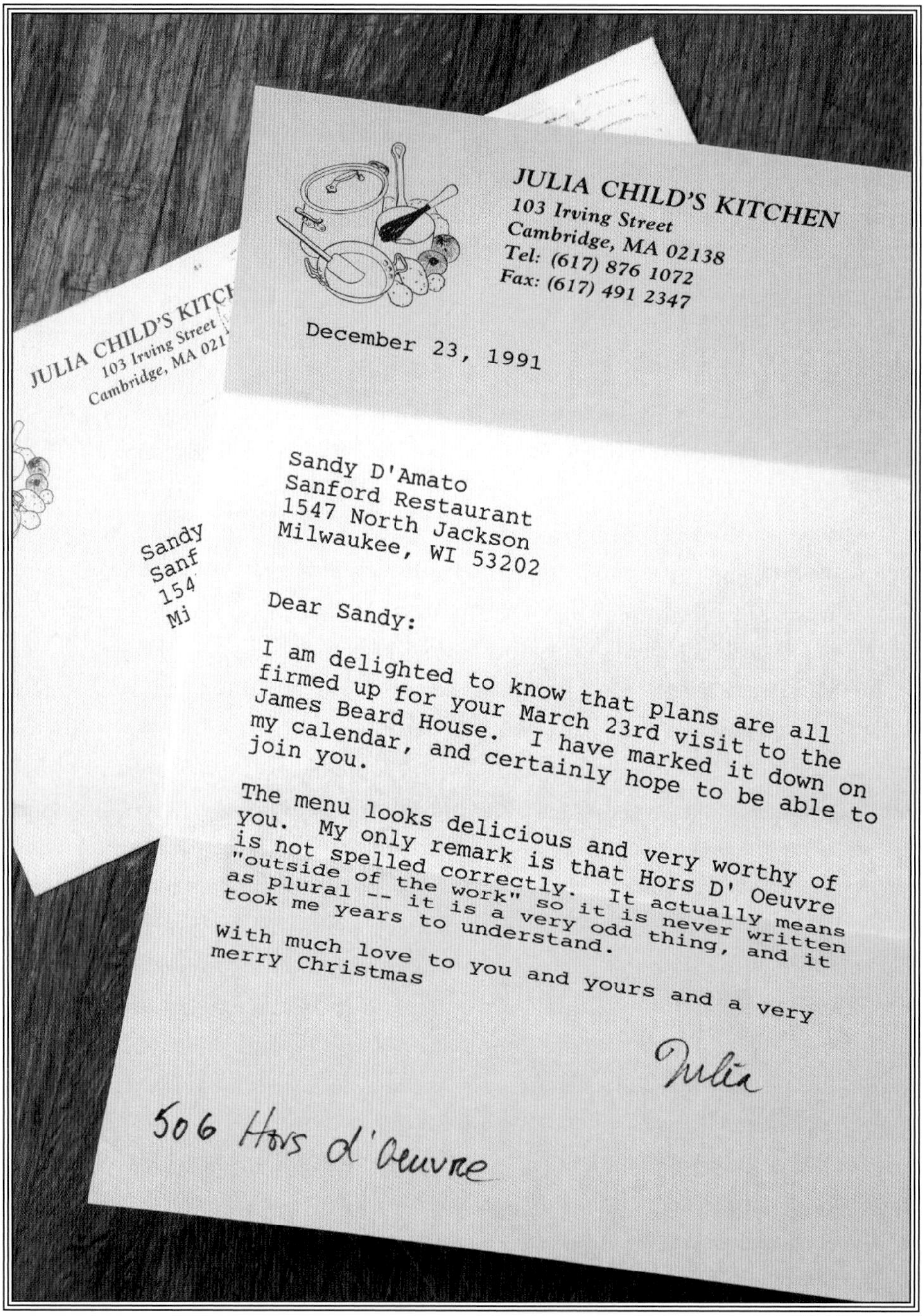

JULIA CHILD'S KITCHEN
103 Irving Street
Cambridge, MA 02138
Tel: (617) 876 1072
Fax: (617) 491 2347

December 23, 1991

Sandy D'Amato
Sanford Restaurant
1547 North Jackson
Milwaukee, WI 53202

Dear Sandy:

I am delighted to know that plans are all firmed up for your March 23rd visit to the James Beard House. I have marked it down on my calendar, and certainly hope to be able to join you.

The menu looks delicious and very worthy of you. My only remark is that Hors D' Oeuvre is not spelled correctly. It actually means "outside of the work" so it is never written as plural -- it is a very odd thing, and it took me years to understand.

With much love to you and yours and a very merry Christmas

Julia

506 Hors d'Oeuvre

Original letter from Julia Child

working when everyone else is playing, this hard-drinking, instant-gratification bunch always tends to feel they have to quickly catch up with the rest of the world after finishing work around midnight.

In the pastry world you find the most antisocial attitudes just due to the fact that most pastry chefs work alone in a very precise and measured world, usually when no one else is in the kitchen. They are impeccably set up and don't take well to anyone moving in on their territory. Also, their handiwork is at the mercy of whoever is executing their desserts in the evening during service.

As challenging as Nate could be, he was one of the best. At the other end of the spectrum was the fellow who replaced Nate after he left. He was a "protractor-carrying freak," and I should have taken a hint from the fact that he tucked his chef coat into his pants and topped his look off with a red bandana tied ascot-style around his neck. A self-proclaimed "ar-teest" and lady's man, he offended one too many female staff members (while engaged to and living with his fiancée) and we were happy to see him finally move on.

Nate fit the classic pastry chef profile, which was fine with me since my personality is split between pastry chef and line cook. I can easily work for hours without verbal banter, as long as it eventually leads to a libation.

Besides our dinner course, each chef was responsible for an hors d'oeuvre for the event reception. I decided on our signature grilled pear and Roquefort tart with caramelized onions and walnuts in a scaled-down bite-size barquette. It was a dish that had been on our Sanford menu since opening day and was also the first dish I served Julia the first time she dined at Sanford in 1990.

This was a huge undertaking, even for a hotel of the Copley's status, as none of the food was preplated. The hot items were coming off a line of temporary stoves that were installed in an adjacent outdoor alley (yes, on this cold day in November) so they would be closer to the ballroom. Leading from the stoves and continuing inside to the prep room of the event were rows of white-clothed, draped tables staffed by multitudes of culinary student volunteers and supervised by the dinner's chefs who made sure that every course would be plated to order as perfectly as it would have been in a 50-seat restaurant.

About an hour before the dessert was to be plated, Marcel, Johanne, and myself got together to do a mock-up to show the students and waitstaff how the plate should look and be served. Marcel was doing a slice of his signature "death by chocolate," a chocolate layer cake that registered a good 10.0 on the cocoa Richter scale—sure to have you vibrating if you came within five feet of it.

Johanne's contribution was the Al Forno signature tiramisu, an espresso-soaked pillow of creamy indulgence. As Johanne placed a sample square of her dessert on the plate, it was like a total solar eclipse over the 10-inch circle.

Marcel's eyes widened, and he said, "Well, Sandy, we might as well go home right now."

Johanne replied, "You think it's too big? That's half the size we serve at the restaurant."

We simultaneously chimed in, "It's too big." She cut it down to a wedge, and we each resumed work on our respective third of the plate.

As the "Boston Pots" opened the evening, my apprehensions about a cheesy display were blown away; I almost welled up at the magnificence of their artistry! They coaxed the most sublime melodies from my everyday *batterie de cuisine*, producing an almost Gershwinesque sonata—very appropriate for our "American in Paris" guest of honor.

A personal highlight of the evening was that, as each course was served, the individual chefs walked out to greet Julia at the table of honor, which included a lot of the original WGBH Boston Public TV gang like her good friends Russell and Marian Morash. This dinner was unlike any I had ever participated in. All of the chefs were so humbled and honored to be involved that the camaraderie behind the scenes was unprecedented. So when we presented dessert and someone from PBS at Julia's table asked how it was working behind the scenes with all those pressured chef egos, I replied honestly, "Just like Mr. Roger's kitchen."

This seminal moment in my career came about from Julia's generosity. She not only realized her celebrity but also was very comfortable with it; she embraced the power it gave her as she shared it. Just like when she had brought French cuisine and the accompanying cooking culture to the American public years before, she continued to do so by systematically introducing this country to the best up-and-coming and established American chefs through her public programming and verbal encouragement. Julia was a student of food and life, never letting her vast knowledge get in the way of a new learning experience. She always asked the questions that you were thinking (or wished you had thought of), and on the flip side, had astute answers to others' questions, which came from years of knowing who she was. There was a fairness about her, and she had a genuine caring for people. She not only influenced the way I cook and think about food, but also how I act and think about life. And I know I'm certainly far from alone in owing Julia a huge debt of gratitude. Merci.

Compliments to
the Chef

A Tribute to
Julia Child on her
80th Birthday

Menu

Duo: Salami de foie gras fumé, sirop de sureau
Pâté de foie gras truffé à l'ancienne
Chefs Daniel Bruce and Patrick Healy
Robert Mondavi Johannisberg Riesling 1990 *Napa Valley*

Brandade de morue en croûte de pommes de terre
et coquilles Saint Jacques rôties servies à la nage de homard
Chefs Jimmy Burke and Dawn Sieber
Robert Mondavi Fume Blanc Reserve To-Kalon Vineyard 1990 *Napa Valley*

Côtelettes d'agneau et raviolis de flageolets au jus d'agneau
et sauce à la crème d'ail
Chefs Jody Adams and Cindy Pawlcyn
Robert Mondavi Merlot 1989 *Napa Valley*

Salade de craterelles et d'endives
avec confit de poires et deux fromages
Chefs Caprial Pence and Allen Susser

Trio: Cannoli au gingembre et aux cerises sèches
Deux petites bouchées de chocolat extraordinaire
Tiramisu aux framboises
Chefs Sandy D'Amato, Marcel Des...
and George Germon ...

Menu from the Julia Child 80th birthday tribute in Boston

CHAPTER TWELVE RECIPES

◆

Provincial Fish Soup with Rouille
337

*Seared Halibut on Corn and
Pepper Relish, Basil Oil*
341

*Grilled Pear and Roquefort Tart with
Caramelized Onions and Walnuts*
344

Herb-Roasted Chicken
346

*Ginger Snap Cannoli with Wisconsin
Dried Cherry Mascarpone Cream*
349

PROVINCIAL FISH SOUP WITH ROUILLE

This dish has been a signature since I started as chef at John Byron's back in 1980. But its roots went back much earlier to a time when, spurred on by her show on Provence, I first read about bouillabaisse in Julia Child's The French Chef Cookbook.

SERVES 2

For the Fish Broth:

⅓ cup (79 mL) extra virgin olive oil

2 medium onions (about 1 pound [454 g]), sliced ¼ inch (6 mm) thick

1 small leek (about 4 ounces [114 g]), sliced ¼ inch (6 mm) thick

1 stalk celery (about 3 ounces [85 g]), sliced

½ fennel bulb (about 4 ounces [114 g]), thinly sliced

12 whole peppercorns, crushed

6 cloves garlic (about 2 ounces [57 g]), chopped

2 bay leaves

2 sprigs fresh thyme

1 medium bunch fresh Italian parsley stems (reserve leaves for garnish)

¼ teaspoon cayenne pepper

1 pound (454 g) cleaned fish bones (preferably from white-fleshed fish)

½ cup (119 mL) brandy

3 cups (711 mL) dry white wine

Scant teaspoon saffron

1 teaspoon grated orange peel

2 cups (474 mL) water

2 cups (320 g) chopped tomatoes in juice

Kosher salt and freshly ground black pepper, to taste

1. Place a sauce pot over medium heat. Add the olive oil to the pot. Add the onions, leeks, celery, fennel, peppercorns, garlic, bay leaves, thyme, parsley stems, and cayenne pepper and sweat, covered, for about 10 minutes, stirring every few minutes. Add the fish bones and continue sweating for another 3 minutes. Add the brandy, wine, saffron, and orange peel, bring up to a simmer, and cook, uncovered, for 5 minutes. Add the water and tomatoes and continue simmering for about 20 minutes.

2. Mill the mixture through the medium blade of a food mill (that has been placed over a clean pot), then place the pot over high heat and reduce to 2 cups (474 mL). Add the salt and black pepper to taste (slightly under-season as you can make a final adjustment after the broth is cooked with the fish and shellfish).

(RECIPE CONTINUES ON PAGE 339)

(RECIPE CONTINUED FROM PAGE 335)

To Finish the Soup:

>4 thin slices French bread, about ¼ inch (6 mm) thick, cut on bias
>
>Extra virgin olive oil, for brushing bread
>
>1 large clove garlic, peeled
>
>6 (1-ounce [28-g]) pieces fish (you may use salmon, snapper, striped bass, etc.).
>
>12 mussels, scrubbed and de-bearded
>
>12 Manila clams or cockles, scrubbed
>
>2 cups (474 mL) prepared Fish Broth
>
>2 tablespoons Pernod
>
>½ cup (44 g) mixed leeks and fennel thinly sliced into ¼-inch strips
>
>Kosher salt and freshly ground black pepper, to taste
>
>3 tablespoons (11 g) chopped fresh Italian parsley leaves
>
>Rouille (recipe follows)

1. Preheat the oven to 375°F (190°C). For the croutons, brush the French bread slices with the oil and bake for about 4 to 5 minutes, or until golden. While the croutons are still warm, rub with the peeled garlic clove; set aside.

2. Place the fish, mussels, and clams in a large saucepan along with the Fish Broth and Pernod. Bring to a simmer, covered, for about 1½ minutes. Add the leeks and fennel and continue cooking for about 1 minute, or until the fish is just cooked and the mussels and clams are open (discard any that have not opened).

3. Remove the fish and shellfish and divide between 2 bowls. Divide the vegetables over the seafood. Reduce the broth to 2 cups (474 mL). Adjust the seasoning with salt and pepper to taste. Stir in the parsley leaves. Divide the broth between bowls and serve with the croutons and Rouille.

For the Rouille: (Makes about 1¼ cups [296 mL])

>(Note: All ingredients should be at room temperature.)
>
>6 large cloves garlic, peeled
>
>¼ cup (36 g) drained pickled sliced hot jalapeño peppers, plus 1 teaspoon jalapeño juice
>
>1 teaspoon ground chipotle pepper
>
>½ teaspoon cayenne pepper
>
>¼ teaspoon ground habanero pepper
>
>1 large egg yolk
>
>¾ cup (178 mL) extra virgin olive oil (divided)
>
>1 teaspoon saffron, steeped in 1½ tablespoons dry white wine
>
>2 teaspoons fresh lemon juice

(RECIPE CONTINUES ON PAGE 340)

(RECIPE CONTINUED FROM PAGE 339)

¾ teaspoon kosher salt

¾ teaspoon freshly ground black pepper

1. Place the garlic, jalapeños and juice, chipotle, cayenne, and habanero in a food processor and process for about 10 seconds. Scrape down the sides, add the egg yolk, and process for 2 seconds. Add half of the olive oil, slowly drizzling it in with the machine running, to form an emulsion. Add the steeped saffron/wine mixture and continue processing. With the machine running, slowly drizzle in the remaining oil and add the lemon juice, salt, and black pepper.

2. When the ingredients are fully incorporated, transfer the Rouille to a covered container and refrigerate until it is needed.

SEARED HALIBUT ON CORN AND PEPPER RELISH, BASIL OIL

When I was setting up the menu for Julia Child's visit to Milwaukee, it was the end of halibut season. Wisconsin sweet corn was still plentiful and the first peppers were hitting the market so this dish was a natural. I first made this dish at my friend TJ's when he was helping us with the opening of Sanford. As the halibut starts to run, it swims back to our menu every season.

SERVES 4

For the Marinated Halibut:

> Juice of 2 limes
> ½ cup (119 mL) regular olive oil
> 20 grinds freshly ground black pepper
> 1½ teaspoons ground cumin
> 1 teaspoon kosher salt
> ⅛ teaspoon cayenne pepper
> 4 (7-ounce [119-g]) skinless halibut fillets (1 inch (2.5 cm) thick)

1. In a shallow dish, large enough to hold the halibut filets in 1 layer, mix all of the ingredients together. Marinate for 4 hours, turning once.

For the Corn and Pepper Relish:

> 4 tablespoons (59 mL) regular olive oil (divided)
> 1 medium red onion, diced small
> 1 medium red bell pepper, seeded and diced small
> 1 medium green bell pepper, seeded and diced small
> Kosher salt and freshly ground black pepper, to taste
> 2 fresh corn on the cob, corn cut from the cobs and milk scraped down with the back of a knife (reserve corn milk separately)
> ¾ teaspoon ground cumin
> 1/16 teaspoon cayenne pepper
> Juice of ½ lime, plus extra for finishing, if necessary

1. Place a saucepan over medium-high heat. Add 2 tablespoons of the oil, and when hot, sauté the onions and bell peppers for about 1½ minutes, season lightly with salt and black pepper, and remove from the pan.

(RECIPE CONTINUES ON PAGE 342)

(RECIPE CONTINUED FROM PAGE 341)

2. Turn the heat up to high and add the remaining oil. When the oil is very hot, add the corn kernels, cumin, and cayenne pepper. Season lightly with salt and black pepper and sauté for 1 to 2 minutes, or until crisp-tender. Add the lime juice to deglaze the pan. With a slotted spoon, remove the corn and add it to the onion/peppers. Add the reserved corn milk to the pan and reduce to ½ tablespoon.

3. Remove the pan from the heat, add the corn mixture back to the pan, and stir it together. Adjust the seasoning with salt and black pepper and additional lime juice, if necessary.

For the Basil Oil:

1 bunch fresh basil
¾ cup (178 mL) regular olive oil
2 cloves garlic, peeled
¼ teaspoon kosher salt
10 grinds freshly ground black pepper

1. Reserve ¼ of the bunch of the basil for the garnish and pick the leaves from the remaining basil. Add the picked leaves to a blender with the remaining ingredients and purée for about 10 seconds (do not blend too long or the basil will cook from the heat of the friction).

To Finish the Dish:

Prepared Marinated Halibut
Kosher salt and freshly ground black pepper, to taste
Prepared Corn and Pepper Relish
Prepared Basil Oil
Marinated Potatoes (recipe follows)

1. Season the halibut lightly on both sides with salt and pepper. Sauté the halibut in a very hot sauté pan for about 3 to 4 minutes per side, or until medium (just warm in the center).

2. Place on top of the Corn and Pepper Relish and drizzle with the Basil Oil (stir before using it). Garnish with the Marinated Potatoes and the reserved basil.

For the Marinated Potatoes:

1½ cups (356 mL) water

½ cup (119 mL) vinegar

Kosher salt, to taste

2 Idaho potatoes, peeled and diced small

1 tablespoon fresh Italian parsley, chopped

¼ cup (59 mL) extra virgin olive oil

2 cloves garlic, finely chopped

¼ teaspoon red pepper flakes

20 grinds freshly ground black pepper

1. Bring the water, vinegar, and enough salt until the water tastes like sea water up to a boil. Add the potatoes and cook until they are tender. Drain well and place the potatoes in a bowl.

2. Sprinkle the parsley over the potatoes. In a small pan, heat the olive oil, garlic, red pepper flakes, and black pepper until the garlic turns light brown. Pour over the potatoes, mix together, and reserve.

GRILLED PEAR AND ROQUEFORT TART WITH CARAMELIZED ONIONS AND WALNUTS

This dish is one of the three that, from day one, was on my menu at Sanford. For my taste, this is a perfectly balanced dish: The pear and Roquefort are a classic combination; the caramelized onions, deglazed with vinegar, gives it a sweet and sour middle; the crisp and rich pastry plays off well against the grilled pears, walnuts, and Roquefort. That is why I prepared it for Julia Child's 80th Birthday, and it has never left the menu at Sanford since.

MAKES 4 TARTS

For the Short Paste Shells:

> **4 ounces (114 g) all-purpose flour (1 cup loosely packed), plus additional for rolling the dough**
>
> **5 tablespoons (2½ ounces [71 g]) cold salted butter, diced**
>
> **1 large egg yolk**
>
> **1½ ounces (45 mL) ice water**

1. Add the 4 ounces (114 g) of flour and butter to a food processor and pulse until the butter is the size of peas. Whisk the egg yolk and ice water together and, with the machine running, add through the feed tube of the processor. Stop the machine when all of the liquid is added.

2. Place the dough on a work surface and bring together with your hands (do not overmix). Cover the dough with plastic wrap and refrigerate for at least 1 hour.

3. Roll out the dough thinly into an approximately 14x14-inch (36x36-cm) square (use a bit of flour so the dough does not stick to the work surface and brush off the excess before using it). Cut the dough in 4 equal pieces and place in 4 (4x½-inch [10x1.3-cm]) removable-bottom tart shell pans. Let the shells rest for 30 minutes in the refrigerator.

4. Preheat the oven to 350°F (180°C). Remove the shells from the refrigerator and trim the excess dough from the top. Line the shell bottoms with parchment paper and place dry beans or rice to weigh down the center. Bake for about 8 to 10 minutes, or until light brown. Remove the beans or rice and finish baking the shells to brown the center. Unmold the shells when they are cool.

For the Caramelized Onions:

> 2 tablespoons clarified butter
>
> 2 tablespoons regular olive oil
>
> 2 medium (1 pound [454 g]) onions, cut in half and sliced, with the grain, as thin as possible
>
> 2 tablespoons red wine vinegar
>
> ⅛ teaspoon kosher salt
>
> ⅛ teaspoon freshly ground black pepper

1. Heat a sauté pan to very hot. Add the butter and oil and wait until the oil begins to smoke. Carefully add the onions and immediately start stirring with a wooden spoon. Continue stirring regularly for about 20 minutes, or until the onions are golden without having any burnt specks on them.

2. Add the vinegar, salt, and pepper and reduce to dry; reserve. (You may make the onions ahead.)

For the Grilled Pears:

> 1 (8-ounce [227 g]) Bartlett or D'Anjou pear (semi-firm), peeled, cut in half and cored, then each half cut in 6 fans (about 1 to 1½ inches x 1 to 1½ inches [2.5 to 3.8 cm x 2.5 to 3.8 cm] when flattened; you should have 12 fans total)
>
> 1 tablespoon clarified butter
>
> Kosher salt and freshly ground pepper, to taste

1. In a bowl, toss the pears with the butter and season lightly with salt and pepper. Preheat the grill or heat a nonstick grill pan. Grill the pears for 15 to 30 seconds on each side. Immediately cool the pears in the refrigerator until they are needed.

To Finish the Tarts:

> Baked Short Paste Shells
>
> Prepared Caramelized Onions
>
> 2 ounces (57 g) Roquefort cheese, crumbled
>
> Prepared Grilled Pears
>
> 2½ tablespoons (18 g) walnuts, toasted at 375°F (190°C) for 5 to 6 minutes, then coarsely chopped
>
> 4 teaspoons walnut oil
>
> 4 pinches freshly ground black pepper

1. Preheat the oven to 375°F (190°C). On the bottom of each baked shell, place a thin layer of Caramelized Onions. Place ¼ of the cheese on top of the onions. Place 3 pear fans on top of the cheese. Sprinkle ¼ of the walnuts over the pear fans and drizzle 1 teaspoon of the walnut oil. Add 1 pinch of black pepper over all.

2. Bake for about 6 to 8 minutes, or until they are heated through, but do not let the cheese liquefy. Serve them immediately.

HERB-ROASTED CHICKEN

There are five keys to making a great roast chicken. First, truss (tying up the bird with string) the chicken so that it cooks evenly. Second, sear the chicken on the stovetop before placing it in the oven. Third, cook it at a high heat to ensure a crispy skin with a moist interior. Fourth, baste, baste, baste. And last, do not over-cook the poor chicken, as a crispy dry chicken will please no one but the dog. Follow this easy recipe and the only disappointment will be on your pet's face.

SERVES 2

For the Herb Mix:

> 3 bay leaves, crushed
>
> 1½ teaspoons thyme leaves
>
> 1 teaspoon fresh rosemary leaves
>
> 1 teaspoon grated orange peel
>
> 1 teaspoon crushed lavender
>
> 1 teaspoon marjoram
>
> 1 teaspoon ground fennel seed

1. Chop all of the ingredients medium fine and mix together. Reserve.

For the Chicken:

> 1 chicken (3½ to 4 pounds [1.59 to 1.82 kg]), rinsed in cold water and dried with paper towels
>
> Kosher salt and freshly ground black pepper, for seasoning
>
> 3 tablespoons (43 g) salted butter, softened
>
> Prepared Herb Mix
>
> 3 tablespoons (45 mL) regular olive oil

1. Preheat the oven to 450°F (230°C). Remove the wings at the second joint. Season the cavity of the chicken with salt and pepper. To truss the chicken, position the chicken with the legs toward you. Place the center of an 18-inch (46-cm) length of string under the tail (the "pope's nose"). Cross over and loop around the leg about 1 inch (2.5 cm) from the ends and pull lightly. Turn the chicken around and bring both ends of the string along the sides and toward the neck. Tie lightly between the neck and the wishbone. Rub the chicken all over with the softened butter. Season with the Herb Mix, salt, and pepper.

2. Heat a heavy-bottomed sauté pan over medium heat. Add the olive oil and turn the heat to high. Add the chicken, right side down, and brown for about 3 minutes. Turn onto the left side and brown for 3 minutes. Turn breast side down and brown for 3 minutes. Place breast side up and bake for about 45 minutes to 1 hour, depending on the size, basting every 10 minutes.

3. Check the chicken for doneness after 45 minutes using a large kitchen fork to pierce the chicken at the underside of the breast (above the thigh and leg and above the back bone), (do not pierce the breast). Hold the chicken neck-side-up over a white plate and let the juices run out. If the last juices are clear, the chicken is done. Let the cooked chicken rest in a warm spot for at least 10 minutes before carving.

GINGER SNAP CANNOLI WITH WISCONSIN DRIED CHERRY MASCARPONE CREAM

When we opened Sanford in 1989, I wanted a dessert that would bridge the gap between my dad's grocery store and the restaurant; a slight twist on the classic cannoli was perfect. So I took ginger snap batter and made a very thin, crisp tube-shaped wafer, then made a light filling with mascarpone, pastry cream, and bourbon-macerated Wisconsin dried cherries, currants, and grated orange peel. Is it better than the traditional? Well, as my traditional Uncle Ben said upon trying it, "Sandy, it's not a cannoli . . . hey, this is good!" It's been a signature dish ever since.

MAKES 4 CANNOLI

For the Ginger Snap Cannoli Shells:

> 2 tablespoons plus 1 teaspoon (1 ounce [28 g]) granulated sugar
>
> 2 tablespoons (1 ounce [28 g]) salted butter
>
> 2 tablespoons (1 ounce [30 mL]) dark corn syrup
>
> ½ teaspoon ground ginger
>
> ¼ teaspoon fresh lemon juice
>
> 3 tablespoons plus 1 teaspoon (1 ounce [28 g]) all-purpose flour
>
> Tool for forming cookies: 1 (20-inch-long x 1¼-inch-thick [51-cm-long x 3.2-cm-thick]) wooden dowel or similar size rolling pin

1. Combine all of the ingredients, except the flour, in a small stainless steel bowl. Place the bowl in a double boiler. Melt the ingredients slowly over a low simmer and mix periodically with a whisk. When they are blended and warm, add the flour and stir in with a spatula.

2. Preheat the oven to 375°F (190°C). Place the warm mixture into a pastry bag that has been fitted with a #2 round tip (before filling, push part of the pastry bag into the tip to prevent the mixture from running out when filling). Pipe a dab of the mixture under each corner of parchment paper on a baking sheet to hold down the paper. Pipe the mixture in a 4-inch (10-cm) circle and continue in a spiral motion toward the center by holding the tip ¼ inch (6 mm) off of the paper to control the thickness (leave ¼ inch [6 mm] of open space between the spirals as the spaces will fill in while baking)—the ginger snaps should be fairly thin when you are finished piping.

3. Before baking, suspend the wooden dowel or rolling pin over a work surface to keep the baked ginger snaps from touching the surface after forming. Bake the spirals for 2 minutes, rotate the baking sheet, then bake for 3 more minutes, or until golden brown.

(RECIPE CONTINUES ON PAGE 350)

(RECIPE CONTINUED FROM PAGE 349)

4. Take the ginger snaps out of the oven, and not immediately, but while they are still warm (about 45–60 seconds), and not too tightly, form them around the dowel in a tube shape. (If they are not pliable and are too hard to form, don't force them as they will break, just place them back in the oven for 30 seconds and repeat the process.) Carefully remove the cannoli shells from the dowel (they will be fragile). (You may prepare the cannoli shells ahead and store them in a covered container in a cool and dry place.)

For the Pastry Cream: (Makes ½ cup [119 mL])

½ cup (119 mL) whole milk

2 tablespoons plus 1 teaspoon (1 ounce [28 g]) granulated sugar (divided)

1 large egg yolk

1 tablespoon (¼ ounce [7 g]) cornstarch

Dash vanilla extract

1. In a small non-corrosive pot, bring the milk and half of the sugar up to a boil. In a bowl, whisk the egg yolk with the remaining sugar until it is light colored. Whisk in the cornstarch and vanilla. Slowly whisk in the hot milk/sugar mixture. Return the mixture to the pot and continue whisking while bringing it up to a boil so that the mixture does not stick to the bottom. Let it boil for 30 seconds, then place it in a clean bowl. Cover the bowl loosely with plastic wrap and refrigerate.

For the Wisconsin Dried Cherry Mascarpone Cream and to Finish the Cannoli:

(Note: All ingredients must be cold before mixing.)

2 tablespoons dried currants

2 tablespoons coarsely chopped Door County dried cherries

1 tablespoon granulated sugar

1 ounce (30 mL) bourbon

Fine zest of ½ orange

4 ounces (114 g) Wisconsin mascarpone cheese

¼ cup (59 mL) prepared Pastry Cream, whisked to soften and smooth

1½ teaspoons Grand Marnier

¼ cup (59 mL) heavy cream, whipped to soft peaks

Prepared Ginger Snap Cannoli Shells

3 tablespoons (23 g) roasted, chopped pistachios

Confectioners' sugar, for dusting

Mango Lime Sauce (recipe follows)

1. Place the currants, cherries, sugar, bourbon, and orange zest in a nonstick pan and reduce, stirring, until almost dry. Cool in the refrigerator.

2. When cold, add the mixture to the mascarpone in a bowl and mix together with a rubber spatula. Add the Pastry Cream and mix. Add the Grand Marnier and mix. Fold in the whipped cream (do not overmix).

3. Place in a pastry bag that has been fitted with a round tip (approximately #18), then fill the Ginger Snap Cannoli Shells. Dip the ends of the filled shells into the chopped pistachios and dust the exterior with the confectioners' sugar. Place some Mango Lime Sauce and a cannoli on each plate and serve.

For the Mango Lime Sauce:

½ ripe mango, peeled and cut in medium dice
Juice of ½ lime
Pinch kosher salt

1. Purée all of the ingredients in a blender until smooth. Reserve the sauce in the refrigerator.

13

CONTINUING EDUCATION

OR A RESTAURANT TO GROW, YOU MUST TRAVEL. I REALIZED EARLY IN MY career that to compete with the best in the restaurant business, you have to know what makes them the best. From the first trip Angie and I took to Europe in 1985 to our years of teaching cooking classes overseas, travel became an overriding teacher. We had many extraordinary, groundbreaking experiences, but we also found out that the lessons we learned from bad experiences could at times be more valuable than the great ones.

On that first trip to Europe, it was as if Angie and I were auditioning for the original pilot of *Lost*—there just weren't any greener rubes walking off the plane in the Brussels airport. We rented a car and just started driving, without a map, to find our way into Brussels and then through Italy and France. We were looking for the highway to the center of the city, and our first turn out of the airport found us quickly backing out of a secret military installation; two officers with machine guns convinced us that it might be in our best interest to procure a map.

We were staying in Brussels for the first two days of the trip for one reason: to go to Comme Chez Soi. This would be my first three-star experience, and I was as intimidated as hell. With it being a Michelin three-star—the absolute pinnacle of fine dining—if there was a God, I was expecting an appearance there. I had been researching the trip since the early 1970s when I would meticulously cut out articles from the *New York Times* on three-star wonders and file them in order. Then, with the release of *Great Chefs of France* in 1978, I became convinced that, without dining at these places, I would never *fully* understand food.

As we followed the maître d' to our table at Comme Chez Soi, my head was getting lighter. We sat down and were dwarfed by the huge menus. I had told Angie before we arrived that I knew exactly what to order. But as soon as I had the menu in my hands, I was a deer in headlights. I heard my name being called in the distance, and then realized it was Angie across the table. I just looked at her with a blank stare as she asked what we were having. She noticed I had broken out in hives as I answered, "I don't know . . ." The waiter, who couldn't have been nicer, asked if we would like to order, and with my finger shaking I just barely pointed to the prix fixe menu. Yes, I was one messed-up kid. With the roster of two- and three-star places that I had booked by mail months before for the upcoming three weeks, I knew it would be prudent to get it together.

Angie and I were a friendly lot, but without a minimal command of any foreign language, we were quite lost. As we were driving across the border in Switzerland, a stoic Swiss guard decided to pull our car out of line for a full inspection. Questions were fired at us in staccato Swiss, and I feverishly paged through my translation book to no avail.

After about a 30-minute wait, we were deemed worthy of border crossing, but the experience was a reality check, highlighting how unworldly and unprepared we both were. As we crossed the border into the French countryside, it was about 1:30 in the afternoon, and we were starving. We wanted to stop to eat, but we were a bit apprehensive because we were away from any major city and any chance of someone actually understanding us.

We pulled off the highway into a tiny town. The streets were deserted, and the only restaurant we saw was dark and looked closed. We got out of the car and approached the large, ominous wooden door, cautiously cracking it open. We peeked our heads in and were greeted with a booming, lyrical "Bonjour!" from the madame behind the bar. We explained that we spoke very little French, so she just motioned for us to sit down at a cute little table, and the food started to arrive. It was a lovely lunch, topped off with a glistening, rustic fruit galette that was in full view at a side table throughout the meal. That lunch set the tone for the whole trip; we were still naive, but assured that good people and good food were universal.

This was in stark contrast to our pretrip advisories. Before Angie and I left for Europe, everyone warned us about the surly French who would not give us the time of day and the Italians who would just as well "pick your pocket" or "rip your purse off your shoulder" as they sped by on their Vespas. Of course you should be aware in any large city, whether it's Paris, Rome, New York, Chicago, or even Milwaukee.

So what horrors can I remember? In the town of Asti in Italy's Piedmont region, we tightly locked up our rental car, toted our luggage to the hotel, and checked in. The first order of business, as always, was eating. We went to a small restaurant for a pizza and a couple of salads. This was pre-Euro, so every few days we had to change money from Belgian francs to French francs to Italian lire. When the bill came, I placed down my "play money" lire with a little extra for a tip and told the waiter to keep it. He picked up the check, took three steps, and did a quick 180 back to the table.

He put the check and lire down and said, "Excusa me. Whatsa this?"

I looked and after a few seconds said, "Big mistake."

He intoned, "Si, a bigga mistake!" I had left him about an $80 tip on a $6 pizza. He proceeded to spread out the various lire bills and gave us a quick lesson on what each was worth. And then he wouldn't even accept any tip as he said, "You know, itsa includa?"

◆

EVEN THOUGH SWEET PEPPERS ARE USED IN MANY DIFFERENT COUNTRIES AND VARIED cuisines, the first country they bring to my mind is Italy. Yes, I know—I'm Italian. When I was growing up there never was a sausage served that didn't have a roasted pepper offered alongside it. It seemed odd to me at first, but that feeling lasted only as long as it took for the first bite to go down.

Italians have always accorded the pepper its own rightful place in their cuisine beyond its role as garnish for sausage. In Italy, it seemed that every restaurant that we went into had an antipasti display with burnished, vibrantly colored peppers as a centerpiece.

One particularly great memory was in Lake Como, near Milan. I had booked a small hotel, Hotel Asnigo, in the hills surrounding the lake. I picked it because of the expansive terrace overlooking the lake and the fact that every room had a lake view—and also because it was inexpensive and fit nicely in our limited budget.

It turned out to be quite a trip to find it. Winding up the narrow mountain roads, we almost drove into a construction hole in the road (we missed the Italian sign, as we didn't speak much Italian) and were greeted by two Italian laborers who gave us the international idiot sign. We turned around and finally found our way to the hotel.

We started to understand the inexpensive part; the hotel was a bit frayed and unkempt around the edges. But you could see that years back (probably about 20 or 30) it had been a grand place. The rooms, however, were impeccably clean, and the view was magnificent.

We arrived in time for dinner and sat in the hollow dining room with one other couple. The menu was very small, and I keyed in on the roasted pepper appetizer followed by veal with mushrooms. After dinner we went to a tiny bar in the lobby presided over by the owner, Luigi. He asked how dinner was, and we said it was very good. He replied, "It wasn't good. It was salty, right? It's always salty—the chef smokes too much."

The veal was a bit salty, but the peppers glossed with olive oil were perfect. And as Luigi brought out a special bottle, he gave us more than a few complimentary shots of our first taste of grappa. As the hours passed, it seemed he knew the perfect complement to salty food was a warm, gracious, and welcoming personality.

I WAS KEEPING MY FOOT TO THE FLOOR SO I WOULDN'T LOSE THE FIREFLY-SIZED taillights in front of me. But it was almost a losing battle, as the matchbox Fiat that Angie and I had rented seemed to be powered by a wind-up rubber band. The rain was pummeling the front windshield, and the only thing I was sure about was that there was a large crevasse to the right and left of the road.

We were lost (again) in the second-largest city in Italy, Milan. We started out from the Asnigo, and Luigi had lent us his personal map (which, judging from the condition of the paper, must have been a christening gift) to direct us the 40-some miles to Milan from Cernobbio.

We arrived in Milan a few hours before our 8 p.m. dinner reservation. Because it was sunny and light out, we didn't really need the map as the route was very well posted, with signs directing us to Milan every few miles.

After exploring the city on foot, we arrived at the traditional Milanese restaurant and put ourselves in the hands of the waiter. He brought us a selection from the copious antipasti table that we'd had to maneuver around as we were seated. The plate contained grilled and roasted vegetables—some sweet and sour, some stuffed or crusted—flanked by paper-thin regional cured meats and salamis.

For the entrée course we had piccata of chicken and veal cotoletta. All was delicious, but the star of the dinner arrived between the antipasto and entrée. This was usually the position reserved for pasta in Italy, but we were in the north, which meant we ate rice. The waiter brought two of the special seafood risottos. It was cooked *all'onda*, which loosely translates to "wavy." When we tapped the rim of the dish, the creamy rice undulated slightly like ocean waves, with the chunks of seafood looking like little bouncing buoys. It was absolutely luscious, and each perfectly cooked kernel of rice exploded with briny crustacean goodness.

By the time we walked out of the restaurant after dinner, the perfect night had given way to an impromptu gale. We ran to the car and unfolded the map, which quickly deteriorated into four separate pieces. Using our best internal GPS, we tried to retrace our way back to the *autostrada* (highway), but soon found ourselves following the only taillights around down a seemingly deserted road. We knew we were in big trouble when the taillights became headlights that started to beam down on us, eventually sliding right past us on the narrow road. That's when we figured out that we might be following another lost traveler.

After an hour of aimless driving, we miraculously ran into the *autostrada* ramp, flanked by a minute arrow sign pointing toward Cernobbio. Saved again from self-destruction.

ABOUT TWO WEEKS INTO OUR TRIP WE WERE FINALLY ON THE FAST TRACK TO BEING seasoned travelers. Actually, we had just become smart enough to realize that wherever we went, we would be lost.

As we arrived in Nice, with three maps spread over the dashboard, we made record time to our hotel, which was conveniently located near the coast. The next day we had a luncheon planned at Restaurant de Bacon in Cap d'Antibes. On the map, it was less than two inches down the coast, which translated to us leaving two hours ahead for a trip that would have taken a local resident only a half hour. It took us exactly one hour and 55 minutes, and we were feeling mighty proud.

There was just one reason we were at Restaurant de Bacon: the bouillabaisse. From the time I started as chef at John Byron's in 1980, my specialty had been a provincial fish soup with rouille. It was the one dish that carried over to Sanford when we opened in 1989 and has been a personal signature dish for 33 years. So anytime I have a chance, I want to try great fish soup.

We walked into the courtyard and were greeted and led to a large table with crisp white linens brightly reflecting the sun streaming through a huge picture window. The window just happened to overlook the Mediterranean Sea. Two windsurfers skimmed the impossibly saturated azure water, and across from us sat an impeccably dressed couple taking bites of a whole roasted John Dory, with every second bite being popped into the mouth of the regal woman's lap dog.

The waiter brought over a silver vessel filled with saffron-infused broth. On the side was a dish of crisp, flat croutons and garlicky rouille to float in the ruddy broth. Then came a huge platter of the fish, traditional to the bouillabaisse, which were infused with the broth. The bouillabaisse at de Bacon was spectacular. Along with our meal, we sipped a perfectly chilled bottle of Chapoutier Hermitage blanc, and even though the smiling pup may have disagreed, we just knew that there wasn't anyone anywhere in the world having a better lunch than us.

TO GET A REAL FEEL FOR THE CUISINE OF FRANCE, YOU HAVE TO TRAVEL THROUGH THE different regions. Even though most of the regions are represented in Parisian restaurants, and I do love eating in Paris, the true essence of regional dishes is best experienced at the source.

One evening in Burgundy we had a reservation at Lameloise, a Michelin three-star restaurant in Chagny. Since Angie and I were still new to the power-eating game, we thought we would stop for a *light* lunch at a small bistro on the road to Chagny. As we sat down and I was handed a menu, my vision started to spiral—boeuf bourguignon, quenelle of pike with crayfish, escargot, and jambon persillé! These were all dishes I had been taught to make over the years, and here I was at the source, where the dishes originated. We had to try them all—so much for a light lunch and having an appetite six hours later when we sat down for dinner. I do remember walking the room after dinner in a now-ritual patting of the stomach and drinking of Alka-Seltzer. And by this time in the trip, I was starting to rethink the miniature car that we had rented; the space between my stomach and the steering wheel seemed to be getting tighter as we racked up dinner after dinner. Well, as one gets older and a bit wiser, one learns to pace oneself a little—but we were still young and dumb.

We were on our way to Tours, the old capital of France, to stay at Jean Bardet. I was really looking forward to staying there. We had a lavish, terraced room that overlooked the outdoor dining courtyard. After snacking in the town all afternoon, we were not really hungry at dinnertime, but after the first bite, we kicked into machine mode and mowed through course after course. When dessert arrived, I had one bite and was done—we learned nothing at Lameloise and could barely make it up to the room.

We couldn't sleep, so we changed into expand-o clothes and planted ourselves on the terrace. Below us, the courtyard dining tables were full, a real United Nations scene. The hushed tones of the German couple in the corner and the Italian family next to them mixed with the large table of 12 Japanese men, seemingly carrying out respectful business conversation.

For a moment the courtyard was completely void of conversation, and the only sounds were the tinkling of silverware against fine bone china. That was until a loud, long noise pierced through the courtyard, echoing from side to side. I looked over at Angie, who had a horrified look on her beet-red face. What had started as a one-cheek sneak had erupted into a Concorde-level sonic boom. I was frightened, strangely proud, and a little challenged that Angie was that gifted. We both hit the ground and crawled into the room, where we peeked out the curtain. Because of the configuration of the courtyard, everyone was confused about where the sound had come from. The men at the large table were accusatorily pointing at one another, and all were shaking their heads as if to deny guilt. Angie decided to ride out the rest of the night in the room.

◆

WHAT IS THE BEST RESTAURANT IN THE WORLD? YOU MIGHT GET AS MANY ANSWERS TO that question as the number of people you ask; everyone has different criteria for what their best is.

By the time we arrived in Paris at the end of the three weeks, we had devoured our wish-list roster of three-star restaurants, a lineup that could put any normal person in a food coma just from reading through it. We had incredible meals at Auberge de l'Ill in Illhaeusern, Georges

Blanc in Vonnas, Alain Chapel in Mionnay, and Lameloise in Chagny. But the consensus best restaurant in France was Taillevent in Paris. Surprisingly, unlike the others, Taillevent was not a chef-owned restaurant. It was under the inescapable watchful eye of Jean-Claude Vrinat, the undisputed restaurateur's restaurateur.

We made our reservation for lunch at Taillevent months before arriving in Paris. We also had a note of introduction from our friends Ihab and Sally Hassan, who were close compatriots with Monsieur Vrinat. Upon entering, we were warmly greeted by Monsieur Vrinat himself. With a few words of fractured French, we passed along the note. He responded in perfect, French-accented English with an aplomb and sweet warmness that reminded me of Maurice Chevalier in Gigi.

"How are the Hassans doing?" he asked. "We do miss them here—please pass along my best." With that interchange, we settled into one of the great shows of our restaurant lives—absolutely wonderful food with unparalleled service.

As we were looking over our menus, we heard a sharp squeak followed by a loud, female Texas drawl: "Honey, look at that big ol' link! Plop it right down here on my plate!"

The woman whose voice we heard was commenting on Taillevent's signature dish, boudin de homard à la nage, a blend of seafood mousse studded with all sorts of shellfish goodness and served in an ethereal beurre blanc. The waiter cut thick tranches of the sausage and soundlessly floated them in front of the Texans.

As he glided away, the woman shrieked, "Where you goin' with the rest of that sausage and gravy?"

He replied, "We are keeping it warm for you on the side until you are ready for more."

"No, no, no!" she said. "We're paying for it *all*, so just leave it here on the table."

"Of course, madame," was the unflappable server's only reply.

We also ordered the boudin de homard—but with a bit less flair than our Southern neighbors. Exquisitely textured, it was just a cloud of shellfish essence as it dissipated across our palates.

At the end of dinner, Angie ordered tea with milk, and as we were talking, a cup appeared in front of her and then simultaneously a looping stream of perfectly steeped tea from the right was met in the cup with a measured touch of warm milk from the left. Angie looked up and melted as she sipped the golden elixir. This was ballet in the guise of service.

Best restaurant in the world? That day, Taillevent was it.

◆

IN OCTOBER OF 2000 I WAS STARTING MY FIRST GUEST-CHEF BIKE TRIP IN UMBRIA, A region in the heart of Italy, with Bike Riders of Boston. Angie and I found ourselves in a small café near the train station in Perugia, waiting for our guides to pick us up. We met the rest of the bikers in the van and were off to the hotel to check in, freshen up, and then take a short warm-up ride to get us mentally *ready* for the week.

Angie and I thought we were in pretty good shape as we had been biking on the weekends and using a cycling machine when we couldn't get outside. As we approached the first uphill section of the journey, my bike mysteriously started to go sideways, and my legs began to shake. After only three minutes I was totally out of breath and gasping. I might as well have been riding a couch, as that is how far I got up the hill. The next couple of days went a bit better, but for future bike trips, we realized that we really had to train if we wanted less pain.

As guest chef, my primary responsibility, which occurred toward the middle of the trip, was to lead the other bikers through the local markets, plan a menu according to what was in season, and pick up all the ingredients. Then we'd go back to the kitchen and together prepare a feast for the evening.

We were staying at a 17th-century mansion in Spoleto that had been converted into a small hotel. When we got back with the food, I went looking for cooking equipment and utensils but came up dry because the only cooking done at the hotel was making coffee for breakfast. This was a big problem because we were supposed to be cooking a six-course meal for 10 people. We went to the local "Everything's a Euro" store and picked up mixing bowls, sauté pans, whisks, and so on. The store, like its counterparts in the United States, carried equipment of suspect quality. Hence, within the first half hour of cooking, the handle fell off the sauté pan, the bowl sprung a leak, and the whisk exploded into strands of aluminum. One of the guides saved the day by taking me over to a local restaurant where we had eaten the previous evening. They were kind enough to let me borrow everything I needed to finish the dinner.

One of the dishes that was inspired by that trip was a combination of perfect, tiny brown lentils from Castelluccio (a stone's throw from Spoleto), that were stewed to a creamy lushness, topped with well-grilled, local, slightly aged, spicy sausage links. These lentils take longer to cook than the conventional US supermarket variety, but that longer cooking time helps infuse them with extra layers of flavor. The beauty of the dish is that it can be completed with one pot and a small sauté pan that even the Italian discount equipment store could have supplied.

Besides the big group dinner that I was responsible for, I was supposed to participate in a short class on antipasti from the region one afternoon. Since I had never been to Umbria before, my appetizers were a touch more "inspired" by the region than literal classic Umbrian dishes. The setting for the class was an *agriturismo* (an Italian farm property/bed and breakfast/restaurant) run by Fabio, a wonderful character who was missing a few too many teeth to

Angie and me when I was cooking as a guest chef on a bike trip in Gordes, France

live up to the aura of his name but whose bravado and genuine warmth made him appealing and memorable.

I had been warned by our guide Mims that in one of the past classes the guest chefs had prepared Franco-Japanese appetizers that had nothing to do with Umbria, and Fabio and his family had been insulted and politely refused to join the group to eat and drink. Consequently I felt I was under pressure to bring them back around.

The class was started by a stout Italian cook who had forearms like rock-hard Brunswick bowling pins from years of rolling out dough for pasta and bread. She made a classic torta al testo, a simple, somewhat bland flatbread of the region that is cooked on a testo, or flat iron griddle, which replaced the original hot stones that it might have been cooked on in Etruscan times.

Within a few seconds she had swirled together the flour, a bit of yeast, sparkling water, and golden Umbrian olive oil. She kneaded it together like a well-oiled machine, let it rest, and then tossed it on the hot testo. When it was golden brown on both sides, she split the bread open while it was still hot, and then layered it with thin slices of fat-edged prosciutto. We all ate the wedges as the fat melted into the hot crispy torta.

I was up next. This is like following Pavarotti at La Scala in Milan. I started by making a simple crostini with local grilled pears, Gorgonzola, and onions. As I started to grill the pears, searing them with olive oil and pepper, I saw Fabio's wife instinctively slapping her cheek and murmuring "O Dio Mio" as she looked over at him. You have to understand, in Italy, when you have a fresh ripe pear, you eat it—you don't grill it or sprinkle it with pepper.

Along with that I made sautéed chard and pancetta-wrapped mozzarella with mint sauce and a few other items, and added half of a leftover pine nut tart from the previous evening's dinner.

We all sat down, and I asked Fabio and his wife to join us. He said they could sit for just *un momento*. His wife picked up the pear crostini and looked it up, down, and around before taking a bite. She called her young son over, and he put a piece in his mouth. He grinned and said, "Buono." All of a sudden the food started to disappear. An hour and a half later, we were still there.

Fabio offered us some of his stash of grappa, and we exchanged recipes for his torta and my pine nut tart. He said, "This is a good exchange. We both learn something today. Of course, you learn more than we do, but it's still good."

◆

THE GOLDEN SPANISH SUN TEMPORARILY BLINDED ME AS I SWUNG OPEN THE weathered wooden shutters. As soon as my eyes came back into focus, they revealed the bustling activity of a packed Plaza Mayor.

Angie and I were just waking up at one in the afternoon. Although we've been known to sleep for 9 or 10 hours on occasion, this would have been overkill even for us—if we hadn't gotten to bed at 6 a.m.

After our third day in Madrid, we were officially on Madrileños time. The previous evening we had met up with Simon, a former coworker who was now cooking in Madrid. We were familiar with the fact that the Spanish eat later, but when he had suggested that we start the evening at 11:30 p.m., I thought he was joking.

The city was just starting to get into full swing as we went through a bevy of tapas bars, with Simon pointing out the specialties of each establishment. It was a brilliant night of wonderful bites that added up to a perfectly satisfying traveling dinner.

But by that night we had to get back on Sandy-and-Angie time because we had an early flight the next morning to Catania, Sicily, where we were starting a bike trip. Consequently, we had a light lunch and planned to have an early dinner at a small restaurant next door to our hotel. They opened at 8:30, and we were the first and only customers in the dining room. On our first day in Madrid, we had already had one of the local can't-miss dishes, oven-roasted baby pig. So when I saw another signature of the city, the rabo de toro—a bull tail braised in red wine to a fragile tenderness, I was in.

Angie was having no part of the tail and went for a large, steaming bowl of hearty chickpea soup. I did talk her into having a bite of my dish, and she said it was a bit tart, which I thought must be from the inclusion of vinegar in the braising process. Unfortunately, as I started to find out the next morning, it wasn't vinegar at all. I woke up just not feeling quite right, and the feeling escalated as we boarded the plane.

After 40-plus years of flying, I finally got to use everything in the seat pocket in front of me. Thank God for that bag. It only got worse after we landed in Catania and we were shoved in the back of a hot, windowless van for a cross-country drive to the coast. Then we boarded an ancient ferry for a bobbing three-hour trip to the island of Lipari. It took three days for my green face to return to its regular color.

This experience should have put me off oxtail for life, but our next trip to Rome found us at Piperno, a restaurant located in the old Jewish ghetto, where the food is classic Roman with the influence of Jewish culture. The main difference from other Roman restaurants is the predominance of perfectly crispy fried foods. The squash blossoms, vegetable, salt cod, and more are lightly batter dipped, quickly fried in olive oil, and served on folded white napkins—as the best fast food should be. We were there specifically for the star of all fried food, the carciofi alla giudia. This is a young, stem-on Roman artichoke trimmed, fried once, and then flattened face down so the leaves fan out like an overblown rose.

We could not reach the restaurant by phone, so we just stopped by right when they opened at noon. The restaurant was very old-school formal, with beautifully starched linens and silver. Four or five tables were already occupied with regulars who must have had papal dispensation to get in before noon. We were seated across from a prime corner table occupied by a strikingly beautiful older woman in her 70s. She was dressed as impeccably as a mannequin in a Roman couture showroom window and had the stateliness and grace of a countess.

The waiter came to our table, and I immediately ordered the artichokes to start. Angie was enraptured looking across at the woman delicately spooning a thick liquid to her lips, and she asked the waiter, "What is that woman having?"

"Ahh, that is the pasta e ceci"—pasta and chickpeas—"a very special preparation."

Angie, who's never met a legume or starch she doesn't love, was ecstatic. "That's perfect. I'll have a bowl."

Now I was stuck. The other specialty of Piperno was the Roman classic coda alla vaccinara, or braised oxtail! I don't have a short memory, but in the spirit of "blame the restaurant, not the tail," I went for it. The artichokes were wonderful, as expected. The soup was a luscious, molten amalgamation of luscious chickpeas, almost bursting and loaded with flavor, juxtapositioned with the silken, melting texture of perfectly cooked pasta. I realized all of this as it slid across my palate, the one measly bite that Angie gave up.

But the dish that I will always lust after is the coda; it was viscous, deep, and brooding with a kick of white wine and tomato acid that kept my fork returning for more. With a side of puntarelle (tart seasonal Roman greens) with a bracing anchovy dressing, it may well be my favorite lunch in Rome. Who knew (besides the thousands of native Romans)?

◆

ARE FOODS ALWAYS BETTER AT THE SOURCE? IS A FRENCH BAGUETTE BETTER IN Paris or Peoria? Thai green curry better in Bangkok or Bangor, Maine? Saltimbocca—Rome or Racine?

I found over the years that eating food at the source can be an enlightening experience with that moment of *Aha!* That's *what it's supposed to taste like!* It can also be an incredible letdown as you begin to wonder, *Does anyone know how to cook here?*

Often a specific regional dish can be influenced by the setting. Imagine sitting on a sunny patio overlooking the Mediterranean and consuming a quintessential salade Niçoise. With that type of setting, a passable salad can become memorable.

For years I had been looking forward to visiting Austria, the home of napkin dumplings, tafelspitz, kaiserschmarren (a dessert omelet), and one dish I've had many times in my working life, zwiebelrostbraten. Zwiebelrostbraten is basically a flattened steak, quickly seared or braised, accompanied by a tart, rich sauce and topped with zwiebel, or crispy onions.

My first experience with this dish came while I was working in the Escoffier Room at the Culinary Institute. For Chef Von Erp's rendition, we took strip steaks that were pounded to half-inch thickness, lightly slathered them with mustard and peppercorns, dusted them with flour, and quickly seared the beef in a very hot pan. They were then deglazed with a shot of red wine vinegar, a bit of veal glaze, and a small hunk of butter. On the side, a sauté pan was used to shallow fry some thinly sliced onions to add a crispy counterpoint.

When Angie and I finally traveled to Vienna, we were hard-pressed to find a menu without zwiebelrostbraten on it. We went to a small gastropub serving modern Austrian food. The zwiebelrostbraten I had was very straightforward and a bit sad: a tough slice of beef with pedestrian gravy and a ton of greasy fried onions on top, and a big honkin' pickle spear next to it. I'm sure there is better zwiebelrostbraten in Austria, but I think Peter's version—tart, piquant, rich, crispy, and savory—would be a star right there at the source.

In contrast, as a chef visiting a city for the first time, it is my sworn duty to find the best food that city has to offer. In Vienna, I had a goal—and it was tafelspitz. There is much more modern food in Vienna, the same type of cutting-edge gastronomy that you'll find in many large cities throughout the world. Great food, yes, but at times it has no sense of place.

A few years back, Johnny Apple, the legendary *New York Times* political writer and prodigious gourmet bon vivant, stopped in for dinner at Sanford. He and his wife Betsy had made our restaurant a regular visit anytime they were in Milwaukee. I had first met them at John Byron's in 1984, and it was always a treat listening to Johnny expound his encyclopedic knowledge and opinion with such firm conviction that you knew, even if you disagreed, he wouldn't waiver. They stopped in once after a trip to Vienna, and he told me that he had had the single-greatest dish of his life, tafelspitz. He described it as simply braised beef in a clear, limpid, root vegetable-infused broth that, in and of itself, tasted like liquid meat jelly.

Angie and I had our epiphany at Plachutta in Vienna. We picked two cuts of beef from the multiple options offered on the menu. The waiter started the ceremony by serving us china bowls full of golden broth that he had ladled from a large copper pot. Then came the melting meat and vegetables along with a bit more of the delicious broth elixir. On the side were creamed spinach and roasted potatoes, but it was with the tangy sauce of apple and horseradish and a bottle of Grüner Veltliner that made us just settle back and bask in the soul of Vienna.

Best dish ever? Who'd argue with Johnny Apple?

◆

ONE OF THE MOST FASCINATING LARGE CITIES I'VE BEEN TO HAS TO BE ISTANBUL. THIS bustling metropolis is situated with one foot in Europe and the other in Asia, divided by the Bosphorus strait.

I was a guest chef on Seabourn Cruise Line, and Angie and I decided to spend three days in Istanbul before we embarked. We flew into the city and were met at the airport by a driver who whisked us through the winding traffic to our hotel. Along the way, our faces were glued to the window as we passed glowing domes and towers, the sun shooting off them in every direction. Street vendors manned small carts either studded with wooden poles looped by simit (circular, pretzel-looking, darkly burnished breads shrouded with sesame seeds) or piled high with skewers of glistening crispy meat that perfumed the air.

Our hotel was the Çirağan Palace, aptly named because it had once been an Ottoman royal palace. As we were escorted through the door to our room, it opened onto a 15-foot terrace that overlooked the Bosphorus. In the center of the terrace was a large, hammered-metal tray filled with exquisite dried fruits, cured olives, fresh sheep's cheese, and cooling citrus drinks. As we sat at the table, a haunting drone floated through the air, and we found out it was the call to prayer emanating from the minaret at the mosque. We were enchanted.

Angie on hotel terrace in Istanbul overlooking the
Bosphorus prior to the Guest Chef Seabourn Cruise

That evening we dined in the hotel's restaurant, which featured outdoor tables right on the water and a spectacular view of the Asian side of Istanbul. As we settled into dinner, the food flowed like a sultan's feast, and as we slumped back in our armchairs, our hands slightly sticky from too much baklava, we waited for the dancers to appear.

My obligations once we boarded the ship were to prepare and oversee two four-course dinners (one each week) in conjunction with a one-hour cooking class on the days of the two dinners. Upon boarding the ship, I immediately sought out the food service manager, Johan, who assured me everything was in place. He told me they had all the products for the menu and to just really relax and enjoy the cruise, as the first dinner wasn't for five days. In that short five days, we not only explored a lot of the Mediterranean, we also formed a fast friendship with Bob and Jenny from NYC; this started as a friendship by default as we were the only two couples on the ship under Medicare age—by a good 20 years. But we soon realized why we were the two odd couples: Bob was writing a story about the cruise and I was the guest chef—so both of us were sailing free. (This turned out to be more than a "default" friendship; and to this day Bob and I are still arguing on a daily basis as we try to manage our fantasy baseball team with as much detente as a lifelong New York Yankee and a Milwaukee Brewer fan can muster.)

On the fifth day I sought out the chef, a young Swiss fellow named Jurgen, who proceeded to tell me, in a thick Swiss accent, the insider's version of the cruise kitchen: "Zis is a fookin 'ospital. Speecial zis, speecial zat, no zucher, no kreem. Oh, and by zee way, we didn't get all zee products for your menu. But vee do have zuper fresh corn for your corn relish."

I was now a little worried because I would have to change half of my menu on the fly. I jumped right in and started prepping. The corn was indeed fresh, but the kernels looked like they had mutated during some nuclear accident. They were huge and had faces—tough faces, at that—a cruel joke to pull on a Midwesterner. After about two and a half hours of braising, the corn became passable digestible feed.

For dessert I was making baked semolina pudding. The semolina Jurgen gave me was white and very fine. I told him it didn't look right, but he said, "Eet's OK—eet's a zuper European brand!" The key to the pudding recipe is making sure that, when you heat up the semolina, you don't let it boil. If it boils, it will immediately seize up and get too thick; it should be at a pourable texture when ready. When I added the "European semolina," it instantaneously seized up, forming a huge, beige hockey puck in the bottom of the pan. This confirmed my hunch that it was really farina. After three adjustments to the recipe, the puddings came out pretty well, considering the circumstances, and the plates came back empty. It was a real learning experience for me, and surprisingly, they even loved the corn relish (probably because the guests were mostly European and fresh corn was almost exotic to them).

YOU DON'T ALWAYS GET A DO-OVER IN A RELATIONSHIP.

On our first trip to Europe, Angie and I had really looked forward to Venice. We pulled our rental car into a dingy garage near the waterfront. The guy at the front motioned that it was full; then he stuck out his hand. A bunch of liras miraculously opened up a space.

We took the *vaporetto* (water bus) across the water to the city and were immediately accosted by a rotund, mustached Super Mario look-alike—overalls and hat included. He grabbed our luggage, slapped it on his handcart, and asked, "Whitcha 'otel?" Then he stuck out his hand. Venice is one of the biggest tourist towns in Europe, but this was over the top because we had arrived on Easter weekend. We had to sprint to keep up with the mustache and our luggage, as we went up and down the individual canal bridges on our way to the hotel. Angie was almost gleeful as she pointed out the gondolas gliding along the canals as we passed over them.

I should have gotten with the program, but all I saw was a backup of eight or so boats butting one another, all filled with loud, sweaty, and unhappy-looking people—kinda cheesy. I decided that I wasn't going to be pulled into that tourist stereotype and fill yet another outstretched hand, this time belonging to a suave gondolier.

Although I had made many small mistakes along the way, in retrospect, I can see that this was a really huge one. We had a spectacular dinner at Harry's Bar on Easter; the menu was filled with Venetian specialties. After signature bellinis and carpaccio, an undulating spring risotto gave way to simply roasted baby lamb. The food was traditional magic and should have been a defining memory of Venice. But after we returned home, anytime the trip came up and Venice was mentioned, the "gondola glare" exploded from Angie's eyes, directed right at me.

Many years later, our cruise, which had started in Istanbul, was ending in my chance for redemption, Venice. We took a dusk-to-night gondola ride, and the canals were so quiet. As we lay back in our lush, pillow-backed seats, passing under open Venetian windows, you could hear the tinkling of silverware on plates and muffled dinner conversations. It was as perfect as a movie set but better because it was real. It takes some of us a while to grow up.

◆

ANGIE AND I WERE CELEBRATING OUR 25TH ANNIVERSARY WITH AN ASIAN CRUISE. Starting in Hong Kong, we went through China, Korea, Japan, Russia, and Alaska, and ended up in Vancouver.

Our second stop was an overnight in Shanghai. As this was our first trip to China, we didn't know what to expect. On one side we saw a mega-crane that was working on an ultra-modern fantasy skyscraper that would make the Empire State Building blush. Then we turned the corner to see another type of construction: a throng of workmen repairing a fifth-century edifice. They dangled from precarious bamboo scaffolding five stories up that seemed to be lashed together with nothing more than reeds. At the traffic light were two older cars surrounded by at least 400 bikes, all anxiously waiting for the light to change. It went green, and we witnessed what looked like a Tour de France start, except everyone was on a rusted Chinese version of a large Huffy.

We stopped to rest on a pedestrian mall, surrounded by a sea of heads covered with beautiful black hair glistening in the sun. I noticed a group of school children completely fixated as they stared and pointed. It took a moment to realize they were pointing with wonder and curiosity at Angie, a five-foot-seven blonde who stuck out like a unicorn in a herd of stallions.

We were fortunate to be able to spend the day with a couple of friends, Nan and Dody, who were there on business. That evening we went to a Hunan restaurant in the French Concession part of the city. As we walked up to the door, a yawning, entertaining rabbit sat in a colorful circus-like cage—always a good sign for the D'Amatos.

We had a phenomenal and inexpensive dinner—about $25 for the four of us—which included seven dishes, each one better than the one before. After the head-on, impossibly

Posing with Angie, the chef, and the manager of Seabourn Cruise in the 1990s

crispy shrimp buried in a mountain of golden chopped garlic, and the Hunan hot pot, who would have thought that a plate of ribs would steal the show? Tossed with chunky pieces of cumin, coriander, and fennel seed, they were rich, fragrant, a bit mouth searing, and bursting with juicy goodness—some of the best pork I've ever had.

◆

AS ANGIE AND I GOT OUT OF THE VAN AT THE MASSERIA TORRE COCCARO, I IMMEDIATELY walked to my right and found myself in the middle of a garden fully in bloom. All types of greens—rapini, spinach, and dandelion—grew next to wispy fennel fronds, and vibrant basil and dusty sage bent seductively as they yielded to the warm breezes off the Adriatic. These were surrounded by plump figs, yellow quince, and bursting pomegranates that were literally spitting out bright red seeds from the raw crevasses of their splitting, ruddy shells. You might have heard the culinary expression, "The fruits and vegetables were talking to me." Well, these rowdy guys were screaming, "*Scusi!* You, with the sunglasses! Get your skinny American legs over here and use us!"

We were in Brindisi (in Puglia) for another bike tour, getting ready to lead a hands-on cooking class, and I had conveniently been dropped off in Italian raw food heaven. Along with the garden of delights, I had at my disposal the most beautiful leg of baby lamb, rustic spicy sausages, shelves filled with Puglia's golden extra-virgin olive oil, salt-cured capers and anchovies, rustic ground semolina, dried chickpeas, and a platter of bright-red, head-on Adriatic shrimp thrown in for good measure.

The menu was planned: Adriatic shrimp soup with chickpeas and saffron, hand-rolled orecchiette with rapini and sausage, roast leg of lamb with rosemary, crisp olive oil potatoes and lemon-glazed fennel, and roasted pomegranate-glazed figs with fresh ricotta.

As we finished the preparation and family-style plating of the dinner, we walked across the glowing courtyard to the large, square dining room table positioned in front of the fire. The waiters brought the food over and started service. I had my head buried in the soup bowl and was lifting the spoon to my mouth when, out of nowhere, I was severely punched in the right arm. My soup spoon went flying, and I almost fell out of my seat. Confused, I looked at Dawn, the Bike Riders tour guide sitting to my right.

"What the heck is up with you?" I said.

She exclaimed, "This soup is unbelievable! In New Orleans we call that 'slap yo' mama' good, and I thought this deserved a little more than a slap!" I was truly flattered by the compliment but was on my guard for the rest of the meal in case there was a New Orleans "break your friend's leg" tradition after the lamb course.

◆

I COULDN'T TEAR MY EYES AWAY FROM THE FLOOR. WHAT LOOKED LIKE TWO CORDOVAN schooner hulls sharply protruding from the sea were coming closer and closer. But we weren't near any water. We were entering the dining room of the restaurant at the Torre Coccaro, and the boat hulls were residing on the maître d's feet. This is no exaggeration. His Italian leather shoes came to a perfect point and had to have extended at least eight inches from where any toes could have been, in order to avoid strangulation, let alone be comfortable.

Along with the snappy footwear came spiked, five-inch hair, an over-the-top attitude, and patter that made him a living caricature of the kind of restaurant maître d' that you would expect to find on a Saturday morning cartoon. He certainly kept us entertained throughout the dinner.

The next evening, we were having a before-dinner cocktail in the bar adjacent to the restaurant with a few friends. We were situated right next to a curtain that divided the bar and the dining room, and Angie had her back to the curtain. I was settled back in an oversized plush chair and could hear the low background music interspersed with the gentle hum of the other guests all talking in different languages.

We were sipping perfectly mixed Campari and sodas in between tiny bites of panzarotti (mini calzone-like stuffed pastries of the region). At 6:30 sharp, the curtain was ripped open. A screaming "BUONA SERA!" fog-horned out of the mouth of the maître d'. It would have destroyed Jack Nicholson's "You can't *handle* the truth!" in a fantasy verbal throwdown. Then his giant gunboats collided with our table like the Titanic hitting an iceberg. I had to peel Angie off the ceiling and dust away from everyone at the table the remnants of the antipasti that went flying after the collision.

As we looked up for the maître d', he was already across the room, moving at the speed of light, completely oblivious to his verbal and physical carnage. Was it drugs? One too many doppio espressos? Cramping toes?

Who knows? But it was certainly a show.

◆

I'VE NEVER BELIEVED IN "BIG CIGAR TIME," WHICH, IN THE RESTAURANT BUSINESS, denotes the time when you just sit back with a devil-may-care attitude and arrogantly think that the business will thrive because you are so talented.

During Fashion Week in Paris one year, as the stars shone brightly in the evening Parisian sky, Angie and I found ourselves in the middle of the historic Place Vendôme, with large

Cuban Cohibas dangling from our hands and lips, posing for pictures in front of the mother of all hotels, the original Paris Ritz.

The path that had brought us to that spot had started quite a bit earlier. We were on a river cruise that began in Prague and finished in Paris. We decided to rent an apartment in Paris for a week at the end of the trip and coordinated with our dear friends Ihab and Sally Hassan in order to meet up with them. From that first time in Europe in 1985, they had continued to mentor us on the who, what, and where of Europe—a personal insider's guide. After years of talking about it, this would be the first time we would actually meet in Europe, and Paris was the perfect place.

In all the years that they'd visited Paris, there was only one hotel for them: the Ritz. What the Ritz means to me, being a student of the culinary arts, is Escoffier, the father of French cuisine. He and partner César Ritz started the Paris hotel in 1898, and it became one of the most historically important hotels in the annals of food history. So, when the Hassans asked us to join them for dinner there, we were thrilled.

As we were walking through the Tuileries public garden on our way to dinner, we heard the unmistakable strains of Al Green flowing from a huge tent, and then were slowly surrounded by jaw-dropping, statuesque models and over-the-top fashionistas. We were passing through the middle of Fashion Week headquarters, right near the Place Vendôme.

We entered the majestic Ritz, and our friends met us in the lobby. After a short stroll we were seated in arguably the most famous watering hole in the world, the Hemingway Bar. We sipped perfect aperitifs and consumed bar snacks elevated to the sublime, and then took a short jaunt across the hotel to L'Espadon, the Michelin-starred restaurant that is the centerpiece of the hotel.

Even though it was October, temperatures were in the 80s during the day, so the outside terrace was set up for dinner. With the night sky enshrouding the impeccable soft glow from the flickering candlelight, the setting was a proper, peaceful oasis of gustatory indulgence—a flawless dinner with warm company, wistful service, brilliant food, and extraordinary wine.

Between courses we were led down to Escoffier's kitchen, and I had a chance to speak with the chef de cuisine, Jean-François Girardin, who actually knew some of the French chefs with whom I had trained back in the '70s.

After dinner, Cuban cigars appeared, and even though Angie and I don't smoke, it somehow seemed to make perfect sense as the evening found us hugging Ihab and Sally good-bye in the Place Vendôme and practically floating back to our apartment across the river on a cloud of satisfied pleasure. A night we will never forget.

CHAPTER THIRTEEN RECIPES

◆

*Stewed Umbrian Lentils with
Charred Spicy Italian Sausage*
373

*Braised Oxtails with Sultana,
Fennel, and Celery Salad*
375

Tafelspitz
378

*Crisp-Skinned Red Snapper with Shrimp
Feta Moussaka, Avgolemono Cream*
381

Risi Bisi
384

Hunan Spice-Crusted BBQ Ribs
386

STEWED UMBRIAN LENTILS WITH CHARRED SPICY ITALIAN SAUSAGE

One of the dishes inspired by a bike trip in Umbria was a combination of perfect tiny brown lentils from Castelluccio (a stone's throw from Spoleto) that were stewed to a creamy lushness and topped with well-grilled local and slightly aged spicy sausage links. These lentils take a bit longer than the conventional US supermarket variety, but that longer cooking time helps them infuse extra layers of flavor. The beauty of this dish is that it can be completed with one pot and a small sauté pan.

SERVES 4 TO 6

¼ cup (59 mL) plus 2 tablespoons extra virgin olive oil (divided), plus additional to finish dish

1 medium red onion (6 ounces [170 g]), diced small

4 carrots (8 ounces [227 g]), peeled and diced medium

Kosher salt and freshly ground black pepper, to taste

4 cloves garlic, chopped

2 bay leaves

3 sprigs fresh rosemary (divided)

2 cups (384 g) lentils (I prefer Castelluccio lentils from Umbria), rinsed

6–8 cups (1.42–1.89 L) unsalted chicken stock

1½ tablespoons fennel or anise seeds, ground

4 ounces (114 g) giancuale or pancetta (you will need ½ cup diced), rind reserved, if present, to add to lentils

20 cherry tomatoes, cut in half

½ cup (119 mL) dry white wine

12 links hot Italian sausages, grilled just before the lentils are ready until just cooked through, about 4–5 minutes per side

1. Place a 1-gallon (3.79 L) heavy-bottomed pot over medium heat. When the pot is hot, add ¼ cup (59 mL) of the olive oil. When hot, add the onions (and the rind from the giancuale) and sauté for 2 minutes. Add the carrots, season with salt and pepper, and sauté for 1 minute. Add the garlic, the bay leaves, and 2 of the rosemary sprigs and sauté for 1 minute. Add the lentils and stir. Add 6 cups (1.42 L) of the stock and the ground fennel, partially cover, and simmer, stirring regularly, for 15 to 30 minutes, and adding stock, if necessary, to keep the lentils moist.

(RECIPE CONTINUES ON PAGE 374)

(RECIPE CONTINUED FROM PAGE 373)

2. While the lentils are cooking, place a medium sauté pan over medium heat. When the pan is hot, add the remaining 2 tablespoons of the olive oil. When hot, add the giancuale or pancetta and sauté for 1 minute to render and lightly brown. Add the tomatoes and the remaining rosemary sprig and lightly season with salt and pepper. Add the white wine and reduce to 3 tablespoons (45 mL) of liquid. Reserve.

3. When the lentils are tender, stir in the reserved tomato mixture and adjust the seasoning with salt and pepper (the lentils should be moist with a thick soupy consistency). Serve with the grilled sausages and finish with a bit of olive oil over the top.

BRAISED OXTAILS WITH SULTANA, FENNEL, AND CELERY SALAD

I never should have looked at an oxtail after the Madrid experience cleaned me out, but I had a past history with the "tail" that brought me to Armando Al Pantheon in Rome for their Thursday special, Coda alla Vaccinara. This was the oxtail that brought me back into the "herd."

SERVES 4

5 to 5½ pounds (2.27 to 2.49 kg) oxtails

Kosher salt and freshly ground black pepper, to taste

All-purpose flour, to dust oxtails

7 tablespoons (104 mL) extra virgin olive oil (divided)

1 small (about 6 ounces [170 g]) fennel bulb with stalks and sprigs

2 large stalks celery (1 to braise with oxtails, 1 reserved for garnish)

2 onions (18 ounces [510 g]), diced small

6 cloves garlic, finely chopped

1 teaspoon red pepper flakes

2 cups (474 mL) dry red wine

For the sachet, mix together the following spices in cheesecloth and tie with butcher string:

    2 (3-inch [7.5-cm]) cinnamon sticks

    4 sprigs fresh thyme

    4 bay leaves

    1 tablespoon whole fennel seed

    2 whole star anise

    Zest of ¼ orange

2 (14½-ounce [411 g]) cans diced tomatoes in sauce

2½ cups (593 mL) unsalted chicken stock

Canola oil, for brushing parchment paper

¼ cup (50 g) granulated sugar

¼ cup (59 mL) water

¼ cup (41 g) golden raisins

¼ cup (59 mL) red wine vinegar

1. Season the oxtails lightly with salt and black pepper. Dust them with flour and pat off the excess. Place a large pot over medium-high heat. Add 5 tablespoons (74 mL) of the olive oil, and when hot, sauté the oxtails until they are golden brown on all sides, about 10 minutes.

(RECIPE CONTINUES ON PAGE 377)

(RECIPE CONTINUED FROM PAGE 375)

2. While the oxtails are browning, cut the stalks off of the fennel bulb and tie together with the celery stalk (reserve the bulb for garnish). Remove the oxtails from the pot and drain any oil in excess of 3 tablespoons (45 mL).

3. Preheat the oven to 300°F (150°C). Add the onions to the pot and sauté for 4 minutes. Add the garlic and red pepper flakes and sauté for 1 minute. Add the wine and bring up to a boil for 1 minute. Add the sachet, tied celery and fennel stalks, oxtails, tomatoes, and chicken stock and bring up to a slow simmer.

4. Cover with a piece of parchment paper that has been cut in a circle to fit the interior and brushed on the underside with the canola oil. Bake for about 3 hours, or until the oxtails are fork-tender but not falling apart.

5. Remove the oxtails and discard the sachet and tied celery and fennel. Strain the sauce (reserving the onions and tomatoes) and reduce it to 2½ cups (593 mL). Add the oxtails and reserved onions and tomatoes to the sauce.

6. For serving, prepare the garnish by placing the sugar and water in a small sauce pot. Bring it up to a boil, stirring, then let it boil until the sugar starts to caramelize to a medium-dark color. Carefully add the golden raisins and vinegar, bring up to a simmer, then remove from the heat and cool (you may make this ahead).

7. Cut the reserved fennel bulb in thin slices and cut the reserved celery in thin pieces. Mix together with the raisin mixture and season lightly with salt, black pepper, and the remaining 2 tablespoons of the olive oil. Serve as a garnish over the oxtails.

TAFELSPITZ
(Slow-Braised Beef)

Listening to Johnny Apple was like watching a humorous and ironic National Geographic special. His knowledge was historic, honest, and lashed with measured hyperbole. When he talked about his favorite foods, I listened and salivated at the same time. And as far as Plachutta, he was dead-on, as the Tafelspitz was a revelation of tender, beefy goodness!

SERVES 6

4½ pound (2.04 kg) beef chuck roast (3 inches [7.5 cm] thick), cut in 3 equal pieces, about 4x4-inches (10x10-cm) each

1 large onion (1 pound [454 g]), cut in half with skin on, cut side brushed with 1 tablespoon grapeseed oil and browned, oil side down, in a sauté pan over medium-high heat until lightly blackened, about 5 minutes

12 cups (2.84 L) unsalted chicken stock

1 tablespoon kosher salt

For the sachet, mix together the following spices in cheesecloth and tie with butcher string:

    1 head garlic, cut in half horizontally

    1 bunch fresh parsley stems (1 ounce [28 g])

    40 peppercorns, lightly crushed

    6 juniper berries, lightly crushed

    4 whole allspice, lightly crushed

    3 bay leaves

    3 sprigs fresh thyme

    2 sprigs fresh savory

    2 whole cloves

    1 tablespoon whole caraway seed

    1 teaspoon whole fennel seed

    ⅓ whole nutmeg, grated

2 medium parsnips (about 10 ounces [284 g]), peeled and cut in even wedges

2 turnips (about 8 ounces [227 g]), peeled and cut in even wedges

2 medium carrots (about 8 ounces [227 g]), peeled and cut in even wedges

1 celery heart (about 10 ounces [284 g] and 6 inches [15 cm] long), cut in half from stem to tip, then tied together with kitchen string to hold together

1 large fennel bulb (12 ounces [341 g]), cut in half through core and each half cut in 6 wedges through core to keep intact

2 leeks (10 ounces [284 g]), trimmed to about 6 inches (15 cm), cleaned and tied with kitchen string to hold together

(RECIPE CONTINUES ON PAGE 380)

(RECIPE CONTINUED FROM PAGE 378)

Kosher salt, freshly ground black pepper, and ground nutmeg, to taste

Pickled Horseradish (recipe follows)

Apple, Horseradish, and Parsley Sauce (recipe follows)

1. Place the beef and onions in a large Dutch oven. Cover with the chicken stock and the 1 tablespoon salt. Place the sachet in the pot. Bring up to a very slow simmer, cover, and simmer lightly for about 1½ to 2 hours.

2. Remove the meat, onions, and sachet and strain the stock through 4 layers of cheesecloth. Clean the Dutch oven and place the meat and sachet back in the pot. Cover with the strained stock and continue cooking for about 1 hour, or until the meat is just starting to get fork-tender.

3. Add the parsnips, turnips, carrots, celery, fennel, and leeks and continue simmering for about 30 minutes, or until all of the vegetables are tender. Remove the broth and reduce to about 6 cups (1.42 L). Adjust the seasoning with salt, pepper, and nutmeg, then pour back over the meat and vegetables.

4. For serving, divide the meat and vegetables equally among 6 bowls (you will need to cut the beef in slices and chop the leeks and celery). Scatter over the drained Pickled Horseradish and serve the Apple, Horseradish, and Parsley Sauce on the side.

For the Pickled Horseradish:

4 ounces (114 g) fresh horseradish root, peeled, thinly sliced, then cut into thin strips

Rice wine vinegar, to pickle horseradish

1. Cover the horseradish with vinegar in a small bowl. Cover and marinate in the refrigerator until needed (you may prepare up to 2 days ahead).

For the Apple, Horseradish, and Parsley Sauce

3 large Granny Smith apples

¼ cup (60 g) prepared hot horseradish

¼ cup (60 g) sour cream

Kosher salt and freshly ground black pepper, to taste

½ cup (28 g) Italian parsley leaves, coarsely chopped

1. Peel and grate the apples on the coarse side of a box grater (you will need 2 cups [220 g]). In a bowl, mix with the horseradish, sour cream, and salt and pepper to taste. Mix in the parsley right before serving.

CRISP-SKINNED RED SNAPPER WITH SHRIMP FETA MOUSSAKA, AVGOLEMONO CREAM

Eating in the Greek Islands is the ultimate in outdoor dining. There could not be a more picturesque view at the top of Santorini to partake in a square of tasty Moussaka, bowls of Avgolemono soup, and platters of grilled seafood. That combination inspired this recipe and it always takes me to a beautiful place.

SERVES 4

For the Shrimp and Feta Moussaka:

2 tablespoons extra virgin olive oil, plus some for brushing eggplant

1 shallot, finely diced (you will need 2½ to 3 tablespoons diced [23 to 28 g])

3 cloves garlic, finely chopped (you will need 1 tablespoon chopped)

1 bay leaf

1 (14½-ounce [411-g]) can diced tomatoes in juice, drained

½ teaspoon ground cinnamon

½ teaspoon ground fennel seed

Kosher salt and freshly ground black pepper, to taste

1 tablespoon fresh oregano leaves, coarsely chopped

¼ pound (about 8 [114 g]) peeled and deveined shrimp, tossed with 1 teaspoon extra virgin olive oil

2 tablespoons dry white wine

2 tablespoons heavy cream

½ cup (75 g) small diced feta cheese

1 Japanese eggplant (about 6 ounces [170 g]), outside lightly scored lengthwise with a fork, then cut in 36 (¼-inch-thick [6-mm]) slices

1. Place a nonstick sauté pan over medium heat. Add the 2 tablespoons of oil. Add the shallots, garlic, and bay leaf and sauté for 1 minute. Add the tomatoes, cinnamon, and fennel and lightly season with salt and pepper. Simmer 10 to 15 minutes, stirring regularly, until dry but not scorching. Add the oregano and reserve.

2. Place a sauté pan over high heat. When the pan is very hot, season the shrimp with salt and pepper and sear for 30 to 45 seconds. Add the white wine and reduce to dry. Add the cream and reduce until the shrimp are coated. Remove the shrimp and chop into small pieces. Add to the tomato mixture along with the feta cheese and adjust the seasoning with salt and pepper, if necessary. Remove to a plate to cool.

(RECIPE CONTINUES ON PAGE 382)

(RECIPE CONTINUED FROM PAGE 381)

3. Place a grill pan or a large sauté pan over very high heat. Brush the eggplant slices lightly with olive oil. Season lightly with salt and pepper and grill 1 minute per side, or until they are tender. Remove to a plate to cool.

4. For assembling the Moussaka, place 3 slices of the eggplant next to each other to form a slight circle. Place ⅛ of the shrimp mixture on top. Place 3 slices of the eggplant over the mixture. Place ⅛ more of the shrimp mixture over the eggplant and finish with 3 slices of eggplant. Lightly tap the Moussaka down to form a 2½- to 3-inch (6.4- to 7.5-cm) hockey puck-size disc. Repeat the assembly with the remaining eggplant and shrimp mixture to form 4 total. Reserve in the refrigerator until needed. (You may prepare the Moussaka 1 day ahead.)

For the Red Snapper and to Finish the Dish:

> **4 (6- to 7-ounce [170- to 199-g]) fillets red snapper (skin left on), (1 inch [2.5 cm] thick)**
>
> **Kosher salt and freshly ground pepper, to taste**
>
> **3 tablespoons (45 mL) extra virgin olive oil**
>
> **Prepared Shrimp and Feta Moussaka**
>
> **Avgolemono Cream (recipe follows)**

1. Place a sauté pan, large enough to hold all of the red snapper fillets in 1 layer, over high heat. Season the snapper with salt and pepper. When the pan is hot, add the oil to the pan. When hot, place the fish fillets skin side down and let them sear until crisp, about 2 to 3 minutes. Turn the fillets over and finish cooking until the fish is just cooked through, about 3 minutes.

2. While cooking the fish, reheat the Moussakas lightly in the microwave. Divide the Moussakas onto 4 plates. Place 1 snapper fillet on each Moussaka. Spoon the Avgolemono Cream over and around the snapper and serve.

For the Avgolemono Cream:

1 cup (237 mL) unsalted chicken stock

1 teaspoon ground fennel seed

¼ teaspoon ground nutmeg

¼ teaspoon ground cinnamon

1 teaspoon kosher salt

¼ teaspoon freshly ground black pepper

½ cup (119 mL) heavy cream

5 large egg yolks

2½ tablespoons (37 mL) fresh lemon juice

¼ teaspoon granulated sugar

Kosher salt and freshly ground black pepper, to taste

1. Place the stock, fennel, nutmeg, cinnamon, 1 teaspoon salt, and ¼ teaspoon pepper in a small saucepan and reduce to ¼ cup (59 mL). Add the cream and bring up to a simmer. Place the egg yolks, lemon juice, and sugar in a bowl and whisk until smooth. Slowly whisk in the hot cream mixture and adjust the seasoning with salt and pepper, if needed. Place back in the pan and whisk over medium heat until the mixture starts to thicken, at about 170°F to 175°F (77°C to 79°C) on an instant-read thermometer (do not let the mixture simmer or it will curdle).

2. Immediately strain into a chilled bowl and cover tightly with plastic wrap (punch holes in the wrap). Cool in the refrigerator to set. (You may make the Avgolemono Cream 1 day ahead).

RISI BISI

This is my version of a spring Risi Bisi. Depending on where you have it in Venice, it can be a soupy rice and pea concoction or more of a risotto with peas. What is constant is the rice and peas. I use carnaroli rice, peapods, baked ham, and briny clams to ring in the first days of spring and the good memories of Venice.

SERVES 2

¼ cup (59 mL) extra virgin olive oil

1 small onion, finely diced (you will need ½ cup [75 g])

1 cup (190 g) carnaroli rice

2 tablespoons chopped garlic

½ teaspoon red pepper flakes

2 bay leaves

2 sprigs fresh thyme

1 cup (237 mL) dry white wine, heated

1 teaspoon kosher salt, plus additional to taste

¼ teaspoon freshly ground black pepper, plus additional to taste

2½–2¾ cups (591–651 mL) unsalted chicken stock that has been steeped with ½ cup (70 g) ham trimmings (from ham below), covered, for 1 hour, strained, and reheated before adding to rice (reserve ½ cup [119 mL] for sugar snap peas)

20 Manila clams (or cockles), placed in a covered pot with ¼ cup (59 mL) dry white wine

1 (5-ounce [142-g]) piece baked ham, cut in ½-inch (13-mm) diamond-shaped pieces (use trimmings for stock above)

2 cups (4 ounces [114 g]) sugar snap peas, blanched in boiling water for 30 seconds, then shocked in ice water, half the peas puréed in a blender with ½ cup (119 mL) reserved chicken stock, strained through a medium strainer, and the remaining peas cut in half and reserved to finish rice

1. Place a saucepan over medium heat. Add the oil, then add the onion and cook for about 1 minute. Add the rice, and with a wooden spoon, stir to lightly toast, about 2 minutes. Add the garlic, red pepper flakes, bay leaves, and thyme and stir for 30 seconds. Add the heated wine, continue stirring, add the 1 teaspoon salt and ¼ teaspoon black pepper, and cook until the rice starts to absorb the wine.

2. Start adding the stock by small ladles, just enough to keep the rice liquid and continually absorbing, and keep stirring so the rice does not stick. While the rice is cooking, place the clam pot over medium heat to steam the clams open, about 2 to 3 minutes (remove any unopened clams). Remove from the heat as soon as they are open and keep covered.

3. After adding about 1 cup (237 mL) of the stock to the rice, add all of the liquid from the clams as the next addition. Taste the rice and continue adding the stock until the rice is just cooked but still al dente. At this point, the rice should be creamy and fluid but not watery.

4. Add the diamond-cut ham and reserved sugar snaps peas. Finish the rice by stirring in the sugar snap pea purée and season to taste with salt and pepper. Fold in the clams. Divide the Risi Bisi into 2 bowls and serve immediately.

HUNAN SPICE-CRUSTED BBQ RIBS

We were at a Hunan restaurant in Shanghai in the last throws of a spectacular meal when an American expat couple next to us asked if we had tried the Spice-Crusted Ribs. We were really full but being "good soldiers," we ordered a plate. My God—it would have been a huge mistake to miss those spicy wonders!

SERVES 4

For the Ribs:

> 3 tablespoons (18 g) ground fennel seed
>
> 3 tablespoons (15 g) ground coriander seed
>
> 2 tablespoons plus 1 teaspoon kosher salt
>
> 2 teaspoons medium-hot chili powder
>
> 1 tablespoon plus 1 teaspoon ground cinnamon
>
> 1 teaspoon freshly ground black pepper
>
> 2–2½ pound (0.9–1.1 kg) racks of baby back pork or lamb ribs (you may have your butcher remove the thin inner membrane that covers the inside bone of the ribs)
>
> ¼ cup (59 mL) grapeseed oil
>
> 2 cups (474 mL) Barbeque Sauce (recipe follows)
>
> Coarse Spice Mix (recipe follows)

1. Mix the fennel, coriander, salt, chili powder, cinnamon, and black pepper together (reserve 1 tablespoon for the Barbeque Sauce). Sprinkle over the rib racks on both sides, rubbing in so the spices adhere. Wrap the ribs in plastic wrap and place them in the refrigerator overnight.

2. On the next day, remove the ribs and preheat the oven to 475°F (260°C). Unwrap and separate the ribs, then evenly drizzle the grapeseed oil over them. Place them meat side down on a rimmed baking sheet and bake for 10 minutes. Turn the ribs over and bake for another 15 minutes. Remove the ribs from the oven and let them rest at least 30 minutes (you may refrigerate them at this point for finishing later).

3. Preheat the broiler. Cut the rib racks in individual ribs and toss them in a large bowl with enough Barbecue Sauce to coat all sides but not puddle in the bottom. Sprinkle evenly with the Coarse Spice Mix and toss. Place the ribs on a wire rack that has been placed on a sheet pan, and broil 3 to 4 minutes per side, or until they are caramelized and crispy. Serve.

For the Barbeque Sauce: (Makes about 1 quart [948 mL])

> 2 tablespoons sesame oil
>
> 1 medium onion (12 ounces [341 g]), thinly sliced

8 ounces (227 g) fresh ginger root, peeled and sliced ¼ inch (6 mm) thick

8–10 cloves garlic, thinly sliced

2 serrano chiles (about ¾ ounce [21 g]), stem removed and cut in ¼-inch (6-mm) slices

¼ cup (56 g) brown sugar

¼ cup (59 mL) plus 2 tablespoons red wine vinegar (divided)

1 tablespoon reserved ground spices for the Barbeque Sauce

½ cup (119 mL) dry sherry

1 (28-ounce [784-g]) can tomato purée

1 cup (237 mL) unsalted vegetable stock

6 tablespoons (89 mL) dark soy sauce

2 tablespoons tamarind concentrate

1 tablespoon kosher salt, plus additional to taste

½ teaspoon freshly ground black pepper, plus additional to taste

1 teaspoon unsweetened cocoa powder

1. Place a 3-quart (2.84-L) sauce pot over medium-high heat. When the pot is hot, add the sesame oil, then add the onions and sauté, stirring, for 4 to 5 minutes. Add the ginger, garlic, and serranos and sauté for 4 minutes. Add the brown sugar and sauté, stirring to glaze, for 3 minutes. Add ¼ cup (59 mL) of the vinegar and reduce to almost dry. Add the reserved spice mix and sherry and reduce by half. Add the tomato purée, stock, soy sauce, and tamarind, bring up to a slow simmer, then cover and simmer for 30 minutes.

2. Strain the sauce through a medium strainer, pushing on the solids. Add the 1 tablespoon salt and the ½ teaspoon pepper. In a small bowl, mix together the remaining 2 tablespoons of the vinegar and the cocoa, then whisk into the sauce. Adjust the seasoning with salt and pepper, if necessary.

For the Coarse Spice Mix:

2 tablespoons whole caraway seeds

2 tablespoons whole fennel seeds

2 tablespoons whole coriander seeds

2 tablespoons whole cumin seeds

1 teaspoon red pepper flakes

1. Toast all of the ingredients in a sauté pan over high heat, stirring, for 1 to 2 minutes. Immediately place them in a spice grinder and pulse to grind coarsely (or you may coarsely crush or chop the spices by hand, to about ⅓-size of the whole spices).

14

TABLE 3

HROUGH THE FRONT WINDOW, I COULD SEE GLEN, THE HVAC GURU, carrying out the long, silver radiator with his son Lyle. It was just a fragment within the flurry going on in the restaurant that day during the initial construction. Four years later, I realized that I hadn't once stopped to think, until just then, what that radiator meant.

For Angie and me, those first four years after we opened Sanford had been some of the most sadomasochistic times of our lives. The exhilaration, excitement, and pure pleasure of running one of the best restaurants in the country, playing off against the day-to-day reality of working from 6 a.m. to midnight, six days a week, left us looking and feeling haggard. Mentally, it was all a blur of the unknown as we were learning at an instantaneous pace to keep up with our lack of knowledge. Every day there were bright, shiny new nuggets of information to unwrap and decipher. We knew there was an answer to everything coming our way, but even when we had a good idea about what the right answer might be, it was accompanied by self-doubt and our stressed-out fear of making a bad decision.

To paraphrase Frank Sinatra: Regrets, we had a few, but we were doing it our way. The main reason for that was *we had no other choice*—there was just not a lot of information out there at that time. And even if there had been, we were always too frazzled to step back and be unemotional. At least we didn't repeat mistakes, and we always hoped that a killer mistake—one that could take us down for good—wouldn't appear.

The turning point came around that four-year anniversary. There were three events that changed my attitude. The first was the Boston dinner for Julia Childs's 80th birthday. The night before the dinner, all the participating chefs were being entertained at a local WGBH supporter's Boston home. This was the first time since Sanford had opened that I was among peers in a really relaxed atmosphere. Jimmy Burke, Jody Adams, Caprial Pence, Marcel Desaulniers, Daniel Bruce, and Patrick Healy became my sounding boards as the drinks flowed—it was just what I had been missing. It was so easy to be candid, in an open forum of

Styling a dish for Good Stock *in the Sanford dining room*

conversation, with peers who were not in the same market. All of the "unique" problems that we all had been wrestling with were bundled into a neat package as I realized that they were actually pretty universal.

The second event was a cooking competition run by the Wisconsin Milk Marketing Board at the Culinary Institute of America. On the bus ride from NYC up to Hyde Park, we were caught in a serious thunderstorm that elongated the roughly one-hour trip to three.

I was sitting in back with Janos Wilder, the chef owner of Janos restaurant in Tucson. What started as casual conversation blossomed into a quick friendship as we realized our parallel situations: fine-dining restaurants, both in mid-range cities with limited tourism, lying in the shadow of major cities (Chicago for us, Phoenix for Janos). The numbers, business flow, and even shared clientele with Arizona (the state being a heavy snowbird stop for Wisconsinites) were a comforting revelation.

These events snapped me into reality and alleviated a ton of stress, as I realized that our troubles were not proof that we were doomed but simply the normal day-to-day of running a restaurant.

The third event was a restaurant seminar I attended in Chicago. Even though we were starting to finally understand a few things about the business, Angie and I were feeling burnt out. The restaurant was doing great, but we always felt like we were going at full speed without really moving forward. In a breakout session at the Chicago seminar, we talked about our specific experiences, and during one of the breaks, I struck up a conversation with Justin Rashid, a founder of American Spoon Foods. I was relating our situation at Sanford, and he suggested I read a book that had helped him grow his business—*The E-Myth* by Michael E. Gerber. I picked up the book but never found time to read it.

When our yearly vacation came up in September, Angie and I decided to go back to New Orleans, with no actual plans except to relax and also devote some time to talking about where our business was going. I started reading *The E-Myth* and ended up devouring it in one day. Angie followed the next day, and by the end of the week, our life was changed. The gist of the book was that in order for your business to grow, you must have the time and ability to step back and assess situations, instead of just living in the moment and letting situations control you. This was a turning point in our lives and our business. We were such worker bees that when a situation came up, instead of making a well-thought-out decision, we rushed into a pressured response—sometimes brilliant, but at other times, just stupid.

When we arrived back at work, we started by shifting to a five-day schedule. The additional day away from the restaurant started out as a brutally guilt-ridden day for us. We called the restaurant every hour, afraid it would implode without us there to keep an eye on things—it didn't. Then we moved out of the building. Even though our new place was directly across the street, it did give us a feeling of separation and closure from the business; when we walked out of the restaurant and across the street, we weren't working anymore, a feeling that we had not experienced since leaving Byron's. We eventually looked forward to discussing how we could improve things, instead of just getting by, and consequently the restaurant thrived and got better. And I know we had to be more fun to work with too.

Exterior of Sanford at night

◆

"IT'S TIME TO DRY THE PINKS" BECAME MY DAD'S USUAL EARLY MORNING GREETING TO me as I entered the restaurant. We quickly found out how much cheaper it was to buy aprons and kitchen towels and launder them ourselves rather than renting them from the linen company that supplied our tablecloths and napkins. And after a few months of me doing the previous night's laundry each morning, my dad just took over the position. He was used to getting up early and would beat us to the restaurant every morning by at least two hours before we rolled in around 8 a.m. Where my half-baked system was to quickly separate the towels and aprons into two neat piles after washing them, my dad fashioned individual compartments for each employee and initialed their aprons for identification. Then each day he folded the towels and aprons impeccably before placing them in the individual cooks' compartments. The "pinks" were reusable wet wipes that we bought by the case and were part of my dad's arsenal. He had figured out that washing the pinks on a delicate cycle and letting them air-dry would add at least another 10 washings to their limited lifespan.

At that point in my career, being 44, I didn't feel old, but line cooking is a young man's game; you have to have a clear head and unlimited stamina. I was there when I was in my 20s, and just as a professional ballplayer starts to peak physically from 25 to 29, as he gets to his 30s the added experience overtakes any physical downturn. But by the time he nears his 40s, you usually hear the term "wiley veteran," describing an athlete who pulls out every trick in the book to baffle the opposition with experience, always picking and planning the perfect moment to exert energy. At 40-plus, unless you are Nolan Ryan, you're looking toward using your skills in a managing or teaching scenario.

I was still fast and competent in bursts, but when you are running a station on a busy night, you have to have your head in the game. All of your concentration has to be on the 6 to 12 dishes that you might be working on at any point in the evening. When I had a dozen things going and someone on the other end of the line asked what to do about a problem, I might think, *Hey! I'm buried with my own stuff here—you figure it out!* But acting on that impulse is not an option when you're the chef and owner.

In the dining room, a similar scenario was playing out in Angie's world. After a full day of doing the previous night's books, placing the daily orders, and working on paperwork, she would finish up just in time to man the phones from 1 p.m. until the 5 p.m. opening. Meanwhile, she'd be mapping out the dining room for the evening and running the dining room until the last guest had bid their adieu—and then waiting for the dishwasher to finish up. It had gotten so bad that the servers would wilt before approaching me with a request, and customer problems that used to roll off Angie's back would now bring her to tears.

We each had to free ourselves up; this meant a sous chef for me and an office manager for Angie so we could become true overseers and jump in wherever we were needed. This was an important step for us to become effective owners, managers, and leaders. The mental freedom was incredible; all of a sudden the myriad ideas that were flying through my head were easier to decipher. I gained the organized clarity that had been missing in the beginning and a renewed confidence in the dishes that I was coming up with. I now had time to write down and better catalogue the hits and misses, and it became easier to get from an initial idea to finished dish. Subsequently, I noticed my food becoming more precise and focused as well as simpler and more confident.

In retrospect, I feel this was all part of the cook's journey to craft maturity. Even though I had new dishes appearing weekly, I no longer felt compelled to retire a dish just for the sake of change.

◆

WHILE ANGIE AND I SAT IN THE AUDIENCE, I TUGGED AT THE TIGHT COLLAR OF MY 12-year-old tuxedo shirt, hoping to let in a bit of air. We were at the sixth annual James Beard

Awards, and I was once again up for the Best Chef–Midwest award. It should have been exciting, but I'd been there before, nominated in years one, two, three, four, and five. The last year's winner walked to the podium to announce that year's choice, and I had already resigned myself to the outcome. It was only after Angie began shaking me that I realized, he had called *my* name.

Backstage, the first person I saw was Rick Bayless, who yelled out, "Thank God you won—I'm getting tired of voting for you!" Then Jean Joho came over to congratulate me and introduce me to Eric Ripert and Maguy Le Coze from Le Bernardin. It so happened that, before the awards, Angie and I had made a reservation at Le Bernardin for the next evening—to either celebrate or soothe another loss.

The next night, they were ready for us. As we sat down, Maguy came over to again offer congratulations and welcome us and to tell us that Eric had set up a tasting menu for us.

This was a kismet moment for Angie. On that first trip to Paris in 1985, we had dinner at the original Le Bernardin, run by Maguy and her brother Gilbert, before they moved it to New York City. From the first moment we walked in, Maguy's chic elegance and gracious control were on display. Dressed in leopard skin tights and a couture top, she prowled the room, clearly in control. With almost imperceptible glances she directed every aspect of the service as she glided through the room, never taking an unnecessary step. The food was great, but the show of understated service bordered on magic. At that moment Maguy became an idol and a goal for Angie. The mixture of Vrinat's service ballet at Taillevent and the modern dance of Maguy's Le Bernardin became the blueprint for her service at Sanford. And now Angie had a once-in-a-lifetime chance to tell Maguy how much she had inspired her.

To this day the success of Sanford is commonly attributed to the food accolades that we have received. But people in the know, know better. From the beginning, Angie's impeccable knowledge of real service drove us toward success; she knew how to perfectly take care of our guests in a personal way, recognizing who wanted to be coddled, who wanted to talk, who wanted to be left alone, and who wanted to play. Every night is a show in the restaurant business, and you have many different segments to your audience—so you'd better know how to reach them all.

Early on, critic John Mariani named Sanford one of a handful of restaurants that had service on par with the best restaurants in Europe. Great service should be recognized only in retrospect because if you are completely aware of the service and food, it is really hard to be transported to the comfort zone. It should be like watching a great movie and forgetting you are in a theater. The overall restaurant experience, at its best, is a seamless amalgam of service and food, with neither lagging behind. Any break or misstep would be as flagrant an error as an actor flubbing a line in a play. We treated people not as customers, but as invited guests, and we were thrilled that they could make it. Basically, over the 20-plus years we've had Sanford, we've just been having one long dinner party at our house.

Beyond the service, Angie took care of all the other aspects of running the restaurant—books, payroll, permits, bills, parking—everything except for the kitchen. This gave me unparalleled freedom to solely concentrate on the food and the wine cellar. It was not at all an equitable division of duties, so believe me when I tell you who is responsible for the success of Sanford. It was my dream; but her execution and expertise brought it to life.

Being an owner, from the start, was always an ambiguous feeling to me. *I just never felt like an owner.* Certainly, I did everything that an owner would do, always with the welfare of the restaurant in mind, but the bravado and separation that are equated with ownership are not in my makeup. I had worked for quite a few verbally abusive chefs who regularly erupted and then slipped back into oblivious nonchalance. This was an accepted way of getting the best out of line cooks, but if you abuse and mentally beat someone up, eventually everything good inside dies.

My kitchen was different; it really was built on a model of civility. If one of the cooks could not do his or her job and was not teachable, that cook would be gone. There was no need for me to rant and scream, as fear is an extremely short-term solution. I wanted a kitchen staff of highly self-motivated people who wanted to be at Sanford and wanted to be the best. I would teach, but they had to want to learn. Both Angie and I felt the most important attribute of a person's personality was a great attitude—hands down. Experience and natural physical skills were admirable, but without the right attitude, they were worthless to us.

Along with that attitude, I wanted commitment. Every good chef and restaurant is unique, and what you learn from a chef is not recipes, but technique. When you start in my kitchen I can give you my entire recipe index, but without your knowing me, those recipes would be missing something. Without knowledge of my techniques and the roots of their inception—the recipes' backstory—they are just soul-less frames.

Just as a good recipe is one leg of a personal journey, a good menu should be a roadmap of your overall odyssey, with no end in sight. Your food should tell a story. If you give the same ingredients to five accomplished chefs, they will come up with five distinct dishes, and if you know each chef's individual style, you will easily be able to pick out whose dish is whose. You might also know where they have been and sometimes how they got there.

For example, the difference between Peter's food and Roland's food was dramatic. In art terms, Peter was like Van Gogh, with strong brush strokes—powerful, vivid, and layered; like a wild horse, the flavors bucked off the plate, all crunchy, rich, and savory, with a balanced Dutch bravado.

Roland was like Seurat—polished, controlled, and elegant. He would merge two adjacent flavors to yield a cohesive third element not apparent in the individual ingredients' makeup. The plates were precise and always masterful.

With both of them, the years of honing their individual crafts begot magic in the eyes and palates of their audience. Consequently, I had to learn to cook according to two very different palates in order to reproduce food in the manner that would be acceptable to their visions.

When you got down to the essence of their food, for Peter, it was his pea soup, and for Roland, his veal Franc-Comtois. When I had either of those dishes, which were so close to their hearts, I could taste what *they* tasted, and the essence of their pasts carried over into every dish they made. Learning from Peter and Roland helped me to realize that without understanding a person, no chef could reproduce their recipes.

When I think of defining my style, I think of my favorite artist, Jean Dubuffet, for two reasons: His work displays primitive modernity with an edge. And really, who in their right mind can pass up a good buffet?

◆

I BELIEVE THAT IN PUTTING TOGETHER A MENU, FOOD NEEDS RELIEF. LIKE GREAT MUSIC, you have to know when to pull back so you have somewhere to go—you can't overwhelm your customers repeatedly with crescendos before it starts to hurt. You need decrescendos, peppered with a touch of delicato, to keep them hungry but leave them ultimately satisfied at the finale. If you are not able to pull back, you never had control in the first place.

I want people to work in Sanford's kitchen long enough to learn and understand my technique so that eventually they can look at a recipe or a group of ingredients and inherently know how we would put it together. From there, they can start to develop their own cooking signature. Individual technique is part of that signature, and at times it is shared with fellow cooks. But there are two other personal parts of a cooking signature that only the cook has: his palate and his taste memories, which are his soul.

There's quite a bit of completely proper but soulless food out there. We've all had it: A plate is set before you, and it's stunning. You take the first bite, and it's cooked correctly. After you take the second and third bite, you realize there's just something missing. I've always felt that if you don't have the primal urge to chuck your silverware and plop your face right onto the plate, not coming up for air until the food is gone, something is wrong.

I feel that the majority of this misguided food comes from the pressure on cooks to come up with something new. Cooking used to be like vaudeville, where a performer would put on the same act for life and just move from city to city, performing for sellout crowds. When TV hit, all of a sudden millions were seeing your act, and if you tried to repeat it, their response became, *We've heard that—now what do you have?* Le Veau d'Or had the same menu and specials as when it opened in 1937 and thrived, which is almost unconceivable for a restaurant today. Cooking has become a race for the new and different, and cooks are ubiquitously pushing the envelope before they've put in the time to understand every nook and cranny of what's already in front of them. And often, by parroting whatever hot dish they surf across on the Internet, they either blur or destroy the fine line between culinary inspiration and culinary plagiarism. To be a master craftsman you have to have total control of the basics. Picasso didn't attempt cubism before he had mastered realism.

Every great chef has the combination of impeccable technique, a razor-sharp palate, and personal taste memories that are displayed in every dish. And the good news is that everyone, whether a professional or home cook, has a distinct background of one-of-a-kind food experiences from their personal and family life to draw from. This is just what they should eventually bring out in their food.

◆

MY BELIEFS HAVE BEEN REINFORCED, THROUGH OBSERVATION, BY THE MANY DINNERS I have participated in across the country and by the all-star lineup of the country's brightest stars that we have hosted at Sanford since we opened.

In 1991, right after my first James Beard nomination, I received a call from Charlie Trotter inviting me to his restaurant to cook for one of his early James Beard out-of-house dinners. It was quite an assemblage—including Barbara Tropp, Norman Van Aken, Emeril Lagasse, Carrie Nahabedian—12 in all. I had such a terrific time that I decided to host a chef dinner at Sanford. Six months later I invited Charlie, Paul Bartolotta, Jean Joho, and Celeste Zeccola. This became the inauguration of 12 consecutive years of chef dinners at Sanford. Every year five new chefs would grace our kitchen—some close friends, and all masters in their domains. The list is broad: Rick Bayless, Jody Adams, Bob Kinkead, Janos Wilder, Mark Haugen, Hubert Keller, Robert McGrath, Ken Frank, Michael Schlow, Roland Liccioni, Mary Beth Liccioni, Craig Shelton, Frank Stitt, Bill Cardwell, Didier Durand, Don Yamauchi, Alex Stratta, Ben Barker, Karen Barker, Debbie Gold, Roberto Donna, Elka Gilmore, Douglas Rodriguez, Jim Cohen, Mario Batali, Rocco DiSpirito, Jimmy Sneed, Brian Polcyn, Anne Gingrass-Paik, David Gingrass, Razz Kamnitzer, Monique Barbeau, Greg Higgins, Louis Osteen, Chris Gross, Ann Cashion, Ken Oringer, Paul Kahan, Michael Smith, Roxsand Scocos, George Mahaffey, Terrance Brennan, Mark Baker, Patrick Clark, Jeff Buben, Takashi Yagihashi, Gordon Hamersley, Michael White, Suzanne Goin, Grant Achatz, Barbara Lynch, and Bruce Sherman, to name a few.

Along with wine specialists such as Richard Sanford, Jim Clendenen, Randall Grahm, Bob Lindquist, Terry Theise, Joe Spellman, and my personal wine idol, Larry Stone, they created an extravaganza that showed just what Sanford was capable of.

We scheduled the first few dinners in February thinking it would be a down time and most restaurants and chefs would be freed up to participate—sound thinking. February in Wisconsin—*sound thinking?*

For our second dinner in 1993, we picked up Francesco Ricchi and Jean-Louis Palladin at the airport and headed for the restaurant to drop off their food before taking them to the hotel. It was a brisk, 20-degree day, and Jean-Louis was wearing a fashionable, striking mid-weight jacket in a bright mustard color. They decided to walk back to the restaurant for dinner when they saw how close it was. After dinner we went out to play a few rounds of pool (at Jean-Louis's request) right near the hotel. As they left, I told them I would pick them up in the morning as the temperature was dropping and walking eight blocks in Milwaukee near the lake would be seriously cold.

Jean-Louis looked me right in the eye and said, "What do we look like—little girl? We leeve een D.C.—*we know cold!*"

"OK," I acquiesced. "See you in the morning."

I was inside the front of the restaurant about 8 a.m. the next day, and the door rattled open. There was Francesco with Jean-Louis, whose head looked like an enflamed, hairy tomato, nestled in a puddle of mustard dressing.

He was shaking uncontrollably as he screamed my way, "*What ees zees fucking cold?* Why have you brought me here?! I know cold—*zees ees not natural!*" Anytime I saw him in the future his greeting was always the same: "How do you leeve een that fucking cold place?"

A few years later, after we had moved into a 100-year-old Victorian across from the restaurant, the chef dinner after-parties took on a new dimension as our newly acquired basement was done up in frat house style and outfitted with a professional foosball table and regulation Ping-Pong table. Alongside the keg of beer, the only thing out of place was the selection of special bottles from the wine cellar that we opened for the occasion. All in all, it made for a very convivial soirée.

During one of our later chef dinners, we found ourselves at a Milwaukee treasure, Koz's Mini Bowl on Seventh and Becher, the night before the dinner. This was competitive duck-pin bowling of the highest order. Who knew, with Barbara Lynch trash-talking inches from his face, that Bill "Words" (his bowling nom de plume) Rice, one of the premier food writers in the country, would crush everyone in his path. He had the experienced pinsetters bowing to his majesty by the time we were escorted out at bar closing.

It was late and I was in our living room, after yet another dinner, kibitzing with Don Pintabona, Drew Nieporent, and David Burke when David got up, said he was ready to leave, and walked to the front door. I followed him, and as he hit the icy top step, his feet cleared his head and careened down the eight steps. He immediately snapped up, his arms outstretched as if he had just crossed a finish line, and called out, "I'm OK!"

I brought the car around and took him over to the hotel. We had known each other since 1988 when we had competed together in the Bocuse d'Or. We ended up talking for the next hour in front of the hotel about everything having to do with our restaurant lives. After a slew of his NYC stories, I started to whine that maybe I should have stayed in the city a while longer, and before I could even finish the thought, he punched me in the arm and said, "*Are you an idiot?* You own this small, controllable restaurant, with a loyal clientele, and no outside partners, where you can do whatever you want. You live in a classic Victorian with your beautiful, loving wife—and business partner—right across the street from the restaurant! And you don't even realize *you have what every chef wants!*"

First James Beard Foundation fundraiser at Sanford with visiting chefs and spouses

COOKING FOR HEADS OF STATE SHOULD NOT BE ANY DIFFERENT THAN COOKING FOR anyone else. But if the head of state happens to be a Buddhist monk—well, that might get my attention.

What do you cook for the Dalai Lama? When I was asked to cook for him at an event in Madison in May of 2007, I just assumed it would be vegetarian food. Surprisingly, I was told that the monks were free to eat anything, meat included, as long as it wasn't specifically killed for them—nice loophole!

We wanted to keep the menu seasonal and Wisconsin centric, so I decided on roast Strauss veal loin with grilled escarole and rhubarb essence. Beyond the entrée, we were responsible for dessert (bittersweet Intentional Chocolate tart with coffee ice cream) and all of the bread, which came from our bakery, Harlequin.

As we were going over the lunch setup, we received a short tutorial on accepted protocol around the Dalai Lama. First, we were never to approach or speak to him until he asked; and second, we must never turn our backs to him. And as far as pictures went, he might stop near you, but he wouldn't stop to pose.

Because of heavy security, the lunch was scheduled to start between 11:15 a.m. and 1 p.m. We had arrived early, prepped in the basement kitchen, and were completely set up by 11 in an open adjoining room next to the dining area. Two hours later, with the Dalai Lama nowhere in sight, I was getting antsy and took a walk down the stairs to the basement kitchen. As I was halfway down, I was met by a blast of radiance as I ran into a monk entourage led by the Dalai Lama himself, all resplendent in vibrant, flowing red and gold robes. I froze in place, almost proceeded to utter a greeting—but caught myself—and, remembering protocol, started to moonwalk back up the stairs.

I scampered back to my place behind the tables in the setup room. Within seconds the Dalai Lama appeared at the doorway, hesitating slightly to acknowledge bowing followers. He came to a full stop and looked our way, exclaiming, "Oh, the cooks! You want picture?" *Holy moly!*

He walks behind the serving table and sidled up right next to me, grabbing my hand as the photographers snapped away. My hand was sweating as he asked me, "What's for lunch?"

"I'm making roast veal with rhubarb."

"Oh, I love veal!" he replied, as smiley and giddy as a young kid.

We were told his food regimen was to have a large early breakfast and a larger lunch, and then fast until the next morning. He was not a shy eater either. He chowed throughout the

My dad helping in the kitchen

luncheon, supplementing the plated food with nine slices of our black olive sourdough—not leaving a speck of food on his plates.

At the end of the lunch, he signed a book of his that Angie and I had brought along. He wrote, "I hope you two have wonderful success and wonderful happiness in all your lifetimes."

The experience of cooking for and listening to the Dalai Lama really affected Angie and me. He spoke of compassion and love and ridding yourself of anger. You create the life you live in, so make it right and better. All we ever wanted was a life that we could control and be happy in, and his message reinforced the balance that we always strived for.

And as far as lifetimes go, we should be so lucky as to repeat this one!

◆

I FELT LIKE THE CIRCLE OF LIFE WAS COMPLETE AS I STRETCHED OUT AT TABLE 3, THE only large round at Sanford, set right in front of the radiator, next to the front windows of the restaurant. This is where the original checkout counter of the store was located. It is directly below the living room of the apartment where I lived for the first three years of my life. Just as it was when the store was open and the counter was the center of the neighborhood, this area became the center of the Sanford universe. This table became the comfort zone for family, employees, and guests. This was where we would all meet and plan the future of the restaurant as it was being built. This was where every family celebration was held. This was the spot where everyone was hired (or fired), where we ate our family meal, and the gathering place after a hard night's work. It was where the employees decompressed with a light libation and perhaps a couple hands of Sheepshead. And this was where my dad spent every afternoon, reading the paper and having his lunch, as he worked with us from the day the restaurant opened until the day he passed away.

Enlightenment for me is in the repetition and refinement of my craft. I have the same excitement and satisfaction when preparing an omelet or a triple-decker burger as I do if I come up with a new wild pheasant dish for Sanford. I consciously and unconsciously learned this from each of my mentors, the obvious ones being Peter, Roland, my mother, and my grandfather. More obscure are the apprentices, who after years of stumbling, finally got it. Or the grill cook who was putting together hamburgers and meticulously trimming the crisp iceberg lettuce to perfectly fit the golden, toasted top buns with the precision of a couture dressmaker finishing a seam—all the while surrounded by a loud, crude, hungry, drunken bar crowd at 2:30 a.m. at a Chicago cabbie joint! I almost welled up at the unfettered dedication he displayed, when just being mediocre would have been enough. If all cooks had that inner fortitude, what a wonderful, tasty world this would be.

These are the people who enlightened me, as if they personally unwound the protective gauze from the radiator-burnt hands of my childhood. Each one removed a strip, eventually uncovering the hands of a craftsman.

My real finishing school was my dad, who taught me—from the crib, to the radiator behind the counter, and from Table 3—to be a fair and understanding man. In this black-and-white world, we need more gray.

So, where do I go from here? I'll decide after I finish the pinks.

IN MY PERSONAL REPERTOIRE I HAVE
many favorites that will keep family, friends,
and me sustained until I can't physically
lift a spatula or can direct someone else to
do it. These dishes all have such a personal
connection to my psyche that even if I don't
consume them, their taste memories will still
satisfy me. As I get on in years, my body ages,
but my mind remains in the exact moments
when these tastes and dishes stamped their
imprimatur on my life.

They are all interwoven with a story. Some
are recent, and others are from my childhood,
but they are all inspired by events that propel
me back, at the first scent of their ingredients,
to a place that is as familiar to me as watching
a tall vat of tomato sauce slowly undulate on
the stovetop.

Bittersweet Chocolate Chip Pecan Cookies

I was about eight years old, and we were over at TJ's Aunt Norma's house. Our mothers had unceremoniously dumped us there so they could go out and power shop without the kids in tow. I was not happy being in a strange house, but things soon got better.

Also dropped off at the brat pen were two of TJ's cousins, Raymond and Joanne. I was very noncommittal about Raymond, as I didn't know him very well. But Joanne was a plus. I had had a long-lasting crush on her since the Christmas before when I had spotted her on the other side of the Christmas tree at a holiday party. A bit too shy at the time, I could only make low, guttural animal noises, hoping to catch her eye. For some strange reason she never responded, so I was grateful for a fresh chance to make a lasting impression.

Aunt Norma gathered us together and said we were going to spend the afternoon making chocolate chip cookies. She used the classic Nestlé Toll House recipe that, as we learned, was almost foolproof (with a bit of direction). The duties were split up between us, and I opted to be at the end of the food chain and roll the cookies into balls with Joanne. Having realized that the animal noises hadn't previously worked, I decided to hum themes from Westerns. This led to a low-pitched exclamation: "Roll-um, roll-um, roll-um, keep those doggies moving!" Alas, she wasn't a *Rawhide* fan, but darned if she didn't notice that I was there. Still, as we sat down later to plow through the warm cookies and milk, I thought to myself, "Now this is a pretty good day!"

◆

Rosemary-Skewered Sicilian Mock Chicken Legs

Christmas dinner brought a new dish every year. Except for the time we had a standing beef rib roast, which was for a large dinner party, almost all the dishes had one thing in common: the pig. Over the years we consumed enough pork to make an Iowa farm boy proud, from the perfectly glazed, rotund hams to my mom's magical pork roast with its thick coat of crispy, flavorful fat and bevy of caramelized carrots, onions, and potatoes.

My mother sent me down to the basement on a search-and-retrieval mission for the Sunbeam electric frying pan, and I knew what was coming: the double-cut stuffed pork chops she always cooked in it.

But as she set up the pan and unwrapped the white butcher paper parcel, I grew confused. Before her was a small mountain of large meat cubes—half dark pink, half light pink. I asked her where the pork chops were. Amused, she pulled out 12 thick wooden skewers and showed me how to thread the meat cubes while alternating the veal and pork. Then we set up three pie plates—one with flour, one with beaten egg, and one with breadcrumbs. After the skewers were seasoned liberally with salt and pepper, they went from the flour to the egg to the crumbs, and then I knew—mock chicken legs.

But it was Christmas, and my last experience with those fake gams had been hot lunch at my grade school cafeteria. One of the cafeteria's few flubs, the dry, grizzly chunks of meat, entombed by a flaccid steam table blanket of crumbs, were certainly not holiday worthy. But Christmas is about small miracles, and in my mother's hands, those faux appendages became crisp, burnished morsels bursting with juice and seasoned to perfection.

◆

Dusty Road Plum Soup with Plum Tart and Oven-Roasted Plums

I bounded down the painted cement stairs, half holding on to the concave handrail, which was worn away and heavily patinaed from years of supporting grimy, sweaty hands fresh from the upstairs playground.

As I hit the bottom stair, a stationed nun pointed to the bathroom door, conveniently located to the right. Rough granules spilled from the dry soap dispenser onto my darkened paws, and as I rubbed them under the faucet, they magically brightened before my eyes.

After leaving the bathroom with clean hands, I walked toward the large arch, and it hit me—that smell. It was like an overbaked ziti casserole mixed with pencil shavings and lead. It's hot-lunch time, the best part of my grade school day. As I grabbed my tray I knew that no matter what the daily menu was, I could depend on there being a small parfait glass filled with some type of canned fruit. It ranged from the real crowd-pleasers—fruit cocktail, sliced peaches, or pears—to the almost exotic, apricot halves or the dreaded prunes bobbing in their mud-colored syrup.

I say dreaded because of the vocal angst that would electrically spread through the line as the first person got up to the window. We all knew that you couldn't pass on the shriveled nodules, and after years of seeing them used as milk carton fillers, the nuns were wise to that trick and would make you shake your carton before depositing it in the garbage. It wasn't pretty to have to pour them back out onto your plate and go back to your lunch seat to gag them down.

One of the only ways out was to borrow a leftover wax paper bag from someone who had brought their lunch from home, remove the prune pits, place the pits in the glass dish, deposit the prune flesh in the bag, and then mule it out—all under the eagle eyes of the habit-clad monitors.

But unlike most of my schoolmates, I loved prunes and had ever since my dad explained to me that they were dried plums. I made lots of friends by downing their wrinkled orbs.

◆

Sicilian Spiedini

We always had a very traditional Thanksgiving at the D'Amatos'. As usual, when my mother disappeared into the kitchen the day before, it became off limits for mere mortals to even peek in. The dining room buffet was cracked open, and the good china would make its guest appearance on the table. On Thanksgiving Day, the kitchen door would swing open, and the feast was on. When the food appeared from behind the swinging door, it was like a restaurant experience.

The menu never really varied—stuffed turkey, bread-and-giblets stuffing, pan gravy, candied sweet potatoes, baked mashed potatoes, ground orange and cranberry relish—and, just for me, the perfect jellied cranberry sauce, still with its ribs intact from sliding out of the can. The vegetable could vary, but it was usually string beans amandine. And as the years went on, the salad went from the delicious Jell-O fluff to a more nontraditional mixed green salad.

Then there was the odd year. Two days before Thanksgiving, and then one day before Thanksgiving, nothing was going on in the kitchen. A week prior, my sister and I heard a regular cadence of strong words passing between my parents. These parental voices started out at a controlled but strained level, but by the end of the week, they were reverberating from the basement to the attic.

On Thanksgiving Day, my mother woke us up and told us to get dressed—we were going to my grandparents for dinner. Now the arguing made sense, as my mother and my dad's father had never gotten over their horrible start. My mom had just never filled the role of a traditional Italian spouse, being neither traditional nor Italian. And even though we kids spent a lot of time visiting and eating at our grandparents' house while we worked at the store, beyond the regular Christmas and holiday drive-bys, we didn't spend many mother-included family gatherings at their place. Over the years they had worked out a relationship that could best be described as civil tolerance.

But both my sister and I were only thinking about one thing when my dad mentioned the visit: delicious food. My grandfathers' greatest talent—and this was a point even my mother wouldn't argue—was his ability to coax incredible flavor out of simple ingredients: olive oil-fried potatoes, Sicilian burgers, and mostaccioli with seared sausage bobbing in his slowly bubbling sugu.

With a holiday dinner, chances were very good that his signature would show up: spiedini. This was pounded-out beef, rolled around a breadcrumb mixture that was infused with garlic, onions, parsley, Romano, and tomato sauce, with a small prize—a cube of pork fat—nestled in the middle. They were skewered together, separated by bay leaves and onion pieces, and then cooked in the Nesco until all the ingredients became one. His spiedini embodied the qualities that we wanted in a grandfather—all-loving, caring, nourishing, and coddling. When my grandfather cooked, my dad became happy; those were the only times my grandfather was the father that my dad craved.

We sat down to dinner, with nary a turkey, mashed potato, or candied yam in the vicinity. This wasn't necessarily a bad thing as right next to the glass dish with the red jellied cranberry sauce (thank you) was the spiedini, and a few other Italian cousins. This was a dish capable of soothing many wounds.

◆

Triple-Decker Burger with Sandy's Thousand Island

Hot dogs have always been an obsession with me, but every good obsession should have a topper. My topper is triple-decker burgers, in any guise: from my first Howard Johnson's 3-D burger, to the Pig 'n Whistle's Big Chief, and of course, the namesake offering from that darling pompadoured purveyor of good taste, Big Boy.

My earliest memories of eating out at a restaurant involved Howard Johnson. The whole experience—walking into the front setup of 28 scrumptious flavors of ice cream and the expansive counter fountain; eating the clam roll, clam chowder, or 3-D burger; and maybe finishing up by popping pieces of the pastel-colored salt water taffy into our mouths as we left—was pure perfection, no matter what the mix. I always remember my fingers being covered with a mixture of burger juices, special 3-D sauce, and toasted sesame seeds as I plowed through my burger. It was a precarious situation, as my mother would yell at me not to lick my fingers. But what was a boy to do?

This was a perfect lead-in to the Pig 'n Whistle, located on Capitol Drive across from Estabrook Park, a regular eat-out spot for our family. I always felt the Big Chief was a 3-D knockoff, with its shredded lettuce, sesame seed bun, and its special dressing caught somewhere between ketchup and cocktail sauce. It wasn't the original; still, it was a perfectly acceptable dinner by my standards.

When Big Boy came into town, it filled the HoJo void I felt. I loved the hot fudge sundaes, hand-breaded onion rings, fries dipped in Thousand Island dressing, and of course, the Big Boy. I tried the Swiss Miss and other burger options they offered, but I always went back to the Big Boy. I almost lived at the Big Boy at Fifth and Wisconsin. It was a daily stop after high school at Marquette High; and during the summer, I moved to the Big Boy on North Avenue, just east of Prospect—always good after spending the day at Bradford Beach.

When I returned to Milwaukee in 1980, after having left in 1970, the Big Boy scene in Milwaukee had changed. But falling into old habits, my new outpost became the Juneau Village location, where I would stop after working at John Byron's to pick up a couple of Big Boys to take home for Angie and I.

Then, after years of missing the triple-decker, we were visiting Angie's sister in Cincinnati and, lo and behold, we discovered Big Boy had a stronghold throughout Ohio and Michigan! It was just like coming home—and home never tasted so good.

◆

Dad-Style Tuna Salad

As much as my mother loved chicken salad, my dad was always a tuna guy. The shelves of his grocery store always held StarKist and other water-packed brands, but the star of the tuna shelf was the Genoa brand, an Italian-style tuna packed in olive oil.

At least once a week, as lunchtime rolled around, he would stroll over to the tuna section and pick out a prime can of the Italian brand. He would slice up a few ripe tomatoes, a bit of onion, some thick slices of fresh Italian bread, and then add a bit of salt, pepper, and a final sprinkling of olive oil—it was all we needed for a terrific midday meal. Afterward, I had my pick of the six or seven varieties of Johnston cookies that we received in bulk and sold by the piece (I especially liked the chocolate-covered marshmallow and jam cookies).

As years went on, I maintained my taste for quality canned tuna. On one of my first trips to Rome with Angie, I read about a store that carried high-quality Sicilian canned tuna. We started a trek from the center of Rome to the far suburb, which took about three hours. We came upon a small, fully packed grocery with hanging garlands of fresh garlic and dried red peppers. I asked the proprietor, in my stilted Italian, about the Sicilian tuna. He only had eight cans, and I bought them all. I told him my father had a small grocery in the United States, and it turned out that he was a transplanted Sicilian and knew of Sant'Elia, the village my grandfather was from.

My dad was thrilled with the tuna we brought back and prized every can. From that time on, every trip to Europe meant luggage filled with imported tuna from Italy or Spain.

◆

Eggplant Caponata

Now this was an adventure—going to someone else's house for Sunday dinner for the first time. We were visiting my mother's new friend, Ellie. She was the mother of one of my sister's classmates, and shared chaperone duties with my mother for all us kids as we would visit our official swimming hole Friess Lake, near Holy Hill. After hours and hours of baking in the sun together, they formed a great relationship.

As our family entered their house, I noticed it was quite different from those of any of our relatives. The first oddity was the menacing, wailing, and sputtering aluminum contraption on the stove. It looked like a cartoon boiler ready to explode as the steam shot through the tip of the locked-down top. (Fortunately, though frightening to look at, the pressure cooker produced a rosy, pink pork butt and tender cabbage, carrots, and potatoes.)

The other item I was transfixed by was the white block sitting on the butter dish. This was my first experience with oleo, which was served along with clandestine stories from Ellie's husband Frank about his bimonthly border runs for the illegal contraband.

At the end of dinner, it got even stranger as Frank directed my dad to come in the kitchen for an after-dinner beer, as the ladies moved into the living room. This was strange to me because with my dad's work schedule, I had never seen him in a drinking-beer-and-talking-sports situation before. He was downright animated!

After exhausting the sports conversation, they shifted to favorite foods. They were both so intrigued by the other's ethnic background that they set up a German-Italian snack-off for the upcoming Friday—and I got to tag along.

My dad came loaded with a boxful of food. When we arrived in the kitchen, Earl Gillespie was doing the Braves play-by-play on the transistor in the corner, and almost immediately the food started to flow.

My dad's opening salvo was brooding, oil-cured black olives and chunks of sharp, aged Romano. Frank countered with braunschweiger and raw onions on rye. (Both agreed they went down well with PBR.) Then came my favorite: tart and sweet eggplant caponata versus herring with thinly sliced crock pickles, and more beer. The verbal gamesmanship shifted into high gear.

Frank then served up coarse, garlicky German salami chunks on black pumpernickel showered with freshly grated horseradish that had the entire neighborhood's eyes welling up.

This was crushed (my personal opinion) by sesame-encrusted toasts glistening with olive oil that coddled thin slices of hot capocolla topped with spicy pepperoncini salad.

Frank looked perplexed, but then a sly smile crossed his lips as he strode across the kitchen and dug out a jar from deep inside his refrigerator. As soon as he muscled off the crusted lid, we didn't even have to taste the Limburger—it was game, set, match. I remember how much fun it was to see, for the first time, my dad just being a guy, and having the time of his life.

CHAPTER FOURTEEN RECIPES

◆

Bittersweet Chocolate
Chip Pecan Cookies

411

Rosemary-Skewered
Sicilian Mock Chicken Legs

412

Dusty Road Plum Soup with Plum
Tart and Oven-Roasted Plums

415

Sicilian Spiedini

417

Triple-Decker Burger with
Sandy's Thousand Island

419

Dad-Style Tuna Salad

421

Eggplant Caponata

423

BITTERSWEET CHOCOLATE CHIP PECAN COOKIES

It started with Toll House Cookies and it became a lifelong journey to find my ultimate chocolate chip cookie. When we opened our bakery it became an urgent mission, and after 20-some incarnations, I came up with one I was happy with. But that was then, and since I finally came up with the crunchy, brown sugar, buttery texture and flavor I was craving, I hope you agree.

MAKES 20 COOKIES

2½ sticks (10 ounces [284 g]) salted butter, at room temperature

¾ cup (6 ounces [170 g]) granulated sugar

½ cup packed (4 ounces [114 g]) dark brown sugar

1 large egg, at room temperature

1 large egg white, at room temperature

1 teaspoon vanilla extract

1⅝ cups (8 ounces [226 g]) all-purpose flour

¾ teaspoon baking powder

½ teaspoon kosher salt

10 ounces (284 g) bittersweet chocolate (I use 66%), cut in small pieces

1 cup (4½ ounces [128 g]) coarsely chopped pecans tossed with ½ teaspoon grape-seed oil and salted, then toasted at 375°F (190°C) for 8 to 9 minutes until golden brown

1. Preheat the oven to 375°F (190°C). In the bowl of a stand mixer fitted with the paddle, cream the butter, granulated sugar, and brown sugar on medium until well combined and light, about 3 minutes. Add the egg and egg white, 1 at a time, to emulsify. Add the vanilla extract.

2. Sift the flour, baking powder, and salt together and add to the mixer (set on low) to just combine. Mix the chocolate and pecans together in a bowl and add to the mixer (set on low) to just incorporate.

3. Scoop out the batter with a 2-ounce (60 mL) ice cream scoop onto a Silpat- or parchment paper-lined baking sheet leaving about 2 inches (5 cm) between the cookies. Bake for 12 to 14 minutes, or until they are golden and cooked through. Remove the cookies from the baking sheet and let cool on a cooling rack.

ROSEMARY-SKEWERED SICILIAN MOCK CHICKEN LEGS

In the '40s and '50s, Mock Chicken Legs were made with pork and veal because those meats were actually less expensive than chicken at the time. My recipe for Sicilian Mock Chicken Legs actually uses chicken, but only the thighs—which yield a really juicy bite—and with the tart lemon marinade, crispy cheese crust, and rosemary skewers, I'm betting that just as Betty Grable wisely "insured" her legs, these legs will "ensure" a great holiday dinner.

SERVES 4

> 3 tablespoons (45 mL) fresh lemon juice
>
> ½ cup (119 mL) plus 2 tablespoons extra virgin olive oil (divided)
>
> 2 tablespoons chopped fresh rosemary (from reserved skewer leaves)
>
> 1 tablespoon dry white wine
>
> 1½ teaspoons chopped garlic
>
> 1 teaspoon chopped shallot
>
> ¼ teaspoon kosher salt
>
> ¼ teaspoon freshly ground black pepper
>
> ⅛ teaspoon cayenne pepper
>
> Microplaned zest of 1 lemon
>
> 6 boneless skinless chicken thighs (24 ounces [680 g]), each cut into 4 equal parts (24 pieces total)
>
> 8 (8-inch-long [20-cm]) fresh rosemary sprigs, bottom 4 inches (10 cm) of leaves removed from each sprig and reserved, then bottom ¼-inch (6-mm) of sprig cut on a sharp angle to form a point (sprigs will be used as skewers)
>
> Prepared Seasoned Bread Crumbs (recipe follows)
>
> 2 large eggs, whisked with 2 tablespoons extra virgin olive oil
>
> ½ cup (75 g) all-purpose flour

1. Mix the lemon juice, 2 tablespoons of the olive oil, the chopped rosemary, the wine, the garlic, the shallots, the salt, the black pepper, the cayenne pepper, and the lemon zest together with the chicken pieces in a large bowl and place in a large resealable plastic bag. Let marinate for 8 hours, or overnight.

2. Remove the chicken pieces from the marinade and skewer 3 pieces of chicken onto the bottom of each of the 8 rosemary sprigs (try not to break the sprigs as you push them through the meat).

3. Place the Seasoned Bread Crumbs on a large platter. Place the egg/olive oil mixture in a shallow bowl or baking dish. Place the flour in a shallow bowl or baking dish. One by one, place the rosemary-skewered chicken in the flour (just lightly covering the meat), then lightly pat them to remove the excess flour. Place in the egg mixture, then hold up to drain the excess. Place in the bread crumbs to coat by lightly patting on the crumbs with your hand, then remove the excess.

4. When all of the chicken is breaded, place a 12-inch (30-cm) heavy sauté pan over medium-high heat. When the pan is hot, add the remaining ½ cup (119 mL) of olive oil to the pan. When hot, add the skewers and sauté until they are golden brown on all sides, about 10 to 12 minutes. For serving, place 2 skewers on each of 4 plates.

For the Seasoned Bread Crumbs:

1 cup (108 g) bread crumbs (preferably made from stale bread)
⅓ cup (33 g) grated Pecorino Romano cheese
½ teaspoon kosher salt
¼ teaspoon freshly ground black pepper

1. Place all of the ingredients in a food processor and pulse until well mixed.

DUSTY ROAD PLUM SOUP WITH PLUM TART AND OVEN-ROASTED PLUMS

When I make this dessert all I can think about is that the same people who would have trouble keeping down a slice of prune would be completely smitten with this plum tart and soup. Italian plums are from a European variety of plums, which are the source of all prunes. These dusky ovals are freestone (easy to handle) and have a dry constitution, which during baking causes the internal juices to slowly leach out and form their own delicious sticky glaze. Try out this three-way plum dessert and I think you'll see this is one prune that might make you swoon.

SERVES 6

For the Roasted Plums:

> 6 plums, cut in half, pitted, and each half cut into 4 pieces crosswise
>
> Cinnamon sugar (¼ cup [50 g] granulated sugar mixed with ¾ teaspoon cinnamon; reserve some for the Plum Tarts)

1. Preheat the oven to 275°F (140°C). Place the plums skin side down on a parchment paper-lined baking sheet. Sprinkle the plums with cinnamon sugar and bake for 2 to 2½ hours, rotating the baking sheet every 30 minutes.

2. Cool and place the plums in a covered container.

For the Plum Soup:

> 2 pounds (908 g) plums, pitted and coarsely chopped
>
> 2½ cups (593 mL) dry white wine
>
> ½ cup (100 g) granulated sugar
>
> For the sachet, mix together the following spices in cheesecloth and tie with butcher string:
>
> > 2 teaspoons whole black peppercorns
> >
> > 2 star anise
> >
> > 1½ ounces (43 g) fresh ginger root, peeled and sliced
> >
> > 1 bay leaf
> >
> > 1 teaspoon whole allspice
> >
> > 1 whole clove
> >
> > 1 cinnamon stick
> >
> > Pinch ground nutmeg

1. Place the plums, wine, sugar, and sachet in a stainless pot and simmer slowly over low heat for 2 to 2½ hours, stirring to avoid scorching (try not to reduce the liquid).

(RECIPE CONTINUES ON PAGE 416)

(RECIPE CONTINUED FROM PAGE 415)

2. Remove the sachet, then purée the plum mixture in a blender. Pass through a fine strainer and chill.

For the Plum Tarts and to Finish the Dish:

½ cup (71 g) hazelnuts, toasted at 350°F for 15 to 18 minutes until golden brown and fragrant, then rubbed with a towel while warm to remove skins

½ cup (75 g) plus 3 tablespoons all-purpose flour (divided)

Pinch kosher salt

¼ cup (57 g) salted butter, at room temperature

⅓ cup (33 g) confectioners' sugar, sifted

1 large egg yolk, at room temperature

3 plums, cut in half, pitted, and each half cut in ⅛-inch (3-mm) slices

Reserved prepared cinnamon sugar

6 tablespoons (90 g) sour cream

Prepared Roasted Plums

Prepared Plum Soup

⅓ cup (106 g) malt powder, placed in a shaker, for garnish

1. In a food processor, grind the hazelnuts with 1 tablespoon of the flour for 15 seconds. Add the remaining flour and the salt, pulse 3 times, and remove from the processor bowl. Reserve.

2. Add the butter and confectioners' sugar to the processor and blend for 5 to 10 seconds, or until smooth. Scrape down the side of the bowl. Add the egg yolk and blend for 5 seconds, then scrape down again. Add the reserved hazelnut mixture, pulse 4 times, and remove from the processor.

3. Preheat the oven to 400°F (200°C). Gather the dough with your hands and divide into 6 golf ball-size rounds. Place each ball between 2 pieces of plastic wrap and roll thinly, about ¼ inch thick. Remove the top plastic and cut dough with a 3- to 3½-inch (7.5- to 8.9-cm) round cutter. Invert each circle onto a Silpat- or parchment paper-lined baking sheet. Spiral half of a sliced plum in overlapping slices onto each hazelnut circle. Sprinkle with the cinnamon sugar.

4. Bake for about 6 to 8 minutes, or until the bottoms are brown. (You may serve them warm or cool.)

5. For serving, place 1 tablespoon sour cream in each of 6 bowls. Divide the Roasted Plums among the bowls, standing up around the sour cream, ladle 5 to 6 ounces (150–180 mL) of Plum Soup equally around the plums, rest the tart on top of the plums (not in the soup), and dust over all with the malt powder. Serve with your favorite ice cream.

SICILIAN SPIEDINI

In the beginning, I thought all spiedini were created equal. Years later, I would order spiedini at various restaurants, and they were always different; some simple beef roll-ups with just-seasoned breadcrumbs, some more elaborate with a Sicilian component of raisins and capers in the filling, and the most different, Spiedini alla Romana, no meat, just bread and mozzarella. That's the point when I found out that the word spiedini refers to the skewer that holds all of the ingredients together. My grandfather never had any recipes, but I feel these Spiedini capture the taste that I remember.

SERVES 4

For the Tomato Sauce:

1½ pounds (681 g) Italian sausage

¼ cup (59 mL) extra virgin olive oil

1 large onion (12 ounces [341 g]), diced

2 bay leaves

2 sprigs fresh thyme

4 large cloves chopped garlic

1 ounce (28 g) fresh basil leaves, chopped

½ bunch parsley stems, chopped

½ cup (131 g) tomato paste

1 cup (237 mL) unsalted pork or unsalted chicken stock

2 (28-ounce [784-g]) cans peeled plum tomatoes in juice, puréed in a food processor

Kosher salt and freshly ground black pepper, to taste

1. Preheat the oven to 350°F (180°C). Place a heavy-bottomed pot over medium heat. When the pan is hot, add the olive oil, then the sausage and brown on all sides. Remove the sausage to a plate.

2. Add the onions to the pot and sauté until they are lightly brown. Add the bay leaves, thyme, garlic, basil, and parsley stems and sauté for 1 minute. Add the tomato paste and sauté for 3 minutes, stirring, until the paste darkens (do not burn).

3. Add the stock and tomatoes and stir, then bring up to a boil. Add the browned sausage, cover, and bake for 45 minutes.

4. Remove and discard the bay leaf and thyme. Remove the sausage and reserve for another use. Adjust the seasoning with salt and pepper and cool. Reserve the sauce in the refrigerator (you will need 2 cups (474 mL) of sauce for the filling).

(RECIPE CONTINUES ON PAGE 418)

(RECIPE CONTINUED FROM PAGE 417)

For the Spiedini Filling:

4 ounces (114 g) pancetta, cut in small dice

¼ cup (59 mL) extra virgin olive oil

½ cup (75 g) onions, diced small

1½ tablespoons finely chopped garlic

2 cups (216 g) bread crumbs

½ bunch Italian parsley, chopped

2 cups (474 mL) Prepared Tomato Sauce

6 ounces (170 g) grated Pecorino Romano cheese

Kosher salt and freshly ground black pepper, to taste

1. In a sauté pan, render the pancetta in the olive oil. Add the onions and sauté until lightly browned. Add the garlic, sauté for 1 minute, and strain (reserve the oil). Reserve the mixture.

2. Add the oil back to the pan and sauté the bread crumbs until they are brown, then remove to a bowl. Add the reserved pancetta mixture, parsley, Tomato Sauce, and cheese. Adjust the seasoning with salt and pepper and reserve the filling in the refrigerator.

For the Spiedini:

16 thin slices (about 3 ounces [85 g] each) trimmed strip loin, pounded to ¼-inch (6-mm) thickness and cut in half to yield 32 pieces

Kosher salt and freshly ground black pepper, to taste

Prepared Spiedini Filling

2 onions, cut in quarters, blanched 5 seconds in boiling salted water, then cooled

32 bay leaves (if not pliable, blanched 1 second in boiling onion water from above)

¼ cup (59 mL) olive oil for sautéing

1. Lay the strip loin pieces flat and season the top side with salt and pepper. Divide the reserved Spiedini Filling among the slices, then roll up like egg rolls. Place the Spiedini on 8 (6- to 8-inch [15- to 20-cm]) skewers with 1 onion slice and 1 bay leaf between each 1, using 4 per skewer.

2. Preheat the oven to 350°F (180°C). Preheat a char grill or place a large sauté pan over medium-high heat. Season the Spiedini with salt and pepper and if grilling, brush the Spiedini with the olive oil and grill 2 to 3 minutes per side until nicely charred. If sautéing, place the oil in the pan and when the oil is hot, sauté about 2 to 3 minutes per side until golden brown. Either way, then place the spiedini on a baking sheet and bake for about 10 minutes, or until heated through.

TRIPLE-DECKER BURGER WITH SANDY'S THOUSAND ISLAND

I can't tell you in words how happy Thousand Island dressing makes me. If there was not a question of cholesterol or how long I want to remain on this earth, it might make a daily appearance on my table. As much as I revel in it on a salad, it's best between a crispy grilled soft bun and a burger...or two!

SERVES 2

For the Triple-Decker Burger:

> 2 sesame-coated egg hamburger buns, unsliced
>
> Extra virgin olive oil, to brush on buns
>
> 12 ounces (341 g) ground beef chuck (I prefer about 20–25% fat), divided into 4 portions and each portion formed lightly into a 4-inch (10-cm) patty
>
> Kosher salt and freshly ground black pepper, to taste
>
> 4 slices cheddar cheese
>
> Prepared Sandy's Thousand Island or bottled Thousand Island Dressing
>
> ½ cup (18 g) sliced iceburg lettuce

1. Place a 12-inch (30-cm) sauté pan on the stove over medium-low heat. Cut the buns horizontally into 3 evenly thick slices and brush each cut side with a bit of the olive oil. Place the oiled sides into the skillet and cook until they are golden brown (you'll need to turn the middle piece over once). Remove the buns from the pan and turn the heat up to high.

2. Season the patties with salt and pepper, and when the pan is very hot, place them in the pan. Sauté for about 2 minutes on the first side. Turn the patties over, place a slice of cheese on each 1, and cook for another 2 to 3 minutes, or to your desired doneness; remove from the pan to a plate.

3. Place 1 to 1½ tablespoons of dressing on the 2 bottom bun slices. Over each dressed bottom bun, place ¼ of the lettuce, then a patty, a middle bun, more dressing, ¼ of the lettuce, a second patty, then a top bun. Serve the Triple-Decker Burgers immediately with plenty of napkins.

For Sandy's Thousand Island:

> 1 scallion, end trimmed, sliced very thin, rinsed under warm water, then squeezed lightly between paper towels to dry
>
> ½ cup (115 g) mayonnaise
>
> 3 tablespoons (45 mL) plus 1 teaspoon Heinz Chili Sauce

(RECIPE CONTINUES ON PAGE 420)

(RECIPE CONTINUED FROM PAGE 419)

2 tablespoons chopped dill pickles or dill pickle relish, squeezed lightly between paper towels to dry

2 tablespoons capers, drained and coarsely chopped

1½ teaspoons hot prepared horseradish, liquid squeezed out

1½ teaspoons red wine vinegar

1 teaspoon brandy

½ teaspoon kosher salt, plus additional to taste

⅜ teaspoon freshly ground black pepper, plus additional to taste

1. Place all of the ingredients in a bowl and mix together. Adjust the seasoning, if necessary. Let the dressing rest to meld the flavors in the refrigerator for at least 2 hours.

DAD-STYLE TUNA SALAD

When my dad moved back into the apartment above Sanford after my mother passed away, at least once a week he would break out a few cans of imported tuna and put a simple salad together that he would end up sharing with whoever was around in the restaurant kitchen. So I know I'm not alone in regularly making a version of this totally satisfying lunch.

FOR 2 SERVINGS

For the Dressing:

> 6 tablespoons (89 mL) extra virgin olive oil (I prefer a lighter French provincial oil)
>
> 1½ tablespoons Dijon mustard
>
> 2¼ teaspoons fresh lemon juice
>
> 1½ teaspoons red wine vinegar
>
> ⅜ teaspoon kosher salt
>
> ⅜ teaspoon freshly ground black pepper

1. Mix all of the ingredients together in a bowl. Reserve.

To Finish the Dish:

> 6 cups (216 g) red leaf lettuce, cleaned and spun dry
>
> Reserved prepared Dressing
>
> Kosher salt and fresh ground black pepper, to taste
>
> 2 (115-gram) cans Ortiz Bonito del Norte tuna in olive oil (or good-quality Italian or Spanish tuna)
>
> ½ cucumber (5–6 ounces [142–170 g]), sliced in half lengthwise and cut in ¼-inch (6-mm) slices
>
> ½ avocado, pit removed, flesh scooped out, and diced medium
>
> 2 fresh ripe tomatoes (8 ounces [227 g]), cut in half, then each half cut in wedges
>
> 3 tablespoons (24 g) dried salted capers, soaked for 15 minutes, rinsed, and drained
>
> 1 shallot, cut in half, thinly sliced, rinsed, and drained
>
> ½ bunch fresh Italian parsley leaves (½ ounce [14 g]), coarsely chopped
>
> 2 tablespoons fresh tarragon leaves (¼ ounce [7 g]), coarsely chopped

1. Mix the lettuce with ⅓ of the Dressing and season with salt and pepper; divide onto 2 plates.

2. Toss the remaining ingredients with the remaining ⅔ of the Dressing. Place on top of the lettuce and serve.

EGGPLANT CAPONATA

This dish is all about balance of complex tastes, and a touch of unsweetened cocoa powder is a perfect link to bring them together and give you a real memorable depth of flavor. Just remember that for a great caponata you have to find the best market vegetables, good brine-cured olives, and tasty olive oil.

MAKES 8 SERVINGS

3 or 4 (1 pound [454 g]) Japanese eggplants, tops removed and cut in medium dice (leave skin on)

Kosher salt and freshly ground black pepper, to taste

¾ cup (178 mL) extra virgin olive oil (divided)

1 small onion (6 ounces [170 g]), diced medium

1 stalk celery (3 ounces [85 g]), diced medium

½ small red bell pepper (3 ounces [85 g]), cored, seeded, and diced medium

½ small green bell pepper (3 ounces [85 g]), cored, seeded, and diced medium

1 tablespoon chopped garlic

1 sprig fresh thyme

2 bay leaves

¼ cup (66 g) tomato paste

1 tablespoon cocoa powder

6 ounces (170 g) pitted brine-cured green olives, rinsed, drained, and cut in quarters

⅓ cup (50 g) pepperoncini, stem and seeds removed and cut in very thin rings

⅓ cup (1½ ounces [43 g]) sultanas (yellow raisins), soaked in 4 teaspoons Marsala wine and 2 teaspoons Sambuca

½ cup (119 mL) water

3 tablespoons (45 mL) red wine vinegar

1½ tablespoons salted or brine-cured capers, rinsed and drained

¾ teaspoon granulated sugar

½ cup (135g) toasted salted pine nuts

1. Preheat the oven to 350°F (180°C). Season the eggplant with salt and pepper and toss with ½ cup (119 mL) of the olive oil in a bowl. In a very hot sauté pan, add the eggplant and sauté until crisp-tender, about 2 minutes. Remove from the pan and add the remaining ¼ cup (59 mL) of the olive oil. When the oil is medium-hot, add the onions, celery, bell peppers and cook for 2 minutes (do not brown). Add the garlic, thyme, and bay leaves, season lightly with salt and pepper, and sauté for 1 minute. Add the tomato paste and sauté, stirring constantly, for 2 minutes (do not brown).

(RECIPE CONTINUES ON PAGE 424)

(RECIPE CONTINUED FROM PAGE 423)

2. Add the cooked eggplant, cocoa, olives, pepperoncini, sultanas, water, vinegar, capers, and sugar and bring up to a boil. Bake for about 3 minutes, or until the eggplant is tender. Remove to a non-reactive tray to cool.

3. When cooled, adjust the seasoning with salt and pepper. Garnish the Eggplant Caponata with the pine nuts right before serving by mixing half with the Caponata and sprinkling half on top.

ACKNOWLEDGMENTS

I OWE A BOATLOAD OF GRATITUDE TO SO MANY PEOPLE.

I am pleased to announce that Angie and I are still married after her enduring 4+ years of working with a temperamental and at times unreasonable me on this book. I don't envy her, although I do envy myself for having her help. Without her patience, support, and unrelenting perfectionism, I wouldn't have this book. I'm a lucky guy.

Without my patient, best-in-the-business agent and close friend, Lisa Ekus, her daughter Sally (my mini-evil-agent), and the talented folks they work with—Jaimee, Corrine, Sean, and Samantha—shepherding this book and myself through the process, it would still be just a thought and we would not be living our dream in Hatfield.

To my publisher, Doug Seibold, of Agate Midway, who took a chance on a first time author; my editor, Kate DeVivo; Eileen; Jali; and Zach; who, with their brilliant decisions and amazing professional cooperation, led to a much better book than I submitted, and one that I am extremely proud of.

To the infinitely talented photographer, Kevin Miyazaki, who has the working temperament of a Labrador and is wise enough to always know what to do.

To my *Milwaukee Journal Sentinel* editor, Nancy Stohs, who took a chance on a chef who had never written a column 13 years ago. And after 670 or so Sunday columns, still gives me great feedback and support.

To May Klisch, who pushed me to take the first step toward writing that column by suggesting that I pitch the idea to the paper.

To my close friend and sounding board, author Bob "Babe" Spitz, who told me from day one to just write in the same voice that I tell stories, which has been my best advice.

To my sister, Steph, my sweet younger sibling, who lived a lot of this book in a parallel life, but at times saw it from a different angle, which helped fill in missing pieces.

To my "brother," TJ, who never lets me be less than I should be, and who bet me five bucks I couldn't get the first chapter done in one month (which ultimately got my ass in gear).

To my close family of friends—David Saffer, Julie Mautner, Ihab, and Sally Hassan—and my cheerleader mother-in-law, Felicia, who all read parts of this book in progress and gave me invaluable, honest feedback and encouragement.

To our Sanford family of the last 23 years, especially the new owners Justin and Sarah (as of December 2012); Ralph (who's had my back for 30+ years); Jeff; Petra; Casey; Adan; Brian; and the entire current kitchen and dining room staff, who helped me both physically and mentally to have the time and energy to write this book. And all the while never letting down for one second the standards that have made Sanford the restaurant it is and will continue to be.

And finally, to Leo, for always being "hoppy."

RECIPE INDEX

Appetizers

SHELLFISH

Chilled Lobster with Cauliflower Scallion Cream and Caviar, 182

Dungeness Crab Ceviche with Parma Prosciutto, Candied Serrano Orange Garlic Dressing, 199

Fermented Black Bean Clams with Spicy Salami and Ginger, 145

Mustard-Crusted Stuffies, 257

Poached Oysters with Mint Cream and Papaya Mignonette, 255

Sauté of Boniato, Chayote, Shrimp and Wild Mushrooms, Cilantro Oil, 208

MEAT

Cumin-Dusted Sweetbreads, Lemon Minted Peas, Glazed Carrots, and Morels, 153

Grilled Prosciutto and Escarole Wrapped Tuma Cheese with Anchovy Dressing, 281

Lamb and Currant Stuffed Grape Leaves with Spiced Yogurt Sauce, 291

Pancetta-Stuffed Artichokes, 206

Rhubarb-Glazed Squab on Candied Radish and Scallion, Rhubarb Essence, 317

Veal Ragout Arancini with Smoked Tomato and Mint Emulsion, 309

VEGETABLE & CHEESE

Eggplant Caponata, 423

Grilled Pear and Roquefort Tart with Caramelized Onions and Walnuts, 344

Pasta Cacio e Pepe, 316

Soups

Black Bean Chili with Cheddar Cheese Toast, 259

Charred Corn, Zucchini, and Mussel Soup, 95

Chicken Pastina, 30

Chilled Tomato Soup with Maple Bacon Panzanella, 87

Garam Masala-Spiced Kohlrabi Soup with Tamarind-Glazed Almonds, 177

Manhattan Clam Chowder, 173

Minestrone, 160

Pasta e Fagioli, 71

Provincial Fish Soup with Rouille, 337

Russian Shchi, 237

Sweet Potato Soup with Seared Tomatillos, 197

Waterzooï á la Gantoise, 314

Salads

Dad-Style Tuna Salad, 421

Grilled Belgian Endive and Watercress Salad with Tart Cherry Dressing, 150

Sweet-Sour German Potato Salat, 37

Entrees :: Fish and Shellfish

FISH

Crisp-Skinned Red Snapper with Shrimp Feta Moussaka, Avgolemono Cream, 381

Goujonettes of Perch with Potato Pancakes and Chipotle Green Olive Sauce, 90

Peppered Bluefish with Glazed Baby Turnips, Lemon Turnip Green Broth, 262

Seared Halibut on Corn and Pepper Relish, Basil Oil, 341

Seared Striped Bass on Green Papaya Salad, Green Curry Broth, 320

Skate Saltimbocca with Lemon Jam, 185

Wild Salmon on Potato-Sorrel Egg Salad, Chive Vermouth Caviar Dressing, 122

SHELLFISH

Lemon-Cured Scallops on Bacon Pea Mush, Raisin Vinaigrette, 288

Sautéed Peconic Bay Scallops with Applejack, 263

Sautéed Soft Shell Crabs with Morels, Ramps, Fiddleheads, and Asparagus, 286

Risi Bisi, 384

Entrees :: Poultry

CHICKEN

Coq au Vin, 234

Chicken Scarpariello—My Way, 121

Herb-Roasted Chicken, 346

Risi Bisi, 384

Rosemary-Skewered Sicilian Mock Chicken Legs, 412

DUCK

Breast of Duck Smitane, 229

Maple-Glazed Duck with Burnt Orange Vinaigrette, 157

TURKEY

Olive Oil Confit of Turkey Thighs, Cranberry Vinaigrette, 175

Turkey and Smoked Gouda Tetrazzini with Kluski, 35

Entrees :: Meat

BEEF

Braciola, 57

Braised Oxtails with Sultana, Fennel and Celery Salad, 375

Carbonnades of Beef with Brown Butter Egg Noodles, 93

Juniper-Braised Short Ribs with Hutspot, 147

Sicilian Burger with Marinated Olive Schiacciate, 65

Sicilian Spiedini, 417

Steak au Poivre, 239

Tafelspitz, 378

Triple-Decker Burger with Sandy's Thousand Island, 419

LAMB

Lamb Champvallons, 240

Lamb Shepherd's Pie with Minted Chevre Potato Crust, 180

Navarin of Lamb, 117

PORK & VEAL

Fennel Sausage Lasagna, 31

Fragrant Chili Pepper Cinnamon Ribs, 34

Frikadeller with Pickled Beets and Cucumbers, 115

Grilled Yucatan Pork Chop, Ancho Potatoes, Orange Chili Emulsion, 202

Home-Style Pork Cabbage Rolls, 283

Hunan Spice-Crusted BBQ Ribs, 386

Stewed Umbrian Lentils with Charred Spicy Italian Sausage, 373

Desserts & Pancakes

CHOCOLATE

Bitter Chocolate Cream Pie, 85

Bittersweet Chocolate Chip Pecan Cookies, 411

Dark-Roasted Hazelnut Chocolate Tart, 61

Hot Fudge Toffee Nut Ball, 98

Individual Warm German Chocolate Cake, 312

FRUIT

Dried Blueberry Oatmeal Pancakes, 120

Dusty Road Plum Soup with Plum Tart and Oven-Roasted Plums, 415

Ginger Snap Cannoli with Wisconsin Dried Cherry Mascarpone Cream, 349

Italian Plum Tart with Brown Sugar Almond Crust, 63

Lemon Curd Meringue, 241

Rice Pudding with Late Harvest Wine Gel and Apricot Sauce, 151

Schaum Torte with Brown Butter-Roasted Rhubarb, 38

Tart Cherry Lattice Pie, 69

Tarte Fine aux Pommes, 231

ABOUT THE AUTHOR

SANFORD D'AMATO graduated from the Culinary Institute of America in 1974. In December 1989, he opened Sanford restaurant on the former site of his father and grandfather's grocery store (he sold it to his longtime chef de cuisine in December 2012). It has long been recognized as one of the most respected and top-ranked restaurants in the nation, earning accolades from *Bon Appétit*, *Gourmet*, *Food & Wine*, *Esquire*, *Wine Spectator*, *Zagat*, and the James Beard Foundation. D'Amato has cooked for the Dalai Lama and the 2002 Salt Lake City Olympics, and was one of 12 chefs chosen by Julia Child to cook for her 80th birthday celebration. He and his wife, Angie, live in Milwaukee, Wisconsin, and Hatfield, Massachusetts, where Sandy will be writing and teaching in the future.

To contact the author, go to www.goodstockcookbook.com.

◆

ABOUT THE PHOTOGRAPHER

Kevin Miyazaki is based in the unironically fabulous Milwaukee, Wisconsin, shoots regularly in nearby Chicago, and travels often (for the love of a great woman) to St. Louis.

www.kevinmiyazaki.com